AF295096

Textbooks in Language Sciences

Editors: Stefan Müller, Antonio Machicao y Priemer
Editorial Board: Claude Hagège, Jong-Bok Kim, Marianne Mithun, Anatol Stefanowitsch, Foong Ha Yap

In this series:

1. Müller, Stefan. Grammatical theory: From transformational grammar to constraint-based approaches.

2. Schäfer, Roland. Einführung in die grammatische Beschreibung des Deutschen.

3. Freitas, Maria João & Ana Lúcia Santos (eds.). Aquisição de língua materna e não materna: Questões gerais e dados do português.

4. Roussarie, Laurent. Sémantique formelle: Introduction à la grammaire de Montague.

5. Kroeger, Paul. Analyzing meaning: An introduction to semantics and pragmatics.

6. Ferreira, Marcelo. Curso de semântica formal.

7. Stefanowitsch, Anatol. Corpus linguistics: A guide to the methodology.

8. Müller, Stefan. 语法理论: 从转换语法到基于约束的理论.

9. Hejná, Míša & George Walkden. A history of English.

10. Kahane, Sylvain & Kim Gerdes. Syntaxe théorique et formelle. Vol. 1: Modélisation, unités, structures.

11. Freitas, Maria João, Marisa Lousada & Dina Caetano Alves (eds.). Linguística clínica: Modelos, avaliação e intervenção.

12. Müller, Stefan. Germanic syntax: A constraint-based view.

ISSN: 2364-6209

Germanic syntax

A constraint-based view

Stefan Müller

Freie Universität Berlin

For all those out there trying to save our societies and

ecosystems from collapse.

Contents

Contents

iv

Preface

This book has two purposes: firstly the comparative analysis of the major syntactic properties of the Germanic languages and secondly the introduction of a specific format for the description and comparison of languages. The framework in which the analyses are couched is called *HPSG light*. It is based on Head-Driven Phrase Structure Grammar (HPSG) (Pollard & Sag 1987, 1994, Müller et al. 2021) in the specific version that is described in detail in Müller (2013b). However HPSG light does not contain any complicated attribute value matrices (AVMs). If AVMs are used at all, they are reduced to the minimum containing a reduced set of features like ARG-ST for argument structure, COMPS for complements and SPR for specifier. All other aspects of the analyses are represented in syntactic trees, which are easier to read. The idea behind the introduction of HPSG light is to provide a tool for linguists who want to provide a more detailed description of a phenomenon without necessarily being forced to deal with all the technicalities. The degree of formalization corresponds to what is common in Government and Binding Theory, Minimalism, and the less formal variants of Construction Grammar. As for the one formal version of Construction Grammar that is a variant of HPSG, namely Sign-Based Construction Grammar (SBCG, Sag 2012), HPSG light can be regarded as a light version of SBCG as well, since the differences are neglected in the abbreviated representations and trees that are used in this book. The work presented here differs from non-formal work in GB/Minimalism and Construction Grammar in an important way: it is backed up by implemented grammars that use the full version of HPSG including a semantic analysis in the framework of Minimal Recursion Semantics (MRS, Copestake, Flickinger, Pollard & Sag (2005)). The detailed analyses are described in conference proceedings, journal articles and books, and the reader is invited to consult these resources in case she or he is interested in the details. The implemented grammars are distributed with the Grammix virtual machine (Müller 2007b) and can be downloaded from the author's web-page.[1] Grammix contains the gram-

---

[1] https://hpsg.hu-berlin.de/Software/Grammix/, 21st April 2023.

mars for German[2], Danish[3], English[4] and Yiddish[5] that were developed in the CoreGram project (Müller 2015c). The respective web-pages of the grammars contain a list of test items that are accepted or rejected by the grammars. Readers are invited to enter these sentences into the TRALE system (De Kuthy et al. 2004, Penn 2004) that comes with Grammix and inspect the complete AVMs.

The book starts with two introductiory chapters: the first chapter introduces the Germanic languages providing basic facts like number of speakers, areas where they are spoken, and some historical facts. Chapter two discusses the phenomena that are treated in the rest of the book, e.g., scrambling, placement of adverbials, passive, clause types, nonlocal dependencies. The third chapter is an introduction to Phrase Structure Grammars, which are the foundations of almost all theories since Chomsky's (1957) formalization of structuralist ideas (Bloomfield 1933). Chapter 3 introduces not just phrase structure grammars but also grammars using abstractions over phrase structure rules, ultimately resulting in very abstract grammars of the type also known from $\overline{\text{X}}$ theory (Jackendoff 1977). Chapter 4 explains how the concept of valence is combined with abstract phrase structure rules to make sure that the right number and the right kind of elements is combined with a certain word. For example, a word like *laugh* needs a subject and a word like *read* needs a subject and an object. This has to be represented somewhere in a grammar, and Chapter 4 explains how it is done in HPSG (light). The basic differences in the analyses of SVO and SOV languages are explained. This chapter also explains how the various orders of subject and objects can be explained in a language like German (so-called *scrambling*) and how one can account for the various placement possibilities in languages like English and the North Germanic languages on the one hand, and German, Dutch and Afrikaans on the other hand. Verbal complexes are dealt with in Chapter 5, verb-first position (used for question formation) and verb-second position (for assertions) are explained in Chapter 6. Passive and case assignment in general

---

[2] https://hpsg.hu-berlin.de/Fragments/Berligram/, 21st April 2023. The German grammar is documented in Müller (2013b, 2023a) and Müller & Ørsnes (2011, 2013a).

[3] https://hpsg.hu-berlin.de/Fragments/Danish/, 21st April 2023. The Danish grammar is documented in Müller & Ørsnes (2015, 2013a, 2011, 2013b).

[4] https://hpsg.hu-berlin.de/Fragments/English/, 21st April 2023. The English grammar is smaller than the German and Danish grammar. It is a proof of concept of a lexicalist analysis of passive, benefactive constructons, resultative constructions. See Müller (2018) and Müller & Ørsnes (2013a) for details.

[5] https://hpsg.hu-berlin.de/Fragments/Yiddish/, 21st April 2023. The Yiddish grammar is based on Müller & Ørsnes (2011) and unpublished work by Jong-Bok Kim, Alain Kihm, and me on predicate topicalization in Korean and Yiddish (Müller, Kim & Kihm 2019).

are treated in Chapter 7. The Germanic languages are especially interesting here as Icelandic belongs to this language group and is known for its quirky subjects (subjects in the genitive, dative, or accusative case, Zaenen et al. 1985). Chapter 8 deals with expletive pronouns and how they are used throughout the Germanic languages to help mark clause types. For example, expletives are used in German main clauses to fill the initial position so that the clause is an assertion. Danish uses expletives in embedded sentences with subjects as interrogative elements. Again the differences in general grammatical properties influence the grammar in other parts such as the placements of expletives.

The final chapter, Chapter 9, is a brief summary of what was done in the book and points the interested reader to some further literature on HPSG.

German slides developed for the course I am teaching with this book are available on GitHub.[6] Lectures in German corresponding to the chapters can also be found on YouTube.[7]

On the way this book is published

Teachers at schools and at many universities are paid by the state, that is by the public (you). Among their duties is the creation of teaching material. There is no reason whatsoever to leave the teaching material to profit-oriented publishers. On the contrary, teaching material should be open and adaptable to the needs of the teachers who want to use it.

A study by the American Enterprise Institute shows that the price of college books rose by 812 % from 1978 to 2012 while the general consumer prices rose a mere 250 %.[8] Similar figures exist for scientific books in general and for university textbooks. My favorite example is a thin textbook on logic *Logik für Linguisten*, which is a translation of the English textbook *Logic for Linguists* (Allwood et al. 1973). This book has 112 pages. It was sold for 9,40€ as a paperback by the Max Niemeyer Verlag. This publisher was bought by De Gruyter and the book is now sold for $126.00/89,95€ as an eBook and $133,00/94,95€ for the hardcover book[9] (see Müller 2012 for other examples and a general discussion). Both the eBook and the printed book are unaffordable for students. The way out of this highly problematic situation is to publish books in open access. The PDF version of

---

[6] https://github.com/stefan11/germanic-syntax-slides, 2021-09-14.

[7] https://www.youtube.com/playlist?list=PLXwGGsuPxWRp4AB2LsWH6LKc0II7uc6tg

[8] https://www.aei.org/carpe-diem/the-college-textbook-bubble-and-how-the-open-educational-resources-movement-is-going-up-against-the-textbook-cartel/. 2022-12-22.

[9] I noticed in 2022 that De Gruyter stopped offering this book. I think this is even worse.

this book is free for everybody and the printed copy is available for a reasonable price since the book is licenced under a Creative Commons license and hence is not owned by a profit-oriented publisher and everybody can choose his or her own print on demand service in case the default service provided by Language Science Press is more expensive.

Berlin, 21st April 2023 Stefan Müller

Acknowledgments

I thank Hubert Haider, Matthias Hüning, and Shravan Vasishth for discussion and Martin Haspelmath and Tibor Kiss for detailed comments on an earlier version of this book. I thank Antonio Machicao y Priemer for comments on sections about alternative approaches. I thank Shravan Vasishth for discussion of psycholinguistic issues.

I want to thank all students of my course on the structure of Germanic languages. This book benefited enormously from their questions and the discussion during the lectures. Carolin Ulmer and Bastian Schoenfeld deserve special mention for important comments. I thank Sarah Böke, Alexandra Fosså, Anne Kilgus, Nils P. Kujath and Maya Tabea Wolff for pointing out typos. I thank Hannah Schleupner for help with Figure 1.1.

I thank the Department of English Linguistics at the University of Frankfurt/ Main for inviting me to talk about the approach to Germanic syntax that is the basis for this book.

I want to thank all proofreaders (Amir Ghorbanpour, Wilson Lui, Lachlan Mackenzie, Rebecca Madlener, Katja Politt, Janina Rado, Brett Reynolds, Lea Schäfer, Annika Schiefner, Troy E. Spier, George Walkden, Jeroen van de Weijer), who did much more than usual copy editing and provided feedback on content as well. Spezial thanks go to Brett Reynolds, and Anne Zaenen.

This book was partly funded by the Deutsche Forschungsgemeinschaft (DFG, German Research Foundation) – SFB 1412, 416591334, Project A04.

I thank the Twitter community for discussing gender issues and names in linguistics examples with me. Special thanks go to Lauren Ackerman, Kirby Conrod, and Brianna Wilson for extensive discussion.

Abbreviations

COMPS	complements
H	head
PART	particle
PREP	preposition
SOV	subject object verb
SUBJ	subject
SVO	subject verb object
V2	verb-second
VFORM	verb form

1 A general overview of the Germanic languages

This chapter provides an overview of general facts about the Germanic languages. It derives from slides for teaching courses about Germanic languages that were used by Ekkehard König and passed on to Matthias Hüning and via Matthias to me, which explains the similarity to the introductory chapter by Henriksen & van der Auwera (1994) in the book *The Germanic Languages* edited by König & van der Auwera (1994).

1.1 Languages and speakers

Depending on whom one asks, there are between 5000 and 7000 languages spoken worldwide currently. The Germanic languages are a small subset of these, 15–20 languages depending on the counting because the distinction between language and language variety is not always made according to the same criteria (e.g., varieties of Dutch). According to Max Weinreich (1945: 13), a language is a dialect with an army and a navy. According to this "definition", neither Yiddish nor Faroese would be a language.[1] It is often a political question whether two closely related variants of a language are treated as different languages or not (Slovak vs. Czech, Serbian vs. Croatian, Danish vs. Norwegian). Altogether the Germanic languages have almost 500 million native speakers, which is 1/12 of the whole population of the world. English is especially widespread in terms of regions in which the language is spoken.

1.2 Historical remarks and relatedness between the languages

The Germanic languages constitute a separate branch of the tree representing the Indo-European language family (Fitch 2007: 665). Proto-Germanic formed

---

[1]See Weinreich (1945: 13) on Yiddish: https://en.wikipedia.org/wiki/A_language_is_a_dialect_with_an_army_and_navy.

between 2000 and 1000 BCE. Its origins are in the Baltic region, that is, in northern Germany and southern Scandinavia. About 500 BCE, the area where it was spoken extended from the North Sea to Poland. The first written documents are runes from about 300 CE and the Gothic Bible translation in the fourth century. The First Germanic Sound Shift took place before the second century BCE. In that millennium the Germanic languages developed different consonants from the other Indo-European languages.

Harbert (2006: 8) provides the Figure 1.1 that depicts the development of the Germanic languages. Germanic is divided into East, West, and North Germanic. East Germanic existed in the form of Gothic until about 1800 in Crimea (Crimean Gothic) and is now totally extinct.

West Germanic consists of

- German,

- Yiddish,

- Luxembourgish,

- Pennsylvania Dutch,

- Low German,

- Plautdietsch (also called Mennonite Low German),

- Dutch,

- Afrikaans,

- Frisian, and

- English.

The North Germanic languages are:

- Danish,

- Swedish,

- Norwegian,

- Icelandic, and

- Faroese.

Table 1.1 shows how similar the words from the main vocabulary of the Germanic languages are:

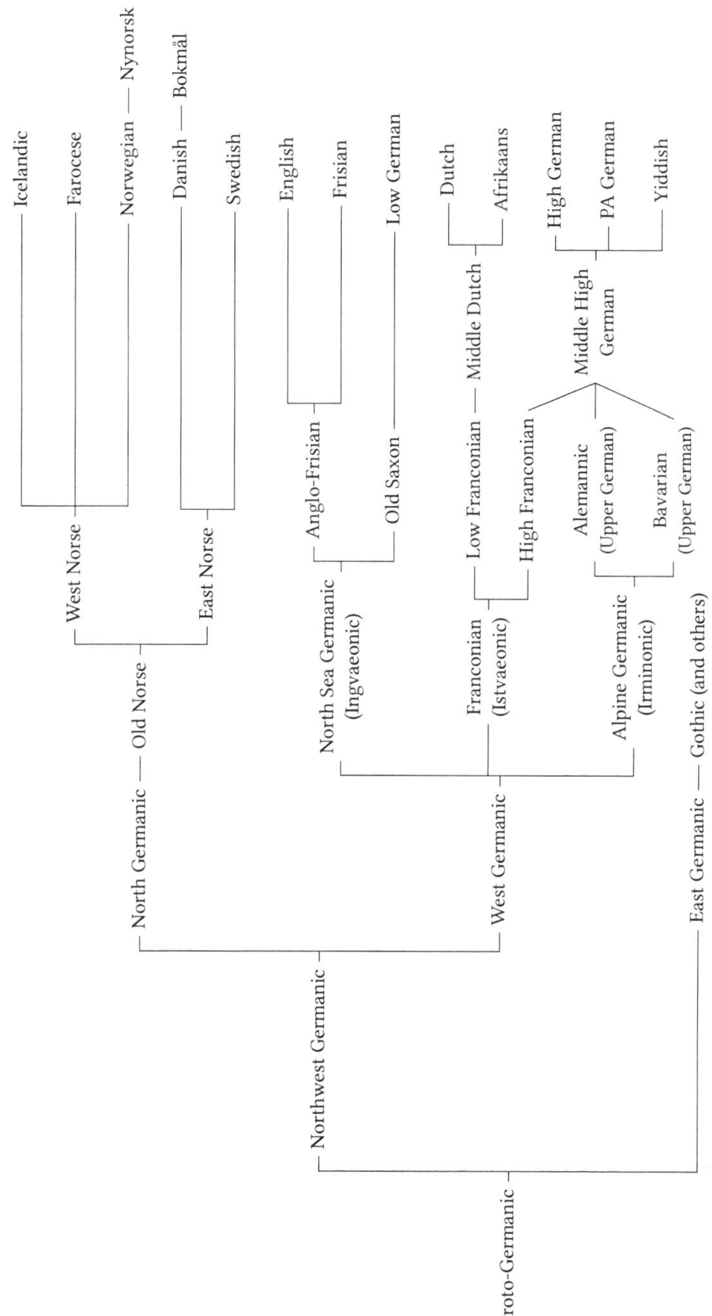

Figure 1.1: Development of Germanic languages according to Harbert (2006: 8)

Table 1.1: Words from the main vocabulary of some Germanic languages

Dutch	vader	vier	vol	huis	bruin	uit	kruid	muis
German	Vater	vier	voll	Haus	braun	aus	Kraut	Maus
English	father	four	full	house	brown	out	crowd (?)	mouse
Frisian	–	fjouwer	fol	hûs	brún	út	krûd	mûs
Swedish	fader	fyra	full	hus	brun	ut	krut	mus
Danish	fader	fire	fuld	hus	brun	ud	krudt	mus
Norwegian	far	fire	full	hus	brun	ut	krydder	mus
Icelandic	faðir	fjórir	fullur	hús	brúnn	út	–	mús

1.3 The three branches of the Germanic family

Proto-Germanic developed into the three main branches East, West, and North Germanic, approximately in the first century CE. The reasons for this development were inherent variations in the respective dialects, migration (language contact) and standardization. This book treats the structure of the Germanic standard languages. This section is divided into three subsections that correspond to the three main Germanic branches. I will sketch the historical developments that lead to the languages spoken today. Many of the details that are covered in Figure 1.1 will be ignored.

1.3.1 East Germanic

It is often claimed that the Goths emigrated to mainland Europe from the Danish islands and South Sweden, but more recent research taking archaeological findings into account assumes that they lived on the European mainland opposite Scandinavia around the Vistula in the first century CE and later moved south to the hinterland of the Black Sea (Heather 1999: 20–30). During this time they were in contact with the Vandals and other tribes. Gothic, Vandalic, and Burgundian and some smaller languages constituted the East Germanic branch, of which only Gothic got passed on. After the decay of the Gothic empires Gothic died out. There were some remnants on the Crimean peninsula until about 1800. The West Gothic bishop Wulfila (or rather a team lead by him, see Ratkus 2018) translated the Bible into Gothic. The best-known version of it is the fragment Codex Argenteus, which belongs to the university library of Uppsala. Figure 1.2 shows a picture of it.[2]

---

[2]Taken from Wikipedia: http://de.wikipedia.org/wiki/Bild:Wulfila_bibel.jpg. 19.10.2014.

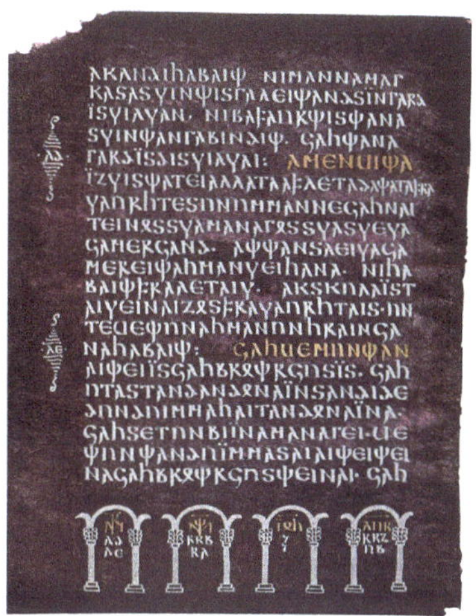

Figure 1.2: The Wulfila Bible (Codex Argenteus), picture from Wikipedia

1.3.2 North Germanic

The first writings on runestones date back to the sixth century. The language
of the Vikings (800–1050) was rather homogeneous and it was only after this
era that two branches started to develop: the East Scandinavian branch with Old
Danish and Old Swedish and the West Scandinavian one with Old Norwegian
and Old Icelandic.

1.3.2.1 Danish

Danish (dansk) is the official language of the Kingdom of Denmark and the second official language of the Faroe Islands and of Greenland, Inuit being the first
official language of Greenland. Danish has about 5.5 million speakers. About
50,000 speakers live in Schleswig-Holstein, the northernmost of the federal states
of Germany. Danish is the Scandinavian language that drifted furthest away from
the common Scandinavian roots.

1.3.2.2 Swedish

Swedish (svenska) is the official language in Sweden with about 8.5 million native speakers. It is the first language of about 300,000 Swedish-speaking Finns
in Finland. Until the times of the Vikings Danish and Swedish were almost indis-

tinguishable. Starting from about 800 they started to diverge. Since about 1300 there have been obvious differences.

1.3.2.3 Icelandic

Icelandic (íslenska) is the West Scandinavian language of Iceland since its settlement over 1000 years ago. There are about 325,000 native speakers. 97 % of the Icelandic population (325,000) has Icelandic as their mother tongue and there are large groups of native speakers in Denmark, the USA, and Canada (about 15,000 in total). There is less variation than in other Germanic languages (no dialects). The language is conservative, in the sense that Icelandic is the language among the Germanic languages that best preserved Germanic vocabulary and inflection. In the beginning there were almost no differences between Norwegian and Icelandic but starting about 1100 the languages diverged. This process continued also due to the Danish influence and nowadays Norwegian is more similar to Danish than to Icelandic. There are many written documents in Icelandic.

1.3.2.4 Norwegian

There are two standard varieties of Norwegian (norsk): Danish-Norwegian (bokmål) and New-Norwegian (nynorsk, landsmål). Both are official languages of Norway. There are about 4,3 million speakers. From 1380 to 1814 Danish was the written language and local dialects were spoken in Norway. It developed into the bokmål standard. A standard that is less influenced by Danish was also developed. This was done by Ivar Aasen (1813–1896), who developed Nynorsk. Nynorsk got an official status in 1885. Bokmål 'book tongue' is the first language of most of the Norwegians.

1.3.2.5 Faroese

Faroese (føroyskt) is – alongside Danish – an official language of the Faroe Islands. There are about 47,000 speakers. The Faroe Islands have belonged to Denmark since 1816. Since 1948 they have been a self-governing country within the Danish Realm. Faroese has a strong Danish influence. The first manuscript transmission is as recent as 1773 and even after that date there are not many written documents.

1.3.3 West Germanic

Opinions on the question whether West Germanic developed from a single source or not differ. Some authors assume that the West Germanic languages do not have a common root, but instead developed from the following three unrelated branches of dialect groups (for instance Robinson 1992: 17–18 and Henriksen & van der Auwera 1994: 9):

- North Sea Germanic

- Weser-Rhine Germanic

- Elbe Germanic

Other authors assume that these three branches had a common ancestor (see Figure 1.1) and some disagree with dividing West Germanic into three subbranches altogether (Stiles 2013). There is no unique mapping of these dialect groups to the languages spoken today.

1.3.3.1 German

German is the official language of

- Germany (about 80 million speakers),

- Austria (about 7.5 million speakers),

- Liechtenstein (about 15,000 speakers),

- Switzerland (4.2 million of 6.4 million Swiss residents),

- Northern Italy/South Tyrol (about 270,000 speakers),

- Belgium (about 65,000 speakers), and

- Luxembourg (about 360,000 speakers).

In addition to German, Luxembourg also has Luxembourgish and French as official languages. There are further countries in which German is a national language or a national or regional minority language: Brazil, Czech Republic, Denmark, Hungary, Namibia, Poland, Romania, Russia, and Slovakia.

There are three main national variants (Germany, Austria, Switzerland). In other countries German is a minority language. There are two large dialect groups: German (Plattdüütsch, Nedderdüütsch; in Standard German: Plattdeutsch or Niederdeutsch) and High German (varieties of German spoken south of the Benrath and Uerdingen isoglosses).

1.3.3.2 Yiddish

Yiddish is one of many languages spoken in the Jewish diaspora. There are no reliable numbers as far as the number of speakers is concenred: some sources assume that 1.5 million people speak this language actively or passively with just 500.000 speakers using the language actively in everyday life. Other sources assume that there are 4 million speakers. In any case, the number of Yiddish speakers was much higher 100 years ago: Birnbaum (1915: 6) estimated the number of speakers at up to 12 million. Most of them lived in the area of the Soviet Union (over 7 million) and there were larger communities in the United States (over 2 million), Austria-Hungary (1.5 to 2 million), Romania (over 250,000), Great Britain (250,000), Palestine, Argentina, and Canada (about 100,000 each). See also Schäfer (2023) for estimations of numbers of speakers and further references.

Yiddish has its roots in medieval German with influences from Hebrew and Aramaic. It is also influenced by Roman languages, especially by Old French and Italian varieties.

1.3.3.3 Pennsylvania German

Pennsylvania German (Pensilfaanish, Deitsch), which is also known as Pennsylvania Dutch, has about 300,000 native speakers, who mainly live in the USA. The most important regions are Pennsylvania, Ohio, and Indiana. Pennsylvania German is the result of immigration in the 17th and 18th century. Members of various protestant religions (Mennonites, Pietists and so on) left Europe for religious reasons but later immigrants that came for economic reasons followed. The language is based on Palatine dialects and is nowadays mainly spoken by Amish and Mennonites.

1.3.3.4 Dutch

Dutch (Nederlands) is the official language of the Netherlands and has about 15 million speakers in that country. Dutch is also one of the official languages of Belgium with about 6 million speakers. Dutch is the sole official language and teaching language in Suriname, and in Aruba and the Netherlands Antilles.

1.3.3.5 Afrikaans

Afrikaans has been one of the official languages of South Africa since 1925, which has eleven official languages. There are about 6.4 million native speakers in South Africa, which is about 15 % of the population, and 150,000 in Namibia. Afrikaans has developed since the 17th century from Dutch dialects and has been seen as an independent language since somewhere between 1775 and 1850 (den Besten 2012: 272). The various African languages spoken in the area interacted with Afrikaans. Today English has a strong influence.

1.3.3.6 Frisian

The three varieties of Frisian are not mutually intelligible. There is North Frisian spoken by about 10,000 speakers mainly on the north Frisian islands Amrum, Sylt, and Helgoland. East Frisian is extinct with the exception of Saterlandic, which is spoken in the three villages of Saterland (Landkreis Cloppenburg) by between 1,000 and 2,500 people. West Frisian is spoken in the northern Dutch province Fryslân (Friesland) and has about 350,000 native speakers.

1.3.3.7 English

All over the world English had about 570 million speakers at the end of the 20th century (337 million native speakers, 235 million speakers with English as a second language[3]). The countries with the most native speakers are listed below:

- USA: 227 million,

- Great Britain: 57 million,

- Nigeria: 43 million,

- Canada: 24 million,

- Australia: 17 million,

- Ireland: 3.5 million,

- New Zealand: 3.2 million.

There are many national variants, which differ mostly in pronunciation. Between 1 and 1.5 billion people have active or passive knowledge of English. English is an official language in 59 states. It is the most important scientific language.

---

[3]The term *Zweitsprache* 'second language' is used to refer to speakers using a language in everyday life since this language is spoken in the environment in which they live. An example would be speakers with Turkish as their first language living in Germany. The German tradition distinguishes *Zweitsprache* from *Fremdsprache* 'foreign language'.

2 Phenomena

This chapter deals with variation in the Germanic languages in what is often called the Core Grammar, that is, in sentences of the *John loves Mary* variety.[1] We will look at differences in the verb position (verb before object and object before verb), the verb-second property, which all of the Germanic languages with the exception of English have, the ordering of subjects and objects with respect to each other, the placement of adverbials, the existence/non-existence of verbal complexes, the obligatoriness/absence of subjects, passive including the personal and impersonal passive, expletive pronouns and various ways to mark the clause type, that is, to signal whether a certain clause is an assertion, a question or an embedded clause.

The purpose of this chapter is to set the scene for the chapters to come. It provides a general discussion of the phenomena covered in this book. The discussion will be extended in Chapter 4–8.

A note of caution is necessary here: especially the following three subsections are potentially confusing. A language like German will be categorized as an subject-object-verb language, a verb-second language and a language with free constituent order (Haftka 1996). This sounds contradictory but it is not. The respective classifications refer to properties of languages as such, not to the form of single sentences.

2.1 Order of subject, object and verb

The languages of the world can be classified according to the order of subject, object, and verb that is dominant (Greenberg 1963). In order to make languages comparable, a very general definition of grammatical functions like subject and

---

[1]Chomsky (1981: 7–8) suggests dividing grammars of natural languages into a "core" part and a "periphery". All regular parts belong to the core. The core grammar of a language is assumed to be an instance of Universal Grammar (UG), the genetically determined innate language faculty of human beings. Idioms and other irregular parts of a language belong to the periphery. This book deals with phenomena usually assumed to be part of the core without assuming this core/periphery distinction and without assuming a UG (Müller 2014, 2015c).

object is used for such a classification. The definition is based on semantic properties: subjects are those arguments that are agent-like and objects are arguments that tend to be patient-like. This definition is not always identical to the language-particular definitions. For instance, the language-particular definition of subject in German (and the Germanic languages in general) refers to properties like nominative case (Reis 1982), subject-verb-agreement, and control. We will deal with this in more detail in Section 7.1.1. According to this definition, the phrase *der Aufsatz* 'the paper' in (1) is the subject although it is inanimate and not an agent:

(1) Der Aufsatz interessiert mich.
     the paper   interests   me
     'I am interested in the paper.'

Figure 2.1 shows the dominant order of subject, object, and verb among the world's languages. According to Dryer (2013a) the dominant order is defined as follows:

> Where a language is shown on one of the word order maps as having a particular order as the dominant order in the language, this means that it is either the only order possible or the order that is more frequently used. (Dryer 2013a)

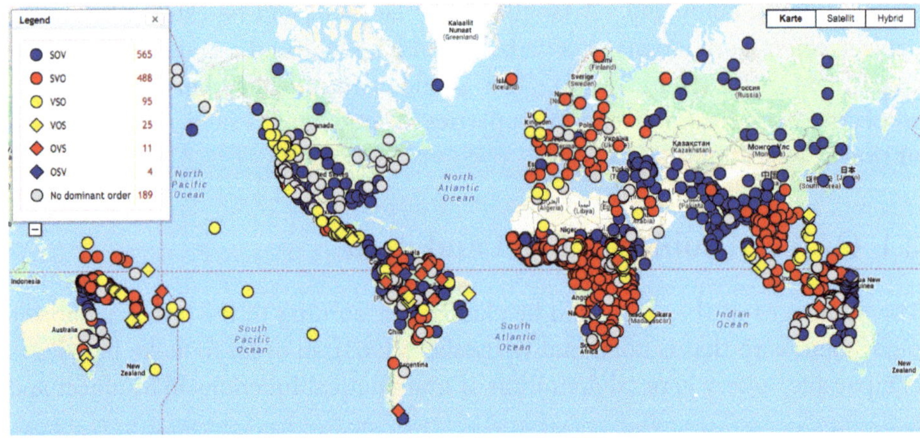

Figure 2.1: Dryer (2013b: Section 1): Feature 81A: Order of subject, object and verb, The World Atlas of Language Structures

If we zoom in to display the European languages we get Figure 2.2. According to the WALS, Icelandic, Norwegian, Swedish, Danish, and English are SVO languages. Dutch, German, and Frisian, however, are marked in gray, that is, these

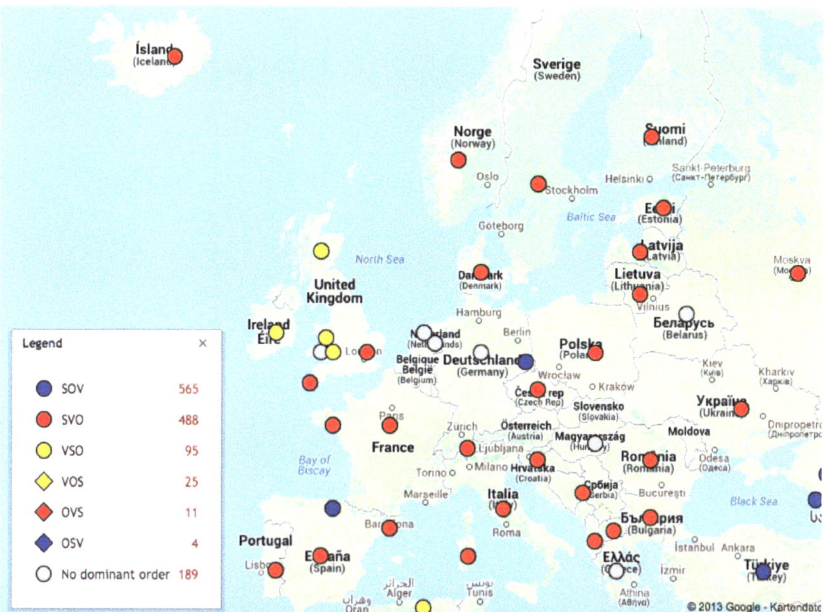

Figure 2.2: Dominant orders of subject, object, and verb in Europe

languages are marked to have no dominant order.[2] According to Figure 2.3, these languages have two dominant orders, namely SOV and SVO. The reason for this classification is that Dryer (2013b: Section 1) distinguishes between sentences in which the finite verb is the main verb (2a) and sentences in which the finite verb is an auxiliary as in (2b):

(2) a. Kim sieht den Fuchs.
     Kim sees the fox
     'Kim sees the fox.'

  b. Kim hat den Fuchs gesehen.
     Kim has the fox   seen
     'Kim has seen the fox.'

According to Dryer the pattern for (2a) is SVO and the one for (2b) is SAuxOV, where Aux stands for the auxiliary verb. Like Greenberg (1963)[3], Dryer counts the latter pattern as having SOV order. The question is whether one can ignore auxiliaries in the examination of constituent order. The auxiliary *hat* 'have' in (2b) syntactically behaves like the full verb *scheint* 'seems' in (3):

---

[2]Greenberg (1963: 87) listed German and Dutch among the SVO languages.

[3]See Höhle (2019: 20–21).

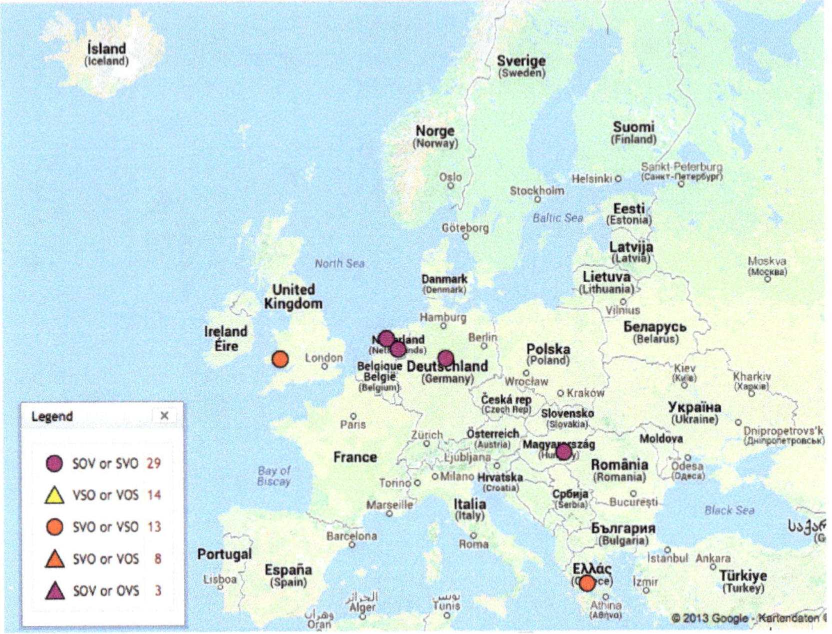

Figure 2.3: Two dominant orders of subject, object, and verb (Dryer 2013b: Section 3)

(3) Kim scheint den Fuchs zu sehen.
     Kim seems the fox   to see
     'Kim seems to see the fox.'

So, here we would have an SVOV order, something that does not exist in the typology under discussion. The languages in Figure 2.3 marked as not having a dominant order use the verb position to mark the clause type: it is just the finite verb that is in first or second position. Non-finite verbs are final:

(4) Kim scheint den Fuchs gesehen zu haben.
     Kim seems the fox   seen   to have
     'Kim seems to have seen the fox.'

In subordinate clauses, both the finite verb and the non-finite verbs appear in final position while the finite verb is in initial position[4] in questions and declar-

---

[4]I use the term initial position to refer to the position the finite verb has in V1 or V2 clauses. The analysis of V2 and V1 involves fronting of the finite verb. In V2 clauses, a constituent is fronted in addition.

ative main clauses. A classification that is entirely based on counting patterns without taking auxiliary verbs and the finiteness/non-finiteness distinction into account cannot tease these properties apart (Höhle 2019: Section 3). In what follows, we will have a look at main and embedded clauses with both finite and non-finite verbs. Embedded clauses reveal differences between OV and VO languages and I will argue that Afrikaans, Dutch, German, and Frisian should be counted among the OV languages and that the other observable pattern SVO is due to other properties of these languages, namely that they mark the clause type by verb position and that they are verb-second (V2) languages.[5]

When one builds more complex German sentences involving several verbs, the embedding verb is usually realized to the right of the embedded verbs. This is shown in (5). (5a) shows a simple sentence with a finite verb. If we form the perfect as in (5b), the perfect auxiliary has to follow the participle. The auxiliary is the finite verb and it determines the form of the participle. Hence the finite verb is the verb that embeds the participle. This is indicated by the lower number of *hat* in comparison to *gesehen*. If we build an even more complex sentence by adding another verb, this verb will be serialized to the right of the present verbs (5c). The Danish example in (6c), adapted from Ørsnes (2009: 146), corresponds to the German example in (5c).

(5)   a. dass sie ihn sieht$_1$ (German)
          that she him sees

          'that she sees him'

     b. dass sie ihn gesehen$_2$ hat$_1$
          that she him seen   has

          'that she has seen him'

     c. dass sie ihn gesehen$_3$ haben$_2$ muss$_1$
          that she him seen   have   must

          'that she must have seen him'

(6)   a. at hun ser$_1$ ham   (Danish)
          that she sees him

     b. at hun have$_1$ set$_2$ ham
          that she has   seen him

     c. at hun må$_1$ have$_2$ set$_3$ ham
          that she must have seen him

---

[5]The property of being a V2 language is independent of the SVO/SOV distinction. All Germanic languages except English are V2 languages. See Section 2.2 on V2.

As the examples in (6) show, the verbs are added in front of the verbs they embed in Danish. This is also the case for English, as is evident from the glosses. In Danish and English the verbs precede the object (*ham*/*him*) and in German they follow it (*ihn*).[6]

Haider (2010: 15, 2020: Section 15.2) pointed out two further differences between the Germanic VO and OV languages: particles precede verbs in OV languages (Vikner 2001: Section 2.4) and the same is true for resultative secondary predicates. In VO languages particles and result predicates follow the verb. This is demonstrated by the following two example sets:

(7)   a.   Kim will look up the information.

      b.   Kim wird die Information nachschlagen.   (German)
         Kim will   the information PART.beat

         'Kim will look up the information.'

(8)   a.   Kim will fish the pond empty.

      b.   Kim wird den Teich leer   fischen.   (German)
         Kim will   the   pond   empty fish

         'Kim will fish the pond empty.'

(7a) shows that *look* precedes the particle *up*, while the verb *schlagen* 'beat' has to follow the particle *nach* in German. Similarly, the secondary resultative predicate *empty* follows the verb in (8a), but *leer* precedes the verb in (8b). Note that I used a future auxiliary in the examples in order to avoid side effects that are due to the verb-second property of German: in declarative main clauses the finite verb always precedes particles and resultative predicates but this is due to the clause type (see Section 2.2).

---

[6]There is a lot of variation in German dialects as far as the order of verbs is concerned and even Standard German allows for orders in which embedding verbs precede embedded verbs (Bech 1955: 63–64, den Besten & Edmondson 1983: 180):

   (i)   weil   er nicht wird$_1$ haben$_2$ kommen$_4$ können$_3$ (German)
          because he not   will   have   come   can

          'because he will not have been able to come.'

The order in which the embedding verb precedes the embedded verb is standard in Dutch (den Besten & Edmondson 1983: 159). Chapter 5 provides an analysis of the verbal complex in the Germanic OV languages. The verbal complexes always follow the objects.

I will return to the SVO vs. SOV order in Chapter 6 and provide more of the evidence that has been used in the literature to argue for the OV status of languages like German and Dutch.

While the Germanic languages can be split nicely into SOV languages with scrambling (see Section 2.3 below) and SVO languages without scrambling, there is one exception: Yiddish. The following data from Diesing (1997: 402) shows that Yiddish can have the order usually observed in SVO languages (9a) and the orders observed in SOV languages with scrambling (9b, c). But it can also have the orders in (9d) and (9e), in which the verb is in the middle and either the direct object or the indirect object precedes the verb.

(9)   a.   Maks hot nit gegebn Rifken dos bukh.   (Yiddish)
             Max   has not given   Rifken the book
             'Max has not given Rifken the book.'

        b.   Maks hot Rifken dos bukh nit gegebn.
             Max   has Rifken the book not given
             'Max has not given Rifken the book.'

        c.   Maks hot dos bukh Rifken nit gegebn.
             Max   has the book Rifken not given
             'Max has not given Rifken the book.'

        d.   Maks hot Rifken nit gegebn dos bukh.
             Max   has Rifken not given   the book
             'Max has not given Rifken the book.'

        e.   Max hat dos bukh nit gegebn Rifken.
             Max has the book not given Rifken.
             'Max has not given Rifken the book.'

Yiddish has been claimed to be a VO language (den Besten & Moed-van Walraven 1986: 113, Diesing 1997: 388, Sadock 1998) or an OV language (Hall 1979, Geilfuß 1990, Vikner 2001: Chapter 2). Some researchers argued that it is neither: it would be a third type of language, one with mixed VO/OV status (Santorini 1993, Schallert 2007: 12, Haider 2010: 161, 2020).

Schallert (2007: Section 2.5) points out that many Germanic languages from earlier stages did not have a fixed VO or OV order and assigns them together with Yiddish to this third class of languages with a rather free verb position. His classification is given in Table 2.1.

Table 2.1: Constituent order typology of the Germanic languages according to
Schallert (2007: 13)

	OV languages	VO languages	OV/VO languages
North Germanic		Islandic, Faroese, Norwegian, Danish, Swedish	Old Nordic, (Old Islandic)
West Germanic	German, Dutch, Afrikaans, Frisian	English	Yiddish, Old English, Old High German,

2.2 V2

The Germanic languages, with the exception of English, are so-called *verb-second languages* (V2 languages). The V2 property can be illustrated with the following German sentences. (10) shows declarative main clauses in which one of the constituents is fronted. (11) shows parallel interrogative clauses.

(10)   a.   Das Kind gibt dem Eichhörnchen jetzt eine Nuss.   (German)
        the child gives the squirrel   now a   nut
        'The child gives the squirrel a nut now.'

      b.   Dem Eichhörnchen gibt das Kind jetzt eine Nuss.
        the   squirrel   gives the child now a   nut

      c.   Eine Nuss gibt das Kind dem Eichhörnchen jetzt.
        a   nut   gives the child the squirrel   now

      d.   Jetzt gibt das Kind dem Eichhörnchen eine Nuss.
        now gives the child the squirrel   a   nut

(11)   a.   Wer gibt dem Eichhörnchen jetzt eine Nuss?   (German)
        who gives the squirrel   now a   nut
        'Who gives the squirrel a nut now?'

      b.   Wem gibt das Kind jetzt eine Nuss?
        who gives the child now a   nut
        'Who does the child give a nut to now?'

      c.   Was gibt das Kind dem Eichhörnchen jetzt?
        what gives the child the squirrel   now
        'What does the child give the squirrel now?'

    d. Wann gibt das Kind dem Eichhörnchen eine Nuss?
        when gives the child the squirrel   a   nut
        'When does the child give the squirrel a nut?'

The finite verb is in second position in all the sentences in (10) and (11).

English, in contrast, does not allow orders in which the object appears immediately before the finite verb.

(12)   a. * This squirrel give I a nut now.

        b. * This nut give I a squirrel now.

        c. * Tomorrow give I the squirrel a nut.

Adverbials and objects can be fronted but then they have to appear before the clause consisting of subject and verb and possibly other constituents.

(13)   a. This nut, I give the squirrel now.

        b. Now, I give the squirrel a nut.

Note also that fronting of objects is restricted to the secondary object for verbs with two objects for some speakers (Hudson 1992: 258).[7] So, while fronting of the secondary object in (14b) is permitted by all speakers, some speakers find extractions like the extraction of the primary object in (14c) unacceptable or marked.

(14)   a.   We give children sweets.

        b.   These sweets, we give children _.

        c. % These children, we give _ sweets.

This is not the case in V2 languages: they are rather liberal as far as fronting is concerned. Basically all constituents can be fronted, exceptions being reflexive pronouns that are selected by inherently reflexive verbs (15), expletive objects (16), and certain modal particles (17). See also Hoberg (1981: 159) on inherently reflexive verbs and modal particles.

(15)   a.   Maria erholt   sich.   (German)
          Maria recovers REFL

          'Maria recovers.'

---

[7]I use the terms *primary object* and *secondary object* in order to avoid the confusion that is sometimes caused by the terms *direct* and *indirect object*. The primary object is the first object in English and the dative object of ditransitive verbs governing the dative in German. The secondary object is the second object in English and the accusative in German ditransitive constructions. The order dative before accusative is also the unmarked order for arguments of most ditransitive verbs (Höhle 1982). For exceptions, see Cook (2006).

      b. * Sich erholt   Maria.
          REFL recovers Maria

(16)   a.   Er bringt es   bis   zum   Professor.   (German)
         he brings EXPL until to.the professor

         'He makes it to professor.'

      b. # Es   bringt er bis   zum   Professor.
         EXPL brings he until to.the professor

(17)   a.   Er geht halt   nicht.   (German)
         he goes PARTICLE not

         'He simply does not go.'

      b. * Halt   geht er nicht.
         PARTICLE goes he not

The element in front of the finite verb is not necessarily a clause mate of the finite verb. In fact, it can belong to a deeply embedded head as is demonstrated by the following example from German:

(18)   [Über dieses Thema]$_i$ habe ich sie gebeten, [[einen Vortrag $\_i$] zu
       about this   topic   have I her asked   a   talk   to
       halten].[8]   (German)
       hold

       'I asked her to give a talk about this topic.'

The PP *über dieses Thema* depends on *Vortrag* 'talk', which is part of the VP headed by *zu halten* 'to hold', which is in turn embedded under *gebeten* 'asked'. Sentences like (18) show that V2 frontings cannot be analyzed as a simple re-ordering of the arguments of a verb. While such an approach would work for the examples in (19), it would not extend to other cases in which the fronted element does not depend on the highest verb in the clause.

(19)   Den   Text kennt er.
      the.ACC text knows he
      'He knows the text.'

The following examples from Danish (SVO) show that the property of being a V2 language is independent of the VO/OV property:

---

[8]Adapted from Hinrichs & Nakazawa (1989a: 21).

(20) a. Gert har læst bogen.   (Danish)
      Gert has read book.DEF

      b. Bogen   har Gert læst.
         book.DEF has Gert read

The example in (20a) shows that the object follows the verbs and (20b) shows that the object *bogen* 'the book' can appear in sentence initial position in front of the finite verb *har* 'have'.

The V2 order is used in declarative main clauses throughout the Germanic languages (except English). Some Germanic languages do not permit V2 order in embedded clauses. For a discussion of embedded interrogatives see Section 2.5.

While English does not allow for the order object-verb-subject, which is possible in the other Germanic languages due to V2 fronting, it allows for the fronting of the object in questions, resulting in structures that are parallel to what we know from the other Germanic languages:

(21) a. Which book did Sandy read?

      b. Which book did Sandy give to Kim?

      c. To whom did Sandy give the book?

English used to be a V2 language but lost this property. The V2 in questions is a residue of earlier stages of the language, which is why English is called a *residual V2 language* (Rizzi 1990: 375).

V2 and verb fronting in general is a way to mark clause types in all Germanic languages. V2 sentences can be declarative clauses in all Germanic languages except English and they can be questions in all Germanic languages including English. In addition, V2 sentences may be imperatives, as (22) shows.

(22) Jetzt gib ihr das Buch!   (German)
      now give her the book

      'Give her the book now!'

Sentences with the finite verb in first position (V1) can be yes/no questions or imperatives:

(23) a. Gibt er ihr das Buch?   (German)
         gives he her the book

         'Does he give her the book?'

      b. Gib ihr das Buch!
         give her the book

Of course the order of elements is not the only cue as far as the clause type is concerned. Intonation and morphological marking of imperative forms plays a role as well.

The property of being a V2 language is exceedingly rare among the world's languages (Holmberg 2015: 343). Apart from the Germanic languages with the exception of Modern English (Haider & Prinzhorn 1986), the only known cases are Estonian (Finno-Ugric, Holmberg 2015: 343), Sorbian (Plank 2003: entry 79) (a Slavic language), the Celtic languages Breton (Borsley & Kathol 2000), Cornish (Borsley, Tallerman & Willis 2007: 287), and Middle Welsh (Willis 1998), Old French (Adams 1987: Section 1.3, Roberts 1993: Section 2.1.2, Vance 1997: Chapter 2), Old Spanish (Fontana 1997: Section 3.3.2), Rhaeto-Romance (Poletto 2002, Anderson 2006), Kashmiri (Bhatt 1999: Chapter 4), two dialects of Himachali, which also belongs to Indo-Aryan and is spoken in regions adjacent to Kashmiri (Hendriksen 1990), the Austronesian languages Taiof and Sisiqa (Ross 2004: 495) and the Brazilian native language Karitiana from the Tupí language family (Storto 2003).

2.3 Scrambling

While the constituent order in languages like English is rather fixed, languages like Dutch and German allow a freer permutation of arguments. In order not to contaminate the effects by reorderings that are due to the V2 property, I use verb last sentences to illustrate the phenomenon in German. Example (24) shows the only possible order for subject and objects of a simple ditransitive sentence in English without extraction:

(24)   because the child gives the squirrel the nut   (English)

If speakers want to realize the secondary object *the nut* before the primary object *the squirrel*, they have to use a prepositional object. This type of reordering is called *dative-shift* and an example is provided in (25):

(25)   because the child gives the nut to the squirrel   (English)

In contrast to this we have the German examples in (26). These examples show that the noun phrases can be freely permuted:

(26)   a.   [weil]   das Kind dem Eichhörnchen die Nuss gibt   (German)
              because the child the   squirrel   the nut   gives

         b.   [weil]   das Kind die Nuss dem Eichhörnchen gibt
              because the child the nut   the   squirrel   gives

c. [weil]   die Nuss das Kind dem Eichhörnchen gibt
because the nut   the child the squirrel   gives

d. [weil]   die Nuss dem Eichhörnchen das Kind gibt
because the nut   the squirrel   the child gives

e. [weil]   dem Eichhörnchen das Kind die Nuss gibt
because the squirrel   the child the nut gives

f. [weil]   dem Eichhörnchen die Nuss das Kind gibt
because the squirrel   the nut the child gives

Not all of these orders can be used in all contexts. Some of the examples require a special, contrastive intonation. The orders can be sorted with respect to the number of contexts in which they can be used. Höhle (1982) suggests calling the order that can be used in most contexts the normal or unmarked order.

The OV languages share a lot of properties, so one would expect that Dutch allows for scrambling as well. However, object NPs cannot be scrambled:

(27)   * Toen hebben de autoriteiten het kind de moeder   (Dutch)
then have   the authorities the child the mother
teruggegeven
back.given
Intended: 'The authorities gave back the child to the mother.'

The reason for this is that NPs are not case marked in Dutch. It would be very difficult for hearers and readers to find out who did what to whom. This is parallel to examples with caseless NPs in German. As noted by Wegener (1985b: 45), (28) is not ambiguous:

(28) Sie mischt Wein Wasser bei.   (German)
she mixes wine water   at
'She mixes wine with water.'

This means that there is wine and water is added to it. This corresponds to the order dat < acc. The situation is different with determiners:

(29) a. Sie mischt dem   Wein das   Wasser bei.   (German)
she mixes the.DAT wine the.ACC water   at
'She mixes wine with water.'

b. Sie mischt das Wasser dem Wein bei.
she mixes the.ACC water the.DAT wine at
'She mixes wine with water.'

With determiners, we get the reading in (28) independent of the order of the noun phrases. If we change the order of determinerless NPs in (28), we get a different reading:

(30) Sie mischt Wasser Wein bei.   (German)
      she mixes water   wine at
      'She mixes water with wine.'

So, without any clues from case marking, one has dat < acc order; with case marking, both orders are possible.

Returning to Dutch, the examples in (31) show that scrambling is indeed possible, if the arguments can be identified (Geerts et al. 1984: 989, Haider 2010: 14, 152):

(31) a. Toen hebben de autoriteiten het kind aan de moeder   (Dutch)
          then have   the authorities the child to   the mother
          teruggegeven.
          back.given

      b. Toen hebben de autoriteiten aan de moeder het kind teruggegeven
          then have   the authorities to   the mother the child back.given

(31) contains examples with NP and PP object. Since the PP is clearly identifiable, the two arguments can appear in either order. Hence, it seems justified to assume that the OV languages (German, Dutch, Afrikaans, Frisian) allow for scrambling with restrictions forbidding scrambling of elements that are not identifiable.

2.4 The position of adverbials

In languages like German and Dutch, the position of adverbials is rather free: the adverb *gestern* 'yesterday' can appear anywhere between the arguments and the verb:

(32) a. weil   das Kind dem Eichhörnchen die Nuss *gestern*   (German)
          because the child the squirrel   the nut yesterday
          gab
          gave
          'because the child gave the squirrel the nut yesterday'

      b. weil   das Kind dem Eichhörnchen *gestern*   die Nuss gab
          because the child the squirrel   yesterday the nut   gave

   c. weil   das Kind *gestern*   dem Eichhörnchen die Nuss gab
       because the child yesterday the squirrel   the nut gave

   d. weil   *gestern*   das Kind dem Eichhörnchen die Nuss gab
       because yesterday the child the squirrel   the nut gave

Dutch has free order of adverbials as well (Neeleman 1994: 387, Koster 1999: 4, Bouma 2003: Section 6). (33) shows the Dutch examples corresponding to (32):

(33)   a. omdat   het kind de eekhoorn de noot *gisteren*   gaf   (Dutch)
         because the child the squirrel   the nut yesterday gave

       'because the child gave the squirrel the nut yesterday'

     b. omdat   het kind de eekhoorn *gisteren*   de noot gaf
         because the child the squirrel   yesterday the nut   gave

     c. omdat   het kind *gisteren*   de eekhoorn de noot gaf
         because the child yesterday the squirrel   the nut   gave

     d. omdat   *gisteren*   het kind de eekhoorn de noot gaf
         because yesterday the child the squirrel   the nut   gave

In contrast, the position of the adverbials is rather restricted in SVO languages like Danish and English. The adverbials usually are placed before or after the VP; that is, verb and objects form one unit and adverbials attach to the left or to the right of this unit. (34) provides an example:

(34)   a.   because the child often [gave the squirrel the nut]   (English)

     b.   because the child [gave the squirrel the nut] often

     c.   * because the child [gave often the squirrel the nut]

     d.   * because the child [gave the squirrel often the nut]

It is assumed that in these languages verb and objects form a structural unit, a verb phrase (VP). Adverbials may attach to this VP forming a larger VP, which is then combined with the subject to form a complete sentence.

The following example, which is due to Quirk et al. (1985: § 8.20, 495), shows that even in very complex combinations of several verbs adverbs may be placed at the left periphery of a VP:

(35)   It [certainly [$_{\text{VP}}$ may [possibly [$_{\text{VP}}$ have [indeed [$_{\text{VP}}$ been
      [badly [$_{\text{VP}}$ formulated]]]]]]]].

It seems then that while the verb and its objects form a unit, the combination of several levels of embedding verbs do not form a unit on their own. This is different from the OV languages where verbs form a verbal complex which usually cannot be interrupted by adverbs.

(36) a. dass das Kind dem Eichhörnchen die Nuss morgen   geben dürfen
          that the child the   squirrel   the nut   tomorrow give   may

          muss

          must

          'that it must be possible that it is allowed that the child gives the
          squirrel the nut tomorrow'

      b. * dass das Kind dem Eichhörnchen die Nuss geben morgen   dürfen
            that the child the   squirrel   the nut   give   tomorrow may

            muss

            must

      c. * dass das Kind dem Eichhörnchen die Nuss geben dürfen morgen
            that the child the   squirrel   the nut   give   may   tomorrow

            muss

            must

2.5 Embedded clauses

This section deals with embedded clauses that are introduced by a complementizer and with embedded interrogative clauses. The Germanic languages vary
with respect to the verb placement in these subordinate clauses and with respect
to the question whether the embedded clauses are V2 or not.

2.5.1 Embedded clauses introduced by a complementizer

As was already mentioned, Afrikaans, Dutch, and German are SOV languages
and this is shown in embedded clauses that are introduced by a complementizer.
(37) is an example:

(37) Ich weiß, dass Aicke das Buch heute gelesen hat.
      I   know that Aicke the book today read   has
      'I know that Aicke read the book today.'

English, being an SVO non-V2 language, allows for SVO order only.

(38) I know that Kim read the book yesterday.   (English)

Interestingly, Danish, also an SVO language, allows both SVO order (39) and V2
order (40) in clauses preceded by a complementizer:

(39)   Jeg ved, at   Gert ikke har læst bogen   i dag.   (Danish)
         I   know that Gert not   has read book.DEF today

         'I know that Gert did not read the book today.'

(40)   a. Jeg ved, at   i dag har Gert ikke læst bogen.   (Danish)
            I   know that today has Gert not   read book.DEF

         b. Jeg ved, at   bogen   har Gert ikke læst i dag.
            I   know that book.DEF has Gert not   read today

The example in (39) includes the negation in order to show that we are indeed
dealing with SVO order here. Without the negation it is not clear whether non-
V2 clauses are allowed in clauses that are introduced by a complementizer since
(41a) has the finite verb in second position. With the negation present, it is clear
that we have a V2 clause if the negation follows the finite verb and that we do
not have a V2 clause if the finite verb follows the negation as in (39) and hence
is in third position.

(41)   a. at   Gert har læst bogen   (V2 or SVO)
            that Gert has read book.DEF

         b. at   Gert har ikke læst bogen   (V2)
            that Gert has not   read book.DEF

For complementizerless sentences the V2 order is the only one that is possible:

(42)   a.   Gert har ikke læst bogen   (V2)
              Gert has not   read book.DEF

         b. * Gert ikke har læst bogen   (SVO)
              Gert not   has read book.DEF

Yiddish and Icelandic are SVO languages as well. The clauses that are combined
with a complementizer are V2:

(43)   a. Ikh meyn az   haynt hot Max geleyent dos bukh.[9]   (Yiddish)
            I   think that today has Max read   the book

            'I think that Max read the book today.'

         b. Ikh meyn az   dos bukh hot Max geleyent.
            I   think that the book has Max read

---

[9]Diesing (1990: 58)

(44) Engum   datt í hug, að vert væri að reyna til   að   (Icelandic)
     no.one.DAT fell to mind that worth was to try   PREP to
     kynnast honum.[10]
     know   him
     'It didn't occur to anyone that it was worth trying to get to know him.'

2.5.2 Interrogative clauses

The OV languages form subordinated interrogative clauses by preposing a phrase containing an interrogative pronoun[11] from an otherwise SOV clause. (45) shows a German example:

(45)   a. Ich weiß, wer heute das Buch gelesen hat.   (German)
          I   know who today the book read   has
          'I know who read the book today.'
       b. Ich weiß, was Aicke heute gelesen hat.
          I   know what Aicke today read   has
          'I know what Aicke has read today.'

Since languages like German allow for scrambling, sentences like those in (45) could just be due to the permutation of arguments of a head. However, the generalization about these *w*-clauses is that an arbitrary *w*-element can be fronted. (46) gives an example from German that involves a nonlocal dependency:

(46)   Ich weiß nicht, [über welches Thema]$_i$ sie versprochen hat,
       I   know not   about which   topic   she promised   has
       [[einen Vortrag $_i$] zu   halten].   (German)
        a   talk   to   hold
       'I do not know about which topic she promised to give a talk.'

Here, the phrase *über welches Thema* 'about which topic' is an argument of *Vortrag*, which is embedded in the VP containing *zu halten* 'to hold', which is in turn embedded under *versprochen hat* 'promised has'. The generalization about interrogative clauses is that an interrogative clause consists of an interrogative

---

[10]Maling (1990: 75)

[11]Most interrogative pronouns start with *w* in German and *wh* in English. Phrases containing an interrogative pronoun are called *w*-phrases or *wh*-phrases, respectively. Interrogative clauses are sometimes called *w*-clauses or *wh*-clauses.

phrase (*über welches Thema* 'about which topic') and a clause in which this interrogative phrase is missing somewhere (*er versprochen hat, einen Vortrag zu halten* 'he promised to give a talk').

In German the order of the other constituents is free as in assertive main clauses and embedded clauses with a complementizer that were discussed earlier.

(47) a. Ich weiß, was keiner diesem Eichhörnchen geben würde. (German)
         I   know what nobody this   squirrel   give   would

         'I know what nobody would give this man.'

    b. Ich weiß, was diesem Eichhörnchen keiner geben würde.
         I   know what this   squirrel   nobody give   would

In Danish and English the interrogative clauses consist of an interrogative phrase and an SVO clause in which it is missing:

(48) a. Gert har givet ham bogen.   (Danish)
         Gert has given him book.DEF

         'Gert gave him the book.'

    b. Jeg ved,   hvad$_i$ [Gert har givet ham $\_i$].
         I   know what   Gert has given him

         'I know what Gert gave him.'

    c. Jeg ved,   hvem$_i$ [Gert har givet $\_i$ bogen].
         I   know who   Gert has given   book.DEF

         'I know who Gert has given the book.'

(48a) shows the clause with SVO order and (48b) is an example with the secondary object as interrogative pronoun and (48c) is an example with the primary object as interrogative pronoun. The position that the respective objects have in non-interrogative clauses like (48a) is marked with $\_i$.

Yiddish is special in that it has V2 order in interrogative clauses as well (Diesing 1990: Sections 4.1, 4.2): interrogatives consist of an interrogative phrase that is extracted from a V2 clause:

(49) Ir   veyst efsher [avu   do   voynt Roznblat der goldshmid]?[12]
     you know maybe   where there lives   Roznblat the goldsmith

    'Do you perhaps know where Roznblat the goldsmith lives?'

---

[12] Diesing (1990: 65). Quoted from Olsvanger, *Royte Pomerantsn*, 1949.

So the variation we find among the Germanic languages is *w*-phrase + SOV, *w*-phrase + SVO, and *w*-phrase + V2.

2.6 The use of expletives to mark the clause type

The Germanic languages use constituent order to code the clause type: V2 main clauses can be assertions or questions, depending on the content of the preverbal material and intonation. Similarly, embedded interrogative clauses consist of a *w*-phrase and an SVO, SOV, or V2 clause. The fronting of a constituent in a V2 clause comes with certain information structural effects: something is the topic or the focus of an utterance. For embedded sentences, it is important for some languages that the structure is transparent, i.e., that we have the *w* + SVO or *w* + V2 order. There are situations in which it is inappropriate to front an element and in such situations the Germanic languages use expletives, that is, pronouns that do not contribute semantically, to maintain a certain order.

German uses the expletive *es* to fill the position before the finite verb, if no other constituent is to be fronted.

(50) a. Drei Reiter ritten zum   Tor hinaus.   (German)
         three riders rode   to.the gate out

         'Three riders rode out of the gate.'

      b. Es   ritten drei Reiter zum   Tor hinaus.
         EXPL rode   three riders to.the gate out

Danish uses the expletive to make it clear that an extraction of a constituent took place (Müller & Ørsnes 2011: 169):[13]

(51) a. Politiet   ved   ikke, hvem der   havde placeret   (Danish)
         police.DEF knows not   who   EXPL has   placed
         bomben.[14]
         bomb.DEF

         'The police does not know who placed the bomb.'

      b. * Politiet   ved   ikke, hvem havde placeret bomben.
         police.DEF knows not   who   has   placed   bomb.DEF

Without the expletive, the pattern would be like the one in (51b). In (51b) we have the normal SVO order and it is not obvious to the hearer that the pattern consists

---

[13]Examples marked with DK are extracted from KorpusDK, a corpus of 56 million words documenting contemporary Danish (http://ordnet.dk/korpusdk).

[14]DK

of an extracted element (the subject) and an SVO clause from which it is missing. This is more transparent if an expletive is inserted into the subject position as in (51a). (52) shows this using the analysis that will be suggested in Chapter 8: (52a) shows the hypothetical structure that would result if one assumed that the subject *hvem* 'who' is extracted. So-called *string-vacuous movement* would result: the subject is moved to a place right next to it. In (52b), on the other hand, the subject position is taken by the expletive and hence it is clear that the embedded sentence has a special structure. There is an overt marker for the hearer or reader of the sentence marking it as an embedded interrogative clause.

(52)   a.   * [hvem$_i$ [$_{-i}$ havde placeret bomben]]   (Danish)
            who   has   placed   bomb.DEF

       b.   [hvem$_i$ [der   havde $_{-i}$ placeret bomben]]
            who   EXPL has   placed   bomb.DEF

Similarly, Yiddish uses an expletive in embedded interrogatives (w + V2) if there is no other element that is information structurally appropriate for the preverbal position. (53) shows examples from Prince (1989: 403–404):

(53)   a.   ikh hob zi gefregt ver es   iz beser far ir   (Yiddish)
            I   have her asked   who EXPL is better for her

            'I have asked her who is better for her.'

       b.   ikh hob im   gefregt vemen es   kenen ale dayne khaverim
            I   have him asked   whom EXPL know all your   friends

            'I asked him whom all your friends know.'

(53a) is an example involving an interrogative pronoun that is the subject and (53b) is an example in which the preverbal position is not filled by an argument of *kenen* 'know' but by an expletive. The subject *ale dayne khaverim* 'all your friends' stays behind and the object *vemen* 'whom' is extracted since it is the interrogative pronoun.

2.7 Verbal complexes in OV languages

The OV languages have a verbal complex, or more general, a predicate complex, since adjectives take part in complex formation as well. (54) gives a German example taken from Haider (1986b: 110; 1991: 128):

(54)   weil   es   ihr   jemand   zu lesen versprochen hat (German)
       because it.ACC her.DAT somebody.NOM to read   promised   has

       'because somebody promised her to read it'

The arguments of the respective verbs can be mixed with arguments of other verbs. In the example above, the *es* 'it' is not adjacent to its verb *lesen* 'to read', neither is *ihm* 'him' adjacent to *versprochen* 'promised' nor *jemand* to *hat* 'has'. In a more "well-behaved" ordering the object of *zu lesen* 'to read' is adjacent to the verb:

(55) weil   jemand   ihr das Buch zu lesen versprochen hat
      because somebody her the book to read promised   has

      'because somebody promised her to read the book'

The ordering in (55) would allow for an analysis in which *das Buch zu lesen* forms a VP which is treated as an argument of *versprochen* 'promised'. However, this is not a viable analysis for (54) if one assumes that phrases have to be continuous.

One explanation of orders like the one in (54) is that the verbs form a unit that behaves like a simplex verb. As with the ditransitive verb *geben* 'to give' all permutations of the arguments of the verbs are possible in principle. So *zu lesen versprochen hat* forms a complex in both (54) and (55) and all permutations of the three arguments are permitted by the grammar.

VO languages like English and Danish do not allow permutations of arguments that belong to different verbs. In VO languages governing verbs always embed VPs. The following example gives an indication of the structure:

(56)   because somebody [will [promise him [to read the book]]]

2.8 Obligatoriness of subjects, case of subjects, and passives

SVO languages like English and Danish require a subject, while OV languages like German allow for subjectless constructions.

(57)   a. Ihm   graut vor   der Prüfung.   (German)
          him.DAT dreads before the exam

          'He dreads the exam.'

       b. Heute wird nicht gearbeitet.
          today is   not   worked

          'There is no working today.'

Reis (1982) developed several tests for subjecthood and according to them, *ihm* 'him' in (57a) is not a subject. German subjects are always in the nominative. As we will see in Section 7.1.1, Icelandic allows for dative subjects, but if we apply the tests that will be developed there (for instance the possibility to omit a subject in infinitival constructions) to cases like (57a), we see that *ihm* is really different from Icelandic dative subjects. So, (57a) is a subjectless construction. In (57b), there is no nominal argument at all.

As is shown in (57b), German allows for so-called impersonal passives. Impersonal passives are a special kind of passives in which no element gets promoted to subject. SVO languages like English and Danish do not allow subjectless constructions. English therefore does not allow impersonal passives at all as (58b) shows:

(58) a. weil   noch gearbeitet wird   (German)
           because still   worked   is
           'because there is still working there'

      b. * because (it) was worked   (English)

Interestingly, Danish found a way to fulfill the subject requirement and at the same time have impersonal passives: Danish simply inserts an expletive pronoun into the subject position:

(59) a. fordi   der bliver arbejdet   (Danish)
         because EXPL is   worked
         'because there is working there'

      b. fordi   der   arbejdes
         because EXPL work.PASS
         'because there is working there'

German does not allow for an expletive subject:

(60) * weil   es noch gearbeitet wird   (German)
        because it still worked   is
        'because there is still working there'

It is possible to have an expletive pronoun in front of the finite verb as in (61), but this is a positional expletive whose purpose it is to mark the V2 sentence type.

(61) Es   wird noch gearbeitet.   (German)
      EXPL is   still worked
      'There is still working there.'

The expletive is not an argument of any verb. The purely positional character of this expletive is shown by the fact that it does not appear in verb last sentences like (60).

As we will discuss in Section 7.1.1, Icelandic has non-nominative subjects (Zaenen et al. 1985), which makes it the most exciting language to study among the Germanic languages. We will see that a uniform analysis of case assignment is possible (Yip, Maling & Jackendoff 1987), although there is some variety in the inflectional systems of the Germanic languages.

2.9 Summary

This chapter has provided an overview of the phenomena that are covered in this book. Of course we will look at everything in much more detail in the chapters to come. Let's start and get our hands dirty.

Comprehension questions

- What are the characteristics of a V2 language?

- If a language has many sentences with subject, verb, object order, does this help to determine whether the language is a V2 language?

Further reading

The book *Germanic languages* edited by König & van der Auwera (1994) provides a descriptive overview of the Germanic languages. Haider's (2010) book about the syntax of German compares German with other Germanic languages. It contains a good description of the syntactic facts compatible with Haider's theoretical approaches within the framework of Government & Binding.

3 Phrase structure grammars and $\overline{\mathrm{X}}$ theory

This chapter introduces phase structure grammars (PSGs), which play an important role in many theories that were developed since Chomsky (1957). The phrase structure grammar developed in this chapter will be the basis for more complicated phenomena covered in the chapters to come. This chapter deals mainly with German and English, which is sufficient for the introduction of the formal apparatus of phrase structure grammars. The result of this chapter is a phrase structure grammar that is similar to $\overline{\mathrm{X}}$ grammars (pronounced: "X-bar grammars") of the style that was developed in the late 1970s and the early 1980s (Chomsky 1970, Jackendoff 1977). The structures argued for in this chapter will also play a role in later chapters, but the lexical items will be much richer: they will contain valence information playing a crucial role in licensing syntactic structure.

Much time is spent on the structure of noun phrases. The main insights on the syntax of German noun phrases can be carried over to other Germanic languages. Later chapters will deal with the differences among the Germanic languages with respect to clause level syntax.

This chapter heavily draws on Müller (2023b: Chapter 2), which is an updated translation of Müller (2013a: Chapter 2). Knowledge of basic concepts like part of speech and constituency tests is presupposed. Readers who feel the need to refresh their knowledge in these areas are referred to Chapter 1 of these textbooks.

3.1 Symbols and rewrite rules

Words can be assigned to a particular part of speech on the basis of their inflectional properties and syntactic distribution. Thus, *weil* 'because' in (1) is a conjunction, whereas *das* 'the' and *dem* 'the' are articles and therefore classed as determiners. Furthermore, *Buch* 'book' and *Kind* 'child' are nouns and *gibt* 'gives' is a verb.

(1) weil   er das Buch dem Kind gibt
     because he the book the child gives
     'because he gives the child the book'

Using the constituency tests introduced in Müller (2023b: Section 1.3), one can show that individual words as well as the strings *das Buch* 'the book' and *dem Kind* 'the child' form constituents. These then get assigned certain symbols. Since nouns form an important part of the phrases *das Buch* and *dem Kind*, these are referred to as *noun phrases* or NPs, for short. The pronoun *er* 'he' can occur in the same positions as full NPs and can therefore also be assigned to the category NP.

The grouping of constituents can be conceptualized and depicted by boxes. For example, *er das Buch dem Kind gibt* can be depicted as in Figure 3.1.

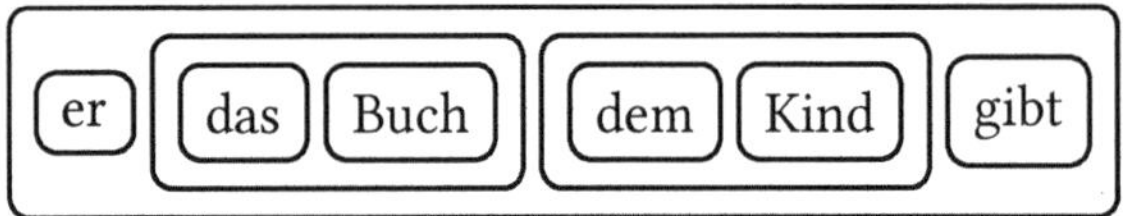

Figure 3.1: Words and phrases in boxes

The categories mentioned above can be integrated into this picture. The resulting picture is given as Figure 3.2. Boxes with the same labels can be replaced

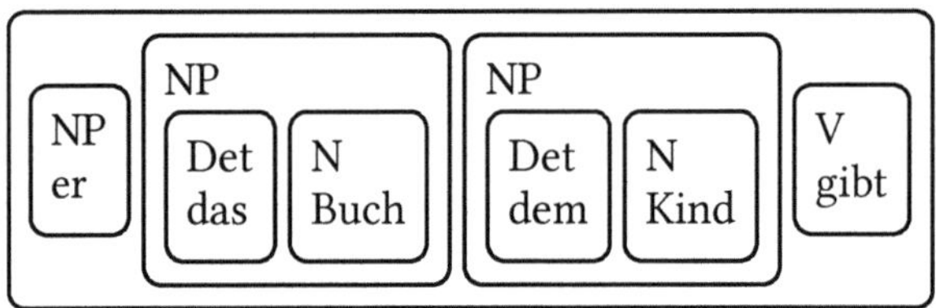

Figure 3.2: Words and phrases in boxes with part of speech labels

by other boxes with the same label. For example, the box for *dem Kind* 'the child' can be replaced by *dem Mädchen* 'the girl'. *Er* can be replaced by *das Mädchen* 'the girl'. This is very intuitive, but it is better to have a tool that can be used to actually derive structures that can be depicted as such boxes or as syntactic trees that you are familiar with from introductory courses. Therefore we will now look at phrsae structure grammars.

Phrase structure grammars come with rules specifying which symbols are assigned to certain kinds of words and how these are combined to create more complex units. A simple phrase structure grammar which can be used to analyze (1) is given in (2):[1,2]

(2)   NP → Det N   NP → er   N → Buch
      S → NP NP NP V   Det → das   N → Kind
                                    Det → dem   V → gibt

We can therefore interpret a rule such as NP → Det N as meaning that a noun phrase, that is, something which is assigned the symbol NP, can consist of a determiner (Det) and a noun (N).

We can analyze the sentence in (1) using the grammar in (2) in the following way: first, we take the first word in the sentence and check if there is a rule in which this word occurs on the right-hand side of the rule. If this is the case, then we replace the word with the symbol on the left-hand side of the rule. This happens in lines 2–4, 6–7 and 9 of the derivation in (3). For instance, in line 2 *er* is replaced by NP. If there are two or more symbols which occur together on the right-hand side of a rule, then all these words are replaced with the symbol on the left. This happens in lines 5, 8 and 10. For instance, in line 5 and 8, Det and N are rewritten as NP.

(3)

	words and symbols						rules that are applied
1	er	das	Buch	dem	Kind	gibt	
2	NP	das	Buch	dem	Kind	gibt	NP → er
3	NP	Det	Buch	dem	Kind	gibt	Det → das
4	NP	Det	N	dem	Kind	gibt	N → Buch
5	NP		NP	dem	Kind	gibt	NP → Det N
6	NP		NP	Det	Kind	gibt	Det → dem
7	NP		NP	Det	N	gibt	N → Kind
8	NP		NP		NP	gibt	NP → Det N
9	NP		NP		NP	V	V → gibt
10						S	S → NP NP NP V

In (3), we began with a string of words and it was shown that we can derive the structure of a sentence by applying the rules of a given phrase structure grammar.

---

[1] I ignore the conjunction *weil* 'because' for now. Since the exact analysis of German verb-first and verb-second clauses requires a number of additional assumptions, we will restrict ourselves to verb-final clauses in this chapter.

[2] The rule NP → er may seem odd. We could assume the rule PersPron → er instead but then would have to posit a further rule which would specify that personal pronouns can replace full NPs: NP → PersPron. The rule in (2) combines the two aforementioned rules and states that *er* 'he' can occur in positions where noun phrases can.

We could have applied the same steps in reverse order: starting with the sentence symbol S, we would have applied the steps 9–1 and arrived at the string of words. Selecting different rules from the grammar for rewriting symbols, we could use the grammar in (2) to get from S to the string *er dem Kind das Buch gibt* 'he the child the book gives'. We can say that this grammar licenses (or generates) a set of sentences.

The derivation in (3) can also be represented as a tree. This is shown by Figure 3.3. The symbols in the tree are called *nodes*. We say that S immediately

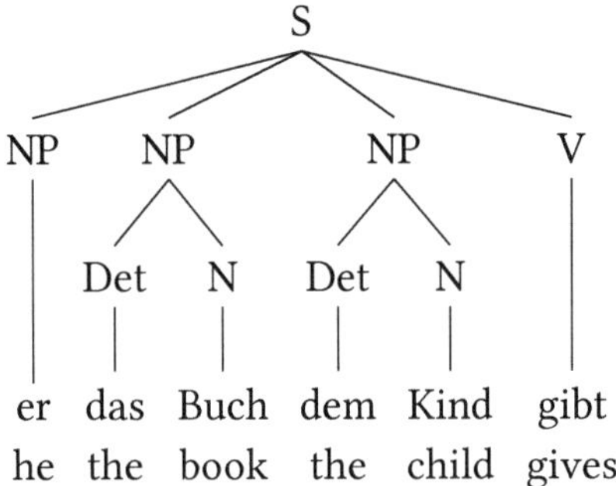

Figure 3.3: Analysis of *er das Buch dem Kind gibt* 'he the book the child gives'

dominates the NP nodes and the V node. The other nodes in the tree are also dominated, but not immediately dominated, by S. If we want to talk about the relationship between nodes, it is common to use kinship terms. In Figure 3.3, S is the *mother node* of the three NP nodes and the V node. The NP nodes and V are *sisters* or *daughters*, since they have the same mother node.[3] If a node has two daughters, then we have a binary branching structure. If there is exactly one daughter, then we have a unary branching structure. Two words or phrases are said to be *adjacent* if they are directly next to each other.

Phrase structure rules are often omitted in linguistic publications. Instead, authors opt for tree diagrams or the compact equivalent bracket notation as in (4).

(4) $[_S [_{NP}$ er$]$ $[_{NP} [_{Det}$ das$]$ $[_N$ Buch$]]$ $[_{NP} [_{Det}$ dem$]$ $[_N$ Kind$]]$ $[_V$ gibt$]]$
       he   the   book   the   child   gives

Nevertheless, it is the grammatical rules/schemata which are actually important because these represent grammatical knowledge which is independent of specific

---

[3] *Parent node* and *child node* are alternative terms. I use *mother* and *daughter* here, since this terminology is also used in formalizations of the theory developed later.

structures. In this way, we can use the grammar in (2) to parse or generate the sentence in (5), which differs from (1) in the order of objects:

(5) (weil)   er   dem   Kind das   Buch gibt
     because he.NOM the.DAT child the.ACC book gives
     'because he gives the child the book'

The rules for replacing determiners and nouns are simply applied in a different order than in (1). Rather than replacing the first Det with *das* 'the' and the first noun with *Buch* 'book', the first Det is replaced with *dem* 'the' and the first noun with *Kind.*

At this juncture, I should point out that the grammar in (2) is not the only possible grammar for the example sentence in (1). There are an infinite number of possible grammars which could be used to analyze these kinds of sentences (see Müller 2023b: Chapter 2, Exercise 1). Another possible grammar is the following one:

(6)   NP → Det N   NP → er   N → Buch
      V   → NP V   Det → das   N → Kind
                          Det → dem   V → gibt

This grammar licenses only binary branching structures, as shown in Figure 3.4. Since the rule V → NP, V is recursive, arbitrarily many NPs can be combined with a V. The result of an NP-V combination is a V, which can be used as a daughter at the right-hand side of the rule again.

Both the grammar in (6) and the one in (2) are too imprecise. If we adopt additional lexical entries for *ich* 'I' and *den* 'the' (accusative) in our grammar, then the grammar would incorrectly license the ungrammatical sentences in (7b–d):[4]

---

[4]With the grammar in (6), we also have the additional problem that we cannot determine when an utterance is complete since the symbol V is used for all combinations of V and NP. Therefore, we can also analyze the sentences in (i) with this grammar provided we add the respective words to the lexicon:

(i) a. * der   Delphin erwartet
         the.NOM dolphin expects

     b. * des   Kindes   er   das   Buch dem   Kind gibt
         the.GEN child.GEN he.NOM the.ACC book the.DAT child gives

The number of arguments required by a verb must be somehow represented in the grammar. In Chapter 4, we will see exactly how the selection of arguments by a verb (valence) is captured in HPSG.

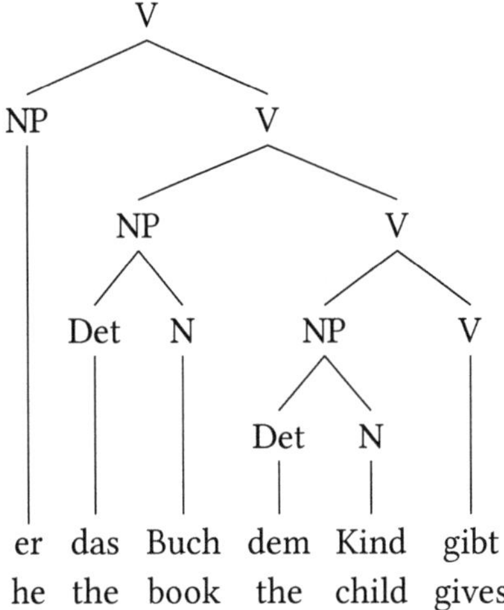

Figure 3.4: Analysis of *er das Buch dem Kind gibt* with a binary branching structure

(7) a. er   das   Buch dem   Kind gibt
         he.NOM the.ACC book the.DAT child gives
         'He gives the book to the child.'

     b. * ich   das   Buch dem   Kind gibt
         I.NOM the.ACC book the.DAT child gives

     c. * er   das   Buch den   Kind gibt
         he.NOM the.ACC book the.ACC child gives

     d. * er   den Buch   dem Kind gibt
         he.NOM the.M book(N) the   child gives

In (7b), subject-verb agreement has been violated. In other words: *ich* 'I' and *gibt*
'gives' do not fit together. (7c) is ungrammatical because the case requirements of
the verb have not been satisfied: *gibt* 'gives' requires a dative object. Finally, (7d)
is ungrammatical because there is a lack of agreement between the determiner
and the noun. It is not possible to combine *den* 'the', which is masculine and
bears accusative case, and *Buch* 'book' because *Buch* is neuter gender. As the
gender properties of these two elements are not the same, the elements cannot
be combined.

In the following, we will consider how we would have to change our grammar
to stop it from licensing the sentences in (7b–d). If we want to capture subject-

verb agreement, then we have to cover the following six cases in German, as the verb has to agree with the subject in both person (1, 2, 3) and number (sg, pl):

(8) a. Ich schlafe. (1, sg)
     I   sleep

  b. Du schläfst. (2, sg)
     you sleep

  c. Er/sie/es schläft. (3, sg)
     he/she/it sleeps

  d. Wir schlafen. (1, pl)
     we sleep

  e. Ihr schlaft. (2, pl)
     you sleep

  f. Sie   schlafen. (3, pl)
     they sleep

It is possible to capture these relations with grammatical rules by increasing the number of symbols we use. Instead of the rule S $\rightarrow$ NP NP NP V, we can use the following:

(9) S $\rightarrow$ NP_1_sg NP NP V_1_sg
   S $\rightarrow$ NP_2_sg NP NP V_2_sg
   S $\rightarrow$ NP_3_sg NP NP V_3_sg
   S $\rightarrow$ NP_1_pl NP NP V_1_pl
   S $\rightarrow$ NP_2_pl NP NP V_2_pl
   S $\rightarrow$ NP_3_pl NP NP V_3_pl

This would mean that we need six different symbols for noun phrases and verbs respectively, as well as six rules rather than one.

In order to account for case assignment by the verb, we can incorporate case information into the symbols in an analogous way. We would then get rules such as the following:

(10) S $\rightarrow$ NP_1_sg_nom NP_dat NP_acc V_1_sg_nom_dat_acc
    S $\rightarrow$ NP_2_sg_nom NP_dat NP_acc V_2_sg_nom_dat_acc
    S $\rightarrow$ NP_3_sg_nom NP_dat NP_acc V_3_sg_nom_dat_acc
    S $\rightarrow$ NP_1_pl_nom NP_dat NP_acc V_1_pl_nom_dat_acc
    S $\rightarrow$ NP_2_pl_nom NP_dat NP_acc V_2_pl_nom_dat_acc
    S $\rightarrow$ NP_3_pl_nom NP_dat NP_acc V_3_pl_nom_dat_acc

Since it is necessary to differentiate between noun phrases in four cases, we have
a total of six symbols for NPs in the nominative and three symbols for NPs with
other cases. Since verbs have to match the NPs, that is, we have to differentiate
between verbs which select three arguments and those selecting only one or two
(11), we have to increase the number of symbols we assume for verbs.

(11) a. Aicke schläft.

   Aicke sleeps

   'Aicke is sleeping.'

   b. * Aicke schläft das Buch.

   Aicke sleeps the book

   c. Aicke kennt das Buch.

   Aicke knows the book

   'Aicke knows the book.'

   d. * Aicke kennt.

   Aicke knows

In the rules above, the information about the number of arguments required by
a verb is included in the atomic symbols, e.g., 'nom_dat_acc'.

In order to capture the determiner-noun agreement in (12), we have to incorporate information about gender (fem, mas, neu), number (sg, pl), case (nom, gen,
dat, acc) and the inflectional classes (strong, weak).[5]

(12) a. der Mann, die Frau, das Buch (gender)

   the.M man(M) the.F woman(F) the.N book(N)

   b. das Buch, die Bücher (number)

   the book.SG the books.PL

   c. des Buches, dem Buch (case)

   the.GEN book.GEN the.DAT book

   d. ein Beamter, der Beamte (inflectional class)

   a civil.servant the civil.servant

Instead of the rule NP → Det N, we will have to use rules such as those in (13).[6]
(13) shows the rules for nominative noun phrases. We would need analogous
rules for genitive, dative, and accusative. We would then require 24 symbols for
determiners (3 * 2 * 4), 24 symbols for nouns and 24 rules rather than one. If

---

[5]These are inflectional classes for adjectives which are also relevant for some nouns such as
Beamter 'civil servant', *Verwandter* 'relative', *Gesandter* 'envoy'.

[6]To keep things simple, these rules do not incorporate information regarding the inflection
class.

inflection class is taken into account, the number of symbols and the number of rules doubles.

(13) NP_3_sg_nom → Det_fem_sg_nom N_fem_sg_nom
      NP_3_sg_nom → Det_mas_sg_nom N_mas_sg_nom
      NP_3_sg_nom → Det_neu_sg_nom N_neu_sg_nom
      NP_3_pl_nom → Det_fem_pl_nom N_fem_pl_nom
      NP_3_pl_nom → Det_mas_pl_nom N_mas_pl_nom
      NP_3_pl_nom → Det_neu_pl_nom N_neu_pl_nom

3.2 Expanding PSG with features

Phrase structure grammars which only use atomic symbols are problematic as they cannot capture certain generalizations. We as linguists can recognize that NP_3_sg_nom stands for a noun phrase because it contains the letters NP. However, in formal terms this symbol is just like any other symbol in the grammar and we cannot capture the commonalities of all the symbols used for NPs. Furthermore, unstructured symbols do not capture the fact that the rules in (13) all have something in common. In formal terms, the only thing that the rules have in common is that there is one symbol on the left-hand side of the rule and two on the right.

We can solve this problem by introducing features which are assigned to category symbols and therefore allow for the values of such features to be included in our rules. For example, we can assume the features person, number and case for the category symbol NP. For determiners and nouns, we would adopt an additional feature for gender and one for inflectional class. (14) shows two rules augmented by the respective values in brackets:[7]

(14) NP(3,sg,nom) → Det(fem,sg,nom) N(fem,sg,nom)
      NP(3,sg,nom) → Det(mas,sg,nom) N(mas,sg,nom)

If we were to use variables rather than the values in (14), we would get rule schemata as the one in (15):

(15) NP(3,Num,Case) → Det(Gen,Num,Case) N(Gen,Num,Case)

The values of the variables here are not important. What is important is that they match. For this to work, it is important that the values are ordered; that is,

---

[7]In the following chapters, attribute value structures will be used. In these structures, we always have pairs of a feature name and a feature value. In such a setting, the order of values is not important, since every value is uniquely identified by the corresponding feature name. Since we do not have a feature name in schemata like (13), the order of the values is important.

in the category of a determiner, the gender is always first, number second and so on. The value of the person feature (the first position in the NP(3,Num,Case)) is fixed at '3' by the rule. These kind of restrictions on the values can, of course, be determined in the lexicon:

(16) NP(3,sg,nom)   → es
      Det(mas,sg,gen) → des

The rules in (10) can be collapsed into a single schema as in (17):

(17) S → NP(Per1,Num1,nom)
         NP(Per2,Num2,dat)
         NP(Per3,Num3,acc)
         V(Per1,Num1,ditransitive)

The identification of Per1 and Num1 on the verb and on the subject ensures that there is subject-verb agreement. For the other NPs, the values of these features are irrelevant. The case of these NPs is explicitly determined.

3.3 Phrase structure rules for some aspects of German syntax

Whereas determining the direct constituents of a sentence is relatively easy, since we can very much rely on the movement test due to the somewhat flexible order of constituents in German, it is more difficult to identify the parts of the noun phrase. This is the problem we will focus on in this section. To help motivate assumptions about $\overline{X}$ syntax to be discussed in Section 3.4, we will also discuss prepositional phrases.

3.3.1 Noun phrases

Up to now, we have assumed a relatively simple structure for noun phrases: our rules state that a noun phrase consists of a determiner and a noun. Noun phrases can have a distinctly more complex structure than (18a). This is shown by the following examples in (18):

(18) a. ein Buch
          a   book

      b. ein Buch, das wir kennen
          a   book that we know

      c. ein Buch aus Japan
          a   book from Japan

    d. ein interessantes Buch
        an interesting   book

    e. ein Buch aus Japan, das wir kennen
        a   book from Japan that we know

    f. ein interessantes Buch aus   Japan
        an interesting   book from Japan

    g. ein interessantes Buch, das wir kennen
        an interesting   book that we know

    h. ein interessantes Buch aus Japan, das wir kennen
        an interesting   book from Japan that we know

In addition to determiners and nouns, noun phrases can also contain adjectives, prepositional phrases and relative clauses. The additional elements in (18) are adjuncts. They restrict the set of objects which the noun phrase refers to. Whereas (18a) refers to an entity which has the property of being a book, the referent of (18b) must also have the property of being known to us.

Our previous rules for noun phrases simply combined a noun and a determiner and can therefore only be used to analyze (18a). The questions we are facing now is how we can modify this rule or which additional rules we would have to assume in order to analyze the other noun phrases in (18). In addition to rule (19a), one could propose a rule such as the one in (19b).[8,9]

(19)   a. NP → Det N

        b. NP → Det A N

However, this rule would still not allow us to analyze noun phrases such as (20):

(20)   alle weiteren schlagkräftigen Argumente
        all   further   strong   arguments
    'all other strong arguments'

In order to be able to analyze (20), we require a rule such as (21):

(21) NP → Det A A N

It is always possible to increase the number of adjectives in a noun phrase and setting an upper limit for adjectives would be entirely arbitrary. Even if we opt for the following abbreviation, there are still problems:

(22) NP → Det A* N

---

[8]See Eisenberg (2004: 238) for the assumption of flat structures in noun phrases.

[9]There are, of course, other features such as gender and number, which should be part of all the rules discussed in this section. I have omitted these in the following for ease of exposition.

The asterisk in (22) stands for any number of iterations. Therefore, (22) encompasses rules with no adjectives as well as those with one, two or more.

The problem is that according to the rule in (22), adjectives and nouns do not form a constituent and we therefore cannot explain why coordination is still possible in (23):

(23)   alle [[großen Seeelefanten] und [grauen Eichhörnchen]]
       all   big   elephant.seals and gray   squirrels
       'all big elephant seals and gray squirrels'

If we assume that coordination involves the combination of two or more word strings with the same syntactic properties, then we would have to assume that the adjective and noun form a unit.

The rules in (24) capture the noun phrases with adjectives discussed thus far:

(24)   a. NP → Det N̄
       b. N̄ → A N̄
       c. N̄ → N

These rules state the following: a noun phrase consists of a determiner and a nominal element (N̄). This nominal element can consist of an adjective and a nominal element (24b), or just a noun (24c). Since N̄ is also on the right-hand side of the rule in (24b), we can apply this rule multiple times and therefore account for noun phrases with multiple adjectives such as (20). Figure 3.5 shows the structure of a noun phrase without an adjective and that of a noun phrase with one or two adjectives. The adjective *grau* 'gray' restricts the set of referents

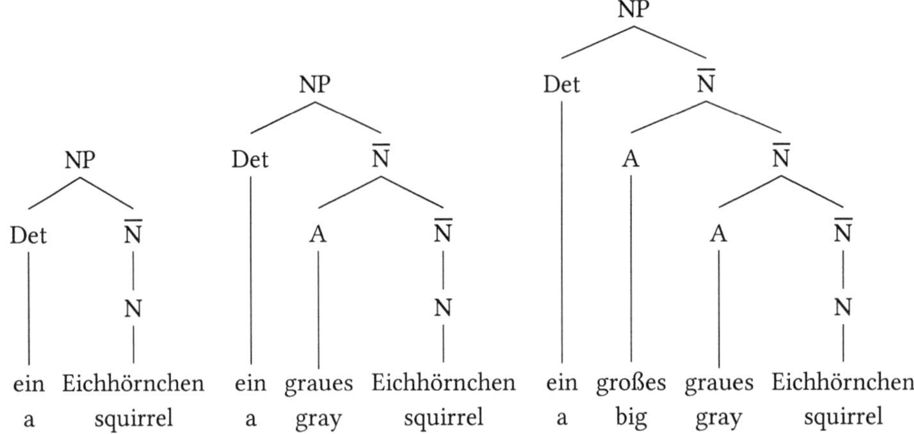

Figure 3.5: Noun phrases with differing numbers of adjectives

for the noun phrase. If we assume an additional adjective such as *groß* 'big', then it only refers to those squirrels who are gray as well as big. These kinds of noun phrases can be used in contexts such as the following:

(25) A: Alle grauen Eichhörnchen sind groß.
      all   gray   squirrels   are big
      'All gray squirrels are big.'
    B: Nein, ich habe ein kleines graues Eichhörnchen gesehen.
      no   I   have a   small   gray   squirrel   seen
      'No, I saw a small gray squirrel.'

We observe that this discourse can be continued with *Aber alle kleinen grauen Eichhörnchen sind krank* 'but all small gray squirrels are ill' and a corresponding answer. The possibility of having even more adjectives in noun phrases such as *ein kleines graues Eichhörnchen* 'a small gray squirrel' is accounted for in our rule system in (24). In the rule (24b), $\overline{\text{N}}$ occurs on the left-hand as well as the right-hand side of the rule. This kind of rule is referred to as *recursive*.

We have now developed a nifty little grammar that can be used to analyze noun phrases containing adjectival modifiers. As a result, the combination of an adjective and a noun is given constituent status. One may wonder at this point if it would not make sense to also assume that determiners and adjectives form a constituent, as we also have the following kind of noun phrases:

(26) diese schlauen und diese neugierigen Eichhörnchen
     these smart   and these curious   squirrels

Here, we are dealing with a different structure, however. Two full NPs have been conjoined and part of the first conjunct was not pronounced.[10]

(27) diese schlauen ~~Eichhörnchen~~ und diese neugierigen Eichhörnchen
     these smart   squirrels   and these curious   squirrels

---

[10]Note that one cannot claim that the second conjunct in (23) is a full NP and *alle* 'all' is just not pronounced. If the determiner is omitted in German NPs, we need a different inflection:

(i) a. Alle grauen   Eichhörnchen sind groß.
       all   gray.NOM squirrels   are big
       'All gray squirrels are big.'
   b. Graue   Eichhörnchen sind groß.
       gray.NOM squirrels   are big
   c. * Grauen   Eichhörnchen sind groß.
       gray.DAT squirrels   are big

Hence what is coordinated in (23) is two adjective–noun combinations and the result is combined with a determiner.

One can find similar phenomena at the sentence level (28a) and even at the word level (28b):

(28) a. dass Conny dem Kind das Buch ~~gibt~~ und Aicke der Frau   die
         that Conny the child the book gives and Aicke the woman the
         Schallplatte gibt
         record   gives
         'that Conny gives the book to the child and Aicke the record to the woman'

      b. be-   und ent-laden
         PRFX and PRFX-load
         'load and unload'

Coordination is a complex phenomenon. See Abeillé & Chaves (2021) for an overview.

Thus far, we have discussed how we can ideally integrate adjectives into our rules for the structure of noun phrases. Other adjuncts such as prepositional phrases (18c) or relative clauses (18b) can be combined with $\overline{\text{N}}$ in an analogous way to adjectives:

(29) a. $\overline{\text{N}} \rightarrow \overline{\text{N}}$ PP
      b. $\overline{\text{N}} \rightarrow \overline{\text{N}}$ relative clause

With these rules and those in (24), it is possible – assuming the corresponding rules for PPs and relative clauses – to analyze all the examples in (18).

(24c) states that it is possible for $\overline{\text{N}}$ to consist of a single noun. A further important rule has not yet been discussed: we need another rule to combine nouns such as *Vater* 'father', *Sohn* 'son' or *Bild* 'picture', so-called *relational nouns*, with their arguments. Examples of these can be found in (30a–b). (30c) is an example of a nominalization of a verb with its argument:

(30) a. der Vater von Peter
         the father of   Peter
         'Peter's father'

      b. das Bild   vom   Gleimtunnel
         the picture of.the Gleimtunnel
         'the picture of the Gleimtunnel'

      c. das Kommen der   Installateurin
         the coming of.the plumber
         'the plumber's visit'

The rule that we need to analyze (30a,b) is given in (31):

(31) $\overline{\text{N}} \to$ N PP

Figure 3.6 shows two structures with PP-arguments. The tree on the right also contains an additional PP-adjunct, which is licensed by the rule in (29a).

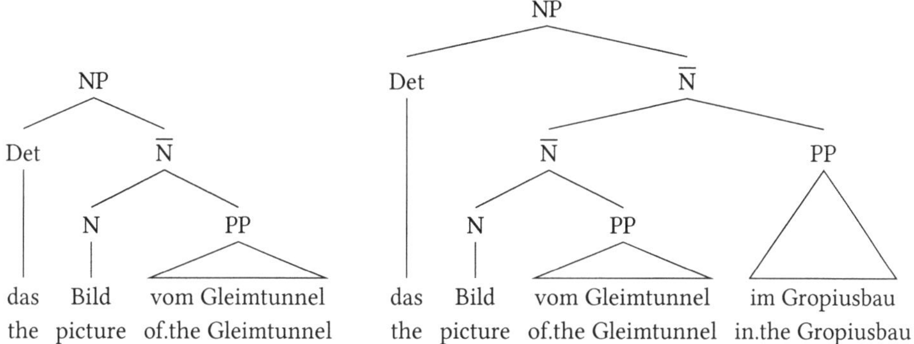

Figure 3.6: Combination of a noun with PP complement *vom Gleimtunnel* to the right with an adjunct PP

In addition to the previously discussed NP structures, there are other structures where the determiner or the noun is missing. Nouns can be omitted via ellipsis. (32) gives an example of noun phrases where a noun that does not require a complement has been omitted. The examples in (33) show NPs in which only a determiner and a complement of the noun has been realized, but not the noun itself. The underscore marks the position where the noun would normally occur.

(32) a. ein interessantes _
          an interesting
          'an interesting one'

      b. ein neues interessantes _
          a   new   interesting
          'a new interesting one'

      c. ein interessantes _ aus Japan
          an interesting   from Japan
          'an interesting one from Japan'

      d. ein interessantes _, das wir kennen
          an interesting   that we know
          'an interesting one that we know'

(33) a. (Nein, nicht der Vater von Klaus), der _ von Peter war gemeint.
       no   not the father of Klaus the of Peter was meant
      'No, it wasn't the father of Klaus, but rather the one of Peter that was
      meant.'

   b. (Nein, nicht das Bild   von der Stadtautobahn), das _ vom
      no   not the picture of the motorway   the of.the
      Gleimtunnel war beeindruckend.
      Gleimtunnel was impressive
      'No, it wasn't the picture of the motorway, but rather the one of the
      Gleimtunnel that was impressive.'

   c. (Nein, nicht das Kommen des   Tischlers), das _ der   Installateurin
      no   not the coming of.the carpenter the of.the plumber
      ist wichtig.
      is important
      'No, it isn't the visit of the carpenter, but rather the visit of the
      plumber that is important.'

In English, the pronoun *one* must often be used in the corresponding position,[11]
but in German the noun is simply omitted. In phrase structure grammars, this
can be described by a so-called *epsilon production*. These rules replace a symbol
with nothing (34a). The rule in (34b) is an equivalent variant which is responsible
for the term *epsilon production*:

(34) a. N →
   b. N → ϵ

The corresponding trees are shown in Figure 3.7. Going back to boxes as the one
in Figure 3.2, the rules in (34) correspond to empty boxes with the same labels
as the boxes of ordinary nouns. As we have considered previously, the actual
content of the boxes is unimportant when considering the question of where we
can incorporate them. For example, the noun phrases in (18) can occur in the
same sentences. Similarly, the empty noun box behaves like one with a genuine
noun: if we do not open the empty box, we will not be able to notice the difference
to a filled box.

  It is not only possible to omit the noun from noun phrases, but the determiner
can also remain unrealized in certain contexts. (35) shows noun phrases in the
plural:

---

[11]See Fillmore et al. (2012: Section 4.12) for English examples without the pronoun *one*.

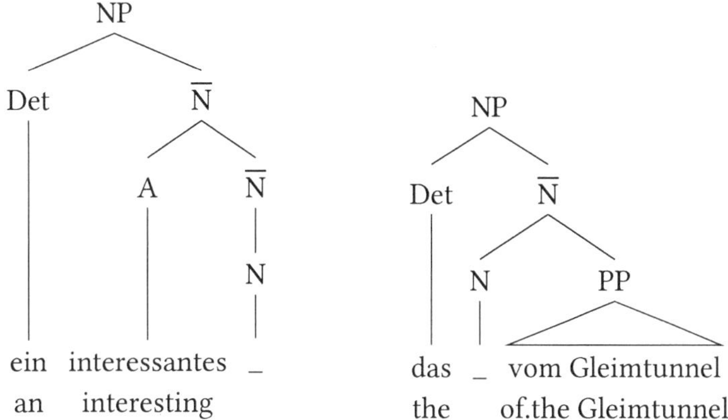

Figure 3.7: Noun phrases without an overt head

(35) a. Bücher
         books

      b. Bücher, die wir kennen
         books   that we know

      c. interessante Bücher
         interesting   books

      d. interessante Bücher, die wir kennen
         interesting   books   that we know

The determiner can also be omitted in the singular if the noun denotes a mass noun:

(36) a. Getreide
         grain

      b. Getreide, das gerade gemahlen wurde
         grain   that just   ground   was
         'grain that has just been ground'

      c. frisches Getreide
         fresh   grain

      d. frisches Getreide, das gerade gemahlen wurde
         fresh   grain   that just   ground   was
         'fresh grain that has just been ground'

Finally, both the determiner and the noun can be omitted:

(37) a. Ich lese interessante.
          I   read interesting
          'I read interesting ones.'

      b. Dort drüben steht   frisches, das gerade gemahlen wurde.
          there over   stands fresh   that just   ground   was
          'Over there is some fresh (grain) that has just been ground.'

Figure 3.8 shows the corresponding trees.

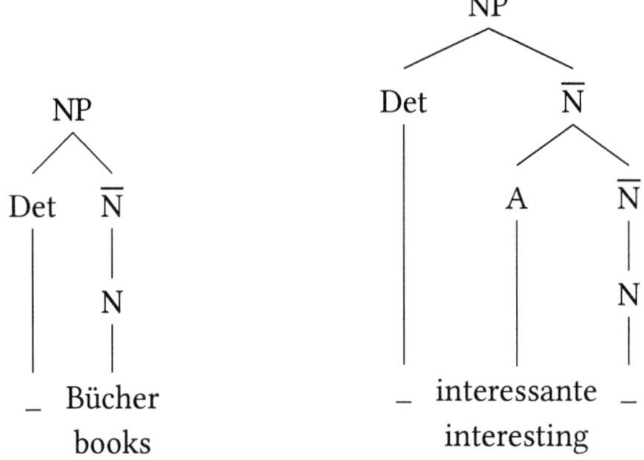

Figure 3.8: Noun phrases without overt determiner

It is necessary to add two further comments to the rules that were developed up to this point: up to now, I have always spoken of adjectives. However, it is possible to have very complex adjective phrases in pre-nominal position. These can be adjectives with complements (38a,b) or adjectival participles (38c,d):

(38) a. der seiner Frau treue   Mann
          the his.DAT wife faithful man
          'the man faithful to his wife'

      b. der auf seinen Sohn stolze Mann
          the on his.ACC son   proud man
          'the man proud of his son'

      c. der seine   Frau   liebende Mann
          the his.ACC woman loving   man
          'the man who loves his wife'

      d. der von seiner Frau geliebte Mann
          the by his.DAT wife loved   man
          'the man loved by his wife'

Taking this into account, the rule (24b) has to be modified in the following way:

(39) $\overline{N} \rightarrow AP\ \overline{N}$

An adjective phrase (AP) can consist of an NP and an adjective, a PP and an adjective or just an adjective:

(40)   a. $AP \rightarrow NP\ A$

      b. $AP \rightarrow PP\ A$

      c. $AP \rightarrow A$

There are two imperfections resulting from the rules that were developed thus far. These are the rules for adjectives or nouns without complements in (40c) as well as (24c) – repeated here as (41):

(41) $\overline{N} \rightarrow N$

If we apply these rules, then we will generate unary branching subtrees, that is trees with a mother that only has one daughter. (See Figure 3.8 for an example of this.) If we maintain the parallel to the boxes, this would mean that there is a box which contains another box which is the one with the relevant content.

In principle, nothing stops us from placing this information directly into the larger box. Instead of the rules in (42), we will simply use the rules in (43):

(42)   a. $A \rightarrow kluge$

      b. $N \rightarrow Mann$

(43)   a. $AP \rightarrow kluge$

      b. $\overline{N} \rightarrow Mann$

(43a) states that *kluge* 'smart' has the same properties as a full adjective phrase, in particular that it cannot be combined with a complement. This is parallel to the categorization of the pronoun *er* 'he' as an NP in the grammars (2) and (6).

Assigning the category $\overline{N}$ to nouns which do not require a complement has the advantage that we do not have to explain why the analysis in (44b) is possible as well as (44a) despite there not being any difference in meaning.

(44)   a. $[_{NP}$ einige $[_{\overline{N}}$ kluge $[_{\overline{N}}\ [_{\overline{N}}\ [_N$ Frauen $]$ und $[_{\overline{N}}\ [_N$ Männer $]]]]]]$
             some   smart   women   and   men

      b. $[_{NP}$ einige $[_{\overline{N}}$ kluge $[_{\overline{N}}\ [_N\ [_N$ Frauen $]$ und $[_N$ Männer $]]]]]$
             some   smart   women   and   men

In (44a), two nouns have projected to $\overline{N}$ and have then been joined by coordination. The result of coordination of two constituents of the same category is always a new constituent with that category. In the case of (44a), this is also $\overline{\text{N}}$. This constituent is then combined with the adjective and the determiner. In (44b), the nouns themselves have been coordinated. The result of this is always another constituent which has the same category as its parts. In this case, this would be N. This N becomes $\overline{\text{N}}$ and is then combined with the adjective. If nouns which do not require complements were categorized as $\overline{\text{N}}$ rather than N, we would not have the problem of spurious ambiguities.[12] The structure in (45) shows the only possible analysis.

(45) [$_{\text{NP}}$ einige [$_{\overline{\text{N}}}$ kluge [$_{\overline{\text{N}}}$ [$_{\overline{\text{N}}}$ Frauen] und [$_{\overline{\text{N}}}$ Männer]]]]
        some   smart   women   and   men

3.3.2 Prepositional phrases

Compared to the syntax of noun phrases, the syntax of prepositional phrases (PPs) is relatively straightforward. PPs normally consist of a preposition and a noun phrase whose case is determined by that preposition. We can capture this with the following rule:

(46) PP → P NP

This rule must, of course, also contain information about the case of the NP. I have omitted this for ease of exposition as I did with the NP-rules and AP-rules above.

The Duden grammar (Eisenberg et al. 2005: § 1300) offers examples such as those in (47), which show that certain prepositional phrases serve to further de-

---

[12]Natural language utterances are often ambiguous. For example, the following sentence has two readings.

(i) Unbekannte haben Mittwochabend   bei einer FDP-Wahlkampfveranstaltung mit
     strangers   have Wednesday.evening at a   FDP-campaign.rally   with
     FDP-Chef   Guido Westerwelle Farbbeutel   geworfen. (taz, 21.5.2004, p. 7)
     FDP-leader Guido Westerwelle paint.bombs thrown

     'Strangers threw paint bombs Wednesday evening during a FDP campaign rally with
     FDP leader Guido Westerwelle.' or 'Together with FDP leader Guido Westerwelle,
     strangers threw paint bombs Wednesday evening during a FDP campaign rally.'

The two readings correspond to two different structures. In the first reading, the *with* PP attaches to the campaign rally, which means that Guido Westerwelle was at the rally. In the second reading, the PP modifies the verb *threw*, which corresponds to a meaning in which Guido Westerwelle threw paint bombs together with strangers. This is normal ambiguity. What linguists usually want to avoid is spurious ambiguity: cases in which we have the same semantics but two different syntactic structures.

fine the semantic contribution of the preposition by indicating some measurement, for example:

(47) a. [[Einen Schritt] vor   dem Abgrund] blieb   er stehen.
          one   step   before the abyss   remained he stand
       'He stopped one step in front of the abyss.'

     b. [[Kurz]   nach dem Start]   fiel die Klimaanlage   aus.
          shortly after the take.off fell the air.conditioning out
       'Shortly after take off, the air conditioning stopped working.'

     c. [[Schräg]   hinter der Scheune] ist ein Weiher.
          diagonally behind the barn   is a   pond
       'There is a pond diagonally across from the barn.'

     d. [[Mitten] im   Urwald] stießen   die Forscher   auf einen alten
          middle in.the jungle   stumbled the researchers on an   old
       Tempel.
       temple
       'In the middle of the jungle, the researches came across an old temple.'

To analyze the sentences in (47a,b), one could propose the following rules in (48):

(48)   a. PP → NP PP

       b. PP → AP PP

These rules combine a PP with an indication of measurement. The resulting constituent is another PP. It is possible to use these rules to analyze prepositional phrases in (47a,b), but it unfortunately also allows us to analyze those in (49):

(49)   a. * [PP einen Schritt [PP kurz   [PP vor   dem Abgrund]]]
              one   step   shortly   before the abyss

       b. * [PP kurz   [PP einen Schritt [PP vor   dem Abgrund]]]
              shortly   one   step   before the abyss

Both rules in (48) were used to analyze the examples in (49). Since the symbol PP occurs on both the left and right-hand side of the rules, we can apply the rules in any order and as many times as we like.

We can avoid this undesired side-effect by reformulating the previously assumed rules:

(50)   a. PP → NP $\overline{\text{P}}$

       b. PP → AP $\overline{\text{P}}$

    c. PP $\rightarrow \overline{P}$
    d. $\overline{P} \rightarrow$ P NP

Rule (46) becomes (50d). The rule in (50c) states that a PP can consist of $\overline{P}$. Figure 3.9 shows the analysis of (51) using (50c) and (50d) as well as the analysis of an example with an adjective in the first position following the rules in (50b) and (50d):

(51)   vor   dem Abgrund
        before the abyss
        'in front of the abyss'

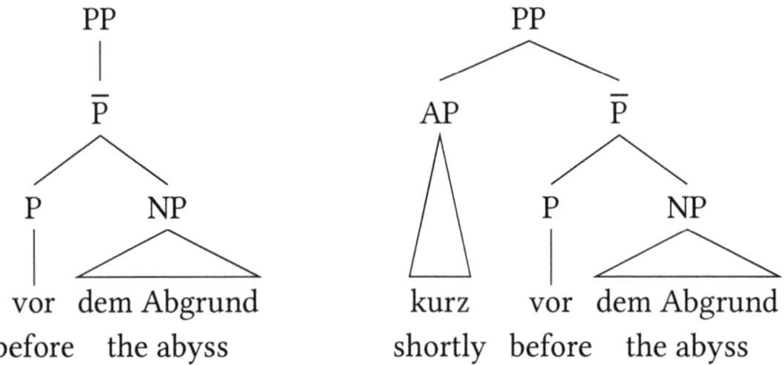

Figure 3.9: Prepositional phrases with and without measurement

At this point, the attentive reader is probably wondering why there is no empty measurement phrase in the left-hand figure of Figure 3.9, which one might expect in analogy to the empty determiner in Figure 3.8. The reason for the empty determiner in Figure 3.8 is that the entire noun phrase without the determiner has a meaning similar to those with a determiner. The meaning normally contributed by the visible determiner has to somehow be incorporated in the structure of the noun phrase. This can be done by the empty determiner with an appropriately specified meaning contribution.

Unlike determiner-less NPs, prepositional phrases without an indication of degree or measurement do not lack any meaning component for composition. It is therefore not necessary to assume an empty indication of measurement, which somehow contributes to the meaning of the entire PP. Hence, the rule in (50c) states that a prepositional phrase consists of $\overline{P}$, that is, a combination of P and NP.

3.4 $\overline{\text{X}}$ theory

If we look again at the rules that were formulated in the previous section, we see that heads are always combined with their complements to form a new constituent (52a,b), which can then be combined with further constituents (52c,d):

(52) a. $\overline{\text{N}} \rightarrow$ N PP

b. $\overline{\text{P}} \rightarrow$ P NP

c. NP $\rightarrow$ Det $\overline{\text{N}}$

d. PP $\rightarrow$ NP $\overline{\text{P}}$

Grammarians working on English noticed that parallel structures can be used for phrases which have adjectives or verbs as their head. I discuss adjective phrases at this point and postpone the discussion of verb phrases to Chapter 4, since the assumptions regarding the structure of clauses in both German and English deviate from $\overline{\text{X}}$ theory as it is commonly assumed today. As in German, certain adjectives in English can take complements with the important restriction that adjective phrases with complements cannot realize these pre-nominally in English. (53) gives some examples of adjective phrases:

(53) a. Kim and Sandy are proud.

b. Kim and Sandy are very proud.

c. Kim and Sandy are proud of their child.

d. Kim and Sandy are very proud of their child.

Unlike prepositional phrases, complements of adjectives are normally optional. *proud* can be used with or without a PP. The degree expression *very* is also optional.

The rules which we need for this analysis are given in (54), with the corresponding structures in Figure 3.10.

(54) a. AP $\rightarrow \overline{\text{A}}$

b. AP $\rightarrow$ AdvP $\overline{\text{A}}$

c. $\overline{\text{A}} \rightarrow$ A PP

d. $\overline{\text{A}} \rightarrow$ A

As was shown in Section 3.2, it is possible to generalize over very specific phrase structure rules and thereby arrive at more general rules. In this way, properties

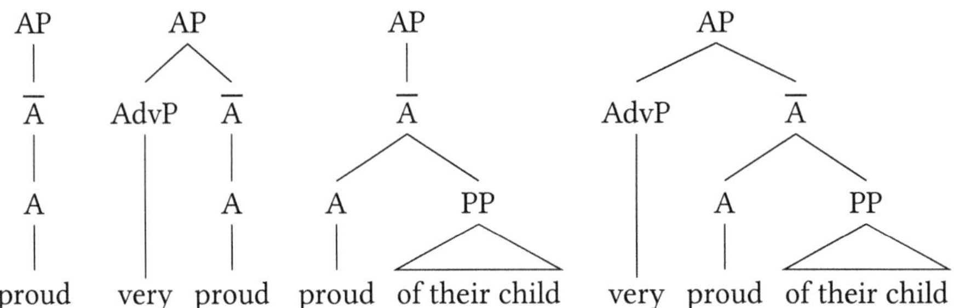

Figure 3.10: English adjective phrases

such as person, number and gender are no longer encoded in the category symbols, but rather only simple symbols such as NP, Det and N are used. It is only necessary to specify something about the values of a feature if it is relevant in the context of a given rule. We can take this abstraction a step further: instead of using explicit category symbols such as N, V, P and A for lexical categories and NP, VP, PP and AP for phrasal categories, one can simply use a variable for the word class in question and speak of X and XP.

This form of abstraction can be found in so-called $\overline{\text{X}}$ theory (or X-bar theory, the term *bar* refers to the line above the symbol), which was developed by Chomsky (1970) and refined by Jackendoff (1977). This form of abstract rules plays an important role in many different theories. For example: Government & Binding (Chomsky 1981), Generalized Phrase Structure Grammar (Gazdar et al. 1985, Uszkoreit 1987) and Lexical Functional Grammar (Bresnan 1982, Bresnan et al. 2016). In HPSG, the theory assumed in this book, $\overline{\text{X}}$ theory also plays a role, but not all restrictions of the $\overline{\text{X}}$ schema have been adopted.

(55) shows a possible instantiation of $\overline{\text{X}}$ rules, where the category X has been used in place of N, as well as examples of word strings which can be derived by these rules:

(55)

$\overline{\text{X}}$ rule	with specific categories	example strings
$\overline{\overline{\text{X}}} \rightarrow \text{specifier } \overline{\text{X}}$	$\overline{\overline{\text{N}}} \rightarrow \overline{\text{DET}} \ \overline{\text{N}}$	the [picture of Paris]
$\overline{\text{X}} \rightarrow \overline{\text{X}} \text{ adjunct}$	$\overline{\text{N}} \rightarrow \overline{\text{N}} \ \overline{\text{REL\_CLAUSE}}$	[picture of Paris] [that everybody knows]
$\overline{\text{X}} \rightarrow \text{adjunct } \overline{\text{X}}$	$\overline{\text{N}} \rightarrow \overline{\overline{\text{A}}} \ \overline{\text{N}}$	beautiful [picture of Paris]
$\overline{\text{X}} \rightarrow \text{X complement*}$	$\overline{\text{N}} \rightarrow \text{N} \ \overline{\overline{\text{P}}}$	picture [of Paris]

Any word class can replace X (e.g., V, A or P). The X without the bar stands for a lexical item in the above rules. If one wants to make the bar level explicit, then it is possible to write X^0. Just as with the rule in (15), where we did not specify the case value of the determiner or the noun but rather simply required that the values on the right-hand side of the rule match, the rules in (55) require that the word class of an element on the right-hand side of the rule (X or $\overline{\text{X}}$) matches that of the element on the left-hand side of the rule ($\overline{\text{X}}$ or $\overline{\overline{\text{X}}}$).

A lexical element can be combined with all its complements. The '*' in the last rule stands for an unlimited amount of repetitions of the symbol it follows. A special case is zero"fold occurrence of complements. There is no PP complement of *Bild* 'picture' present in *das Bild* 'the picture' and thus N becomes $\overline{\text{N}}$. The result of the combination of a lexical element with its complements is a new projection level of X: the projection level 1, which is marked by a bar. $\overline{\text{X}}$ can then be combined with adjuncts. These can occur to the left or right of $\overline{\text{X}}$. The result of this combination is still $\overline{\text{X}}$, that is the projection level is not changed by combining it with an adjunct. Maximal projections are marked by two bars. One can also write XP for a projection of X with two bars. An XP consists of a specifier and $\overline{\text{X}}$. Depending on one's theoretical assumptions, subjects depending on a verb are specifiers of a verb phrase (Sag, Wasow & Bender 2003: 100–103; Müller & Ørsnes 2011: Section 3.1) and determiners are specifiers in NPs (Chomsky 1970: 210). Furthermore, degree modifiers (Chomsky 1970: 210) in adjective phrases and measurement indicators in prepositional phrases are also counted as specifiers.

Non-head positions can only host maximal projections and therefore complements, adjuncts and specifiers always have two bars. As already mentioned above, HPSG does not stick to the $\overline{\text{X}}$ theory. For example, arguments maybe words or intermediate, non-complete phrases (see Chapter 5 about the verbal complex in Germanic SOV languages). Figure 3.11 gives an overview of the minimal and maximal structure of phrases.

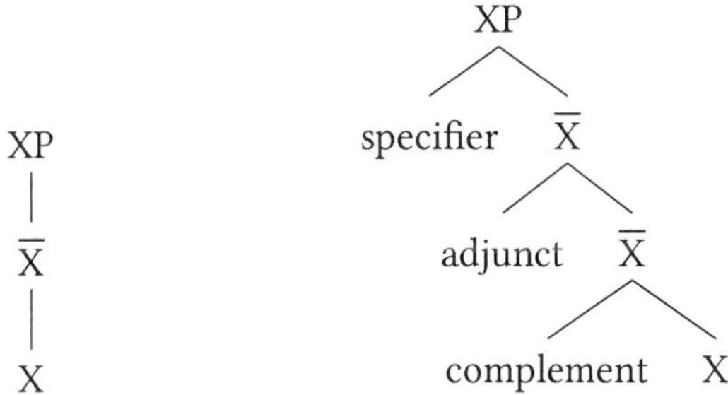

Figure 3.11: Minimal and maximal structure of phrases

Some categories do not have a specifier or have the option of having one. Adjuncts are optional and therefore not all structures have to contain an $\overline{\text{X}}$ with an adjunct daughter. In addition to the branching shown in the right-hand figure, adjuncts to XP and head-adjuncts are sometimes possible. There is only a single rule in (55) for cases in which a head precedes the complements, however an order in which the complement precedes the head is of course also possible. This is shown in Figure 3.11.

Figure 3.12 shows the analysis of the NP structures *das Bild* 'the picture' and *das schöne Bild von Paris* 'the beautiful picture of Paris'. The NP structures in Figure 3.12 and the tree for *proud* in Figure 3.10 show examples of minimally populated structures. The left tree in Figure 3.12 is also an example of a structure without an adjunct. The right-hand structure in Figure 3.12 is an example for the maximally populated structure: specifier, adjunct, and complement are present.

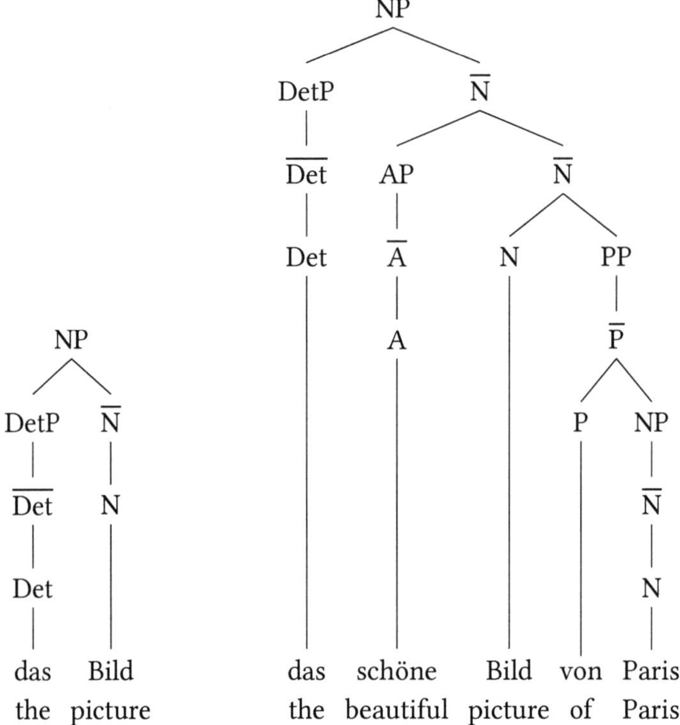

Figure 3.12: $\overline{\text{X}}$ analysis of *das Bild* 'the picture' and *das schöne Bild von Paris* 'the beautiful picture of Paris'

The analysis given in Figure 3.12 assumes that all non-heads in a rule are phrases. One therefore has to assume that there is a determiner phrase even if the determiner is not combined with other elements. The unary branching of determiners is not elegant but it is consistent.[13] The unary branchings for the NP *Paris* in Figure 3.12 may also seem somewhat odd, but they actually become more plausible when one considers more complex noun phrases:

(56)   a. das Paris der   dreißiger Jahre
          the Paris of.the thirty   years
          '30's Paris'

       b. die Maria aus   Hamburg
          the Maria from Hamburg
          'Maria from Hamburg'

Unary projections are somewhat inelegant but this should not concern us too much here, as we have already seen in the discussion of the lexical entries in (43) that unary branching nodes can be avoided for the most part and that it is indeed desirable to avoid such structures. Otherwise, one gets spurious ambiguities. In the following chapters, I show how HPSG (light) can analyze determiners and noun, adjective, and verb phrases without assuming unary rules. So instead of assuming the structures in Figure 3.12, the much simpler ones in Figure 3.13 will be used.

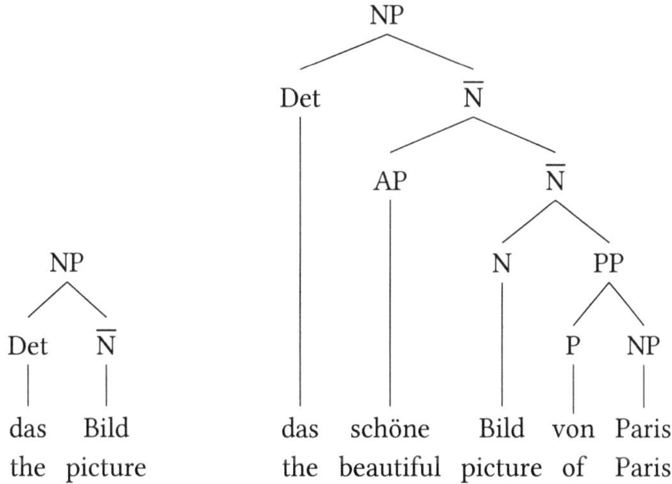

Figure 3.13: HPSG analysis of *das Bild* 'the picture' and *das schöne Bild von Paris* 'the beautiful picture of Paris'

---

[13]For an alternative version of $\overline{X}$ theory which does not assume elaborate structure for determiners see Muysken (1982).

Comprehension questions

1. Why are phrase structure grammars that use only atomic categories inadequate for the description of natural languages?

2. Assuming the grammar in (6), state which steps (replacing symbols) one has to take to get to the symbol V in the sentence (57).

   (57) er das Buch dem Kind gibt
         he the book the   child gives
         'He gives the book to the child.'

   Your answer should resemble the analysis in (3).

Exercises

This chapter is in large part identical to Chapter 2 of Müller (2023b). Since the focus of this book is different from the textbook about grammatical theory, I decided to provide a different set of exercises here. Those who are interested in doing more exercises may consult the grammatical theory textbook in addition. It is published by Language Science Press and hence open access, that is, it is freely available.

1. Draw trees for the following phrases. You may use the symbol NP for proper names and $\overline{\text{N}}$ for nouns not requiring complements (as in Figure 3.13).

   (58) a. eine Stunde vor   der Ankunft des   Zuges
            one hour   before the arrival of.the train
            'one hour before the arrival of the train'

    b. kurz   nach der Ankunft in Paris
       shortly after the arrival   in Paris
       'shortly after the arrival in Paris'

    c. das ein Lied singende Kind aus dem Allgäu
       this a   song singing   child from the Allgäu
       'the child from the Allgäu singing a song'

2. Use the online version of SWI-Prolog[a] to test your grammar using a computer. Details regarding the notation can be found in the English Wikipedia entry for Definite Clause Grammar (DCG).[b]

------

[a]https://swish.swi-prolog.org/, 2020-06-07.

[b]https://en.wikipedia.org/wiki/Definite_clause_grammar, 2020-06-07.

Further reading

The expansion of phrase structure grammars to include features was proposed as early as 1963 by Harman (1963).

The phrase structure grammar for noun phrases discussed in this chapter covers a large part of the syntax of noun phrases but cannot explain certain NP structures. Furthermore, it has the problem, which Exercise 3 of Müller (2023b: Chapter 2) is designed to show. A discussion of these phenomena and a solution in the framework of HPSG can be found in Netter (1998). For a discussion of the question whether Det or N is the head in nominal structures see Müller (2022) and Machicao y Priemer & Müller (2021). Van Eynde (2021) is an overview of work on the NP in HPSG.

The discussion of the integration of semantic information into phrase structure grammars was very short. A detailed discussion of predicate logic and its integration into phrase structure grammars – as well as a discussion of quantifier scope – can be found in Blackburn & Bos (2005).

4 Valence, argument order and adjunct placement

This chapter deals with the representation of valence information and sketches the basic structures that are assumed for SVO and SOV languages. I provide an account for scrambling in those languages that allow for it and discuss the fixed vs. free position of adjuncts.

4.1 Valence representations

The word sequences in (1) were already discussed in footnote 4 on page 39.

(1) a. * der   Delphin erwartet
        the.NOM dolphin expects

   b. * des   Kindes   der   Delphin den   Ball dem   Kind gibt
        the.GEN child.GEN the.NOM dolphin the.ACC ball the.DAT child gives

The problem is that there are too few (1a) or too many NPs (1b) present. The concept that is needed here is valence: like in chemistry it is assumed that heads have a certain potential to enter into stable relations with other material (Tesnière 2015: 239). For example, the verb *erwarten* 'to expect' requires an NP in the nominative and one in the accusative. *geben* 'to give' is the prototypical ditransitive verb: it can be combined with an NP in the nominative, an NP in the dative and an NP in the accusative, but as (1b) shows, a genitive object could not be integrated into a sentence.

The NPs in the examples in (2) are arguments of the respective verbs:

(2) a. [dass] der   Delphin den   Menschen erwartet
        that the.NOM dolphin den.ACC human   expects
        'that the dolphin expects the human'

   b. [dass] der   Delphin dem   Kind den   Ball gibt
        that the.NOM dolphin the.DAT child the.ACC ball gives
        'that the dolphin gives the child the ball'

Most syntactic arguments also fill a so-called *semantic role* in the semantic representation of the head. For example, the dolphin is the giver, the child is the recipient, and the ball is the item given. Tesnière (2015: Chapter 48) suggested using the analogy of dramas for the explanation of valence: if we imagine the scene of giving, what has to happen on stage to call an event that is acted out a giving event? There have to be the three participants, a giver, a recipient and something that is given. Without these participants, we do not have a proper giving event.

In addition to elements like the NPs in the examples above, which are called arguments, there are also so-called adjuncts. *schnell* 'quickly' (3a) and *quickly* (3b) are examples of adjuncts:

(3) a. [dass] der   Delphin dem   Kind schnell den   Ball gibt
        that   the.NOM dolphin the.DAT child quickly the.ACC ball gives
     'that the dolphin gives the child the ball quickly'

    b. that the dolphin gives the child the ball quickly

The adverbials provide additional information about the giving event, but they do not fill a semantic role.

To make things complicated not all arguments have to be realized in a sentence. The ditransitive verb *geben* can be realized with any subset of its arguments, provided the context fills in the missing information.

(4) a. Sie gibt Geld.
        she gives money
        'She gives money.'

    b. Sie gibt den Armen.
        she gives the poor
        'She gives to the poor.'

    c. Sie gibt.
        she gives

    d. Gib!
        give

In the case of (4a), a certain charity setting could have been established and one can either donate food or money or contribute some voluntary work. In such a situation, (4a) is perfectly fine. The transferred object in (4b) is probably money. A possible context for (4c) and (4d) is the card game skat where the person who is dealing rotates among the players. (4d) is an imperative. Even subjects can be dropped in imperatives since the referent of the subject is obvious: it is the addressee of the utterance.

The examples in (4) show that the arguments of *geben* 'to give' may be omitted. This is not the case for the accusative object of *erwarten* 'to expect': it is obligatory. So arguments may be optional or obligatory, but adjuncts are always optional. While the number of arguments is limited (by the number of available slots), the number of adjuncts is not: there can be arbitrarily many adjuncts in a phrase. (5) shows an example with two adjuncts:

(5) [dass] der   Delphin jetzt dem   Kind schnell den   Ball gibt
       that the.NOM dolphin now the.DAT child quickly the.ACC ball gives
     'that the dolphin now gives the child the ball quickly'

The analogy with chemistry and drama may be confusing since H_2O is a very nice and stable molecule and it is helpful to imagine the parallel combination of a verb with its two arguments. Figure 4.1 shows H_2O and the parallel combination of a verb with its arguments corresponding to (6a). The problem is that a single H and an O do not form a stable combination, while (6b) is fine:

(6)   a. Kirby helps Sandy.
      b. Kirby helps.

Figure 4.1: Combination of hydrogen and oxygen and the combination of a verb
           with its arguments

Of course one can simply assume that there is a version of *helps* that has a valence different from the two-place valence usually assumed. Here is where the parallel breaks down since we do not have an oxygen atom with just one open slot for the hydrogen atom. The drama analogy adds to the confusion since the helping event described in (6b) of course involves somebody who is helped. The solution to this problem is to distinguish between syntactic and semantic valence (Jacobs 2003: Section 3). The drama analogy helps us to find the semantic valence, the chemistry analogy is more about syntactic valence.

Given that chemistry and drama have their problems, we may go for another analogy: food. Let's assume you want to prepare a meal with pasta, tofu and a tomato sauce. For the tomato sauce you also need some onions. You put all the ingredients onto a shopping list and go to the shop. Once in the shop you realize that they have run out of tofu. Your meal will work without tofu. Tofu is optional.

Fortunately, the shop has plenty of pasta. You may choose between the different types and select the pasta type and brand you prefer. Some onions, tomatoes and you are done. Wait, next to the cashier there are these gummy bears. OK, you take some of these as well although you did not want to and they have nothing to do with your meal and your shopping list. The gummy bears are the adjuncts.

Back to linguistics: there are two ways of ensuring that arguments are realized together with their heads. The first one uses techniques that were introduced in Chapter 3. If one uses flat phrase structure rules, one can make sure that certain arguments appear together with certain heads. A schema similar to the one in (7) was discussed as (17) on page 44.

(7) S → NP[*nom*] NP[*dat*] NP[*acc*] V[*ditransitive*]

Such schemata were used in Generalized Phrase Structure Grammar (Gazdar, Klein, Pullum & Sag 1985, Uszkoreit 1987), but they were abandoned later in favor of lexicalist models, that is, models assuming that information about arguments of a head is encoded in the lexical description of the head rather than in phrase structure rules (Jacobson 1987b, Müller 2016: Section 5.5, Müller & Wechsler 2014a). Reasons for abandoning the phrasal approach of GPSG were problems with so-called partial verb phrase frontings (Nerbonne 1986, Johnson 1986) and with accounting for interactions with morphology (Müller 2016: Section 5.5.1).[1]

In lexical approaches, the valence of a head is represented in its lexical entry in the form of a list with descriptions of the elements that belong to the head's valence. (8) provides some prototypical examples:

(8) a. *schläft* 'sleeps': ⟨ NP[*nom*] ⟩
  b. *kennt* 'knows': ⟨ NP[*nom*], NP[*acc*] ⟩
  c. *hilft* 'helps': ⟨ NP[*nom*], NP[*dat*] ⟩
  d. *gibt* 'gives': ⟨ NP[*nom*], NP[*dat*], NP[*acc*] ⟩
  e. *wartet* 'waits': ⟨ NP[*nom*], PP[*auf*] ⟩

---

[1]Starting with influential work by Adele Goldberg (1995) in the framework of Construction Grammar, the phrasal approaches had a revival (Goldberg & Jackendoff 2004). Phrasal approaches are widespread and also assumed in other frameworks (Haugereid 2007, 2009, Culicover & Jackendoff 2005, Alsina 1996, Christie 2010, Asudeh et al. 2008, 2013). The problems that led to the abandonment of GPSG are ignored in the literature and newly introduced ones are not properly addressed. See Müller 2006, 2010, 2013c, Müller & Wechsler 2014a,b, Müller 2017, 2018, 2019, 2023b, 2021b for some discussion. Note that there are also lexical variants of Construction Grammar. Sag, Boas & Kay (2012), introducing Sign-Based Construction Grammar, explicitly argue for a lexical view citing some of the references just given. The framework underlying the proposals sketched in this book is Constructional HPSG (Sag 1997).

The elements in such lists come in a fixed order. The order corresponds to the order of the elements in English and to the so-called unmarked order in German, that is, for ditransitive verbs the order is usually nom, dat, acc (see Höhle (1982) for comments on the unmarked order). This fixed order is used to establish the link between syntax and semantics. This will be briefly discussed in Section 4.9.

Given such a valence representation for a verb like *kennen* 'know', one can assume a schema that combines an element from the valence list with the respective head and passes all unsaturated elements on to the result of the combination. Alternatively, one could assume a flat structure in which all arguments are combined with a head in one go (Ginzburg & Sag 2000: 34, Müller 2021a: Section 3). I do not assume such flat structures since this would make the account of adjuncts (see Section 4.8) more difficult (Müller 2021a: 377–378). The first step of the analysis of (9) is provided in Figure 4.2.[2]

(9) [dass] niemand   ihn   kennt
       that nobody.NOM him.ACC knows

     'that nobody knows him'

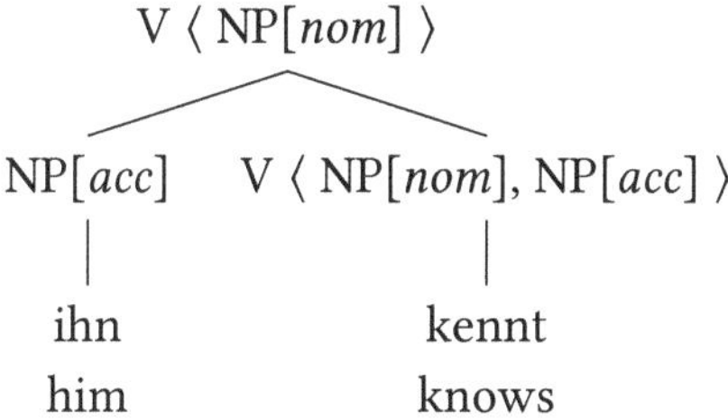

Figure 4.2: Analysis of *ihn kennt* 'him knows', valence information is represented in a list

The lexical item for *kennt* 'knows' has a valence description containing two NPs. In a first step *kennt* is combined with its accusative object. The resulting phrase *ihn kennt* 'him knows' is something whose most important constituent is a verb. Therefore it has V as its category label. Certain important properties of linguistic objects are called *head features*. Part of speech is one of these properties. It is assumed that all head features are passed up from the head in the tree automatically.

---

[2]Note that this sounds as if there were an order in which things have to be combined. This is not the case. HPSG grammars are sets of constraints that can be applied in any order. It is for explanatory purposes only that analyses are explained in a bottom-up fashion throughout the book.

The element that is not yet combined with *kennt* 'knows' is the NP[*nom*]. It is still represented in the valence list of *ihn kennt* 'him knows'. Figure 4.3 shows the next step combining *ihn kennt* with the subject *niemand* 'nobody'. The result is

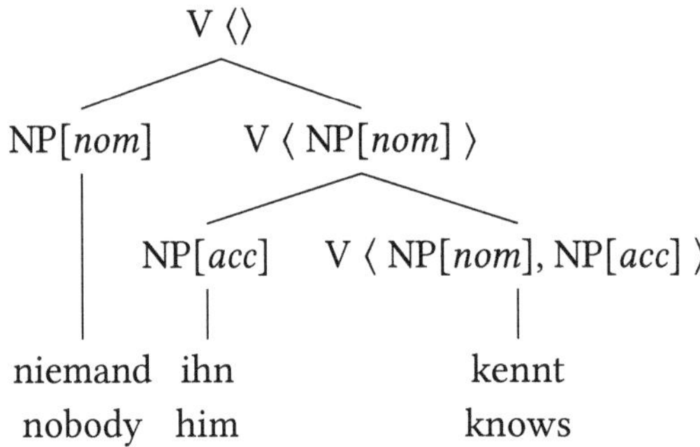

Figure 4.3: Analysis of (*dass*) *niemand ihn kennt* 'that nobody knows him'

a linguistic object of category verb with the empty list as valence representation.

As will be shown shortly, the schema that licenses structures like the V ⟨⟩ and V ⟨ NP[*nom*] ⟩ in Figure 4.3 is a more abstract version of the rule in (6) on page 39.

It is probably helpful to return to our meal-shopping analogy. Assume we are using an app to organize our shopping lists. For our current meal we need pasta and tomatoes. They are listed in the app in a certain order (tomatoes, pasta) and there are little images attached to the products. Once we have found something matching the pasta, we remove the pasta from the list and the remaining list contains an icon reminding us of the tomatoes. Once we have those, we remove them from the list and since nothing is left on the list, we pay. Linguistic structures are similar: we start with a verb selecting two NPs, we combine it with one NP and then with the second one. The result is a complete structure, something with an empty valence list.

There are various ways to deal with optional arguments. The simplest is to assume further lexical items selecting fewer arguments. For the example in (4c) one would assume the valence representation in (10a) and for sentences with *warten* 'to wait' without prepositional object, one would assume (10b) in addition to the representations in (8):

(10) a. *gibt* 'gives':   ⟨ NP[*nom*] ⟩
      b. *wartet* 'waits': ⟨ NP[*nom*] ⟩

4.2 Scrambling: The general idea

As we already saw in the data discussion in Section 2.3, some languages allow
scrambling of arguments. For those languages one can assume that a head can
combine with any of its arguments not necessarily beginning with the last one
as was the case in the analysis in Figure 4.3. Figure 4.4 shows the analysis of (11).

(11) [dass] ihn   niemand   kennt
      that him.ACC nobody.NOM knows
      'that nobody knows him'

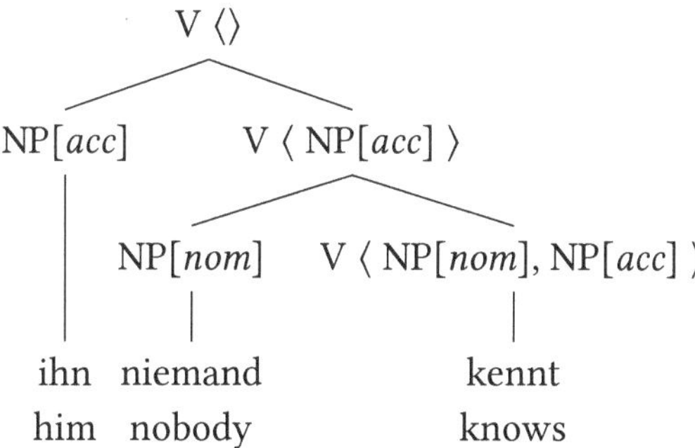

Figure 4.4: Analysis of (*dass*) *ihn niemand kennt* 'that nobody knows him', lan-
        guages that allow for scrambling permit the saturation of arguments
        in any order

Rather than combining the verb with the accusative argument (the object) first,
it is combined with the nominative (the subject) and the accusative (the object)
is added in a later step.

4.3 SVO: Languages with fixed SV order and valence features

The last section demonstrated how verb-final sentences in German can be analyzed. Of course it is easy to imagine how this extends to VSO languages: The
head is initial and combines with the first element in the valence list first and
then with all the other elements. However, nothing has been said about SVO
languages so far. In languages like Danish, English, and so on, all objects are
realized after the verb, as in (12); it is just the subject that precedes the verb.

(12)   Kim gave Sandy the book.

The verb together with its objects forms a unit in a certain sense: it can be fronted (13a). It can be selected by dominating verbs (13b), it can be coordinated (13c), and it is the place where adjuncts attach to (13d–e).

(13)   a. John promised to read the book and [read the book], he will.
      b. He will [read the book].
      c. Kim [[sold the car] and [bought a bicycle]].
      d. He often [reads the book].
      e. ... [often [read the book] slowly], he will.

This can be modeled adequately by assuming two valence lists: one for the complements (COMPS short for COMPLEMENTS) and one for the subject. The list for the subject is called SPECIFIER list (SPR).[3] The specifier list plays a role both in the analysis of sentences and in the analysis of noun phrases. Nouns select their determiner via SPR and all their other arguments via COMPS. Figure 4.5 shows the analysis of sentence (14) using the features SPR and COMPS.

(14)   Nobody knows him.

The COMPS list of *knows* contains a description of the accusative object and the accusative *him* is combined in a first step with *knows*. In addition to the accusative object, *knows* selects for a subject. This selection is passed on to the mother node, the VP. Hence, the SPR value of *knows him* is identical to the SPR value of *knows*. The VP *knows him* selects for a nominative NP. This NP is realized as *nobody* in Figure 4.5. The result of the combination of *knows him* with *nobody* is *nobody knows him*, which is complete: It has both an empty SPR list and an empty COMPS list. The two rules that are responsible for the combinations in Figure 4.5 are called the Specifier-Head Schema and the Head-Complement Schema. I use VP as abbreviation for something with a verbal head and an empty COMPS list and

---

[3]There are various versions of HPSG: Pollard & Sag (1987: Chapter 3.2) assumed that all arguments of a head are represented in one list. This list was called SUBCAT list. Borsley (1987) argued that one should use several valence features (SUBJ, SPR, and COMPS) and this was adopted in Pollard & Sag (1994: Chapter 9): subjects of verbs were selected via SUBJ and determiners via SPR. Sag, Wasow & Bender (2003: Chapter 4.3) assume that both subjects and determiners are selected via SPR, which is what is assumed in the grammars developed here too. Sag (2012: Section 3.3) presents a version of HPSG called Sign-Based Construction Grammar (SBCG) which assumes one valence list for all arguments as was common in 1987. This return to an abandoned approach came without any argumentation. Hence, I do not adopt this variant of HPSG but stick to the separation of subjects and other arguments to SPR and COMPS. I will not use SUBJ as a valence feature, but it will be introduced in the analysis of verbal complexes in Chapter 5.

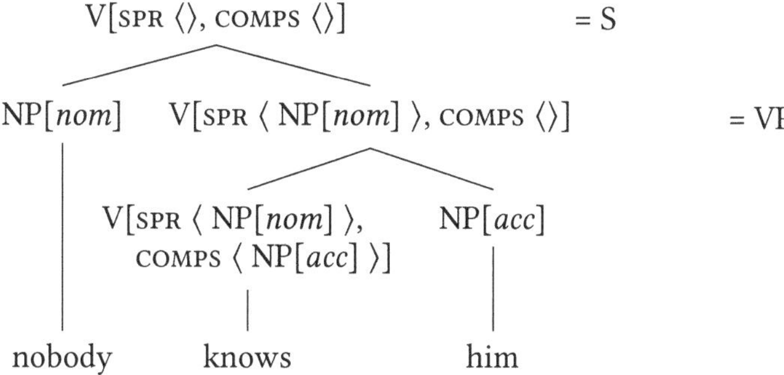

Figure 4.5: Analysis of the SVO order with two separate valence features

at least one element in the SPR list, and S as abbreviation for something with a verbal head and empty lists for both the SPR and the COMPS value.

In Section 4.2, it was explained how scrambling can be accounted for: the rules that combine heads with their arguments can take the arguments from the list in any order. For languages with stricter constituent order requirements, the rules are stricter: the arguments have to be taken off the list consistently from the beginning or from the end. So for English and Danish, one starts at the beginning of the list, and for head-final languages without scrambling, one starts at the end of the list. Figure 4.6 shows the analysis of a sentence with a ditransitive verb. The accusative object is the first element in the COMPS list and it is combined with the verb first. The result of the combination is a verbal projection that has the PP[*to*] as the sole element in the COMPS list. It is combined with an appropriate PP in the next step resulting in a verbal projection that has an empty COMPS list (a VP).

The analysis of our first German example in Figure 4.3 did not use a name for the valence list. So the question is: How does the analysis of German relate to the analysis of English using SPR and COMPS? A lot of researchers from various frameworks have argued that it is not useful to distinguish the subjects of finite verbs from other arguments in grammars of German. All the tests that have been used to show that subjects in English differ from complements do not apply to the arguments of finite verbs in German. For example, it is argued that subjects – in contrast to objects – are extraction islands (Chomsky 1973: 249–250, Fanselow 1987: 76, Grewendorf 1989: 35–36), that is, nothing can be fronted out of a subject. But Haider (1993: 173) discussing the examples in (15) shows that this is not true for German.

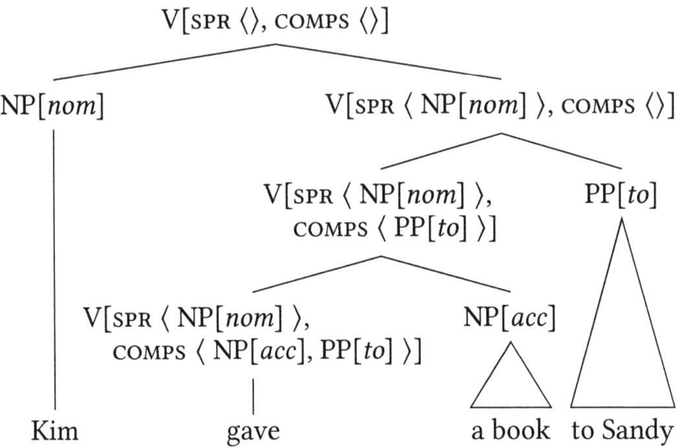

Figure 4.6: Analysis of the SVO order with two separate valence features and two elements in COMPS

(15) a. [Über Strauß]$_i$ hat [ein   Witz $_{-i}$] die Runde gemacht.   (German)
      about Strauß has a.NOM joke   the round made
      'A joke about Strauß went round.'

   b. [Zu drastischeren Maßnahmen]$_i$ hat ihm [der   Mut $_{-i}$]
      to more.drastic measures   has him the.NOM courage
      gefehlt.
      lacked
      'He has lacked the courage for more drastic measures.'

   c. [Zu diesem Problem]$_i$ haben uns noch [einige   Briefe $_{-i}$]
      to this   problem have us still some.NOM letters
      erreicht.[4]
      reached
      'Some letters concerning this problem reached us afterwards.'

The $_{-i}$ indicates the place where the fronted element, the element in the *Vorfeld*, belongs. It is within the subject NP in all three examples. Since no subject-object asymmetries exist in German, researchers like Pollard (1996: 295), Haider (1993: Section 6.3.2), Eisenberg (1994: 376), and Kiss (1995a: 57, 78) argued for so-called "subject as complement" analyses. Figure 4.7 shows the adapted analysis of (9) – repeated here as (16):

---

[4]Oppenrieder (1991: 79)

(16) [dass] niemand   ihn   kennt
     that   nobody.NOM him.ACC knows
    'that nobody knows him'

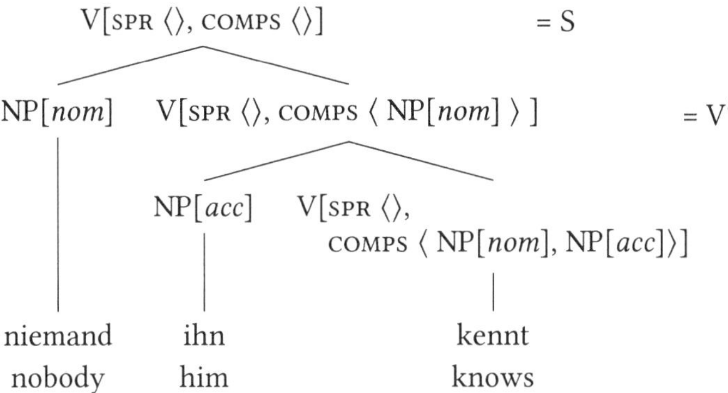

Figure 4.7: The analysis of a German sentence with SPR and COMPS list

The difference between German and English is that German contains all arguments in the COMPS list of the finite verb and no arguments in the SPR list. Since the elements in the COMPS list can be combined with the head in any order, it is explained why all permutations of arguments are possible. Specifiers are realized to the left of their head. This is the same for German and English. For German this is not relevant in the verbal domain, but the Specifier-Head Schema, which will be introduced shortly, is used in the analysis of noun phrases.

Throughout the remainder of this book, I use the abbreviations in Table 4.1.

Table 4.1: Abbreviations for S, VP, and V′ and NP, N′

S	= V[SPR ⟨⟩, COMPS ⟨⟩]
VP	= V[SPR ⟨ NP[*nom*] ⟩, COMPS ⟨⟩]
V′	= all other V projections apart from verbal complexes
NP	= N[SPR ⟨⟩, COMPS ⟨⟩]
N′	= N[SPR ⟨ DET ⟩, COMPS ⟨⟩]

4.4 Immediate dominance schemata

In Section 4.1, I already mentioned that the non-terminal nodes in a tree, that is, the nodes that are not the leaves of the tree, are licensed by schemata similar to those introduced in Chapter 3.2 and 3.4. In fact, the schemata are even more abstract than $\overline{\text{X}}$ schemata since they do not make any statements about linear order of the daughters. The two schemata discussed in this section are sketched here as (17):

(17)   Specifier-Head Schema and Head-Complement Schema (preliminary)
   H[SPR ①]   → H[SPR ① ⊕ ⟨ ② ⟩, COMPS ⟨⟩]   ②
   H[COMPS ①] → H[COMPS ⟨ ② ⟩ ⊕ ①]   ②

Syntactic rules as used here are usually called schemata since they are rather abstract: they do not mention specific categories but instead identify certain information in the mother and the daughter descriptions. The details about such schemata are given in more formal HPSG literature like Müller (2013b: Chapter 4) or Abeillé & Borsley (2021), but Figure 4.8 and Figure 4.11 provide the respective tree representations. The H stands for *head*. The term *head daughter* is used

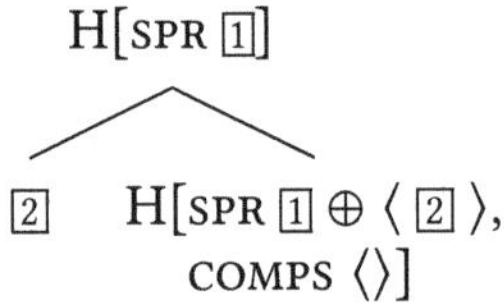

Figure 4.8: Sketch of the Specifier-Head Schema (preliminary)

for the daughter that either is the head of a phrase or contains the head of the phrase (e.g., the verb in a sentence or the noun in a noun phrase). *append* (⊕) is a relation that concatenates two lists. For instance, the concatenation of ⟨ a ⟩ and ⟨ b ⟩ is ⟨ a, b ⟩. The concatenation of the empty list ⟨⟩ with another list yields the latter list. To give some examples that are of relevance in this chapter consider the list ⟨ NP[*nom*], NP[*dat*], NP[*acc*] ⟩. *append* can be used to append two lists resulting in our list in the following ways:

(18)   a.   ⟨⟩ ⊕ ⟨ NP[*nom*], NP[*dat*], NP[*acc*] ⟩ = ⟨ NP[*nom*], NP[*dat*], NP[*acc*] ⟩
   b.   ⟨ NP[*nom*] ⟩ ⊕ ⟨ NP[*dat*], NP[*acc*] ⟩ = ⟨ NP[*nom*], NP[*dat*], NP[*acc*] ⟩
   c.   ⟨ NP[*nom*], NP[*dat*] ⟩ ⊕ ⟨ NP[*acc*] ⟩ = ⟨ NP[*nom*], NP[*dat*], NP[*acc*] ⟩
   d.   ⟨ NP[*nom*], NP[*dat*], NP[*acc*] ⟩ ⊕ ⟨⟩ = ⟨ NP[*nom*], NP[*dat*], NP[*acc*] ⟩

The schema in Figure 4.8 takes a list apart in such a way that a list with a singleton element (⟨ ② ⟩) and a remaining list (①) results. Assuming the three-element list with nom, dat and acc elements, this would be the case in (18c) and ② would be NP[*acc*] and ① would be ⟨ NP[*nom*], NP[*dat*] ⟩. In this book, the SPR list has at most one element.[5] It can be an NP[*nom*] in the case of verbs in the SVO languages or the determiner, if the head is a noun. If one splits a list with a singleton element into a list containing one element and a rest, the rest will always be the empty list. Hence, with the lists on the right-hand side of the equations in (19), ① will be the empty list and ② will be NP[*nom*] and Det, respectively.

(19)   a. $\langle \rangle \oplus \langle$ NP[*nom*] $\rangle = \langle$ NP[*nom*] $\rangle$

       b. $\langle \rangle \oplus \langle$ DET $\rangle = \langle$ DET $\rangle$

For a schema like the one in Figure 4.8 to apply, the descriptions of the daughters have to match the actual daughters. For instance, *sleeps* is compatible with the right daughter: it has an NP[*nom*] in its SPR list. When *sleeps* is realized as a daughter of the schema in Figure 4.8, ② is instantiated as NP[*nom*]. Therefore the left daughter has to be compatible with an NP[*nom*]. It can be realized as a simple pronoun like *she* or a complex NP like *the brown squirrel*. Two analyses are shown in Figure 4.9. The ① in Figure 4.9 says that whatever is in the SPR list is

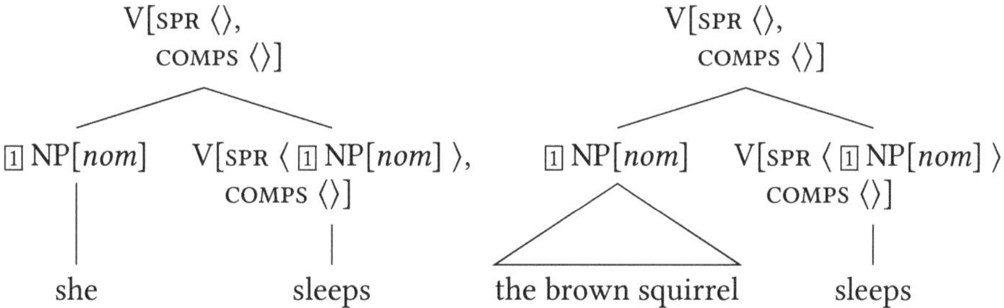

Figure 4.9: Head-Specifier phrases with a subject and an intransitive verb

identified with whatever is the other element in the tree. I wrote down NP[*nom*] following the ① in both the NP node and within the SPR list, but it would have been sufficient to mention NP[*nom*] at one of the two places. The actual number in the box does not matter. What matters is where the same number appears in the trees or structures. I usually start with ① at the top of the tree and use consecutive numbers for the following sharings.

Figure 4.12 on p. 79 below shows an example analysis with a ditransitive verb also involving the Specifier-Head Schema. The specification of the COMPS value of the head daughter in the Specifier-Head Schema ensures that the verb is combined with its complements before the specifier is added.

---

[5]But see Müller & Ørsnes (2013b) for an analysis of object shift in Danish assuming multiple elements in the SPR list.

Apart from its use for the analysis of subject–VP combinations in the SVO languages, the Specifier-Head Schema is also used for the analysis of NPs in all the Germanic languages. Figure 4.10 shows the analysis of the NP *the squirrel.* *squirrel* selects for a determiner and the result of combining *squirrel* with a de-

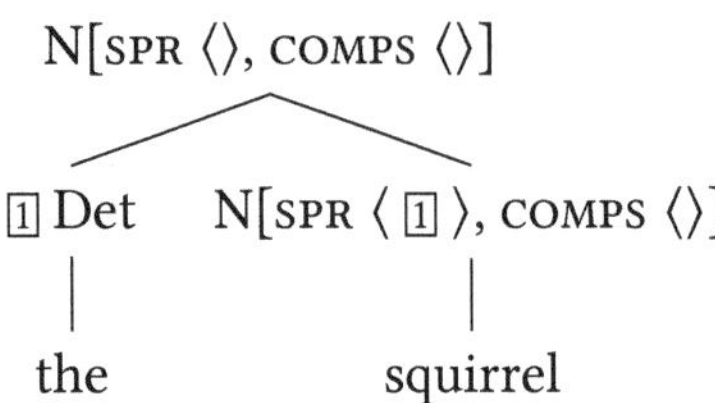

Figure 4.10: Analysis of the NP *the squirrel*

terminer is a complete nominal projection, that is, an NP. There are also nouns like *picture* that take a complement in addition to a determiner:

(20) a picture of Kim

The combination of *picture* and its complement *of Kim* is parallel to the combination of a verb with its object in VO languages with fixed constituent order. For such combinations we need a separate schema: the Head-Complement Schema, which is given in Figure 4.11. The schema splits the COMPS list of a head into an

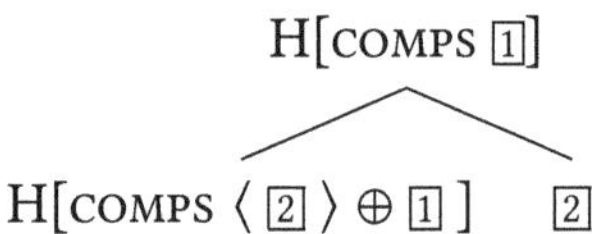

Figure 4.11: Sketch of the Head-Complement Schema (preliminary)

initial list with one element (②), which is realized as the complement daughter to the right.[6] This schema licenses both the combination of *gave* and *the child* and the combination of *gave the child* and *a book* in Figure 4.12, which shows the analysis of (21).[7]

---

[6]In principle, daughters are unordered in HPSG as they were in GPSG (Gazdar et al. 1985). Special linearization rules are used to order a head with respect to its siblings in a local tree. So a schema licensing a tree like the one in Figure 4.11 would also license a tree with the daughters in a different order unless one had linearization rules that rule this out. See Müller (2021a) for an overview of approaches to constituent order in HPSG. Linear precedence rules are discussed in more detail in Section 4.6.

[7]English nouns and determiners do not inflect for case. However, case is manifested in pronouns: *he* (nominative), *his* (genitive), *him* (accusative). Hence, verbs in double object constructions select for two accusatives rather than for dative and accusative as in German.

(21) Nobody gave the child a book.

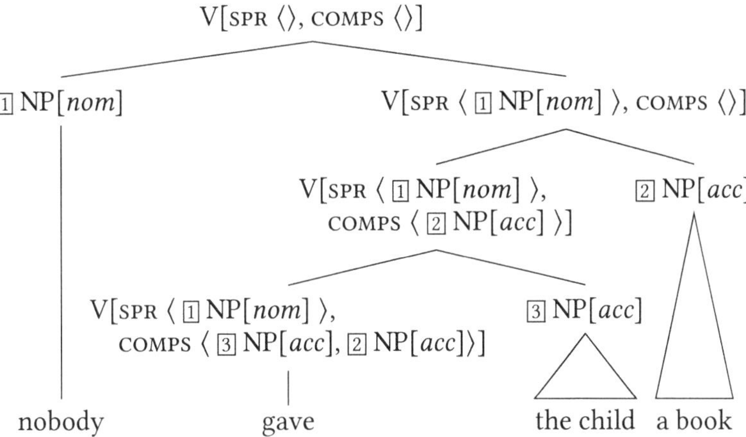

Figure 4.12: Analysis of the sentences with a ditransitive verb

To keep things simple, the Specifier-Head Schema did not mention the COMPS value of the mother. The Head-Complement Schema neither mentioned the SPR value of the head daughter nor that of the mother. But the respective values are important, since something has to be said about these values in structures that are licensed by these schemata. If the SPR value in the combination of *gave* and *the child* were not constrained by the Head-Complement Schema, any value would be possible. This includes a SPR list containing two genitive NPs and an accusative NP. Sequences like (22) would be licensed:

(22) * his his him gave the child a book

To avoid such unspecified SPR values, the SPR value of the head daughter is identified with the SPR value of the mother node in the schema. This is the ① in (23b). Similarly, the COMPS value of the mother in Specifier-Head phrases has to be specified to be identical to the COMPS value of the head daughter (② in (23a)) and hence the empty list.

(23) Specifier-Head Schema and Head-Complement Schema (final)
      a. H[SPR ①, COMPS ②] → H[SPR ① ⊕ ⟨ ③ ⟩, COMPS ② ⟨⟩]   ③
      b. H[SPR ①, COMPS ②] → H[SPR ①, COMPS ② ⊕ ⟨ ③ ⟩]   ③

Figure 4.13 shows the final versions of the two schemata.

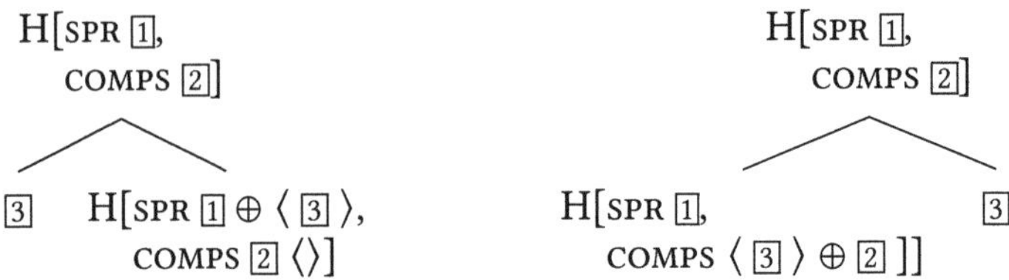

Figure 4.13: Sketch of the Specifier-Head and Head-Complement Schema

4.5 Scrambling: The details

Now, in order to analyze languages with free constituent order, a more liberal variant of the schema in Figure 4.11 is needed. Figure 4.14 splits the COMPS list of a head into three parts: a list ①, a list containing exactly one element ⟨ ③ ⟩ and a third list ②. The element of the second list is realized as the complement of the head. The length of the lists ① and ② is not restricted. For our example list

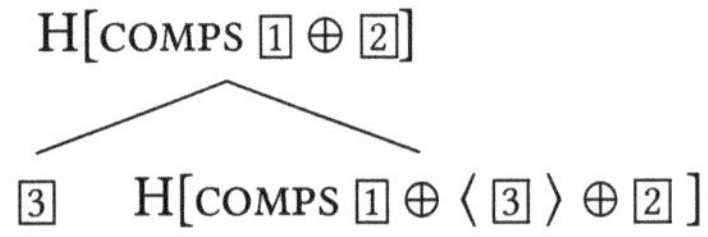

$$\text{H[COMPS ①} \oplus \text{②]}$$

$$\text{③} \quad \text{H[COMPS ①} \oplus \langle \text{③} \rangle \oplus \text{②]}$$

Figure 4.14: Sketch of the Head-Complement Schema for languages with free constituent order

containing a nom, a dat and an acc element, there are the following possibilities to split the list:

(24)   a. ⟨⟩ ⊕ ⟨ NP[*nom*] ⟩ ⊕ ⟨ NP[*dat*], NP[*acc*] ⟩

        b. ⟨ NP[*nom*] ⟩ ⊕ ⟨ NP[*dat*] ⟩ ⊕ ⟨ NP[*acc*] ⟩

        c. ⟨ NP[*nom*], NP[*dat*] ⟩ ⊕ ⟨ NP[*acc*] ⟩ ⊕ ⟨⟩

So ③ in Figure 4.14 would be NP[*nom*] in (24a), NP[*dat*] in (24b) and NP[*acc*] in (24c).

If one restricts ① to be the empty list, one gets grammars that saturate complements from the beginning of the list (VO languages with fixed order like English) and if one restricts ② to be the empty list, one gets grammars that take the last element from the COMPS list for combination with a head (this would be an OV language with fixed order, if such a language existed). Scrambling languages like German allow any complement to be combined with its head since there is neither a restriction on ① nor one on ②.

4.6 Linear precedence rules

The abstract schemata are similar to the schemata that were gained by abstracting over simple phrase structure rules in Chapter 3. They are similar to abstract $\overline{\text{X}}$ rules. However, there is an important difference: the elements on the right-hand side of a rule and the daughters in the corresponding treelets in the figures visualizing the schemata are not ordered. This means that a schema like the one in (25) can be used to analyze configurations with a preceding b and with b preceding a.

(25) m → a b

As will be shown shortly, this comes handy in situations in which one wants to leave the actual order underspecified.

For the Head Complement Schema discussed above this means that actually two orders can be analyzed: head-daughter before complement and complement before head-daughter. Hence the Head-Complement Schema is general enough to analyze the German and English phrases in (26):

(26) a. dem Kind ein Buch gibt
          the child the book gives
      b. gives the child the book

But such a general schema without restrictions would also allow an analysis for (27b) and (27c):

(27) a. [dass] niemand dem Kind ein Buch vorliest
              that nobody the child a   book PART.reads
          'that nobody reads a book to the child'
      b. * [dass] dem Kind niemand vorliest   ein Buch
              that the child nobody PART.reads a   book
      c. * [dass] niemand vorliest   dem Kind ein Buch
              that nobody PART.reads the child a   book

The structures licensed by the Head-Complement Schema without any restrictions are shown in Figure 4.15 and Figure 4.16.

Now, this problem is easy to fix: what is needed is a binary feature specifying whether a head is initial or not. The feature is called INITIAL (abbreviated as INI). All head-daughters that are INI+ are always serialized to the left of their complement and all those that are INI− are serialized to the right. The linearization rules are provided in (28):

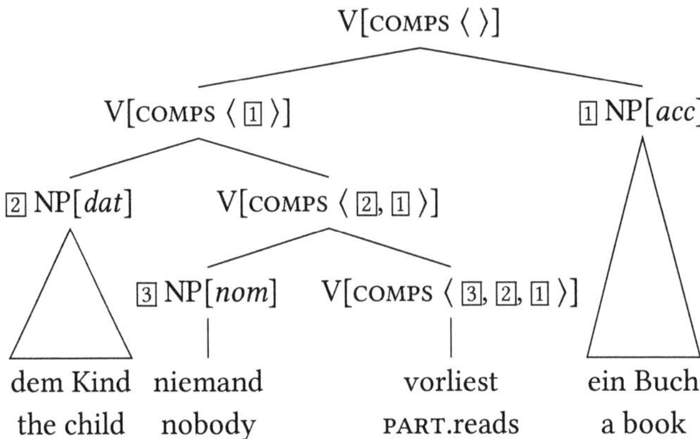

Figure 4.15: Unwanted analysis using the Head-Complement Schema without linearization constraints

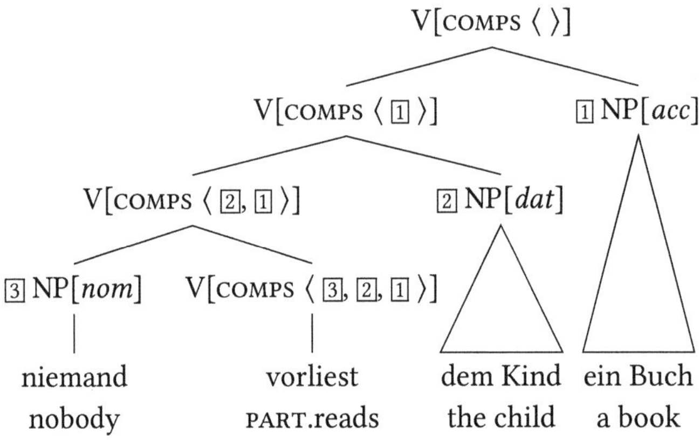

Figure 4.16: Unwanted analysis using the Head-Complement Schema without linearization constraints

(28) a. HEAD [INITIAL+] < COMPLEMENT

 b. COMPLEMENT < HEAD [INITIAL−]

German verbs are specified to be INITIAL−, while English verbs are INITIAL+. Because of this specification and the linearization rules in (28), verbs are always ordered after their complements in German (and other SOV languages) and before their complements in English (and other SVO languages). Of course, there are sentences in German in which the verb is in first or second position and there are sentences in the Germanic SVO languages in which the object precedes the verb. These sentences will be covered in Chapter 6.

Haider (2020: 342) claims that scrambling is only possible in head-final projections. If this claim is correct (at least for the languages under consideration here),[8] the Head-Complement Schema in Figure 4.13 has to be restricted to head-initial projections and the Head-Complement Schema in Figure 4.14 to head-final projections. Nouns in all Germanic languages are head-initial, that is, they take their complements to the right and these are not allowed to scramble. Genitive NPs have to be adjacent to the noun that governs them:

(29)   a.   das Verlesen des   Entwurfes durch die Vorsitzende   (German)
           the reading   of.the draft   by   the chair.woman

       b.   * das Verlesen durch die Vorsitzende   des   Entwurfes
           the reading   by   the chair.woman of.the draft

Verbs in SVO languages like English and the Scandinavian languages are INITIAL+ and hence form a VP via the schema in Figure 4.13, augmented as the left schema in Figure 4.17. Verbs in SOV languages are INITIAL− and combine with their complements via the schema in Figure 4.14, augmented as the right schema in Figure 4.17.

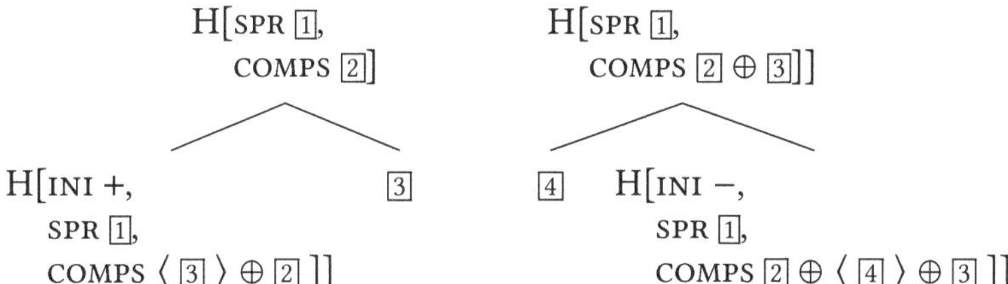

Figure 4.17: Head-Complement Schemata with ordered daughters and instantiated INITIAL values. Left schema for SVO languages and NP structures (no scrambling), right schema for SOV languages (scrambling)

Yiddish with its mix of VO and OV structures poses an interesting formal puzzle, which is addressed in the following section.

---

[8]Santorini (1993: 244) claims that Old French, Old Spanish, Middle English and Russian are VO languages allowing scrambling. Thuilier, Grant, Crabbé & Abeillé (2021) show that French allows postverbal arguments to be reordered. More careful examination of the VO status and scrambling properties of these languages is needed. For example, Haider (2021: Section 3) assigns languages like Russian to a third type (T3) allowing both OV and VO structures. I leave this for further research. See the following section for a T3-analysis of Yiddish.

4.7 Free VO/OV order

As already mentioned in Section 2.1, Yiddish has mixed VO/OV properties and researchers like den Besten & Moed-van Walraven (1986), Schallert (2007: 12), and Haider (2010: 161, 2020) see this language as belonging to a third type.[9] Example (9) from Diesing (1997: 402), which was discussed on p. 17 and is repeated below as (30), shows that Yiddish can have the order usually observed in SVO languages (30a) and the orders observed in SOV languages with scrambling (30b, c). But it can also have the orders in (30d) and (30e), in which the verb is in the middle and either the direct object or the indirect object precedes the verb.

(30)   a. Maks hot nit gegebn Rifken dos bukh.   (Yiddish)
          Max has not given   Rifken the book

          'Max has not given Rifken the book.'

      b. Maks hot Rifken dos bukh nit gegebn.
          Max has Rifken the book not given

          'Max has not given Rifken the book.'

      c. Maks hot dos bukh Rifken nit gegebn.
          Max has the book Rifken not given

          'Max has not given Rifken the book.'

      d. Maks hot Rifken nit gegebn dos bukh.
          Max has Rifken not given   the book

          'Max has not given Rifken the book.'

      e. Max hat dos bukh nit gegebn Rifken.
          Max has the book not given Rifken.

          'Max has not given Rifken the book.'

Haider (2010: 161) argues that Yiddish is a mixed VO/OV language and that heads just may combine with their complements in any order. Haider claims that scrambling is only possible in head-final projections. So, a variant of (30a) with initial verb and scrambled objects is predicted to be impossible. Now, freedom seems to be easy to achieve as the absence of constraints. Yiddish would be a language

---

[9]Santorini (1993) also argues for a classification of Yiddish as a mixed VO/OV language but assumes that this means that particular sentences may be either VO or OV, but verbs cannot govern both to the left and to the right Santorini (1993: 240). The solution outlined below will not assume this but rather assume that Yiddish verbs have neither an INITIAL value of + (VO) nor − (OV) but a third value and hence can be placed in the middle of their arguments without any movement.

in which the INITIAL value is just unspecified.[10] But this is not sufficient since if *Rifken* is combined with *nit gegebn* to form *Rifken nit gegebn*, the result is an INITIAL− projection. This projection cannot be used as the daughter in the head-initial schema since it is incompatible with INITIAL+.

Fortunately, there is a solution to such problems that was developed for accounts of case syncretism (Daniels 2002). It makes use of the type system that is part of the formalism for specifying linguistic constraints (Abeillé & Borsley 2021: Section 3, Richter 2021: Section 2). Values like part of speech are types and types can have subtypes. For example, there can be a type *part-of-speech* with the subtypes *noun, verb, adj, prep* and others. There can be a type *vform* with the subtypes *fin, bse, ppp, inf* for finite verbs, infinitives without *to*, participles, and infinitives with *to*. For our problem at hand, one would need a type *bool* for boolean values (+ or −). Normally, the subtypes of *bool* would be just + and −, but since the requirements from the schemata have to be allowed to be compatible, the type hierarchy has to be more complex. It is given in Figure 4.18. There

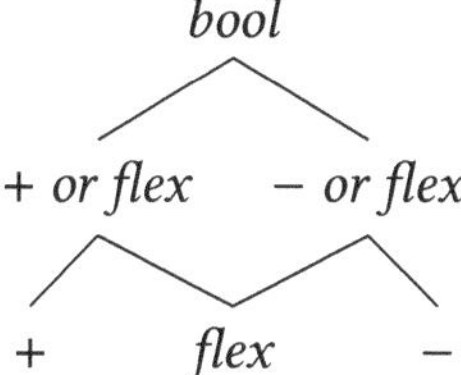

Figure 4.18: Extended hierarchy for boolean types

are two new types + *or flex* and − *or flex. flex* is the INITIAL value of Yiddish verbs. The schemata require their head daughters to be of type + *or flex* or − *or flex*. SVO languages have verbs with INITIAL value + and SOV languages have verbs with INITIAL value −. + and − are compatible with the requirements of the schemata but they do not allow a switch in the direction of government as is possible in Yiddish.

4.8 Adjuncts

While arguments are selected by their head, adjuncts select the head. The difference between languages like Dutch and German on the one hand, and Danish

---

[10]See for example Haider (2010: 7) for the suggestion of an "underspecification of the directionality feature".

and English on the other hand, can be explained by assuming that adjuncts in the former languages are less picky as far as the element is concerned with which they combine. Dutch (31) and German (32) adjuncts can attach to any verbal projection, while Danish (33) and English (34) require a VP (see also Section 2.4):

(31) a. [dat] onmiddellijk iedereen   het boek leest   (Dutch)
             that promptly   everybody the book reads

             'that everybody reads the book promptly'

     b. [dat] iedereen   onmiddellijk het boek leest
             that everybody promptly   the book reads

     c. [dat] iedereen   het boek onmiddellijk leest
             that everybody the book promptly   reads

(32) a. [dass] sofort   jeder   das Buch liest   (German)
             that   promptly everybody the book reads

             'that everybody reads the book promptly'

     b. [dass] jeder   sofort   das Buch liest
             that   everybody promptly the book reads

     c. [dass] jeder   das Buch sofort   liest
             that   everybody the book promptly reads

(33) a. at   hver   læst bogen   straks   (Danish)
             that everybody reads book.DEF promptly

             'that everybody reads the book promptly'

     b. at   hver   straks   læst bogen
             that everybody promptly reads book.DEF

             'that everybody promptly reads the book'

(34) a. that everybody reads the book promptly

     b. that everybody promptly reads the book

For the selection of arguments the features SPR and COMPS are used. In parallel there is a MOD feature that is part of the lexical description of a head of a phrase that can function as an adjunct (MOD is an abbreviation for *modified*). The value of MOD is a description of an appropriate head. Head-adjunct structures are licensed by the schema in Figure 4.19. For instance, attributive adjectives have $\overline{\text{N}}$ as their MOD value, where $\overline{\text{N}}$ is an abbreviation for a nominal projection that has an empty COMPS list and a SPR list that contains a determiner. (35) shows the lexical item for *brown*:

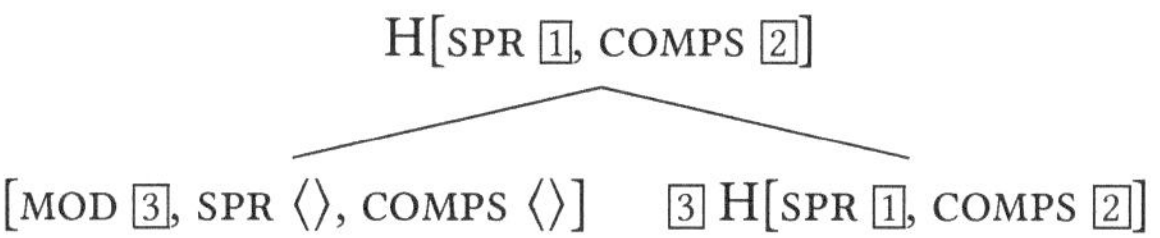

Figure 4.19: Sketch of the Head-Adjunct Schema

(35) Lexical item for *brown*:

$$\begin{bmatrix} \text{PHON} & \langle\ brown\ \rangle \\ \text{MOD} & \overline{\text{N}} \\ \text{SPR} & \langle\rangle \\ \text{COMPS} & \langle\rangle \end{bmatrix}$$

The analysis of the phrase *brown squirrel* is shown in Figure 4.20. In languages

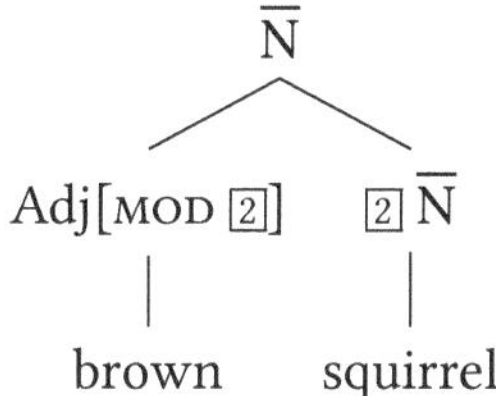

Figure 4.20: Analysis of the head-adjunct structure *brown squirrel*

like German in which the adjective agrees with the noun in gender, number, and inflection class (Pollard & Sag 1994: Section 2.2.5, Müller 2013b: Section 13.2), the properties that the noun must have can be specified inside the MOD value. For instance, *kleiner* selects a masculine noun and *kleine* selects a feminine one:

(36) a. ein kleiner Hund   (German)
          a   little   dog

      b. eine kleine Katze
          a   little   cat

For German adverbials, the value restricts the part of speech of the head to be verb (or rather verbal since, as (37b) shows, adjectival participles can be modified as well) and the value of INITIAL to be −.

(37) a. dass es oft   lacht   (German)
          that it often laughs

          'that he/she laughs often'

   b. das oft   lachende Kind
      the often laughing child
      'the child who laughs often'

The specification of the modified element to be INITIAL− ensures that the adjunct attaches to verbs in final position only (verb-initial sentences are discussed in Chapter 6). A linearization rule has to make sure that adverbials are serialized to the left of the verb, that is, somewhere in the *Mittelfeld*. The MOD value of English adverbials is simply VP. Without any further restrictions, this allows for a pre- and a post-VP attachment of adjuncts.

- SOV (Dutch, German, …): MOD V[INI−]

- SVO (Danish, English, …): MOD VP

The analysis of (32a) is shown in Figure 4.21, the analysis of (32b) in Figure 4.22, and the analysis of (32c) in Figure 4.23. The only difference between the figures is the respective place of attachment of the adverb. I marked the parts of the tree that are licensed by the Head-Adjunct Schema by including them in a box. All other nodes in the tree are licensed by the Head-Complement Schema in Figure 4.11.

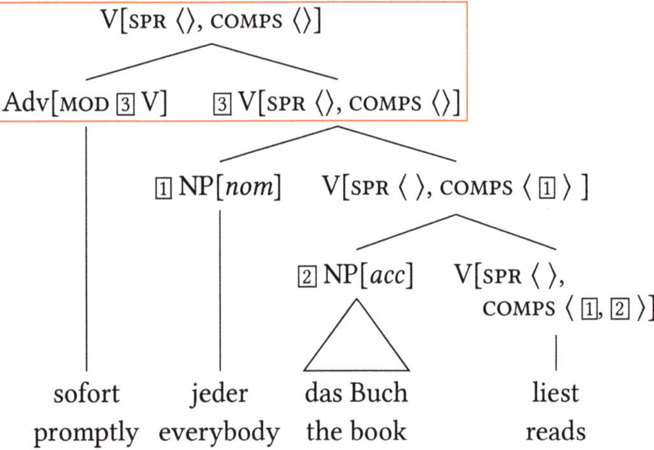

Figure 4.21: Analysis of [*dass*] *sofort jeder das Buch liest* 'that everybody reads the book promptly' with the adjunct attaching above subject and object

The attentive reader will notice that there is a description following the ③ in the MOD value of the adverbials, while there is no such description in the MOD

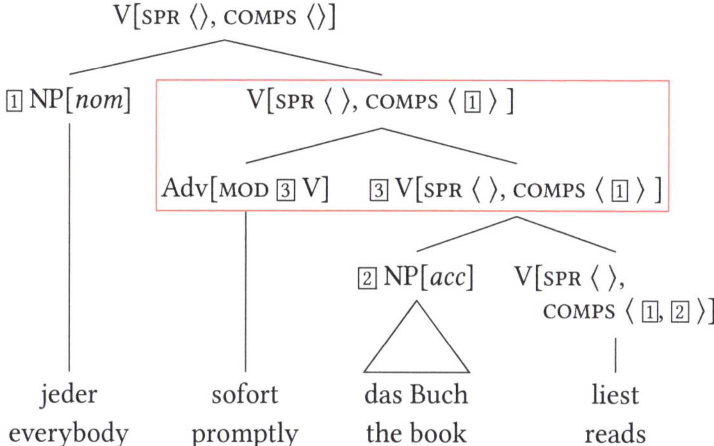

Figure 4.22: Analysis of [*dass*] *jeder sofort das Buch liest* 'that everybody reads the book promptly' with the adjunct attaching between subject and object

values of the English examples that follow. Of course this is purely notational since the numbered boxes identify all values with the same numbers, but the convention behind this is to state the description if it differs from what is given in other places where the box occurs. In the case of German, the MOD value of adverbials is just *verb* without any restrictions regarding valence features. The valence features are given at the modified node (e.g., SPR ⟨⟩, COMPS ⟨ 1, 2 ⟩ in Figure 4.23), but not in the MOD value. Since English adverbials modify VPs and since the modified node is a VP, the value of the MOD value is not given in detail in the figures below, but is just shared with the properties of the modified node.

The Figures 4.24 and 4.25 show the analysis of adjunction with the adverb in pre-VP and post-VP position respectively.

The values of SPR and COMPS in the schema in Figure 4.19 on page 87 have not been explained so far. First there is the sharing of the SPR and COMPS values between mother and head-daughter. Whatever element an adjunct attaches to, the valence requirements of the mother are always identical to the valence requirement of the head-daughter. Nothing is added, nothing is missing. Adjuncts are additional elements that are not selected for via valence features, hence nothing has to be discharged. This can be seen by looking at the German examples in Figures 4.21 to 4.23: *sofort* 'promptly' attaches to a node with certain valence requirements and the dominating node has exactly the same valence requirements.

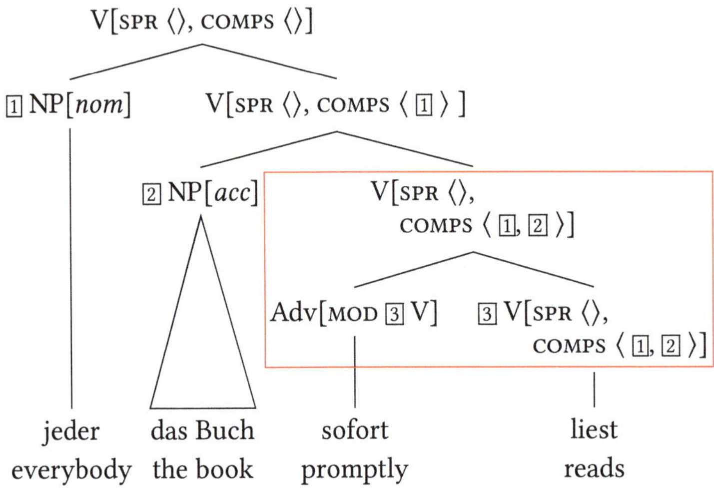

Figure 4.23: Analysis of [*dass*] *jeder das Buch sofort liest* 'that everybody reads the book promptly' with the adjunct attaching between object and verb

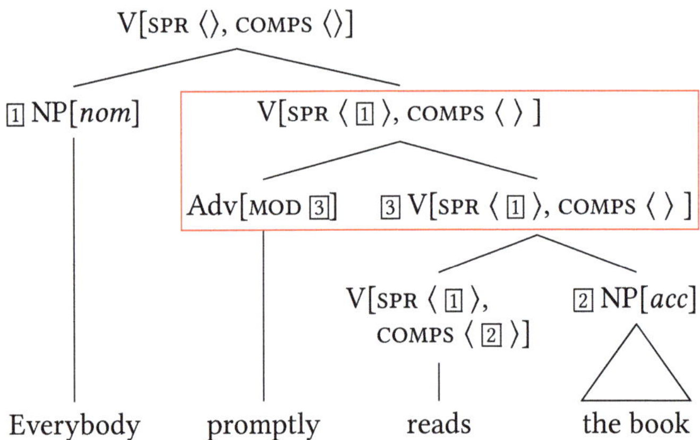

Figure 4.24: Analysis of adjuncts in SVO languages: the adjunct is realized left-adjacent to the VP.

In principle, the figures should have little numbered boxes in them indicating the identity of the valence requirements of mother and head daughter in head-adjunct combinations. I omitted these so-called structure sharings to keep things simple and readable.

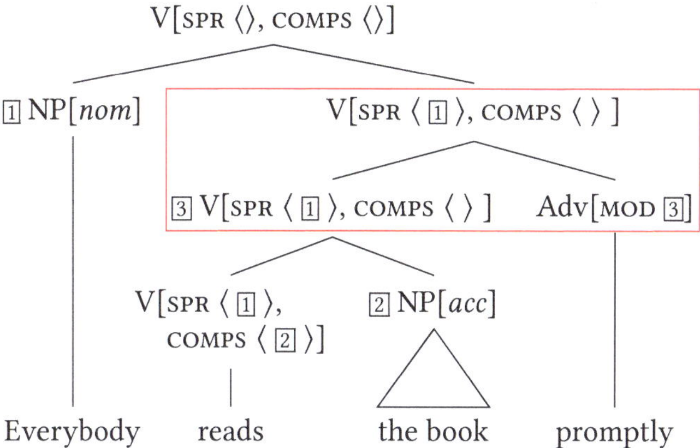

Figure 4.25: Analysis of adjuncts in SVO languages: the adjunct is realized right-adjacent to the VP.

The adjunct itself has to have empty valence lists, that is, it has to be complete. Without this requirement, sentences like the one in (38) would be licensed:

(38)   * Sandy read the book in.

in is a preposition that has an NP[*acc*] in its COMPS list. If the Head-Adjunct Schema did not specify the COMPS list of the adjunct daughter to be empty, a preposition could function as the adjunct daughter and a structure for ungrammatical sentences like (38) would be licensed by the grammar.

The specifier specification is as important as the specification of the COMPS list. If non-empty SPR lists were allowed, the contrast in (39) could not be explained:

(39)   a.   dass jeder   eine Stunde liest   (German)
            that everybody an   hour   reads

            'Everybody is reading for an hour.'

       b. * dass jeder   Stunde liest
            that everybody hour   reads

The analysis of (39a) is shown in Figure 4.26. The adjunct is a full NP. The schema requires the adjunct daughter to be fully complete. If it did not have this requirement, a noun without a determiner like *Stunde* 'hour' in (39b) could enter the schema as adjunct daughter and ungrammatical sentences like (39b) would be licensed.

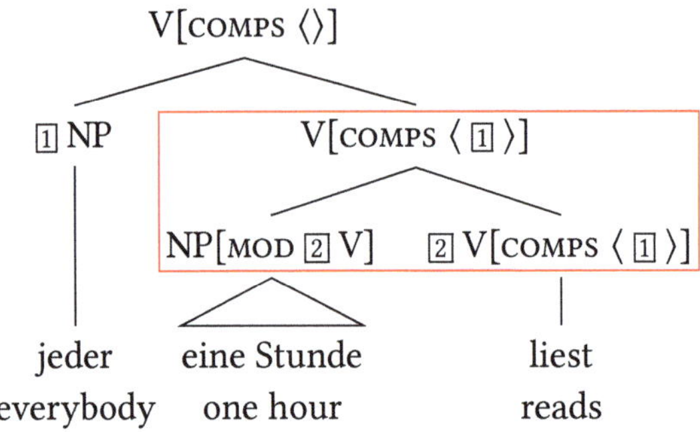

Figure 4.26: Analysis of an adverbial NP in *dass jeder eine Stunde liest* 'that everybody is reading for an hour'

4.9 Linking between syntax and semantics

HPSG assumes that all arguments of a head are contained in a list that is called ARGUMENT STRUCTURE (ARG-ST, Davis, Koenig & Wechsler 2021).[11] This list contains descriptions of the syntactic and semantic properties of the selected arguments. For instance, the ARG-ST list of English *give* and its German, Danish and Dutch and Icelandic variants is given in (40):

(40) ⟨ NP, NP, NP ⟩

The case systems of the languages in question vary a bit as will be explained in Chapter 7, but nevertheless the orders of the NPs in the ARG-ST list are the same across these languages.[12] They correspond to nom, dat, acc in German (41a) and subject, primary object, secondary object in English (41b):

(41) a. dass das Kind dem Eichhörnchen die Nuss gibt
         that the child the squirrel   the nut gives
         'that the child gives the squirrel the nut'

      b. that the child gives the squirrel the nut

In addition to the syntactic features we have seen so far, semantic features are used to describe the semantic contribution of linguistic objects. (42) shows some aspects of the description of the English verb *gives*:

---

[11]See Pollard & Sag (1994: 28–29), Wechsler (1995), Davis (2001), and Müller (2007a: Section 5.6) for argument linking in HPSG. Davis, Koenig & Wechsler (2021) is a handbook article on linking in HPSG.

[12]Interestingly, Haider (2010: 15) also states that the argument structure is the same across the Germanic languages, although he makes different assumptions as far as the structure of OV and VO clauses is concerned.

(42) Lexical item for *gives*:

$$\begin{bmatrix} \text{ARG-ST} & \langle\, \text{NP}_{[1]},\, \text{NP}_{[2]},\, \text{NP}_{[3]}\, \rangle \\[2ex] \text{CONT} & \begin{bmatrix} give \\ \text{AGENS} & [1] \\ \text{GOAL} & [2] \\ \text{TRANS-OBJ} & [3] \end{bmatrix} \end{bmatrix}$$

The lowered boxes refer to the referential indices of the NPs. One can imagine these indices as variables that refer to the object in the real world that the NP is referring to. These indices are identified with semantic roles of the verb *give*. Finding reasonable role names is not trivial and some authors just use ARG1, ARG2 and ARG3 to avoid the problems (see Dowty 1991 for discussion).

The representations for the other languages mentioned above is entirely parallel. Therefore it is possible to capture crosslinguistic generalizations.[13] Nevertheless there are differences between the Germanic OV and VO languages. As was explained above the VO languages map their subject to SPR and all other arguments to COMPS, while the finite verbs of OV languages have all arguments on COMPS. (43) shows some examples.[14]

(43) a. Linking and argument mapping for an English finite verb (SVO):

$$\begin{bmatrix} \text{SPR} & \langle\, \text{NP}_{[1]}\, \rangle \\[1ex] \text{COMPS} & \langle\, \text{NP}_{[2]},\, \text{NP}_{[3]}\, \rangle \\[1ex] \text{ARG-ST} & \langle\, \text{NP}_{[1]},\, \text{NP}_{[2]},\, \text{NP}_{[3]}\, \rangle \\[2ex] \text{CONT} & \begin{bmatrix} give \\ \text{AGENS} & [1] \\ \text{GOAL} & [2] \\ \text{TRANS-OBJ} & [3] \end{bmatrix} \end{bmatrix}$$

---

[13] See also Haider's (2010: 14–15) Observation 3. The relative order of arguments in OV and VO is identical. Haider also assumes that the ranking of arguments in the argument structure of lexical items is identical in the Germanic languages. He assumes a different branching for OV and VO languages though. See Section 6.3.2.

[14] For readability, I just listed the NPs on the respective lists. In actual analyses, the ARG-ST list is split into two sublists [4] and [5] and [4] is the SPR list and [5] the COMPS list. The SPR list contains just one element in languages like English and no element for finite verbs in languages like German. See Ginzburg & Sag (2000: 171), Bouma et al. (2001: 12) and Abeillé & Borsley (2021: 17) for details on argument realization.

b. Linking and argument mapping for a German finite verb (SOV):

$$
\begin{bmatrix}
\text{SPR} & \langle\,\rangle \\[4pt]
\text{COMPS} & \langle\, \text{NP}_{1}, \text{NP}_{2}, \text{NP}_{3} \,\rangle \\[4pt]
\text{ARG-ST} & \langle\, \text{NP}_{1}, \text{NP}_{2}, \text{NP}_{3} \,\rangle \\[4pt]
\text{CONT} & \begin{bmatrix}
\textit{geben} \\
\text{AGENS} & 1 \\
\text{GOAL} & 2 \\
\text{TRANS-OBJ} & 3
\end{bmatrix}
\end{bmatrix}
$$

This provides a connection between arguments of a head and the semantic roles they fill. While this is a first step towards semantics, a lot remains to be said. For example, the contribution of quantifiers like *every* and *a* in (44) and the determination of the scope they take is not explained yet.

(44)   Every squirrel wants to eat a nut.

But this introduction to syntax is not the place to do this. The reader is referred to Koenig & Richter (2021) for an overview of approaches to semantics in HPSG. The implemented fragments of German, Danish, English and Yiddish mentioned in the preface assume Minimal Recursion Semantics (MRS; Copestake et al. 2005), which is also covered by Koenig & Richter (2021: Section 6.1).

4.10 Alternatives

This section is for advanced readers. Subsection 4.10.1 compares the theory developed here with approaches to German developed in the theory of Government & Binding (GB) (Chomsky 1981, 1986). Subsection 4.10.2 contains a comparison to certain approaches to syntax in GB and Minimalism (Chomsky 1995). I argue for an approach to syntactic categories and phrases that is normally used rather than the more recent approaches that include semantic and pragmatic notions in syntactic structures. Like Subsection 4.10.1, Subsection 4.10.2 is optional and it is possible to understand the rest of the book without reading it. I suggest reading it nevertheless since it may deepen the understanding of syntax in general.

4.10.1 CP/TP/VP models

Grewendorf (1988, 1995), Lohnstein (2014) and many others assume that German sentences have a constituent structure that is parallel to the structure that is assumed by Chomsky (1986) for English. As for English, the verb is assumed to form a phrase with its objects and this VP functions as the argument of a Tense head to form a maximal projection together with the subject of the verb, which is realized in the specifier position of the TP.[15] Figure 4.27 shows the analysis of (45) with the respective VP, TP, and CP layers.

(45) dass jeder   dieses Buch kennt
      that everybody this   book knows
      'that everybody knows this book'

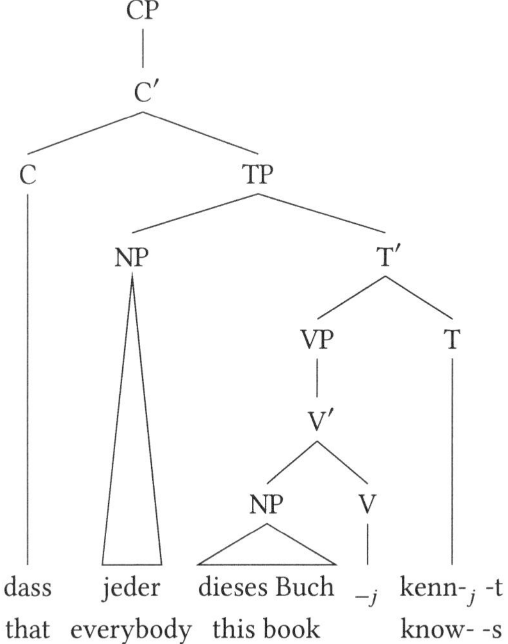

Figure 4.27: Sentence in the CP/TP/VP model

Such CP/TP/VP systems are motivated for English, since auxiliary verbs and modals behave differently from main verbs. These verbs are assumed to be of category T. For finite verbs, T is assumed to hold inflectional affixes and the stem of the finite verb moves to T to "check" inflectional information. Such analyses are not just assumed within the Government & Binding framework and in Minimalism (so-called Mainstream Generative Grammar) but also in frameworks like

---

[15]The Tense Phrase roughly corresponds to the Inflection Phrase (IP) in earlier publications. Pollock (1989: 397) assumes further functional projections. This is called the Split-IP approach. See also Section 4.10.2 on functional projections.

LFG (Bresnan 2001: Section 6.2; Dalrymple 2001: Section 3.2.1). However, languages like German differ from English in that the auxiliaries behave like main verbs, so placing them in T would not be warranted. For this reason and further points discussed below, researchers working on German in non-MGG never assume an IP or TP (see Berman 2003: Section 3.2.3.2 on LFG and Müller 2023a on HPSG). Haider (2010: Chapter 2) discusses IP/TP-based approaches in detail and shows their many problems. See Bayer & Kornfilt (1990), Höhle (1991a: 157), Haider (1993, 1997a, 2010), Sternefeld (2006: Section IV.3), and Beck & Gergel (2014: 172) for MGG approaches without an IP or TP.

In what follows, I want to discuss a problem with scrambling, the phenomenon discussed in the present chapter. See Section 6.3.4 for further problems. The problematic aspect of the TP analysis with respect to scrambling is the realization of the subject in the specifier position of TP. Therefore there is no way of serializing the accusative object before the subject unless one assumes that the object is moved to a higher position in the tree, e.g., adjoined to TP as in Figure 4.28.[16]

While researchers like Frey (1993: 185) argued that quantifier scopings are evidence for movement-based approaches, they actually provide evidence against movement-based approaches. Let us consider Frey's examples. Frey argues that sentences without movement have only one reading and sentences like (46b) in which – according to the movement-based theory – movement is involved have two readings: one corresponding to the visible order and one to the order before movement, the so-called underlying order.

(46) a. Es ist nicht der Fall, daß er mindestens einem Verleger   fast
         it is not   the case that he at.least   one   publisher almost
         jedes Gedicht anbot.
         every poem   offered
         'It is not the case that he offered at least one publisher almost every poem.'
      b. Es ist nicht der Fall, daß er fast   jedes Gedicht$_i$ mindestens einem
         it is not   the case that he almost every poem   at.least   one
         Verleger _$_i$ anbot.
         publisher   offered
         'It is not the case that he offered almost every poem to at least one publisher.'

---

[16]Note that this is a general property of analyses introducing arguments in different projections. For example, analyses that introduce arguments in separate verb shells like little v (Larson 1988, Adger 2003: 331) are also forced to assume movement to account for orders involving arguments licensed by different heads.

96

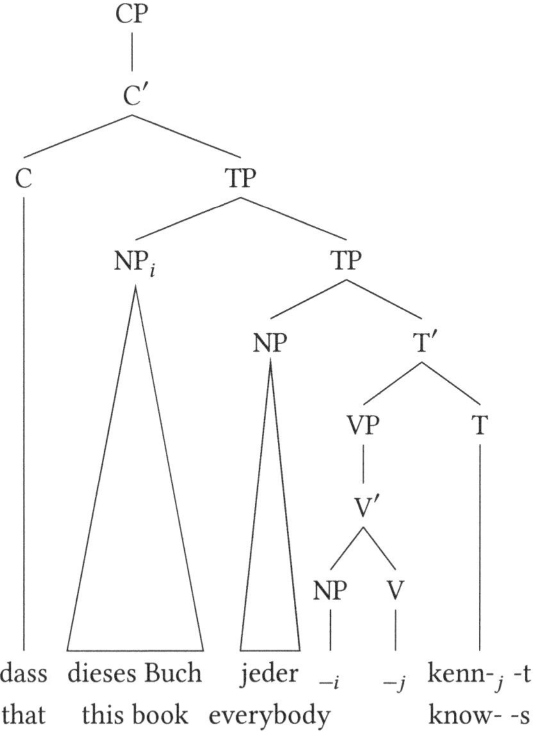

Figure 4.28: Scrambling has to be movement in the CP/TP/VP model

However, Kiss (2001: 146) and Fanselow (2001: Section 2.6) pointed out that such approaches have problems with multiple moved constituents. For instance, in an example such as (47), it should be possible to interpret *mindestens einem Verleger* 'at least one publisher' at the position of $_{-i}$, which would lead to a reading where *fast jedes Gedicht* 'almost every poem' has scope over *mindestens einem Verleger* 'at least one publisher'. However, this reading does not exist.

(47) Ich glaube, dass mindestens einem Verleger$_i$ fast   jedes Gedicht$_j$ nur
      I   believe that at.least   one   publisher almost every poem   only
      dieser Dichter $_{-i}$ $_{-j}$ angeboten hat.
      this   poet   offered   has
      'I think that only this poet offered almost every poem to at least one
      publisher.'

This means that one needs some way to determine the deviation with respect to an unmarked order, but movement is not the solution. See Müller (2023b:

Section 3.5) for further discussion and Kiss (2001) for an approach to scope within the framework assumed here.

4.10.2 Syntax and other levels of description

Chapter 3 relied on constituency tests that are standardly assumed in the syntactic literature (Borsley 1991: 24–31, Haegeman 1994: 35–36, Huddleston & Pullum 2002: 20–23, Sag et al. 2003: 29–33, Kim & Sells 2008: 19–22, Müller 2023b: Chapter 1.3, Machicao y Priemer 2022). It is usually assumed that phrases are assigned categories that correspond to distribution classes. For example, a complex noun phrase can be replaced by other complex noun phrases or by pronouns.

(48) a. der   Tisch
          the.NOM table

    b. der   Tisch aus   Japan
          the.NOM table from Japan

    c. der   alte Tisch aus   Japan
          the.NOM old table from Japan

    d. er
          he

Features like case, person, and gender are important for the distribution of noun phrases. An accusative pronoun cannot be replaced by a nominative pronoun. Similarly, person and number are important for the distribution of noun phrases since they have to match the properties of the verb. Similarly, gender is important for the distribution of noun phrases and pronouns: *der Tisch* 'the table' is masculine and can be replaced by the pronoun *er* 'he' but it cannot be replaced by *sie* 'she', which is feminine. *der Tisch* 'the table' and *die Vase* 'the vase' differ in gender but can be exchanged in many contexts, since both of these phrases are NPs. The phrases in (49) are different, since they lack a determiner. We used the category $\overline{\text{N}}$ for such phrases. Again, the phrases in (49) can be replaced by other phrases of this category: wherever we use *Vase aus China*, we can also use *alte Vase aus China*. This is why the same category is assigned to all these phrases.

(49) a. Vase
          vase

    b. Vase aus   China
          vase from China

    c. alte Vase aus   China
          old vase from China

The phrases in (48) and (49) differ in terms of completeness and in their gender. HPSG models this by assuming the categories can be complex. They consist of various features like gender, number, person, part of speech, valence and so on.

In fact, the reason for these features to be assumed in grammars is that they play a role in the distribution of words and larger units of words. If we were to discover the structure of an unknown language, this would be the task: replace certain units in an utterance and see how things change. Dan Everett did this when studying Pirahã.[17] He first pointed at objects to learn the words used for them. Then he let a stick fall down and asked how this is expressed in Pirahã. Then he let a leaf fall down and asked for the expression. He can then try and identify the words he learned in other environments and maybe, depending on the language, with different inflections. So, syntax is about the distribution of words and groups of words. The classes that can be found this way correspond to parts of speech and morpho-syntactic features like gender, number, and case. The phrase structure grammar introduced in Chapter 3 follows this tradition, which goes back to Bloomfield (1926), Harris (1946), and Wells (1947). To give a simple example of a traditional phrase structure grammar, consider the grammar in (2) on p. 37 – repeated here as (50) for convenience:

(50) NP → Det N   NP → she   N → child
      S   → NP VP   Det → the   N → book
      VP → V NP   V → reads

This little grammar assigns categories to words: *she* is an NP, *the* is a determiner, *child* and *book* are nouns, *reads* is a verb. In addition, there are several phrase structure rules. The NP rule states that an NP may consist of a Det and an N. The S rule says that an S may consist of an NP and a VP. The VP rule states that a VP may consist of a V and an NP. While such rewrite rules are independent of the notion of head in principle, heads play an important role in linguistics. Usually, we talk about NPs because the phrase under consideration contains an N as the most important element.

Starting with Larson (1988) and Pollock (1989) different views entered into Mainstream Generative Syntax. They culminated in the cartographic work of Cinque and Rizzi, who assume at least 400 so-called functional heads in an analysis of a sentence, most of them invisible (Cinque & Rizzi 2010: 57). The following subsections are devoted to such approaches and I want to argue that syntax should be about distribution classes rather than fixed cascades of functional heads.

---

[17] See https://youtu.be/5NyB4fIZHeU?t=868, 2022-03-31.

4.10.2.1 Autonomy of Syntax, resulting problems and syntactification of other descriptive levels

Chomsky argued for the autonomy of syntax and developed architectures in which there was a syntactic component that fed information into a phonology module and into a semantics module. Figure 4.29 shows the so-called T model from Chomsky (1981: 5). The problem with such an architecture is that syntax

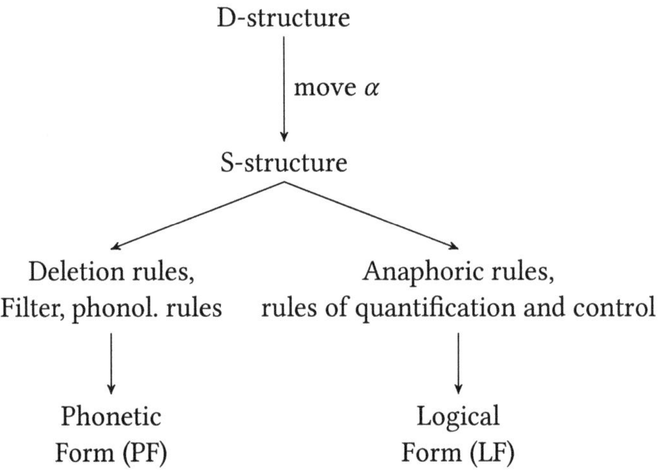

Figure 4.29: The T model as described by Chomsky (1981: 5)

interacts with phonology, semantics, and information structure and that this cannot be captured if one deals with syntax alone. As a result of this, semantic and information-structural notions entered certain flavors of syntax in the GB/Minimalism framework. For example, so-called Cartographic approaches in the tradition of Cinque & Rizzi (2010) assume phrases called Topic Phrase or Focus Phrase although these phrases are simply clausal projections. So, in "normal" syntax they would be verb phrases (VPs) or sentences (S). Figure 4.30 shows an (abbreviated) analysis of a German clause in this tradition.[18] The syntax tree contains a wild mix of categories including a Topic Phrase (TopP), Subject Phrase (SubjP), a Negation Phrase (NegP), an Auxiliary Phrase (AuxP), a Manner Phrase (MannP), an Aspect Phrase (AspP) and the more common Determiner Phrase (DP; our NP) and Verb Phrase (VP). Categories like Topic Phrase and Focus Phrase are

---

[18]Fronted phrases and adverb phrases are assumed to be in specifier positions of respective projections. This means that the actual Topic, Aspect, Manner, and Negation heads are missing in the figure. The technical details of such approaches are discussed in Section 4.10.2.4.

information-structural categories. The topic and focus of a phrase can be some parts of the phrase, for example, fronted constituents. The information that there is a topic within a phrase concerns the relevant parts and should not be the name of the complete phrase. See De Kuthy (2021) for an overview of the analyses of information structure in HPSG. Manner, aspect, negation are semantic categories and of course this information is important in grammatical theory and should be represented somewhere in a grammar, but it should not be the part of speech label (based on the meaning-contribution of a non-head). See Section 4.9 for the place of semantic information in HPSG and a sketch of the connection between syntax and semantics. Further details about semantics in HPSG can be found in Koenig & Richter (2021). Subject and object are grammatical functions. Frameworks like Lexical Functional Grammar use grammatical functions as primitives of their theories. They state formally that a certain phrase is the subject or object of a head, but they do not assume Subject Phrases or Object Phrases. For more on Cinque & Rizzi style analyses and part of speech information see Müller (2023b: Section 4.6.1.1).

The labels of the nodes are created according to the specifier and not to the most important element in the phrase. For example, the Subject Phrase is called Subject Phrase since a DP in its specifier position is the subject of the clause. Similarly Topic Phrases are called Topic Phrases since the DP in the specifier position is a topic. In comparison to so-called Cartographic approaches, the model of syntax argued for in this book is very simple: categories stand for linguistic objects with certain properties that belong to the same distribution class. For example an NP with masculine gender in the third person singular (48) or an $\overline{\text{N}}$ with feminine gender in the third person singular as in (49). Since the phrases/words in (48) and (49) share the respective properties, they can be exchanged. These categories can be selected by other heads. As was described in this chapter, a verb may select an NP in the nominative. This is not possible in theories with "creative" categories. I will explain this with respect to Cinque's (1999) adverb analysis in Section 4.10.2.4, but before going into adverbs in general, I examine a specific case in Section 4.10.2.3: negation analyses with a Negation Phrase. Section 4.10.2.5 deals with Cartography and coordination in general and with approaches to coordination assuming a Conjunction Phrase in particular.

4.10.2.2 Information structure projections

Figure 4.30 shows Laenzlinger's (2004: 224) approach with a Topic Phrase at the beginning of the *Mittelfeld*. Similar suggestions were made by Müller & Sternefeld (1993: 485, 495), Haftka (1995), Frey (2004a) and Grewendorf (2005: 87). The

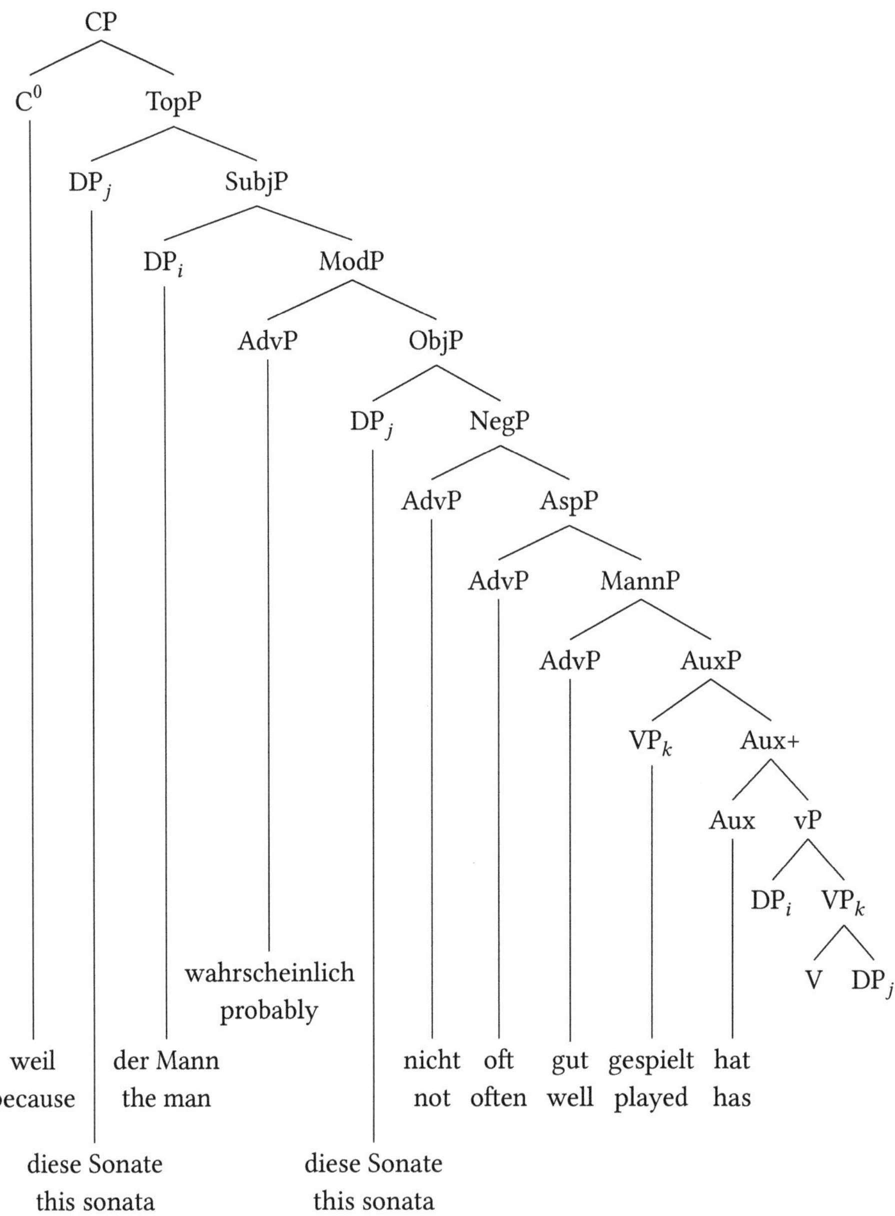

Figure 4.30: Analysis of sentence structure with functional heads following Laenzlinger (2004: 224)

assumption is that topics are initial in the *Mittelfeld* and that they are moved to the specifier position of a designated phrase. To falsify these approaches it is sufficient to point to the problems resulting from movement and reconstruction in terms of scope that were discussed in Section 4.10.1 with respect to TP–VP approaches. But Cartographic approaches face further problems, some of which will be discussed here.

The analysis suggested in this chapter is based on "pure syntax uncontaminated by information structure" (to quote the title of a paper by Fanselow 2006). Syntax is a system of well-formedness constraints that is independent of the context of an utterance (Fanselow 2006: 138). Information structure is context dependent. HPSG approaches to scrambling go back to Gunji (1986) in assuming the view more recently expressed by Fanselow (2003a, 2006), Neeleman & van de Koot (2008), Struckmeier (2017: 3) and Haider (2021): syntax is about distribution of material and category formation. Information structure constraints can be stated with respect to syntactic structure (Engdahl & Vallduví 1994, 1996, De Kuthy 2021) and to prosodic information, but the three components are not conflated. Topic and focus are not syntactic categories.

Fanselow (2006) pointed out that Frey's view that there is a designated position for sentence adverbials and topics have to move to a position left to it is considerably weakened by the existence of sentences with NPs between two sentence adverbs as in (51):

(51) Ich denke, dass wahrscheinlich mindestens zwei   (German)
      I   think   that probably   at.least   two
      leider   ihren Vortrag absagen werden.
      unfortunately their talk   cancel   will
      'I think that probably at least two will cancel their talks,
      unfortunately.'

Frey notices these examples and says that these are unproblematic for his account since *mindestens zwei* 'at least two' is not a topic. But, as Fanselow points out, this means that there is a way to have non-topic NPs precede sentence adverbials and this makes sentences like (52) with a topic to the left of a sentential adverb ambiguous: they can be analyzed as sentences with an NP in the specifier position of the Topic Phrase or as sentences with an NP adjoined to a projection hosting the sentential adverb (similar to the adjunction to TP in Figure 4.28).

(52) Ich denke, dass Julia leider   ihr   Hund gebissen hat. (German)
      I   think   that Julia unfortunately her.NOM dog   bitten   has
      'I think that unfortunately, her dog bit Julia.'

Similarly, non-referential quantified DPs can be placed to the left of sentence adverbs:

(53) dass sie wen aus Hamburg wahrscheinlich / leider   (German)
      that she one from Hamburg probably   unfortunately
      nicht heiraten würde
      not   marry   would
      'Probably/unfortunately, she would not marry anybody from
      Hamburg.'

Fanselow concludes that the existence of such examples undermine the predictive power of Cartographic approaches and that one could simply assume a more traditional scrambling approach using adjunction but avoiding information structural phrasal categories.

Fanselow (2006) also points out that topics do not have to be placed in front of the sentence adverbs. One situation in which this is possible is the presence of a sentence adverb next to a narrow focus. In such situations, the topic is not in the way and fronting is unnecessary. (54) is Fanselow's example:

(54) Gibt's was neues über das Stadtschloss? "Any news about the city castle?"
      Laut   dem Bürgermeister wird man wahrscheinlich in Zukunft nur
      according the mayor   will one probably   in future   only
      am SAMSTAG dieses Gebäude besichtigen können.
      on Saturday this   building visit   can
      'According to the mayor, one will only be able to visit that building on
      Saturdays in the future.'

I already discussed examples in which the arguments are not sufficiently case marked for disambiguation. In such situations scrambling is strongly dispreferred. See example (28) on p. 23. Interestingly, this means that topics can stay in their normal positions despite being topics, as Fanselow (2006) pointed out:

(55) Was schreiben die Zeitungen über Prinzessin Julia? "What do the papers
      write about princess Julia?"
      Der Hofkurier   schreibt, dass leider   erneut eine Maklerin die
      the Court.Courier writes   that unfortunately again a   broker.F the
      Prinzessin um 100.000 Euro betrogen hat.
      princess   by 100,000 Euro cheated   has
      'The Court Courier writes that unfortunately a broker cheated the
      princess once more out of 100,000 Euro.'

Eine Maklerin and *die Prinzession* are both feminine NPs and both could be nominative or accusative. If the NP *die Prinzessin* is palced to the left of *eine Maklerin*, the reading changes so that the princess cheated the broker. In this situation, the topic *die Prinzessin* 'the princess' stays in its unmarked position to the right of the sentence adverb *leider* 'unfortunately'.

The examples discussed so far show that elements to the left of sentence adverbs do not have to be topics and that topics may not move that is they may stay to the right of the sentence adverb. It follows that the assumption of Topic positions in the clause is not really helpful and scrambling should be explained uniformly as a purely syntactic phenomenon.

Before turning to functional adverbial projections in the next section, let us have a brief look at another problem with information structure in the Cinque & Rizzi world (Rizzi 1997: 297): several analyses of the left periphery assume that the *Vorfeld* consists of Topic and Focus Phrases (Grewendorf 2002: 85, 240, 2005: 87, 93, 2009). Grewendorf (2005: 87) explicitly states that the Topic and Focus projections in the *Mittelfeld* are the same as in the *Vorfeld*. According to him, the order in the *Mittelfeld* is as given in (56) and Topic – Focus – Topic is the order that Rizzi (1997: 297) and Grewendorf (2002: 240) assume for the left periphery of main clauses.

(56)   C0 – Topic – Focus – Topic – sentence adverbial – subject

If these phrase categories have anything to do with distribution and complementizers can combine with Topic Phrases as in Figure 4.30, then it follows that complementizers like *dass* can be combined with the Topic Phrases that are parts of V2 sentences as for example (57a). However, examples like (57b) are ungrammatical.

(57)   a.   Den Roman hat   Peter gelesen.   (German)
            that the   novel has   Peter   read
            'Peter has read the novel.´

       b.   * dass den Roman hat Peter gelesen
            that the novel   has Peter read
            intended: 'that Peter has read the novel´

So phrases in the *Mittelfeld* with a topic in the specifier position crucially differ from phrases with a topic in specifier position that are part of a V2 clause. This is not captured by Cartographic approaches unless one assumes different syntactic categories for the respective phrases. Something like VF Topic Phrase and MF Topic Phrase, a rather ad hoc move to fix an otherwise inappropriate grammatical system.

Fanselow (2006) also has a look at fronted NPs in V2 sentences. According to Cartographic approaches the fronted elements should be topics or foci. However, the sentence in (58) can be the answer to the question *What have you done this morning?*.

(58) Ein   Buch hab ich   gelesen.   (German)
      a.ACC book have I.NOM read

      'I've read a book.'

The fronted NP *ein Buch* 'a book' is a part of the focus *ein Buch gelesen* 'a book read' rather than the complete focus.

Similarly, Fanselow's example in (59) has a part of an idiom fronted:

(59) Den   Nagel hat er   auf den Kopf getroffen, als   er   sagte,
      the.ACC nail   has he.NOM on the head hit   when he.NOM said

      dass ....
      that

      'He found the optimal expression when he said that ...'

The fronted material does not contribute any meaning. It is neither the topic nor the focus of the utterance.

I conclude with Fanselow (2006) that information structure categories should not be part of the syntax. Scrambling provides various constituent orders and creates structures that can be combined with constraints on prosody and information structure.

The next two subsections deal with adverbs. We first look at negation and its Cartographic treatment and then at Rizzi-style analyzes of adverbs in the German *Mittelfeld*.

4.10.2.3 Negation as adverb or as special projection

As described above, approaches assuming functional heads often assign category labels to phrases that would correspond to the non-head in more traditional approaches. This subsection has a closer look at negation and approaches assuming a Negation Phrase. Ernst (1992) examined an analysis of negation in which the negation element is analyzed as the head. Ernst pointed out that it is not just verbs that can be negated. Negation can attach to different verbal projections (60a,b), to adjectives (60c) and adverbs (60d).

(60)   a. Ken could not have heard the news.

       b. Ken could have not heard the news.

       c. a [not unapproachable] figure

       d. [Not always] has she seasoned the meat.

But the respective phrases have different distributions. They are not just NegPs. We need information about the part of speech of the head and about the verb form. It may be possible to solve these problems by assuming extensions for functional projections like the ones to be discussed in Subsection 4.10.2.4. Alternatively, it may be possible to use constraints that can search in trees for information and find out that the NegP *not always* contains an adverb, that the NegP *not have heard the news* contains a verb in the base form and that *not heard the news* contains a verb in the perfect participle form, but any such non-local approach would be more complicated than the approach taken here and all other non-Minimalist theories (for explicit discussion see Sag 2007) and also many Minimalist theories (e.g., Abraham 2005: 223). The approach that was discussed in this chapter just compares a requirement of a head with the properties of the complement or specifier daughter. In comparison, Laenzlinger's (2004) approach has to find the verb in *nicht oft gut gespielt hat* 'not often well played has' somewhere deeply embedded in a cascade of NegP, AspP, MannP, AuxP, Aux+.

Concluding this subsection, I follow all work in GPSG and HPSG and other frameworks in assuming that negation particles are not heads but adjuncts. See Kim & Sag (2002) and Sag et al. (2020: Section 6) on negation in English and Kim (2021) for an overview of analyses of negation in HPSG in general.

The next subsection deals with Cinque's theory of adverbs in general. It examines similar problems of category labeling and selection.

4.10.2.4 Functional projections hosting an adverb in their specifier position

It is claimed by Cinque & Rizzi that the hierarchy of functional projections is the same across languages and in principle one could also imagine that this array of functional projections is present in all languages and in all sentences even if some adverbs are not realized in a sentence or do not exist in the language under consideration (Cinque & Rizzi 2010: 55). For example, Cinque (1999: 106) suggests the following hierarchy of functional heads:

(61) The universal hierarchy of clausal functional projections (Cinque 1999: 106) [*frankly* $\text{Mood}_{\text{speech act}}$ [*fortunately* $\text{Mood}_{\text{evaluative}}$ [*alledgedly* $\text{Mood}_{\text{evidential}}$ [*probably* $\text{Mood}_{\text{epistemic}}$ [*once* T(Past) [*then* T(Future) [*perhaps* $\text{Mood}_{\text{irrealis}}$ [*necessarily* $\text{Mood}_{\text{necessity}}$ [*possibly* $\text{Mod}_{\text{possibility}}$ [*usually* $\text{Asp}_{\text{habitual}}$ [*again* $\text{Asp}_{\text{repetitive(I)}}$ [*often* $\text{Asp}_{\text{frequentative(I)}}$ [*intentionally* Modvolitional [*quickly* $\text{Asp}_{\text{celerative(I)}}$ [*already* T(Anterior) [*no longer* $\text{Asp}_{\text{terminative}}$ [*still* $\text{Asp}_{\text{continuative}}$ [*always* $\text{Asp}_{\text{perfect(?)}}$ [*just* $\text{Asp}_{\text{retrospective}}$ [*soon* $\text{Asp}_{\text{proximative}}$ [*briefly* $\text{Asp}_{\text{durative}}$ [*characteristically*(?) $\text{Asp}_{\text{generic/progressive}}$ [*almost* $\text{Asp}_{\text{prospective}}$ [*completely* $\text{Asp}_{\text{SgCompletive(I)}}$ [*tutto* $\text{Asp}_{\text{PICompletive}}$ [*well* Voice [*fast/early* $\text{Asp}_{\text{frequuentative(II)}}$ [*completely* $\text{Asp}_{\text{SgCompletive(II)}}$

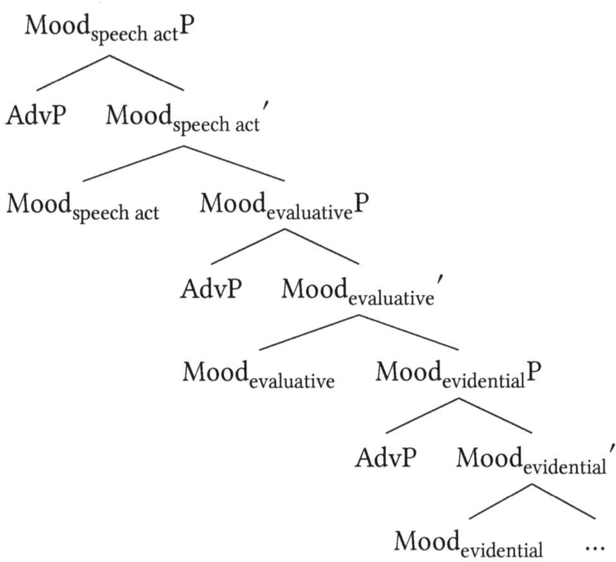

Figure 4.31: Topmost part of Cinque's (1999) functional hierarchy of adverbial projections

Starting with some of the functional heads from the top of this hierarchy, all sentences in all languages are claimed to have structures as in Figure 4.31 as part of their clausal structure. The actual adverbs are assumed to be realized in specifier positions of the functional heads (Mood$_{\text{speech act}}$, Mood$_{\text{evaluative}}$, Mood$_{\text{evidential}}$). In order to enforce the sequence stated in (61), the functional head Mood$_{\text{speech act}}$ has to select a Mood$_{\text{evaluative}}$P and the Mood$_{\text{evaluative}}$ head has to select a Mood$_{\text{evidential}}$P and so on. Since it is assumed that all languages have these structures even if there is no language internal evidence for them, this requires a rather strong conception of Universal Grammar: it is assumed in Mainstream Generative Grammar that language acquisition is guided by innate knowledge about language, the so-called Universal Grammar (UG), and Cinque & Rizzi (2010) are proponents of a rather extreme position claiming that at least 400 syntactic categories are part of this genetically specified linguistic knowledge (Cinque & Rizzi 2010: 57). Since there is no evidence for this and since it is rather unclear how and why categories like case, gender and even nationality (Cinque 1994: 96, 99, 100, Scott 2002: 114) should enter the human genome[19], the overall approach seems dubious. But even

---

[19]See Bishop (2002) and Elman, Bates, Johnson, Karmiloff-Smith, Parisi & Plunkett (1996) about genetics and linguistic information. See also Hauser, Chomsky & Fitch (2002) for a statement about a rather general UG.

if one follows Cinque & Rizzi, the fixed battery of functional projections approach does not work without further add-ons, as the following example from Haider (2022: 210) based on Quirk et al. (1985: § 8.20, 495) shows:

(62)   The new theory certainly may possibly have indeed been badly formulated.

The point here is that adverbs of the same type appear at various places in the sentence. They are attached to VPs whose heads differ in their verb forms. These verb forms are selected by the governing head. Figure 4.32 shows the structure assumed in this book. Figure 4.33 shows the structure with Cinque-style empty

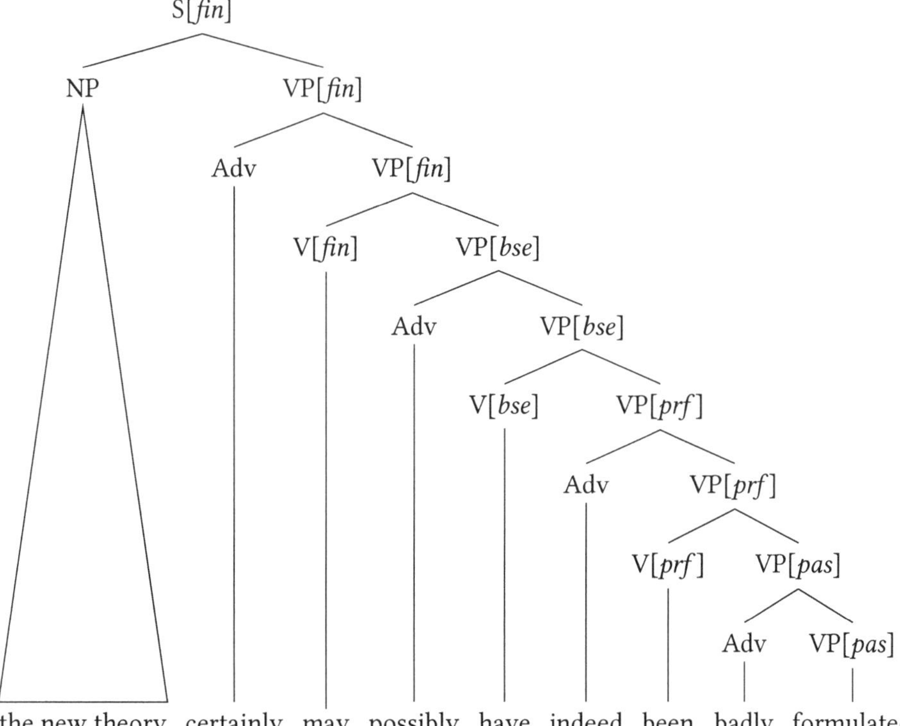

Figure 4.32: Cascade of selections including adverbs as suggested in this book

adverbial heads (here F-Adv). The actual adverbs are analyzed as specifiers of these heads.

The analysis also contains some details that can be ignored here. For example, passive is analyzed as movement: the object of the verb *formulated* moves to the

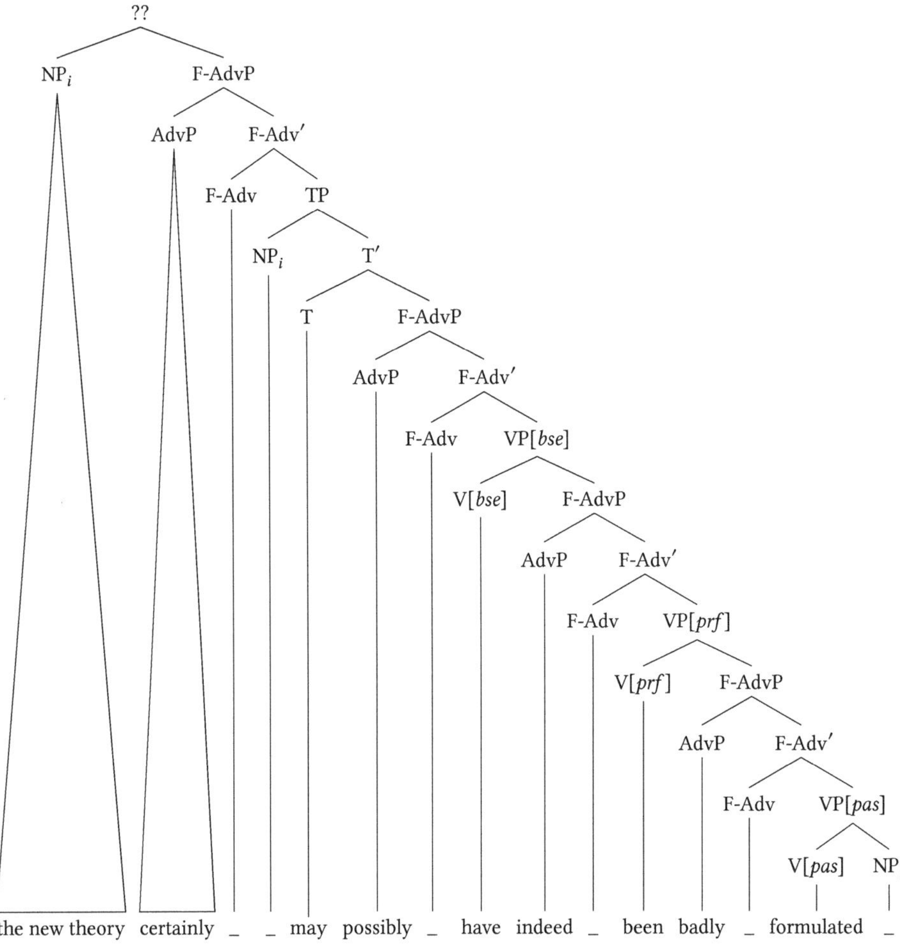

Figure 4.33: VP cascade including empty functional heads hosting adverbial phrases in specifier positions as suggested by Cinque (1999)

specifier position of a Tense head. Auxiliaries are usually classified as Tense elements in grammars of English. Since the adverb *certainly* attaches to T, the NP *the new theory* has to move to a higher position at the beginning of the clause. The figure shows that we have four projections with the label F-AdvP. Three of them have the same semantic type (*certainly, possibly, indeed*) and hence should have the same category label in a Cinque & Rizzi system. But they do not have the same distribution. So even in a system with fixed arrays of functional projections, something would be missing. Even with different category labels for the respective adverbs, the problem would not be fixed since *possibly, certainly* and *indeed* may all appear above and below the VP nodes in Figure 4.33. The only way to enforce correct distribution via a local selection mechanism would be to include the verb form in the category label. Grimshaw (2000), developing a theory of extended projections, suggested something along these lines. See also Riemsdijk (1998). One could have a category that is determined by the lexical head (noun, verb, adjective) and a second category determined by the functional head (determiner, I or T, or any of the Cinque & Rizzi categories).[20]

Figure 4.34 may serve as an example. It shows the analysis of the phrase *the president* in the DP analysis, in which the determiner is assumed to be the head. Instead of just projecting the category of the functional head D, one could project

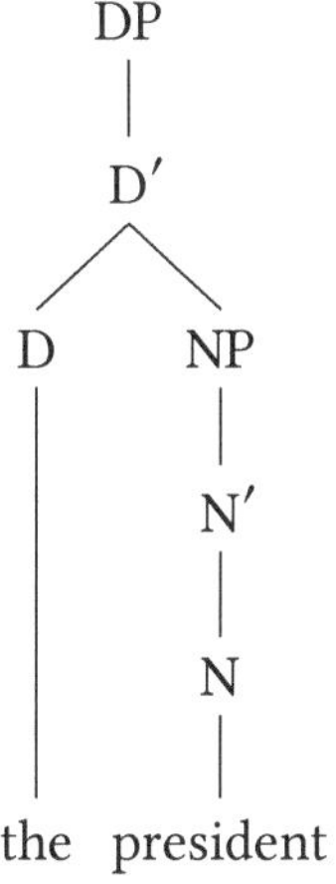

Figure 4.34: *the president* in the DP analysis

information about the lexical category as well. This would make information about verbs and nouns available at the top node of functional projections. Let us assume the feature F for functional categories and the feature L for lexical categories. Figure 4.35 shows the analysis of the DP *the president* with such features.

---

[20]This idea is actually much older. Klaus Netter suggested an analysis of the DP in German assuming MAJOR and MINOR head features (Netter 1994: Section 9.3.1). Wolfe (2015: 134, 2016: 289) suggested the phrasal C hierarchy in (i):

(i) $C_{Frame} > C_{Force} > C_{Top} > C_{Foc} > C_{Fin}$

These categories are closer to traditional conceptions of phrase structure systems. Of course, the approach is not fully formalized. So it remains unclear what the predictions with respect to coordination and other phenomena are.

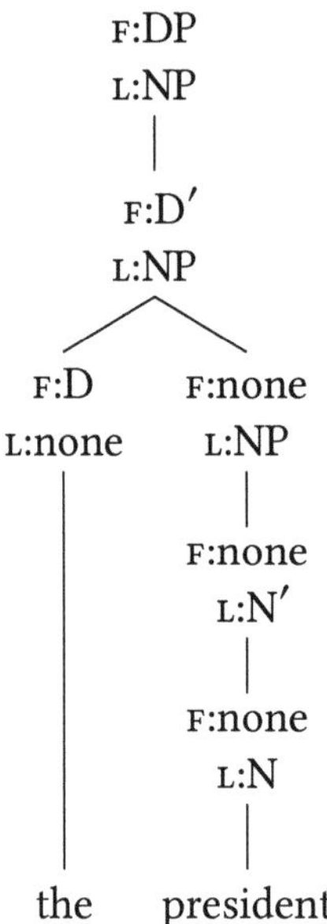

Figure 4.35: *the president* in the DP analysis with functional and lexical features

The phrase *possibly have indeed been badly formulated* would then have the category F:Mod$_{possibility}$,L:VP[*bse*]. This makes it possible to select for the correct part of speech and the correct verb form by looking at the L value.

So, I – or rather Klaus Netter – solved the selection problem for Cartographic approaches. But note two things: firstly, there is a much simpler – and I would argue more appropriate – solution to the goals of Cartography (see Section 4.10.2.6) and secondly, the solution does not solve problems with coordination to be discussed in more detail in Section 4.10.2.5.

As a teaser for the section on coordination consider the example in (63), which shows that verb phrases with different adverbials may be coordinated:

(63)   Kim [unfortunately sang a song] and [allegedly ruined the evening].

According to Cinque (1999: 106) *fortunately* is Mood$_{evaluative}$ and *allegedly* is Mood$_{evidential}$. Hence the two verb phrases in (63) have different categories in Cinque's analysis. In the analysis suggested here, they are just verb phrases containing different adverbials. Since both verb phrases are finite in (63) the coordination is an instance of symmetric coordination in the theory defended here. So, we are back at a point where Chomsky started: syntax is about distribution of words and phrases, not about semantics. And hence it is clear that examples like Chomsky's (1957: 15) (64) are syntactically well-formed although they do not make sense:

(64)   Colorless green ideas sleep furiously.

Note that HPSG has semantic information and information concerning information structure within the information that can be selected by selecting heads (Pollard & Sag 1994: Section 2.4, Bildhauer & Cook 2010: 74). HPSG categories are complex, containing phonological, morphological, syntactic, semantic and information-structural properties. This means that relations between linguistic objects can refer to these properties. This is needed for approaches to language that take all these descriptive levels into account. What is not needed – and in fact strongly rejected here – is semantic or information-structural information within part of speech labels.

For further criticism of Cartographic approaches to scrambling see Struck-meier (2017) and Haider (2021). For more on Cinque & Rizzi-style analyses and the locality of selection see Müller (2023b: Section 4.6.1.3).

4.10.2.5 Coordination and the ConjP analysis

Figure 4.36 shows a sketch of the analysis in which a ConjP is projected from the coordinating conjunction. This analysis is assumed by Larson (1990: 596), Radford (1993: 89), Johannessen (1998: 109), Van Koppen (2005: 8), Bošković (2009: 474), Citko (2011: 27), Lohnstein (2014: 9, 19, 20), and others. The problem is that the coordination of two NPs should be an NP, the coordination of two VPs a VP and so on. It should not be a ConjP since a ConjP is different from an NP or VP and selecting heads require NPs or VPs.[21]

(65)   a. [NP [NP Kim] and [NP Sandy]] laugh.
        b. Kim wants to [VP [VP sing a song], [VP dance], and [VP not worry about tomorrow]].

Grimshaw (2000: 122) states that symmetric coordination could be handled as extended projection. She states that in coordinations functional and lexical information has to be identified. But note that this is actually not easy to establish

---

[21]Johannessen (1996: 669) suggests an analysis in which a coordinate structure has the features of the first conjunct. This does not help since a projection can be either an NP or a ConjP. Approaches assuming two categories per head, a functional and a lexical one, are discussed below. They do not work either. Furthermore, the coordination of two singular NPs is a plural NP not a singular NP as would be predicted by Johannessen's account. See Borsley (2005) for details.

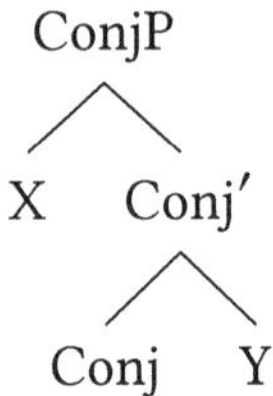

Figure 4.36: Analysis of coordination with ConjP

if the conjunction is seen as a head contributing its part of speech information to a phrase. Consider the following example:

(66) the president and the general

If the conjunction is treated as a functional head, the analysis in Figure 4.37 results. Now, the interesting thing is that the coordination of two bare NPs without a determiner would have exactly the same category, which is wrong since they do not have the same distribution:

(67) a. the president and general

     b. * a the president and general

Figure 4.38 shows the coordination of two NPs. The point is clear: a coordination has to reflect both the functional category and the lexical category of the conjunctions (as Grimshaw 2000: 122 pointed out). Making this information available is impossible if information about a conjunction is projected instead.

Note also that the example in (65b) shows that the assumption that a negated VP is a VP rather than a NegP provides a simple analysis of coordination: it is just VPs that are coordinated and hence (65b) is an instance of symmetric coordination. In a NegP approach, more would have to be said about matching categories in the coordination. And while we want the functional information to be projected in DP coordination, projecting NegP information in VP/NegP coordination is counterproductive.[22] A traditional, clean syntax seems to be highly preferable here. See Borsley (2005) and Borsley & Müller (2021) for more on the ConjP approach.

The points discussed so far in this subsection on coordination have to do with the status of the conjunction: Is it a head? What does it project? But there are

---

[22]The difference between DP coordination and NegP/VP coordination is of course that specifiers in the DP/NP are part of the information that signals completeness of a phrase, while adjuncts are not relevant for this.

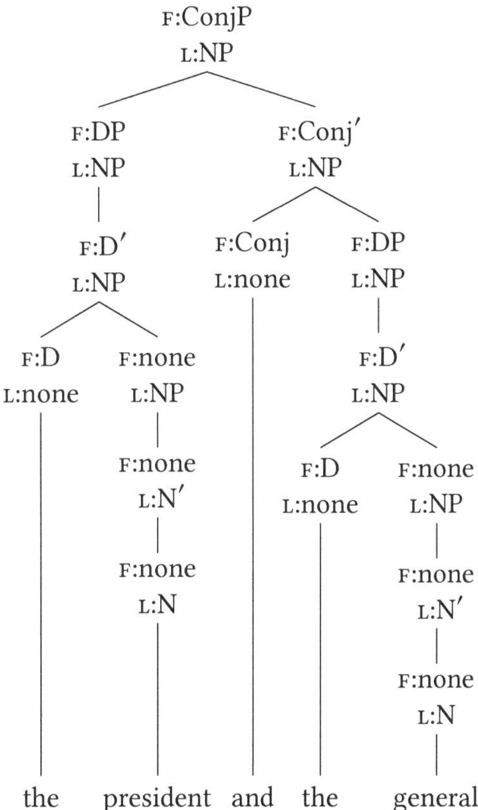

Figure 4.37: Functional and lexical categories and coordination of two functional projections

questions concerning the conjuncts as well. As was pointed out at the beginning of this section, constituency tests determine distribution classes. Coordination is one of these tests and if we find two conjoinable constituents this indicates that they should be assigned to the same category. Cinque (1999: 106) suggests the hierarchy of functional heads already given in (61). Now, consider the sentence in (68):

(68)   She [probably goes by train] and [possibly changes in Ostkreuz].

In the theory developed in this book, *probably goes by train* and *possibly changes in Ostkreuz* are VPs. They can be coordinated with unmodified VPs or with VPs modified with any of the adjuncts listed in (61). But according to Cinque these

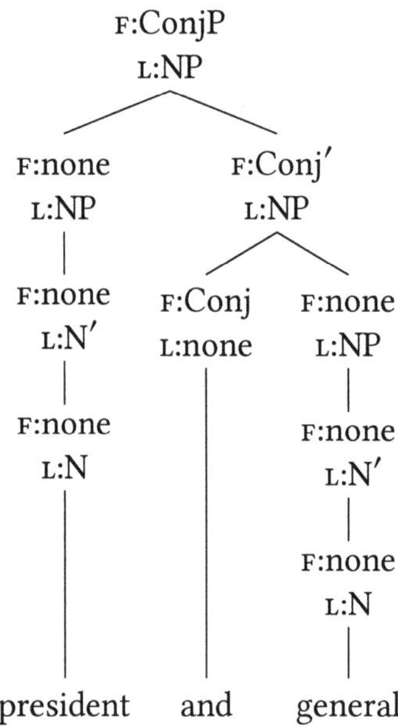

Figure 4.38: Functional and lexical categories and coordination of two lexical projections

phrases are of different categories: the first VP is $\text{Mood}_{\text{epistemic}}$ and the second is $\text{Mood}_{\text{possibility}}$. Does this mean that these VPs cannot be coordinated? No it does not since the category of the second VP is below the category of the first in Cinque's hierarchy and since he assumes that all these nodes are present in all sentences even if the respective adverbial elements are not present. This means that *possibly changes in Ostkreuz* is not just $\text{Mood}_{\text{possibility}}$ but also $\text{Mood}_{\text{necessity}}$, $\text{Mood}_{\text{irrealis}}$, T(Future), T(Past), $\text{Mood}_{\text{epistemic}}$. Since it is $\text{Mood}_{\text{epistemic}}$, it can be coordinated with *probably goes by train*, which is $\text{Mood}_{\text{epistemic}}$ as well. But apart from these categories, it is also $\text{Mood}_{\text{speech act}}$, $\text{Mood}_{\text{evaluative}}$, $\text{Mood}_{\text{evidential}}$. In fact both VPs are. All VPs are combined with all functional projections in Cinque's system. This means that VPs without adjuncts are combined with (at least) 27 empty heads and are (at least) 27fold ambiguous as far as their part of speech label is concerned. When two such VPs are coordinated there are 27 ways of coordinating them without any difference in meaning that could be assigned to the different structures. Such ambiguities are calls *spurious ambiguities* and they are generally frowned upon in syntactic research. See also Müller (2016: 70–71) on the N–N̄ projection in nominal structures without complements. This projection poses the same problem with coordinations as the one discussed in this subsection: whenever there are unary projections that do not add semantics, the result is spurious ambiguities in coordinations.

4.10.2.6 Reaching Cartography's goals

As was shown in the previous subsections, there are a lot of arguments against Cinque & Rizzi approaches, but a lot of researchers assume such approaches anyway. Why? The advantage of these approaches is that they can relate linear order and semantics. As Felix Bildhauer pointed out to me a long time ago: researchers assuming Cinque-style analyses are entertaining some kind of Construction Grammar approach. There are slots for certain elements at a certain position in the sentence. We have seen many instances of these analyses above. Some categories are just unnecessary: SubjP and ObjP, for example. The effects could be done by adjunction, that is, nodes would be doubled as in Figure 4.28. Alternatively, one could assume what is called "base generation": rather than moving constituents they are licensed in the places where they are visible. See Fanselow (2001) for such an approach within the Minimalist Program. Furthermore, the information about adverbials could be made accessible within the semantic contribution of linguistic signs. One representation format of semantics in HPSG is Minimal Recursion Semantics (Copestake et al. 2005). All semantic contributions are contained in lists of elementary predications. Such lists can be augmented by a pointer pointing to the elementary predication that was added by the last adverbial. Similar pointers are used in MRS already. They are called KEY or ALTKEY (Flickinger et al. 2003: Section 3.7, Copestake et al. 2005: 299). So, the contribution added by an adverbial can be singled out by a feature called MODKEY. Since a modifier selects the VP it modifies, it can also access the value of MODKEY and hence a modifying adverbial can state constraints on the adverbial that is to the right of it within the VP it modifies. The selection would refer to semantic properties of the selected linguistic object. This is, of course, also the case in the Cinque–Rizzi system, except that there the semantics is pushed into syntax.

4.10.2.7 Summary

I have shown that Cartographic approaches are not compatible with traditional models of syntax since syntactic categories are mixed with all kinds of information that is not part of syntactic categories as such. Classical distribution tests fail on Cartography constituents. I have shown that the normal mechanisms are not sufficient for selection and that the general architecture would have to be extended. I furthermore showed that this would still not be enough because the proposal fails to interact properly with approaches to coordination. While there may be ways to fix the remaining problems, it is clear that the traditional approach to syntax does not have such problems and is simpler and hence has to be preferred on Occamian grounds.

Exercises

1. Provide the valence lists for the following words:

   (69)   a. laugh
          b. eat
          c. to douse
          d. bezichtigen   (German)
             accuse
          e. he
          f. the
          g. Ankunft   (German)
             arrival

   If you are uncertain as far as case assignment is concerned, you may use the Wiktionary: https://de.wiktionary.org/.

2. Draw trees for the NPs that were also used in Exercise 1 on page 62 in Chapter 3.

   (70)   a. eine Stunde vor   der Ankunft des   Zuges
             one hour   before the arrival   of.the train
             'one hour before the arrival of the train'
          b. kurz   nach der Ankunft in Paris
             shortly after the arrival   in Paris
             'shortly after the arrival in Paris'

c. das ein Lied singende Kind aus   dem Allgäu
   this a   song singing   child from the   Allgäu
   'the child from the Allgäu singing a song'

3. Draw trees for the following examples. NPs can be abbreviated.

(71) a. weil   Aicke dem   Kind ein   Buch   (German)
         because Aicke the.DAT child a.ACC book
         schenkt
         gives.as.a.present
         'because Aicke gives the child a book as a present'
      b. because Kim gave a book to him
      c. Sandy saw this yesterday.
      d. at   Bjarne læste bogen   (Danish)
         that Bjarne read book.DEF
         'that Bjarne read the book'

5 The verbal complex

5.1 The phenomenon

SOV languages like Dutch and German form verbal complexes, that is, combinations of verbs excluding the non-verbal arguments of the verbs. For example, it is assumed that *zu lesen* 'to read', *versprochen* 'promised' und *hat* 'has' form a constituent in Haider's example (1986b: 110; 1991: 128) in (1) to the exclusion of the arguments of the verbs *es* 'it', *ihr* 'her' and *jemand* 'somebody'.

> (1) weil   es ihr jemand   zu lesen versprochen hat
> because it her somebody to read   promised   has
> 'because somebody promised her to read it'

There are several indicators of verbal complex formation that were worked out in detail by Gunnar Bech (1955). As indicated above, one way to analyze such verbal complexes is to assume that the verbs in a sentence form a unit that basically behaves like a simplex verb. This explains for instance why the arguments of the three verbs in (1) can be scrambled: *es* depends on *zu lesen* 'to read', *ihr* 'her' depends on *versprochen* 'promised' and *jemand* is the subject and agrees with the finite verb *hat* 'has' (usually it is also treated as a dependent of the auxiliary *hat*).

It should be said that there is extreme variation in German dialects as far as the serialization of elements in the verbal complex is concerned. The governing[1] verb is realized to the right of the embedded verb in Standard German: $V_3 V_2 V_1$ as in (1), but there are examples like (2) taken from Müller (1999: 376).[2]

> (2) a. Ich hätte stapelweise Akten können haben.   (German, Berlin dialect)
> I   had   by.the.pile files can   have
> 'I could have had files by the pile.'

---

[1]The term *govern* is used equivalently to *select*. When a verb requires an accusative object it is said to govern the accusative/an accusative object. Verbs can also govern other verbs and determine the form the governed verb has to take, e.g., perfect/passive participle, infinitive with or without *zu* 'to'.

[2]Interview partner in: *Insekten und andere Nachbarn – ein Haus in Berlin*, ARD 1995-11-15.

> b. weil   ich mir das nich hab' lassen gefallen
>   because I   me that not have let   please
>   'because I did not put up with it'
>
> c. wenn se   mir hier würden rausschmeißen, ...
>   if   they me here would   out.throw
>   'if they would kick me out here'

The orders in (2) correspond to the order that is most natural in Dutch. (3) shows some Dutch examples:

> (3)   a. dat Kim het boek wil   lezen
>   that Kim the book wants read
>   'that Kim wants to read the book'
>
>   b. dat Kim Sandy het boek laat lezen
>   that Kim Sandy the book lets read
>   'that Kim lets Sandy read the book'
>
>   c. dat Kim Sandy het boek wil   laten lezen
>   that Kim Sandy the book wants let   read
>   'that Kim wants to let Sandy read the book'

SVO languages like Danish and English do not allow the arguments of embedded verbs to be scrambled with arguments of higher verbs. All arguments stay in their VP (modulo extraction, of course).

5.2 The analyis

The technique that is used to analyze the verbal complexes is called *argument attraction* or *argument composition* and was developed by Geach (1970) in the framework of Categorial Grammar and adapted for HPSG by Hinrichs & Nakazawa (1994). The analysis of *lesen wird* 'read will' as it occurs in (4) is shown in Figure 5.1.

> (4)   dass keiner das Buch lesen wird
>   that nobody the book read will
>   'that nobody will read the book'

wird 'will' selects an infinitive without *zu* and in addition its arguments. This infinitive (*lesen* 'read') is combined with the verb and hence is not contained in the valence list of the mother node.

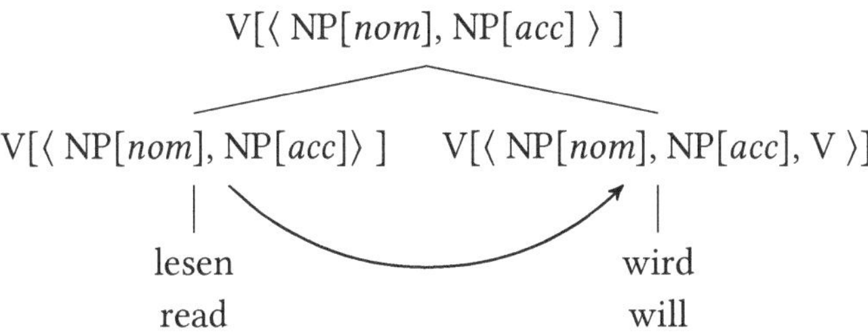

Figure 5.1: Analysis of the verbal complex formation of *lesen wird* 'read will' using argument composition (preliminary version)

Returning to our meal-shopping analogy from p. 67, the verbal complex formation can be envisaged by imagining a young and helpful auxiliary verb helping out a person from a high-risk group in the middle of a pandemic. Since high-risk persons are not supposed to do shopping, the helpful person takes over their shopping list and does the shopping for them. In the case of auxiliary verbs the auxiliary verb just selects the main verb and does not require any further arguments apart from the ones taken over from the embedded verb. This means the auxiliary verb just does the shopping for the main verb. A very altruistic verb it is. Later we will have a look at verbs like *try* and *let* that do require their own arguments in addition to those of the embedded verb. This will be parallel to a shopping event where the helping person buys their own goods in addition to buying goods for somebody else.

The combination of *lesen* and *wird* behaves like a simplex verb in that it can be combined with its arguments in any order. Figure 5.2 shows the analysis of (5a) and Figure 5.3 shows the analysis of (5b).

(5)   a. [dass] keiner   das Buch lesen wird
              that   nobody the book read will
              'that nobody will read the book'

    b. [dass] das Buch keiner   lesen wird
              that   the book nobody read will
              'that nobody will read the book'

I follow Kiss (1995a: Section 3.1.1) and represent the subject of non-finite verbs as the value of a special feature SUBJ. SUBJ differs from SPR and COMPS in that it is not a valence feature. The reason for this special treatment is that the subject cannot be realized as a part of a non-finite verb phrase. This is especially clear for infinitives with *zu*:

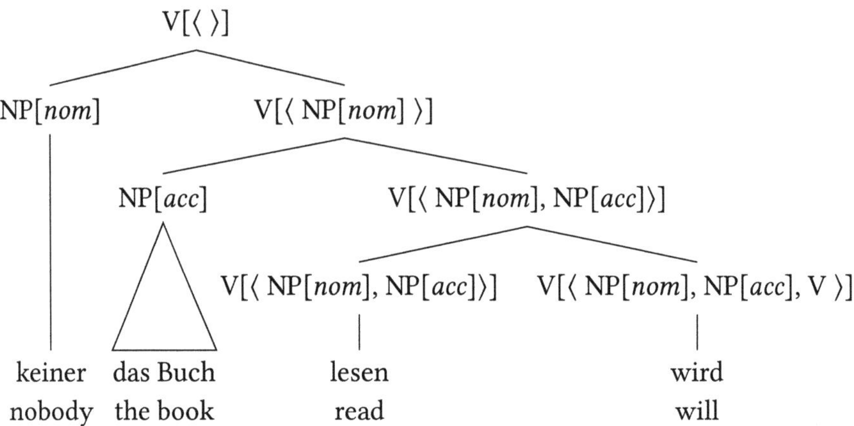

Figure 5.2: Formation of a verbal complex and realization of arguments in normal order (preliminary version)

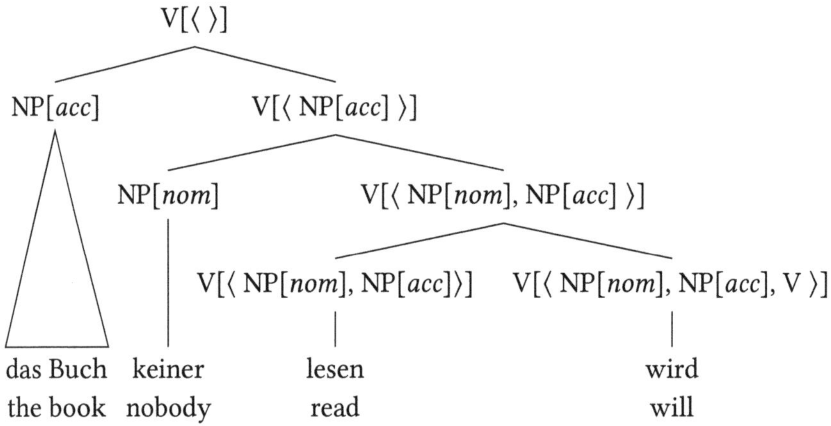

Figure 5.3: Formation of a verbal complex and scrambling of arguments (preliminary version)

(6)   a.   Aicke hat Conny versprochen, [das Buch zu lesen].
          Aicke has Conny promised   the book to read

          'Aicke promised Conny to read the book.'

     b. * Aicke hat Conny versprochen, [sie das Buch zu   lesen].
          Aicke has Conny promised   the book to   read

          Intended: 'Aicke promised Conny that she will read the book.'

Other non-finite verbs (bare infinitives and participles) cannot be placed in the *Nachfeld*, but they can be fronted. (7) shows that the subject cannot be realized together with other arguments of the verb in the *Vorfeld*.

(7)   a.   [Das Buch lesen] wird Aicke morgen.
           the book read   will Aicke tomorrow

          'Aicke will read the book tomorrow.'

     b. * [Aicke lesen] wird das Buch morgen.
          Aicke read   will the book tomorrow

     c. ?* [Aicke das Buch lesen] wird morgen.
          Aicke the book read   will tomorrow

The lexical item for the non-finite form of *lesen* 'to read' is given in (8):

(8)   *lesen* 'to read' non-finite form:

$$\begin{bmatrix} \text{SUBJ} & \langle \text{NP}[\textit{nom}] \rangle \\ \text{COMPS} & \langle \text{NP}[\textit{acc}] \rangle \end{bmatrix}$$

The following Attribute Value Matrix (AVM) is a representation of the auxiliary verb *werden* 'will':

(9)   *werden* 'will' non-finite form:

$$\begin{bmatrix} \text{SUBJ} & \boxed{1} \\ \text{COMPS} & \boxed{2} \oplus \langle \text{V}[\text{VFORM } \textit{bse}, \text{ LEX+}, \text{ SUBJ } \boxed{1}, \text{ COMPS } \boxed{2}] \rangle \end{bmatrix}$$

werden selects a verb that has the *bse* form, that is an infinitive without *zu* 'to'. The embedded element has to be lexical (LEX+), that is, a single word or a verbal complex. All phrases that are licensed by the Head-Complement Schema and the Specifier-Head Schema are assumed to be LEX−. The boxes with numbers are basically variables. Their values depend on the values of the embedded verbs. Therefore this lexical item can be used with a verb like *lesen* 'to read', which takes a nominative and an accusative argument, but also with a verb like *helfen* 'to help', which takes a nominative and a dative argument.

Before I turn to the details of the analysis, I have to provide the lexical items for the finite form of auxiliaries. Since the subject of finite verbs can of course be realized, it has to be represented in one of the valence lists. As was discussed in Section 4.3, German subjects are represented in the COMPS list of finite verbs. Hence the lexical item for *wird* 'will' has the following form:

(10) *wird* 'will' finite form:

$$\left[\begin{array}{ll} \text{SUBJ} & \langle\rangle \\ \text{COMPS} & \boxed{1} \oplus \boxed{2} \oplus \langle\, \text{V[VFORM } \textit{bse}, \text{LEX+, SUBJ } \boxed{1}, \text{COMPS } \boxed{2}] \,\rangle \end{array}\right]$$

This basically says that the valence of *wird* consists of an embedded verb and whatever the SUBJ list of this verb is plus whatever the COMPS list of this verb is. This is exemplified for *lesen wird* in Figure 5.4.[3] The auxiliary selects an

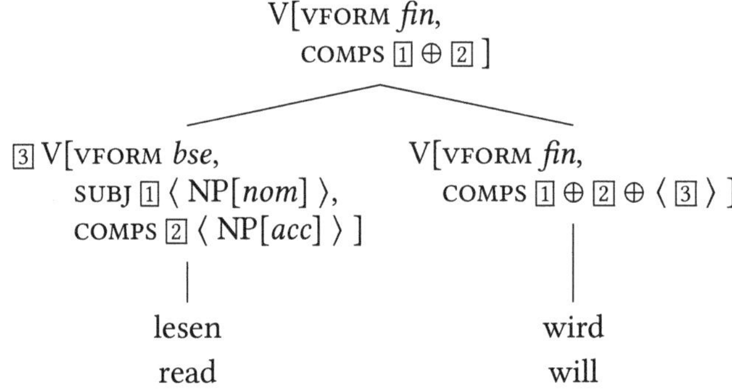

Figure 5.4: Detailed analysis of a verbal complex

infinitive without *zu* 'to' (\boxed{3}). This is ensured by the value *bse* for the VFORM feature of the selected verb: *bse* stands for infinitive without *to/zu/...*, *inf* stands for an infinitive form with marker, *ppp* stands for participle and *fin* for a finite verb. The subject of the selected infinitive (\boxed{1}) and the complements (\boxed{2}) are taken over. The result is that *lesen wird* has the same arguments as *liest* 'reads'.

To make all of this even more fun, we can make it more complex and look at verbal complexes with three verbs. Figure 5.5 shows the analysis of the verbal complex *lesen können wird* 'read can will' in sentences like (11):

---

[3]The lexical items of complex-forming predicates require their verbal argument to be LEX+. So in Figure 5.4, *lesen* 'read' is LEX+ as well. Since this information is not relevant for the discussion of argument attraction it is omitted in Figure 5.4 and the following figures. *lesen* and *lesen können* are required to be LEX+ in the verbal complexes depicted in Figures 5.5 and 5.6. Of course, lexical items like *wird* 'will' and *können* 'can' are LEX+ as well, due to the fact that they are words. Displaying this information in the trees would be confusing rather than adding to the explanation and hence, I decided to omit the LEX information.

(11) [dass] sie das Buch lesen können wird
      that   she the book read can   will

The analysis of (11) is provided in Figure 5.5.

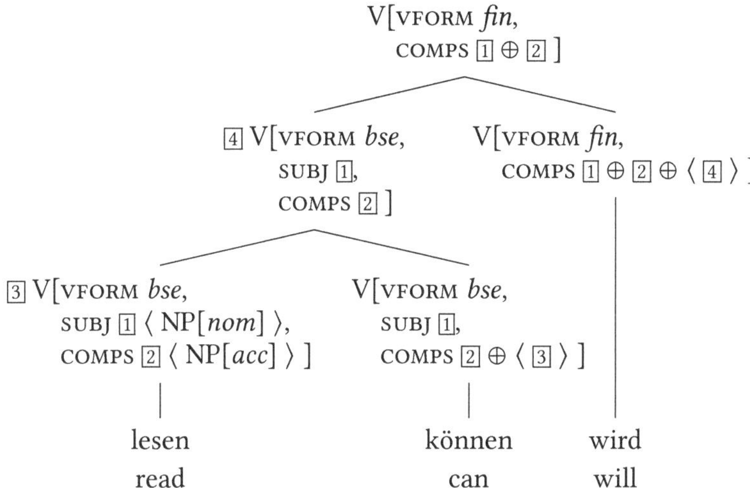

Figure 5.5: Analysis of a German verbal complex with three verbs in canonical
order

One interesting aspect of the analysis is that it can explain a phenomenon that
is called Auxiliary Flip or *Oberfeldumstellung*. German optionally allows verbs
that govern a modal to be placed to the left of the verbal complex rather than to
the right of the modal. So instead of (11) one can also use the order in (12):

(12) [dass] sie das Buch wird lesen können
      that   she the book will read can

After having discussed the analysis of verbal complexes as they are known from
the OV languages like German, Dutch, and Afrikaans, I want to briefly comment
on the SVO languages like Danish and English. Usually a head requires its argument to be saturated, that is, the COMPS value has to be the empty list for NP,
PPs, APs, CPs and sentential and VP arguments. Verbal complexes are different:
words are combined directly. The VO languages differ from the OV languages
in not allowing this. In VO languages the verb forms a phrase with its complements and this verb phrase may be embedded under another verb. (13a) shows
an example with auxiliary verbs, (13b) is an example with a full verb that takes
an infinitive verb phrase with *to* and an object in addition.

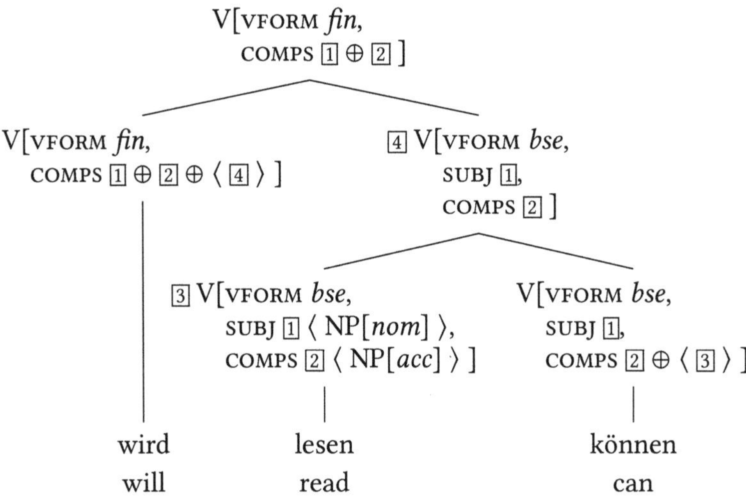

Figure 5.6: Analysis of a German verbal complex with three verbs with Auxiliary Flip

(13) a. Kim [will [have [read the book]]].

  b. Somebody [promised her [to read it]].

Languages like Danish and English only have the Head-Complement Schema and the Specifier-Head Schema, while languages like Dutch and German have an additional schema that can combine unsaturated words. The schema for predicate complex formation is sketched in Figure 5.7. This schema is very similar

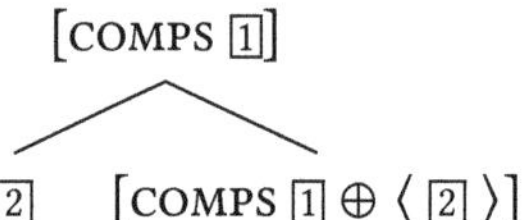

Figure 5.7: Sketch of the Predicate Complex Schema

to the Head-Complement Schema that was given on page 78. The difference is that this schema does not license LEX− elements as the Specifier-Head and Head-Compelement Schema do. Therefore, the combination of two verbs is compatible with LEX+ requirements by governing verbs and an embedding in even more complex verbal complexes is possible. Figure 5.5 is an example: the combination of *lesen* 'read' and *können* 'can' is compatible with the LEX+ requirement of *wird* 'will'. The Predicate Complex Schema also differs from the Head-Complement

Schema in German in that it combines the head with the last element of the valence list. This is the embedded verb and it has to be combined with the head before any other argument since one would not know what the other arguments are because they are taken over from the embedded verb.

Before turning to the next phenomenon, I want to briefly discuss an alternative to the verb complex analysis presented here. One alternative suggestion was to analyze auxiliaries in German as VP embedding verbs (Wurmbrand 2003a). Our standard example would then have the analysis in (14):

(14) dass keiner [[das Buch lesen] wird]
      that nobody   the book read   will

The question that such analyses have to answer is how scrambling of arguments of the involved verbs can be accounted for. The answer is often that it is assumed that the object of the embedded verb is extracted from the VP and moved to the left periphery of the clause. This is shown in (15):

(15) dass [das Buch]$_i$ keiner [[_$_i$ lesen] wird]
      that the book   nobody   read   will

      'that nobody will read the book'

However, analyses that treat scrambling as movement are problematic since they predict additional readings of sentences that have quantifiers in their NPs (Kiss 2001: 146; Fanselow 2001: Section 2.6).

Before I turn to the analysis of the verb position, I want to show how sentences with several verbs in SVO languages can be analyzed. Figure 5.8 shows the analysis of the English version of sentence (5a). The verb *reads* selects a sub-

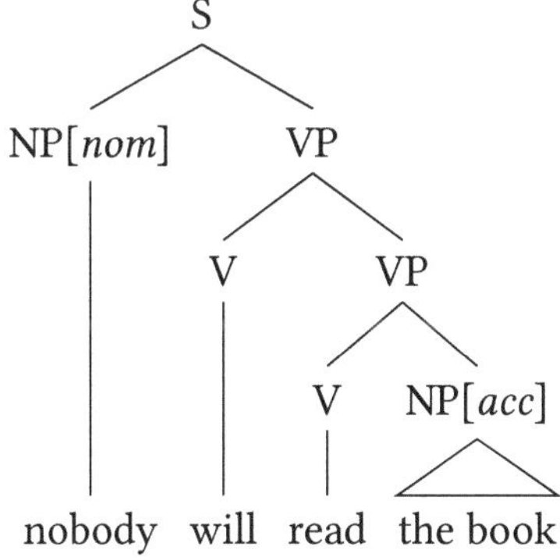

Figure 5.8: Embedding of a VP in SVO languages

ject and an object. The verb forms a VP with the NP *the book*. This VP is still lacking a subject. The auxiliary *will* selects a VP and a subject that is identical with the subject of *read*. The combination of *will* and the VP is licensed by the Head-Complement Schema that was sketched in Figure 4.11.

The equivalent of *lesen können wird* 'read can will' cannot be given here, since English modal verbs do not have non-finite forms, but one can construct examples with modals as the highest verb:

(16)   She [must [have [seen it]]].

This sentence has a structure that is similar to the one in Figure 5.8: *must* and *have* both embed VPs.

Finally, Figure 5.9 shows the translation of (1):

(17)   Somebody has promised her to read it.

promise is a verb that takes a subject, an object, and a VP complement. As in the

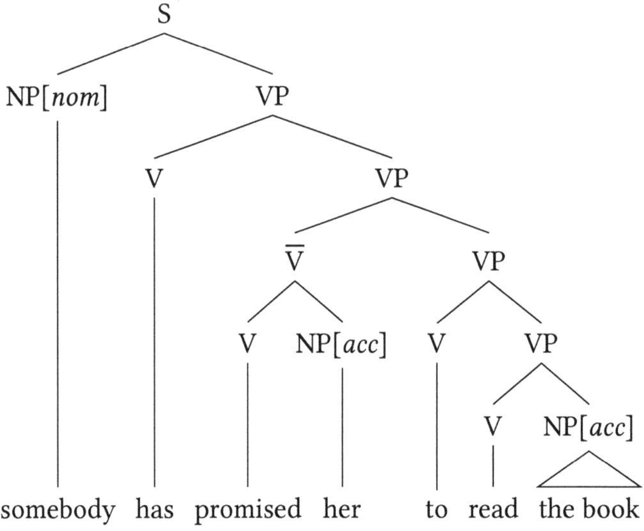

Figure 5.9: Embedding of a VP with verbs that take an additional object

analysis of (21) on page 79 – which is repeated here as (18) for convenience – the verb *promised* is combined with its NP complement first and then with its VP argument.

(18)   Nobody gave the child a book.

The VP argument of *promised* in Figure 5.9 consists of *to* and another VP with an infinitive in base form. *to* is analyzed as an auxiliary verb (Gazdar et al. 1982: 600, Sag et al. 2020: 147). It is important to note that the object *him* cannot appear in any other position (apart from extraction to the left periphery). For instance, it cannot appear in the position of *the book* and the same holds for *the book*: This phrase cannot appear in any other place than in the object position.

Exercises

1. Sketch the analysis of the verbal complexes in the following examples:

   (19) a. dass sie darüber   lachen muss   (German)
            that she there.about laugh   must

            'that she has to laugh about it'
         b. dass sie darüber   hat lachen müssen
            that she there.about has laugh   must

            'that she had to laugh about it'
         c. dass sie darüber   wird haben lachen müssen
            that she there.about will have   laugh   must

            'that she will have had to laugh about it'

   You may omit the SPR values, since they are the empty list for all German verbs anyway.

2. Search for two sentences with a verbal complex in a newspaper or in corpora (for example the COSMAS corpus[a]) and analyze the verbal complexes.

3. Search for verbal complexes with more than four verbs in a corpus and document your search.

---

[a]https://cosmas2.ids-mannheim.de, 2020-05-11.

Further reading

The analysis of verbal complexes in HPSG was first developed by Hinrichs & Nakazawa (1989a,b). Hinrichs & Nakazawa (1994) is the first peer reviewed publication on this topic by Hinrichs & Nakazawa. Kiss (1995a) is a monograph dealing with verbal complexes. Meurers (2000) also deals with verbal complexes including difficult cases like the so-called *Zwischenstellung*, which is not treated here. Müller (2002) treats not just verbal complexes but also other types of complex predicates like adjective verb complexes, resultative constructions and particle verbs.

Godard & Samvelian (2021) provide an overview of analyses of complex predicates in HPSG.

Haider (2010: Chapter 7) discusses various proposals in the Government & Binding framework.

6 Verb position: Verb-first and verb-second

This chapter deals with the analysis of the position of the finite verb in V2 languages. I will concentrate on Danish and German, which may serve as prototypical examples: Danish is an SVO language, while German is SOV. I will first discuss arguments for the classification of German as an SOV language and provide the necessary data on Danish and then explain the respective analyses.

6.1 The phenomena

Section 2.1 contains a discussion of the basic order of subject, object and verb in the languages of the world, and in the Germanic languages in particular. I discussed the classification provided by the World Atlas of Language Structures (Dryer 2013a), which suggested that German is a language with no dominant constituent order, but two orders that can be observed frequently: SOV (subordinate clauses and clauses containing an auxiliary) and SVO (in main clauses lacking an auxiliary). In the following subsection, I discuss this assumption in more detail. Section 6.1.2 explains why researchers working in Mainstream Generative Grammar[1] and also most of the syntacticians working in other frameworks assume that German is an SOV language. Section 6.1.3 deals with Danish as an instance of the Germanic SVO languages and explains how verb-initial clauses in these languages can be best described. Section 6.1.4 is dedicated to fronting in English and verb-second clauses in German (and the other Germanic languages).

6.1.1 German as SVO language?

Claiming that SVO is a basic order on the basis of pure counting is somehow strange given the fact that most German clauses do not have the subject in first position anyway. The following text may serve as an example:

---

[1]The term *Mainstream Generative Grammar* is used for work in the tradition of Chomsky's (1981) Lectures on Government & Binding and Chomsky's (1995) Minimalist Program.

(1) Für selbstfahrende Autos soll es in Deutschland nach Angaben von Bundes-
     verkehrsminister Alexander Dobrindt (CSU) bald eine Teststrecke geben.
     Auf der Autobahn A9 in Bayern sei ein Pilotprojekt „Digitales Testfeld Au-
     tobahn" geplant, wie aus einem Papier des Bundesverkehrsministeriums
     hervorgeht. Mit den ersten Maßnahmen für diese Teststrecke solle schon
     in diesem Jahr begonnen werden. Mit dem Projekt soll die Effizienz von Au-
     tobahnen generell gesteigert werden. „Die Teststrecke soll so digitalisiert
     und technisch ausgerüstet werden, dass es dort zusätzliche Angebote der
     Kommunikation zwischen Straße und Fahrzeug wie auch von Fahrzeug
     zu Fahrzeug geben wird", sagte Dobrindt zur Frankfurter Allgemeinen
     Zeitung. Auf der A9 sollten sowohl Autos mit Assistenzsystemen als auch
     später vollautomatisierte Fahrzeuge fahren können. Dort soll die Kom-
     munikation nicht nur zwischen Testfahrzeugen, sondern auch zwischen
     Sensoren an der Straße und den Autos möglich sein, etwa zur Übermit-
     tlung von Daten zur Verkehrslage oder zum Wetter. Das Vorhaben solle
     im Verkehrsministerium von einem runden Tisch mit Forschern und In-
     dustrievertretern begleitet werden, sagte Dobrindt. Dieser solle sich unter
     anderem auch mit den komplizierten Haftungsfragen beschäftigen. Also:
     Wer zahlt eigentlich, wenn ein automatisiertes Auto einen Unfall baut?
     [Mithilfe der Teststrecke] solle die deutsche Automobilindustrie auch beim
     digitalen Auto „Weltspitze sein können", sagte der CSU-Minister. Die deut-
     schen Hersteller sollten die Entwicklung nicht Konzernen wie etwa Google
     überlassen. Derzeit ist Deutschland noch an das „Wiener Übereinkom-
     men für den Straßenverkehr" gebunden, das Autofahren ohne Fahrer nicht
     zulässt. Nur unter besonderen Auflagen sind Tests möglich. Die Grünen
     halten die Pläne für unnütz. Grünen-Verkehrsexpertin Valerie Wilms sagte
     der Saarbrücker Zeitung: „Der Minister hat wichtigere Dinge zu erledigen,
     als sich mit selbstfahrenden Autos zu beschäftigen." Die Technologie sei im
     Verkehrsbereich nicht vordringlich, auch stehe sie noch ganz am Anfang.
     Aus dem grün-rot regierten Baden-Württemberg – mit dem Konzernsitz
     von Daimler – kamen hingegen andere Töne. Was in Bayern funktioniere,
     müsse auch in Baden-Württemberg möglich sein, sagte Wirtschaftsminis-
     ter Nils Schmid (SPD). Von den topografischen Gegebenheiten biete sich
     die Autobahn A81 an.[2]

The subjects are marked in red and the non-subjects in green. I also counted
subjects/non-subjects within embedded clauses. The ratio is 11 subjects (including one subject sentence) compared to 16 non-subjects (*ein automatisiertes Auto*

---

[2] *Selbstfahrende Autos: A9 soll Teststrecke werden*, taz, 2015-01-27

and *Autofahren ohne Fahrer* in the SOV sentences were not counted, but these
are of course also counterexamples to the SVO claim). So, the question is: What
does this number tell us? Of course we could now further differentiate the grammatical functions of the fronted material. We would find that we have 3 object
clauses fronted; the rest of the fronted constituents are adverbials. We could conclude that SVO is more common than OVS, but saying that SVO is basic would
not be appropriate. Rather, AdvVSO should be regarded as a basic pattern if we
assume this little text as our empirical basis. Of course, assuming this text as the
basis of scientific claims is not sufficient. Hinrichs & Kübler (2005: Section 4)
examined the *Vorfeld* constituents in the TüBa-D/S and Z corpora. The S corpus
contains spoken German from the machine translation project Verbmobil and the
Z corpus sentences from the German newspaper taz. Both corpora are annotated
for grammatical function. The TüBa-D/S consisted of a total of 38,342 trees and
the TüBa-D/Z treebank had 22,087 trees when the paper was written in 2005.
The two corpora had subjects in the *Vorfeld* in 50.3 % and 52.1 % of the sentences
with a *Vorfeld*, respectively. So, assuming SVO as the basic order would not be
helpful, since in about 50 % of the clauses and may be even more, one would have
to deal with an order in which the subject is not in initial position. On top of this,
there would be the problem of subordinated sentences, which clearly do have an
SOV order.[3] Therefore syntacticians of various different frameworks (see Müller
2023b for approaches in GB, Minimalism, LFG, Categorial Grammar, and HPSG)
assume that SOV is the base order of German. The finite verb is fronted to mark

---

[3]The clauses in (i) are in SOV order. (id) is non-finite and does not have a subject.

(i)   a. dass es dort zusätzliche Angebote der   Kommunikation zwischen Straße und
           that it there additional offers   of.the communication between street and
           Fahrzeug wie auch von   Fahrzeug zu Fahrzeug geben wird
           vehicle   as   also from vehicle   to vehicle   give   will
           'that there will be additional offers for communication between street and vehicle
           and also between vehicle and vehicle'

      b. wenn ein automatisiertes Auto einen Unfall   baut
           when a   automatic   car an   accident builds
           'when an automatic car causes an accisdent'

      c. das Autofahren ohne   Fahrer nicht zulässt
           that car.driving without driver not   permits
           'that does not permit car driving without driver'

      d. als   sich mit selbstfahrenden Autos zu beschäftigen
           rather.than self with self.driving   cars to deal.with
           'rather than dealing with autonomous cars'

the sentence type and one constituent is put in front of this verb. This fronted constituent can be the subject, an object or any other constituent of the sentence. It may even be a dependent of a deeply embedded element in the clause. So, the position in front of V in the V2 languages has nothing to do with the SVO/SOV dichotomy; it basically disturbs the picture and makes the counting approach pursued in the WALS (see Section 2.1) non-applicable.[4]

In the following I will provide facts that are seen as evidence for SOV as the basic order of German (and other Germanic languages, e.g., Dutch, Frisian, Afrikaans and their regional variants). Before I provide an analysis in Section 6.2, I discuss the verb position in the Germanic SVO languages with Danish as an example in Section 6.1.3.

6.1.2 German as an SOV language

6.1.2.1 The order of particle and verb

Verb particles form a close unit with the verb. The unit is observable in verb-final sentences only, which supports an SOV analysis (Bierwisch 1963: 35).

(2) a. weil   er morgen   anfängt
          because he tomorrow at.catches
          'because he starts tomorrow'

      b. Er fängt   morgen   an.
          he catches tomorrow at
          'He starts tomorrow.'

The particle verb in (2) is non-transparent: its meaning is not related to the verb *fangen* 'to catch'. Such particle verbs are sometimes called mini idioms.

6.1.2.2 Idioms

The argument above can also be made with idioms not involving particle verbs: many idioms do not allow rearrangement of the idiom parts in the *Mittelfeld*:[5]

---

[4]Martin Haspelmath (p.c. 2022) pointed out that the counting approach serves comparative purposes rather than descriptive ones. Haspelmath (2010a) – distinguishing between comparative concepts and descriptive categories – writes that comparative concepts cannot be right or wrong (p. 665), they can just be more or less suited for certain purposes. I agree that the counting approach is useful for comparing the languages of the world, but my point was that it is not suited for Germanic languages since here the V2 phenomenon disturbs the picture. For further discussion of comparative concepts vs. descriptive categories see Newmeyer (2010), Haspelmath (2010b) and Müller (2015c: 43–44).

[5]As the example (3c) shows, the verb may be used in initial position. Müller (2013b: 203) discusses examples in which the phrase *den Garaus* is in the *Vorfeld*.

(3) a. dass niemand dem Mann den Garaus macht
      that nobody   the   man   the GARAUS makes
      'that nobody kills the man'

   b. ?* dass dem Mann den Garaus niemand macht
      that the   man   the GARAUS nobody   makes

   c. Niemand macht ihm den Garaus.
      nobody   makes him the GARAUS
      'Nobody kills him.'

This is an instance of Behaghel's law (1932) that things that belong together semantically tend to be realized together. The exception is the finite verb. The
finite verb can be realized in initial or final position despite the fact that this
interrupts the continuity of the idiomatic material. Since the continuity can be
observed in SOV order only, this order is considered basic.

6.1.2.3 Verbs formed by backformation

Verbs that are derived from nouns by backformation often cannot be separated
and verb-second sentences are therefore excluded (see Haider 1993: 62, who
refers to unpublished work by Höhle 1991b now published in a collection of
Höhle's work by Language Science Press). The examples are on page 370–371):

(4) a. weil   sie   das Stück heute uraufführen
      because they the play   today play.for.the.first.time
      'because they premiere the play today'

   b. * Sie   uraufführen   heute das Stück.
      they play.for.the.first.time today the play

   c. * Sie   führen heute das Stück urauf.
      they guide today the play   PREFIX.PART

Hence these verbs can only be used in the order that is assumed to be the base
order.

6.1.2.4 Double particle verbs

Examples involving backformation as in (4) have been criticized for being special, since they involve backformation. So maybe there is a certain ill-understood
aspect responsible for their properties. But Haider (1993: 63), Vikner (2001: 105),
Fortmann (2007) and Haider (2010: 59–60) found a similar class of verbs resisting
movement: double particle verbs. Verbs like *vorankündigen* 'preannounce' consists of the combination of *an* 'on' and *kündigen* 'announce' with the addition of
another prefix *vor* 'pre'.

(5) dass sie es vor-an-kündigt
    that she it pre-on-announces
    'that she preannounces it'

Now, the interesting thing about these verbs is that they cannot be fronted. The verb stem has to be adjacent to the particle:

(6) a. * Sie kündigt$_i$ es vor-an $\_i$.
        she announces it pre-on

    b. * Sie an-kündigt$_i$ es vor $\_i$.
        she on-announces it pre

    c. * Sie vor-an-kündigt$_i$ es $\_i$.
        she pre-on-announces it

The examples show that double particle verbs are possible in OV order but impossible in VO order.

6.1.2.5 Constructions that only allow SOV order

Similarly, it is impossible to realize the verb in initial position when elements like *mehr als* 'more than' are present in the clause (Haider 1997b: Section 3.1, Meinunger 2001: 732):

(7) a. dass Hans seinen Profit letztes Jahr mehr als   verdreifachte
        that Hans his   profit last   year more than tripled
        'that Hans increased his profit last year by a factor greater than three'

    b. Hans hat seinen Profit letztes Jahr mehr als   verdreifacht.
        Hans has his   profit last   year more than tripled
        'Hans increased his profit last year by a factor greater than three.'

    c. * Hans verdreifachte seinen Profit letztes Jahr mehr als.
        Hans tripled   his   profit last   year more than

So, it is possible to realize the adjunct together with the verb in final position, but there are constraints regarding the placement of the finite verb in initial position.

6.1.2.6 Order in subordinate and non-finite clauses

Verbs in non-finite clauses and in subordinate finite clauses starting with a conjunction always appear finally, that is, in the right sentence bracket. For example, *zu geben* 'to give' and *gibt* 'gives' appear in the right sentence bracket in (8):

(8) a. Der Clown versucht, Kurt-Martin die Ware zu geben.
     the clown tries   Kurt-Martin the goods to give
     'The clown tries to give Kurt-Martin the goods.'

    b. dass der Clown Kurt-Martin die Ware gibt
     that the clown Kurt-Martin the goods gives
     'that the clown gives Kurt-Martin the goods'

6.1.2.7 Scope of adverbials

The scope of adverbials in sentences like (9) depends on their order (Netter 1992: Section 2.3): The leftmost adverb scopes over the following adverb and over the verb in final position. This was explained by assuming the following structure:

(9) a. weil   er [absichtlich [nicht lacht]]
     because he deliberately   not   laughs
     'because he deliberately does not laugh'

    b. weil   er [nicht [absichtlich   lacht]]
     because he not   deliberately laughs
     'because he does not laugh deliberately'

An interesting fact is that the scope relations do not change when the verb position is changed. If one assumes that the sentences have an underlying structure like in (9) and that scope is determined with reference to this structure, this fact is explained automatically:

(10) a. Lacht$_i$ er [absichtlich [nicht $\__i$]]?
     laughs he deliberately   not
     'Does he deliberately not laugh?'

    b. Lacht$_i$ er [nicht [absichtlich $\__i$]]?
     laughs he not   deliberately
     'Doesn't he laugh deliberately?'

It has to be mentioned here that there seem to be exceptions to the claim that modifiers scope from left to right. Kasper (1994: 47) discusses the examples in (11), which go back to Bartsch & Vennemann (1972: 137).

(11) a. Peter liest wegen   der Nachhilfestunden gut.
     Peter reads because.of the tutoring   well
     'Peter reads well because of the tutoring.'

    b. Peter liest gut wegen   der Nachhilfestunden.
     Peter reads well because.of the tutoring

(11a) corresponds to the expected order in which the adverbial PP *wegen der Nach-hilfestunden* 'because of the tutoring' outscopes the adverb *gut* 'well', but the alternative order in (11b) is possible as well and the sentence has the same reading as the one in (11a).

However, Koster (1975: Section 6) and Reis (1980: 67) showed that these examples are not convincing evidence since the right sentence bracket is not filled and therefore the orders in (11) are not necessarily variants of *Mittelfeld* orders but may be due to extraposition of one constituent. As Koster and Reis showed, the examples become ungrammatical when the right sentence bracket is filled:

(12)   a. * Hans hat gut wegen   der Nachhilfestunden gelesen.
           Hans has well because.of the tutoring   read

       b.   Hans hat gut gelesen wegen   der Nachhilfestunden.
           Hans has well read   because.of the tutoring

          'Peter read well because of the tutoring.'

The conclusion is that (11b) is best treated as a variant of (11a) in which the PP is extraposed and scope is determined at the position at which the PP would occur if it were not extraposed.

While examples like (11) show that the matter is not trivial, the following example from Crysmann (2004: 383) shows that there are examples with a filled right sentence bracket that allow for scopings in which an adjunct scopes over another adjunct that precedes it. For instance, in (13) *niemals* 'never' scopes over *wegen schlechten Wetters* 'because of the bad weather':

(13)   Da   muß es schon erhebliche Probleme mit   der Ausrüstung gegeben
      there must it PART severe   problems with the equipment given
      haben, da   [wegen   schlechten Wetters] ein Reinhold Messner
      have   since because.of bad   weather a   Reinhold Messner
      [niemals] aufgäbe.
       never   give.up.would
      'There must have been severe problems with the equipment, since
      someone like Reinhold Messner would never give up just because of the
      bad weather.'

However, this does not change the fact that the sentences in (9) and (10) have the same meaning independent of the position of the verb. The general meaning composition may be done in the way that Crysmann suggested.

Another word of caution is in order here: there are SVO languages like French that also have a left to right scoping of adjuncts (Bonami et al. 2004: 156–161). So, the argumentation above should not be seen as the only fact supporting the SOV status of German. In any case, the analyses of German that were worked out in various frameworks can explain the facts nicely.

6.1.2.8 Position of non-finite verbs in VO and OV languages

Before I turn to the verb position in Danish in the next subsection, I want to repeat Ørsnes' examples containing several non-finite verbs (see (6) on p. 15): the example in (14a) shows a German subordinate clause with a verbal complex consisting of three verbs. The level of embedding is indicated by subscript numbers. As can be seen, the verbs are added at the end of the clause. In the corresponding Danish example which was adapted from Ørsnes (2009: 146), it is exactly the other way around: the embedding verb precedes the embedded verb.

(14) a. dass er ihn gesehen$_3$ haben$_2$ muss$_1$ (German)
        that he him seen   have   must

        'that he must have seen him'

    b. at   hun må$_1$ have$_2$ set$_3$ ham   (Danish)
        that she must have   seen him

The examples in (15) are variants with different complexity. If we replace the simplex verb *sah* 'saw' in (15a) by the perfect form, the auxiliary is placed after the participle as in (15b).

(15) a. dass er ihn sah   (German)
        that he him saw

        'that he saw him'

    b. dass er ihn gesehen hat
        that he him seen   has

        'that he has seen him'

If a modal is added to (15b), the modal goes to the right of the embedded verbs. This order is distorted by the placement of the finite verb in initial position, but this placement is independent of the order of the non-finite verbs. As the examples in (16) show, the finite verb is realized to the left of the subject both in German (SOV) and in Danish (SVO).

(16) a. Muss er ihn gesehen haben?   (German)
        must he him seen   have

        'Must he have seen him?'

    b. Må   han have set   ham?   (Danish)
       must he   have seen him
       'Must he have seen him?'

6.1.3 Verb position in the Germanic SVO languages

During the discussion of scope facts, I already hinted at an analysis in which a trace marks the position of the verb in final position and the verb in initial position is coindexed with this trace. Although the SVO languages are different, a similar analysis has been suggested for languages like Danish. The evidence for this is that adverbials in SVO languages usually attach to the VP, that is, they combine with a phrase consisting of the verb and its object or objects. (17) is an example:

(17)   at   Conny ikke [$_{\text{VP}}$ læser bogen]   (Danish)
       that Conny not   reads book.DEF
       'that Conny does not read the book'

The interesting thing now is that the finite verb is placed to the left of the negation in V2 sentences:

(18)   Conny læser ikke bogen.   (Danish)
       Conny reads not book.DEF
       'Conny is not reading the book.'

This is seen as evidence for verb fronting by many:

(19)   Conny læser$_i$ ikke [$_{\text{VP}}$ $\_i$ bogen].   (Danish)
       Conny reads not   book.DEF
       'Conny does not read the book.'

With this as a background, it should be clear what the analysis of yes/no questions as in (20b) is:

(20)   a. at   Conny læser bogen   (Danish)
           that Conny reads book.DEF
           'that Conny reads the book'

       b. Læser Conny bogen?
           reads Conny book.DEF
           'Does Conny read the book?'

The analysis of the first sentence involves a VP as in (21a), and the second sentence involves a VP with a verbal trace that corresponds to the verb in initial position:

(21) a. at   Conny [$_{VP}$ læser bogen]   (Danish)
          that Conny   reads book.DEF

          'that Conny reads the book'

      b. Læser$_i$ Conny [$_{VP}$ $_{-i}$ bogen]?
          reads   Conny   book.DEF

          'Does Conny read the book?'

It is interesting to note that the German and the Danish question with simplex verbs have exactly the same constituent order. Compare (20b) with (22):

(22)   Liest Conny das Buch?   (German)
       reads Conny the book

       'Does Conny read the book?'

The internal structure of these sentences is quite different though. The different nature of the two languages is of course more obvious when non-finite verbs are involved:

(23) a. Har$_i$ Conny [$_{-i}$ læst bogen]?   (Danish)
          has   Conny   read book.DEF

          'Has Conny read the book?'

      b. Hat$_i$ Conny das Buch [gelesen $_{-i}$]?   (German)
          has   Conny the book   read

          'Has Conny read the book?'

In (23a) the finite verb is connected to a trace in initial position of the VP and in (23b) it is connected to a verb in final position in a verbal complex.

6.1.4 Verb second

Even languages with rather rigid constituent order sometimes allow the fronting of elements. (24) shows English examples of fronting:

(24) a. I read this book yesterday.

      b. This book, I read yesterday.

      c. Yesterday, I read this book.

The object *this book* and the adjunct *yesterday* are fronted in (24b) and (24c), respectively.

The Germanic languages (with the exception of English) place one constituent in front of the finite verb. As the German examples in (25) show, the fronted constituent can be of any grammatical function:

(25)   a. Ich habe das Buch gestern   gelesen.   (German)
            I   have the book yesterday read

            'I have read the book yesterday.'

       b. Das Buch habe ich gestern   gelesen.
            the book have I   yesterday read

       c. Gestern   habe ich das Buch gelesen.
            yesterday have I   the book read

       d. Gelesen habe ich das Buch gestern,   gekauft hatte ich es aber schon
            read   have I   the book yesterday bought had I   it but yet
            vor   einem Monat.
            before a   month

            'I read the book yesterday, but I bought it last month already.'

       e. Das Buch gelesen habe ich gestern.
            the book read   have I   yesterday

Such frontings are not clause-bounded, that is, the fronting may cross one or several clause boundaries and also boundaries of other constituents. (26) shows English examples in which the object of *saw* is extracted across one and two clause boundaries:

(26)   a. Chris, Sandy saw.

       b. Chris, we think that Sandy saw.

       c. Chris, we think Anna claims that Sandy saw.

In German such extractions can be found as well:

(27)   a. Wer$_i$ wohl   meint   er, dass $\_i$ ihm seine Arbeit hier bezahlen
            who perhaps assumes he that   him his   work here pay
            werde?[6]
            shall

            'Who did he perhaps assume would pay him for his work here?'

---

[6]Paul (1919: 321). Paul provides two pages full of attested examples of extractions out of *dass* clauses.

   b. Wen$_i$ glaubst du, daß ich $\_i$ gesehen habe.[7]   (German)
     who believes you that I   seen   have

     'Who do you believe that I have seen?'

   c. „Wer$_i$, glaubt er, daß er $\_i$ ist?" erregte   sich ein Politiker
     who believes he that he   is   was.upset REFL a   politician
     vom   Nil.[8]
     from.the Nile

     'A politician from the Nile was upset: "Who does he believe he is?".'

It is generally said that they are more common in Southern German varieties, but there are other examples that show that nonlocal dependencies are involved. In (28a) the prepositional object *um zwei Millionen Mark* 'around two million Deutsche Marks' depends on *betrügen* 'to cheat'. It does not depend on any of the verbs in the matrix clause. The phrase *eine Versicherung zu betrügen* 'an insurance to betray' is extraposed, that is, it is positioned to the right of the verbal bracket in the so-called *Nachfeld*. The position of *um zwei Millionen Mark* cannot be accounted for by local reordering. Similarly, *gegen ihn* 'against him' depends on *Angriffe* 'attacks', which is part of the phrase *Angriffe zu lancieren* 'attacks to launch'. Again an analysis based on local reordering of dependents of a head is impossible.

(28)   a. [Um   zwei Millionen Mark]$_i$ soll   er versucht haben,
      around two   million   Deutsche.Marks should he tried   have
      [eine Versicherung $\_i$ zu betrügen].[9]   (German)
      an   insurance.company   to deceive

      'He apparently tried to cheat an insurance company out of two million Deutsche Marks.'

  b. [Gegen ihn]$_i$ falle es den Republikanern hingegen schwerer,
     against him fall it the Republicans   however more.difficult
     [[Angriffe $\_i$] zu lancieren].[10]
       attacks   to launch

     'It is, however, more difficult for the Republicans to launch attacks against him.'

---

[7]Scherpenisse (1986: 84).

[8]Spiegel, 8/1999, p. 18.

[9]taz, 04.05.2001, p. 20.

[10]taz, 08.02.2008, p. 9.

6.2 The analysis

This section deals with verb-first sentences in Subsection 6.2.1 and then covers verb second sentences in Subsection 6.2.2. I explain two different mechanisms for the respective analyses: the double slash notation for dependencies involving a head (so-called "head-movement") and the slash notation for nonlocal-dependencies (so-called "constituent-movement").[11] The analysis of "head-movement" goes back to Jacobson (1987a), who suggested such an analysis in the framework of Categorial Grammar for English. Borsley (1989) adapted this analysis for HPSG and Kiss & Wesche (1991), Kiss (1995a,b) suggested a verb-movement analysis for German in HPSG. The analysis of constituent-movement is actually older than the one of head-movement. It goes back to work in Generalized Phrase Structure Grammar (Gazdar 1981) and was adapted to HPSG by Pollard & Sag (1987: Section 3.4) and Pollard & Sag (1994: Chapter 4).

6.2.1 Verb first

The analysis uses a special mechanism that passes up information in a tree. The verbal trace contains the information that a verb is missing locally. This information about the missing verb is passed up to the node that dominates the verbal trace. It is represented using a device that is called "double slash" and is written as //. The respective information is head-information and therefore it is passed up the head-path along with other information, such as part of speech. Figure 6.1 illustrates. The verbal trace is missing a V, the V′ is missing a V, and the S as well. The initial verb selects for a sentence that is lacking a V ⟨ S//V ⟩. The lexical item for the verb in initial position is licensed by a lexical rule that relates a verb to a verb that selects for a sentence that is lacking the input verb. Since the selectional requirement of this verb (S//V) is identified with the sentence lacking a V (Conny das Buch $_{-j}$), the information about the original verb *liest* is identified with the V in S//V. Since the double slash information is head information, it percolates down along the head path to the verbal trace. The information about the initial V is identified with the syntactic and semantic information of the verbal trace in final position, and hence this verbal trace behaves exactly like the verb in initial position that was input to the lexical rule.

---

[11]Note that HPSG differs from theories like Government & Binding (GB, Chomsky 1981) and Minimalism (Chomsky 1995) in that nothing is actually moved. While GB assumes that there are two or more structures related to each other by movement of constituents, HPSG assumes just one structure with an empty element and sharing of information. This is an important difference as far as psycholinguistic plausibility of theories is concerned. See Müller (2023b: Chapter 15) and Wasow (2021: Section 3.2) for discussion.

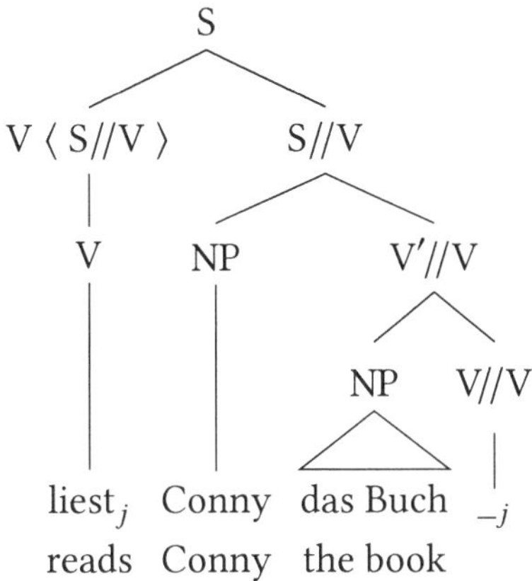

Figure 6.1: Analysis of verb position in German

Various researchers have argued that the finite verb in initial position behaves like a complementizer in subordinated clauses (Höhle 1997, Weiß 2005, 2018). This is captured by the analysis. Compare Figure 6.1 with Figure 6.2. The com-

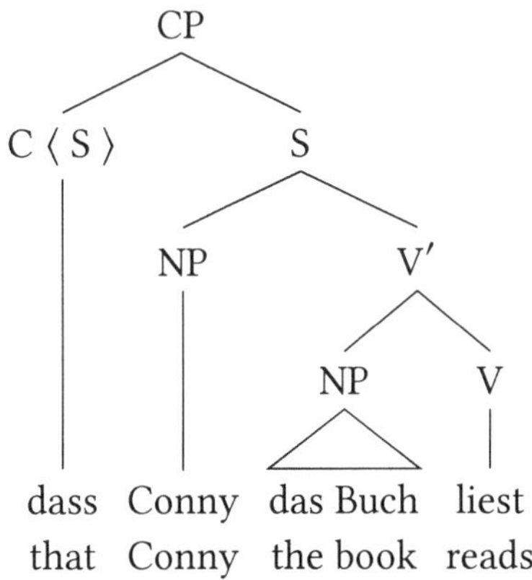

Figure 6.2: Analysis of a verb-final clause with complementizer in German

plementizer *dass* 'that' selects for a complete sentence, that is, a sentence that does not have a missing verb, and the initial verb *liest* 'reads' in Figure 6.1 selects for a sentence that is missing *liest*. So apart from the overt or covert verb, the structures are identical. This fact is important when it comes to the analysis of the scope facts. Since the structure is completely parallel to the one we have in verb-final sentences, the scope facts follow immediately: the trace behaves like the verb in initial position, *absichtlich* 'deliberately' modifies the trace, and the

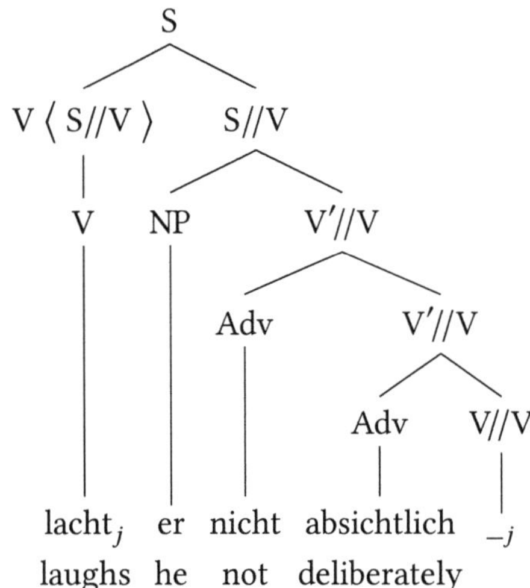

Figure 6.3: Analysis of sentences with adverbials in German

resulting semantics is passed up in the tree (see Figure 6.3). The next step is the modification by *nicht* 'not'. Again the resulting semantics is passed up. *lacht* 'laughs' combines with the clause and takes its semantics over. Since *lacht* is the head the semantics is passed on from there.

The analysis of Danish is completely parallel to the analysis of German. The only difference between Figure 6.1 and Figure 6.4 is the position of the verbal trace relative to the object: the trace follows the object in German, but it precedes it in Danish.

The last thing that is explained in this section is the analysis of negation and verb fronting in Danish. Figure 6.5 shows that the negation attaches to the VP as in verb-final clauses and the verb is fronted so that it appears to the left of the negation. The next section explains the extraction of constituents, and it will then be possible to provide the full structure for sentences like (29a). It will also become clear why the order of negation and verb differs in embedded and main clauses:

(29)   a.   Conny læser ikke bogen.
            Conny reads not   book.DEF

       'Conny does not read the book.'

       b.   at   Conny ikke læser bogen
            that Conny not   reads book.DEF

       'that Conny does not read the book'

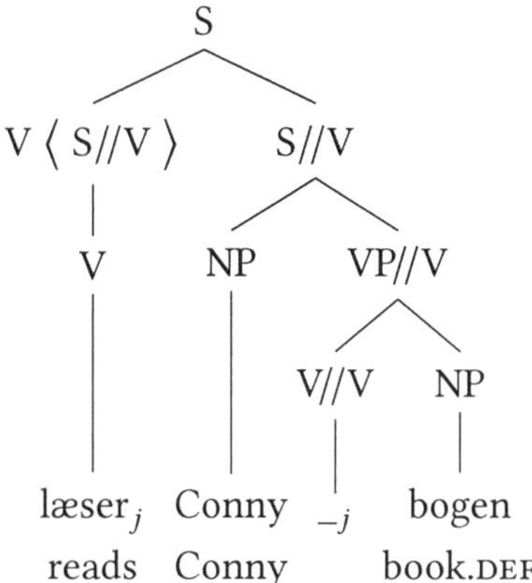

Figure 6.4: Analysis of verb position in Danish

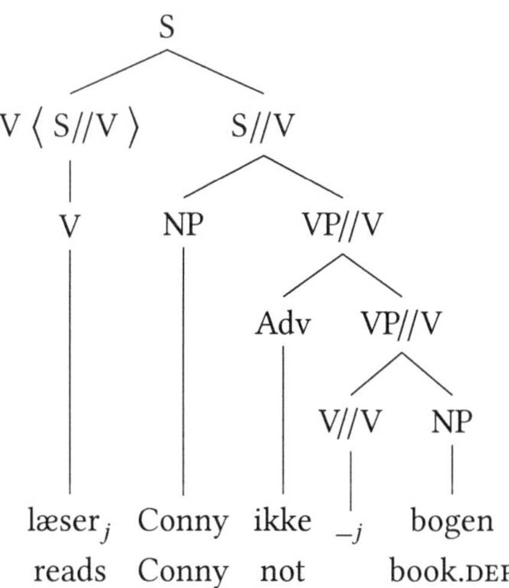

Figure 6.5: The analysis of verb fronting and negation in Danish

6.2.2 Verb second

The technique that is used for the analysis of nonlocal dependencies is the same
that was employed for the analysis of the reorderings of verbs: an empty element
takes the position of the fronted constituent, and the information about the missing constituent (the so-called *gap*) is passed up in the tree until it is finally bound
off by the fronted element, the so-called *filler*. Figure 6.6 illustrates the analysis
of (26a).

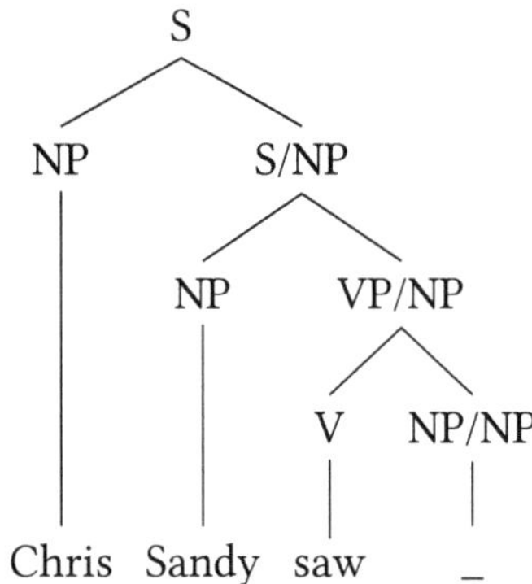

Figure 6.6: The analysis of extraction in English

The category following the slash ('/') stands for the object that is missing locally in the position of the trace. Traces are like jokers in card games: they can fill
(almost) any position. They pretend to be of the category that is required locally
(the NP in the accusative in the example at hand), but the information that this
category is missing locally is passed up (from NP/NP to VP/NP to S/NP). When
a matching filler is combined with a slashed constituent, the information about
the missing element is not passed up any further. The nonlocal dependency is
said to be bound off at this point. In Figure 6.6, S/NP is combined with the filler
NP and hence the mother node is an unslashed S. The verb has all its arguments
and no slashed element is missing in the sentence: the sentence is complete.

Figure 6.7 shows the analysis of example (26b), which really requires a nonlocal dependency. As is shown in the figure, the information about the missing
object is passed up to the sentence level (S/NP), to the CP level (CP/NP) and up
to the next higher S. There it is bound off by the filler *Chris.* The binding off of
the missing element is licensed by a special schema, which is called the Filler-
Head Schema. Figure 6.8 provides a sketch of this schema.

English is the only non-V2 language among the Germanic languages. In what
follows, I show how German (V2+SOV) and Danish (V2+SVO) can be analyzed

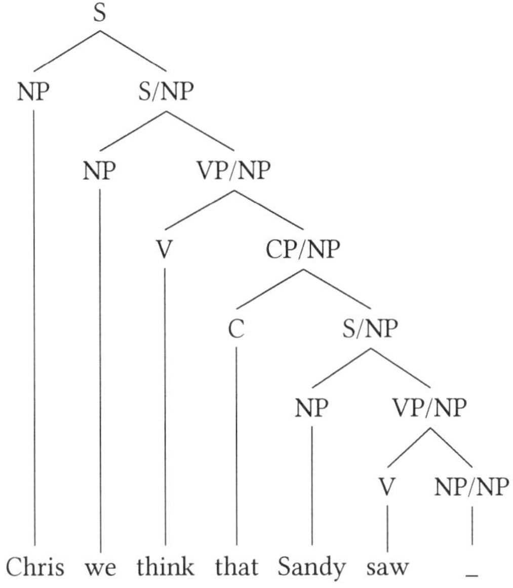

Figure 6.7: Extraction crossing the clause boundary

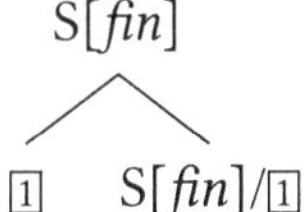

Figure 6.8: Sketch of the Filler-Head Schema

with the techniques that have been introduced so far. Figure 6.9 shows the analysis of (30):

(30)　Das Buch liest　Conny.
　　　the　book reads Conny
　　　'Conny reads the book.'

The analysis of the German example is more complicated than the English one since verb movement is involved. The verb is fronted as was explained with reference to Figure 6.1. In addition, the object is realized by a trace and then filled by the filler *das Buch* 'the book', which is realized preverbally.

I follow Fanselow (2003b) and Frey (2004b), who assume that the position of the object is initial in the *Mittelfeld*. Since German allows for both nominative-accusative and accusative-nominative order, the position of the trace for the extracted object could be initial or final as in (31a) and (31b), respectively:

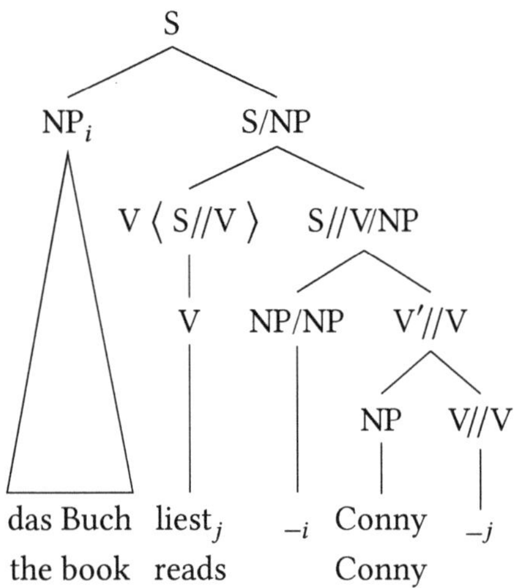

Figure 6.9: Analysis of V2 in German (SOV)

(31) a. [Das Buch]$_i$ liest$_j$ $_{-i}$ Conny $_{-j}$.
          the book   reads   Conny

      b. [Das Buch]$_i$ liest$_j$ Conny $_{-i}$ $_{-j}$.
          the book   reads Conny

Fanselow and Frey argue that fronted elements like *das Buch* 'the book' have information structural properties that correspond to those of non-fronted elements in the initial *Mittelfeld* position:

(32) Liest das Buch Conny?
      reads the book Conny

      'Does Conny read the book.'

They argue that (32) patterns with (31a) rather than with (31b). The complete discussion will not be repeated here, since this would take us too far away, but the interested reader may consult the discussion in Section 4.10.1.

The analysis of the parallel Danish V2 example in (33) is similar.

(33) Bogen   læser Conny.
      book.DEF reads Conny

      'Conny reads the book.'

The analysis consists of two parts: firstly, the analysis of verb-initial position that involves the double slash mechanism and secondly, the fronting of the object using the slash mechanism. Figure 6.10 illustrates.

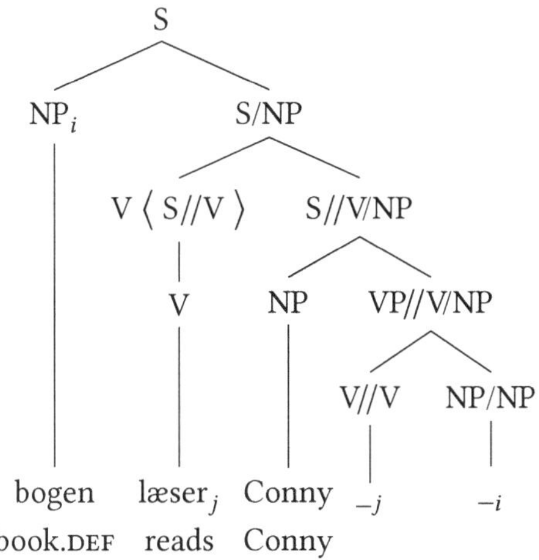

Figure 6.10: Analysis of V2 in Danish (SVO)

The careful reader will ask why we use two different mechanisms to analyze verb movement and extraction. The answer is that these movement types are different in nature: verb movement is clause-bounded, while the movement of other constituents may cross clause boundaries. This is captured by the fact that the double slash information is passed up together with other head features, such as the part of speech information, and the slash information is passed up separately.

Before we deal with passive in the next chapter, we can compare the three sentences in (34):

(34)   a. Conny reads a book.

   b. Conny læser en bog.

   c. Conny liest ein Buch.

Again the order of the elements is the same in all three languages. However, English is an SVO non-V2 language, Danish is an SVO+V2 language, and German is an SOV+V2 language. The analyses in bracket notation are given in (35), the tree structures are depicted in Figure 6.11:

(35)   a. [$_S$ Conny [$_{VP}$ reads [$_{NP}$ a book]]].

   b. [$_S$ Conny$_i$ [$_{S/NP}$ læser$_j$ [$_{S/NP}$ $_{-i}$ [$_{VP}$ $_{-j}$ [$_{NP}$ en bog]]]]].

   c. [$_S$ Conny$_i$ [$_{S/NP}$ liest$_j$ [$_{S/NP}$ $_{-i}$ [$_{\overline{V}}$ [$_{NP}$ ein Buch] $_{-j}$]]]].

It may be surprising that these three sentences get such radically different analyses although the order of elements are the same. The difference in structures is

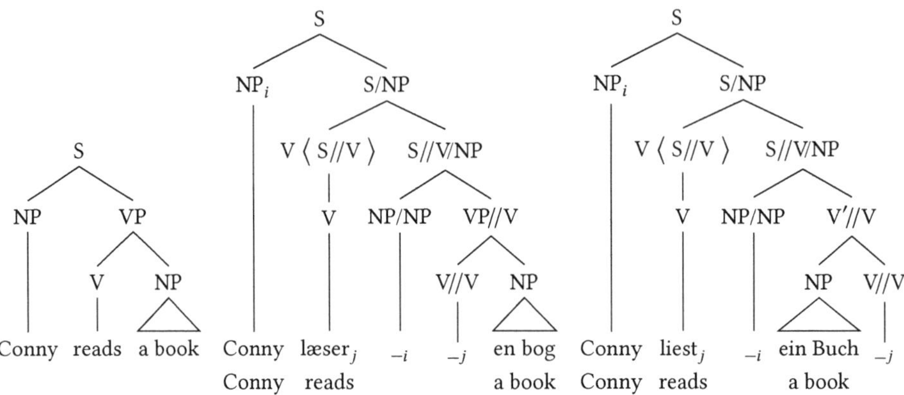

Figure 6.11: Declarative main clauses with subject in initial position in English, Danish and German: despite similar appearance, the syntactic structure is different

the result of the assumption that all declarative main clauses in the Germanic V2 languages follow the same pattern, namely that the finite verb is fronted and then another constituent is fronted. This particular construction is connected to the clause type, that is, to the meaning of the utterance (imperative, question, assertion). The sentences in (27) and (28) show that V2 involves a nonlocal dependency. Therefore the analysis of (35b) is more complex than (36) and involves the fronting of the finite verb to initial position with a successive fronting of the subject:

(36)   [$_S$ Conny [$_{VP}$ læser [$_{NP}$ en bog]]].

The reason is that now all declarative main clauses are subsumed under the same structure, namely (35b). A declarative main clause in all Germanic V2 languages is the combination of an extracted phrase with a verb-initial phrase in which the extracted element is missing. Fronting of the finite verb is a way to mark the clause type: if just the finite verb is fronted, the result is a yes/no question (37a) or an imperative sentence (37b).[12]

---

[12]Verb-initial clauses may also be declarative clauses if so-called *topic drop* (Fries 1988) is involved:

(i)   Was macht Peter? Gibt ihm ein Buch.   (German)
      what does   Peter gives him a   book

      'What does Peter do? He gives him a book.'

The subject of *gibt* 'gives' is dropped. The complete sentence would be a V2 sentence: *Er gibt ihm ein Buch.*

(37) a. Gibt er ihm das Buch?   (German)
          gives he him the book
          'Does he give him the book?'

      b. Gib mir das Buch!
          give me the book

If another constituent is fronted, a question with question word (38a), an imperative (38b) or a declarative clause (38c) results.

(38) a. Wem gibt   er das Buch?   (German)
          who gives he the book
          'Whom does he give the book to?'

      b. Jetzt gib   ihm das Buch!
          now give him the book
          'Give him the book now!'

      c. Jetzt gibt   er ihm das Buch.
          now gives he him the book
          'He gives him the book now.'

The analysis of the semantics of clause types cannot be given here but the interested reader is referred to Müller (2015b, 2023a).

6.3 Alternatives

As with the sections about alternatives in previous chapters, this section is for advanced readers only. It is not necessary to read it in order to understand the rest of the book.

In the preceding section I suggested an analysis in which the basic SVO order is just that: a subject followed by the verb and a verb followed by the objects. The verb-final sentences of SOV languages are analyzed as a verb that is preceded by its arguments. The position of the finite verb is accounted for by fronting it via the double slash mechanism.

There are alternative proposals to SVO and SOV order and also to the placement of the finite verb. The proposal by Kayne (1994) suggests that all languages have an underlying specifier-head-complement order. The orders we see in the Germanic SOV languages would then be derived by movement. The counterproposal by Haider (2000, 2020) does not suggest that all languages are like English or Romance but instead claims that the VO languages are derived from an underlying OV order. These two approaches are discussed in the following two subsections 6.3.1 and 6.3.2. As will be shown, Kayne's proposal makes wrong predictions and Haider's proposal is not without problems either. For both proposals it would be unclear how they should be acquired by learners of the respective languages without the assumption of a rich Universal Grammar.

The third class of proposals to be discussed in Section 6.3.3 does not assume verb movement at all. Rather than assuming a structure with layered VPs and some sort of movement that reorders the finite verb, authors like Gazdar, Klein, Pullum & Sag (1985) and Sag et al. (2020) assume that there are alternative linearizations for finite verbs and their subjects. The pros and cons of such analyses are the topic of Section 6.3.3.

The CP/TP/VP model was already discussed in Section 4.10.1 on scrambling. There are also arguments against this approach when it comes to verb movement. They are discussed in Section 6.3.4.

6.3.1 OV derived from VO: Kayne (1994)

Kayne (1994) stipulates that all sentences in all languages have a Specifier–Head–Complement order. Languages with orders that are not SVO are assumed to be derived by movement from SVO. We already discussed Laenzlinger's (2004: 224) analysis of a German sentence in Section 4.10.2.1. Figure 6.12 shows his analysis without the functional nodes for adjuncts and without the fronting of the object to TopP.

The figure shows a vP to the right of the auxiliary. So the underlying structure without adjuncts is assumed to be (39a) and the derived one in (39b):

(39) a. * weil   hat der Mann gespielt die Sonate
          because has the man   played   the sonata

  b. weil   der Mann die Sonate gespielt hat   (German)
      because the man   the sonata played   has

There is a very simple argument against such derivations: it comes from the Poverty of the Stimulus, an old argument by Chomsky (1980: 34), and I would like to call the argument I am using here the Inverse Poverty of the Stimulus Argument, since I am using the same argument in a different direction. Chomsky argues that knowledge that cannot be learned from the input and can nevertheless be shown to be present must be innate. Since we know by now that it is highly unlikely that elaborated language-specific knowledge is part of our genome (Hauser, Chomsky & Fitch 2002; Bishop 2002, Dąbrowska 2004: Section 6.4.2.2, Fisher & Marcus 2005), it follows that the machinery assumed in linguistics cannot be such that it would not be acquirable. Since the underlying structure assumed by Laenzlinger is not connected to observable material in any way, there would not be a way to learn the transformations to derive German

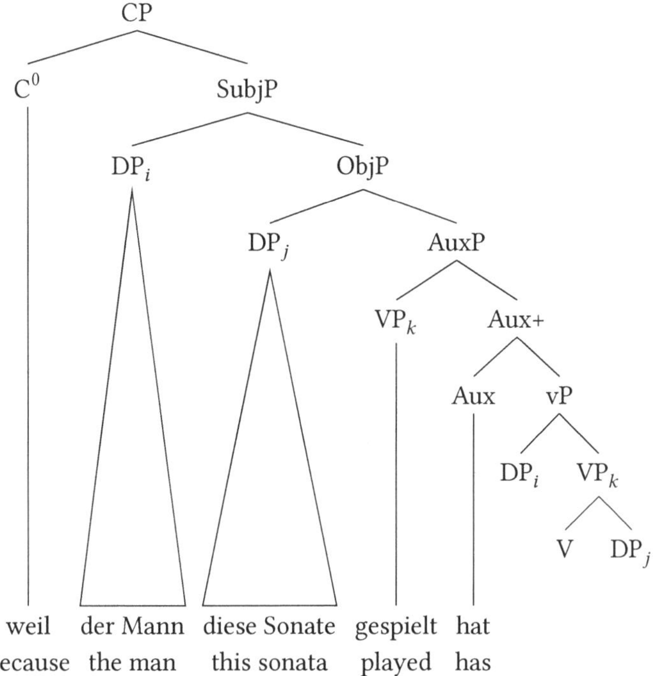

Figure 6.12: Abbreviated analysis of sentence structure with leftward remnant movement and functional heads following Laenzlinger (2004: 224)

sentences. It follows that the complete machinery would have to be part of Universal Grammar, but since it is unclear how it should be gotten there and why one should assume it in the first place, we have to conclude that Kayne's proposal is wrong.

Haider (2000) shows in detail why one should not assume OV to be derived from VO. I will not repeat the discussion here. Haider argues that one should see VO as derived from OV instead. I think that this is not a good idea either and that VO and OV are just different and not derived from each other. I deal with Haider's suggestion and my alternative proposal in the next subsection.

6.3.2 VO derived from OV: Haider (2020)

As was shown in the previous section, SVO approaches to SOV languages are not acquirable in a surface-oriented way, require a large part of innate language-specific knowledge and are hence incompatible with everything we know about language acquisition. Now, Hubert Haider (2000, 2010, 2020) argues with respect to psycholinguistics that a VO language like English has a structure that is basically the structure of OV languages like German with the head moved to an initial position. Haider (2010: 15) compares head-initial and head-final approaches:

(40)   a. $[[[h^0\ A_1]\ A_2]\ A_3]$
       b. $[A_3\ [A_2\ [A_1\ h^0]]]$

He argues that (40a), which is the mirror image of (40b), does not exist crosslinguistically. He argues that the argument structure in VO and OV languages is the same and that VO languages have the same order of arguments as the OV languages. He concludes on p. 28 that the clause structure involving an English three-place verb is as in (41):

(41) $[XP\ [h^0\ [YP\ [h^0\ ZP]]]]$

I argued instead in the previous chapters that the order in which the arguments are combined with their verbs is free. Hence we can combine the verb with A_3 first even if the verb is head-initial:

(42) $[[[h^0\ A_3]\ A_2]\ A_1]$

For English, we get a clause structure as in (43):

(43) $[XP\ [[h^0\ YP]\ ZP]]$

The difference between Haider's structure in (41) and (43) is that Haider assumes that there is head-movement in simple English SVO structures. The head starts out to the left of ZP where it selects the ZP to the right and then moves up to the top of YP. This is shown in the left figure in Figure 6.13.

Haider argues that the structures for English are determined by UG and that there would be too much structure with too many brackets if there were no head-movement to make the structure plausible from a processing perspective.

The question is: what is a psycholinguistically plausible story for the analysis of English sentences? We know for sure now that human language processing is incremental (Marslen-Wilson 1975, Tanenhaus et al. 1996, Sag & Wasow 2011, Wasow 2021). We use information from all available sources as soon as we have it: phonology, syntax, semantics, pragmatics, gestures, world knowledge. When we hear an NP, we entertain hypothesis about how the utterance may proceed. One possible continuation is as a sentence. So, we expect a VP following the NP as in Figure 6.14.[13] After hearing an NP, we expect a VP containing a verb somewhere, but the next upcoming word could be an adverb or two as in (44a):

---

[13]See also Jurafsky (1996) for an explanation of garden-path sentences using a probabilistic chart parser and a phrase structure grammar with feature–value pairs of the kind assumed in HPSG. Jurafsky has probabilities attached to phrase structure rules and to valence information. For the grammar developed here, valence frames play a crucial role in predicting forthcoming constituents.

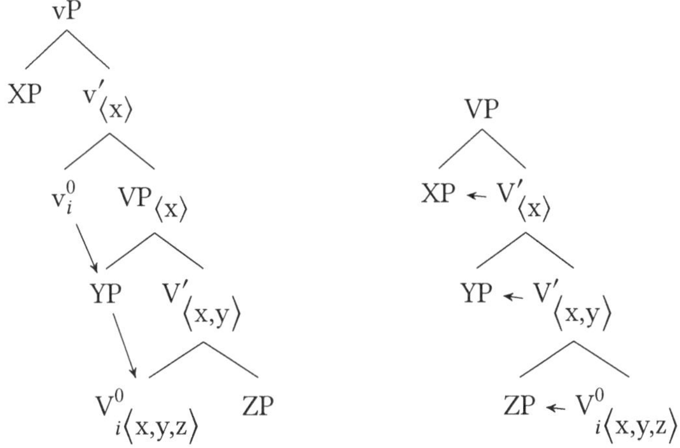

Figure 6.13: English vs. German according to Haider (2010: 29)

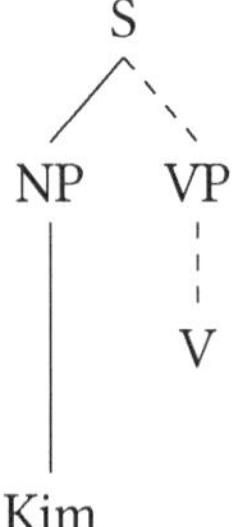

Figure 6.14: A VP is expected to follow the NP to form a sentence

(44)   a. their willingness [[usually [strongly [depends on this]]]][14]

        b. Kim [[promised and gave] Robin a book].

It could also be a verb being part of a coordination of two or more verbs. And combinations are possible of course. The fact that the structure is underdetermined is indicated by a dashed line. When we hear the next word, we can form a more concrete hypothesis though. In the case of a strictly transitive verb we could have it as part of a coordination or, more likely, as a part of a VP consisting of a verb and an NP. The next NP is predicted as in Figure 6.15. If we hear a ditransitive verb instead of a strictly transitive one, the structure in Figure 6.16

---

[14]ENCOW, doc#40288,www.psy.gla.ac.uk

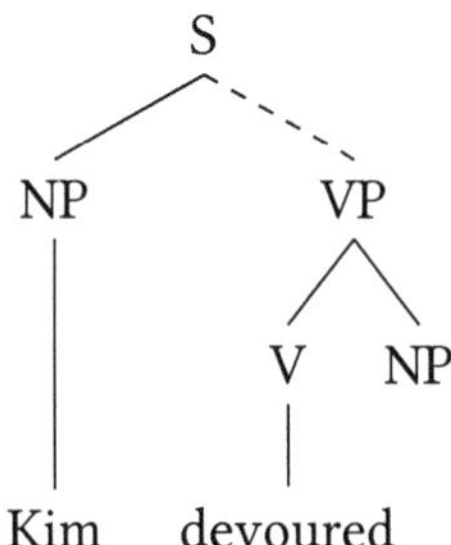

Figure 6.15: An NP is expected to follow the NP + verb to form a sentence with a strictly transitive verb

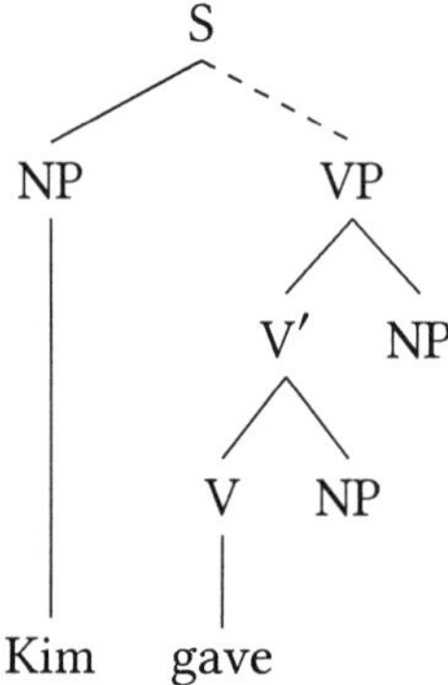

Figure 6.16: Two NPs are expected to follow the NP + verb to form a sentence with a ditransitive verb

is predicted instead.[15] The object NPs have to be filled in as in Figure 6.17, but further adjuncts may be added to the right of the VP. So there has to be room for this. All we know for sure until the end of the sentence is that the S node dominates a VP. There may be more than one VP node.

What all this shows us is that sentences may be internally complex and several adjuncts may be attached to a VP. Nevertheless the human sentence processor can cope with it and the standardly assumed nesting of adverbials and VPs. It follows that it is unnecessary to assume a complicated head-movement approach for English verbal projections.

---

[15]Note that from a psycholinguistic point of view there is no difference between this binary branching VP structure and a flat one. In a flat structure approach, one would assume that one started a VP and would check one daughter after another in a flat structure, while one has more elaborate structures in a binary branching approach checking the NP daughters in seperate subtrees one after the other.

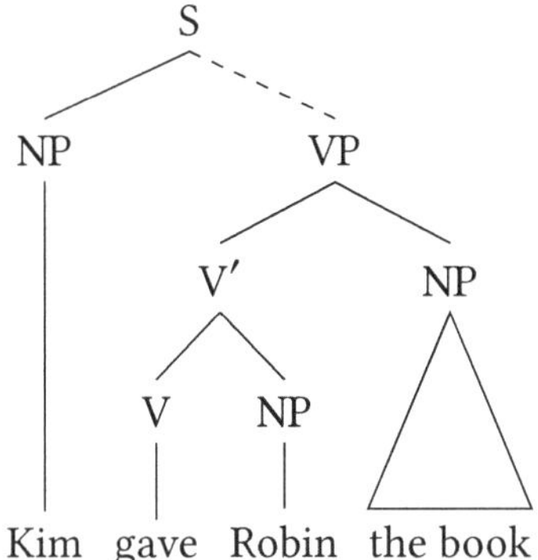

Figure 6.17: NP + ditransitive verb + two objects forms a sentence to which adjuncts can be added.

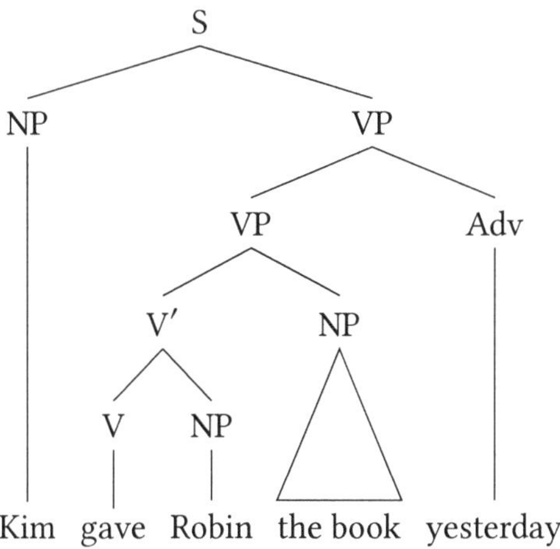

Figure 6.18: Sentence with VP adjunct to the right.

Shravan Vasishth reminds me the "absence of evidence is not evidence of absence". This means that the fact that we cannot find any psycholinguistic reflexes of the structures assumed by Haider does not mean that they are not there. This is true but I would like to argue that evidence of absence together with Occam's razor is an argument against certain structures: if a structure is complex and unnecessary and there is no psycholinguistic evidence *for* it, it should not be assumed.

6.3.3 Analyses of verb-initial sentences in SVO languages without verb-movement

I mentioned in Section 2.2 that English is a residual V2 language. *wh*-questions like the one in (21b) on p. 21, repeated here as (45) are similar in form to what we have seen for the other Germanic languages: a *wh* phrase is fronted and the subject is in the position to the right of the finite verb.

(45)   Which book did Sandy give to Kim?

Borsley (1989) developed a verb-movement account of English clause structure. Figure 6.19 shows the analysis in the notation adopted here.

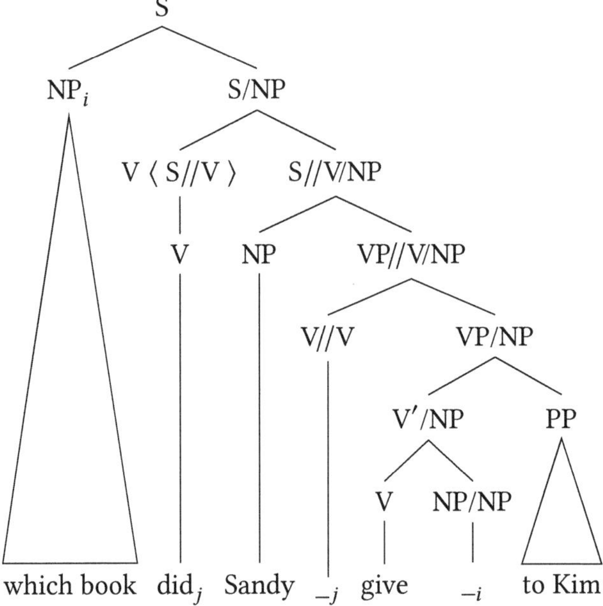

Figure 6.19: Analysis of *wh* interrogatives following Borsley (1989)

While this analysis is compatible with what is stated elsewhere in this book, it is not the analysis usually assumed in HPSG. The standard analysis goes back to Gazdar, Klein, Pullum & Sag (1985) and is taken up by several authors in various forms. The most recent analysis was developed by Ivan Sag and published posthumous as Sag et al. (2020). Sag suggests a flat analysis of English VPs. This means that the verb and all objects are daughters of the same mother. For cases of subject-verb inversion, there have been several suggestions. Figure 6.20 shows

a flat analysis of English verb-initial questions: both the subject and the VP complement are members of the COMPS list and can be combined with the verb in the
direction of complementes.

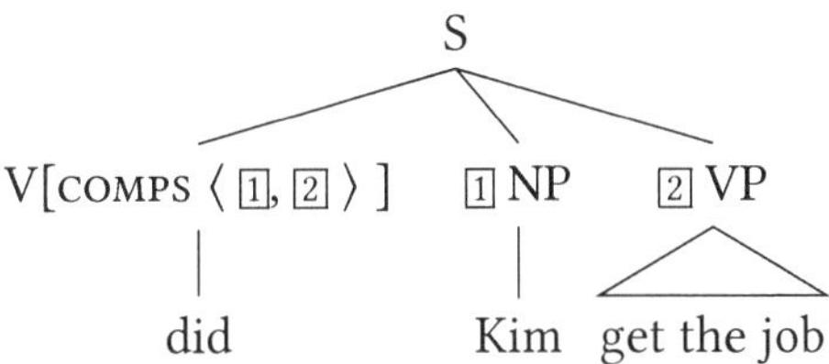

Figure 6.20: Analysis of English auxiliary constructions based on Sag et al. (2020:
117)

With such an approach verb movement is unneccessary. The advantage of
such flat approaches is that various specialized meanings of auxiliary inversion
constructions can be assigned to this configuration. For example, Sag et al. (2020:
116) posit a subtype *polar-int-cl* for polar interrogatives like (46a) and another
subtype *aux-initial-excl-cl* for exclamatives like (46b).

(46)   a. Are they crazy?

        b. Are they crazy!

In the approach developed here, the respective meaning has to be assigned to the
auxiliaries.

It is difficult to decide between the two approaches: on the one hand, the flat
analysis is simpler than the one involving verb-movment. Given that there is no
evidence for a rich Universal Grammar in the Chomskyan sense (Hauser et al.
2002), one can not assume that English has the same structure as the Germanic
V2 langauges, since we cannot rely on knowledge about these structures being
innate. Languages have to be analyzed with respect to data from the language
under consideration allone, since this is the data available to language learners.
From this prespective, the flat analysis wins. On the other hand one should aim
for analyses that are similar across languages. This would be an argument for
the verb-movement analysis. I argued in Müller (2015c) and in Müller (2023b)
that grammars should be written on the basis of data from the language under
consideration alone. If we have several options to analyze a certain phenomenon,
we can choose the analysis that works for several languages and hence capture
crosslinguistic generalizations. In the case of English auxiliary inversion there
seems to be a language internal advantage of the non-movement analysis. It re-

mains to be seen whether there is data that forces us to assume a verb-movement
analysis as it was the case with multiple fronting data for German (Müller 2005,
2023a).

6.3.4 CP/TP/VP

Section 4.10.1 was devoted to the CP/TP/VP analysis and scrambling. Here, I
discuss double particle verbs (Section 6.3.4.1) and landing sites for extraposition
(Section 6.3.4.2).

6.3.4.1 Double particle verbs

Figure 4.27 on p. 95 showed that the verb stem is assumed to move from V to T
to pick up an ending and check inflectional features there. Haider (1993: 63, 2010:
59–60) and Vikner (2001: Section 3.3) found an argument against such proposals:
German has certain verbs with two particles.[16] *vorankündigen* 'preannounce' is
an example. This particle verb consists of the combination of *an* 'on' and *kündigen* 'announce' with the additional addition of another prefix *vor* 'pre'. Example
(5) was already discussed on p. 138, but it is repeated here as (47) for convenience:

(47) dass sie es vor-an-kündigt
      that she it pre-on-announces
      'that she preannounces it'

Now, the interesting thing about these verbs is that they cannot be fronted. The
verb stem has to be adjacent to the particle:

(48) a. * Sie kündigt$_i$ es vor-an $_{\_i}$.
          she announces it pre-on

      b. * Sie an-kündigt$_i$ es vor $_{\_i}$.
          she on-announced it pre

      c. * Sie vor-an-kündigt$_i$ es $_{\_i}$.
          she pre-on-announces it

Haider pointed out that such verbs are predicted to not have finite forms under
approaches assuming that the verb stem moves from V to T to check agreement
features.

The TP-based analysis would have to assume that the verb stem *kündig-* moves
from V to T as in (49), but since this kind of movement is ruled out for double

---

[16]The observation that German has verbs that cannot take part in V2 sentences goes back to
Höhle (1991b).

particle verbs as (48) shows, finite forms of double particle verbs should not exist, not even in clause final position.

(49) dass sie es vor-an _$_i$ kündig$_i$ -t
      that she it pre-on   announce -s
      'that she preannounces it'

But as (47) shows, such sentences do exist. So, as Haider pointed out, a CP/VP model seems to be more appropriate. Verbs do not move to higher functional projections like T to check their agreement features. They just do it in the position they are in: in the V position. The assumption of a T projection for agreement is unnecessary, in fact, it is incompatible with the observable data.[17]

6.3.4.2 VPs as landing sites

Haider (2010: 62–64) examined PP/adverb placement data in relation to the V-to-T movement hypothesis. He noted that prepositional adverbials can be placed in between the verbs of a verbal complex only marginally and full PPs are ungrammatical. Both PPs and pronominal adverbs are completely unacceptable between auxiliaries and modals:

(50) a. ?/* dass er viel   gelernt *dafür* haben muss
            that he much learnt   it.for have   must
         'that he must have learnt much for it'

      b. * dass er viel   gelernt haben *dafür* muss
           that he much learnt   have   it.for must

      c. ?/* ohne   viel   gelernt *dafür* haben zu müssen
            without much learnt   it.for have   to must

      d. * ohne   viel   gelernt haben *dafür* zu müssen
           without much learnt   have   it.for to must

      e. * dass er viel   gelernt *für das Examen* hat
           that he much learnt   for the exam   has

      f. * ohne   viel   gelernt *für das Examen* zu haben
           without much learnt   for the exam   to have

      g. [$_{VP}$ Gelernt haben *dafür / für das Examen*] muss er viel.
            learnt   have   it.for   for the exam   must he much

---

[17] Vikner (2001) assumes a TP for all Germanic languages, even for OV languages. He assumes that there is no V-to-T movement in these languages. However, models that just do not assume this extra layer seem to be more appropriate.

However, as (50g) shows, VPs are a legitimate landing site for PP extraposition and for the extraposition of pronominal adverbs. *Gelernt haben* 'learnt have' forms the right sentence bracket and the PP material is placed in the *Nachfeld* of the fronted VP. Haider continues with the examples in (51):

(51) a. [$_{VP}$ Angefangen damit]$_i$ hat bloß einer $_{-i}$
    on.caught it.with has just one
   'Only one has started with it'

  b. * weil bloß einer an._$_{-i}$ damit fing$_i$
    because just one on   it.with caught

  c. weil bloß einer anfing damit
    because just one on.caught it.with

(51a) shows that *damit* can be placed to the right of a particle verb. If there is a VP embedded under a TP, one would expect this VP also to be a possible landing cite for extraposition as it is in (51a). One would expect that the *damit* can be placed next to the verbal particle *an* as in (51b), but if the pronominal adverb is extraposed, it has to go to the right of the verb as in (51c).[18] There may be ways to explain the problematic data away in a VP/TP system, but the most straightforward explanation is of course not to assume a TP in the first place. If there is a verb *anfing* as the head of the VP, it does not move to a higher head in verb-last sentences and hence, no material has to be blocked from intervening between VP and T.

---

[18]Note that the situation is not as simple as one might expect. Particles can be placed in the *Mittelfeld* in German. But these particle placements are different from movement of the verb to the right. Such movements have to be ruled out in any case.

Comprehension questions

1. How are clause types determined in the Germanic languages?

Exercises

1. Classify the Germanic languages according to their basic constituent order (SVO, SOV, VSO, ...) and V2 assuming that you know that one of the following patterns exists in the language:

   (52) a. NP[acc] V-Aux NP[nom] V NP[dat]
         b. NP[acc] V-Aux NP[nom] NP[dat] V
         c. NP[acc] NP[nom] V NP[acc]
         d. NP[acc] NP[nom] V-Aux V NP[acc]
         e. NP[acc] V-Aux NP[nom] V PP

   Every sentence should be paired with ±V2 and one of the six permutations of S, O, and V.

   If you cannot determine the order unambiguously, please say so. If you think that this pattern does not exist in any of the Germanic languages, say so. Please keep in mind that English is a so-called residual V2 language, which means that there are some traces of V2 left in the grammar. Think about question formation in English.

2. Sketch the analysis for the following examples. Use the abbreviations used in this chapter, that is, do not go into the details regarding SPR and COMPS values but use S, VP, and V′. Verb movement should be indicated with the '//' symbol.

(53)   a. Arbejder Bjarne ihærdigt på bogen?   (Danish)
            works   Bjarne seriously at book.DEF
            'Does Bjarne work seriously on the book?'

        b. Arbeitet Bjarne ernsthaft an dem Buch?   (German)
            works   Bjarne seriously at the book
            'Does Bjarne work seriously on the book?'

        c. Wird sie darüber   nachdenken?   (German)
            will   she there.upon PART.think
            'Will she think about this?'

3. Sketch the analysis for the following examples. Use the valence features SPR and COMPS rather than the abbreviations S, VP, and V′. Since the value of SPR in German is always the empty list, you may omit it in the German examples. NPs and PPs can be abbreviated as NP and PP, respectively. Verb movement should be indicated with the '//' symbol.

(54)   a. dass sie darüber   nachdenkt   (German)
            that she there.upon PART.thinks
            'that she thinks about this'

        b. dass sie darüber   nachdenken wird
            that she there.upon PART.think   will
            'that she will think about this'

        c. Wird sie darüber   nachdenken?
            will   she there.upon PART.think
            'Will she think about this?'

(55)   a. Arbejder Bjarne ihærdigt på bogen?   (Danish)
            works   Bjarne seriously at book.DEF
            'Does Bjarne work seriously on the book?'

        b. Arbeitet Bjarne ernsthaft an dem Buch?   (German)
             works   Bjarne seriously at the book
             'Does Bjarne work seriously on the book?'

4. Sketch the analysis of the following examples. NPs may be abbreviated. Valence features should not be given, but node labels like V, V′, VP and S should be used instead. If non-local dependencies are involved indicate them using the '/' symbol.

(56)   a. Such books, I like.

     b. Solche Bücher mag ich. (German)
       such   books like I
       'I like such books.'

     c. Bøger som det elsker jeg. (Danish)
       books like this like   I
       'I like such books.'

Further reading

The analysis of nonlocal dependencies was developed by Gazdar (1981). Sag (2010) deals with further constraints necessary in a theory of nonlocal dependencies in English and how they can be represented in HPSG. The HPSG Handbook also contains a chapter on constituent order and verb-movement (Müller 2021a) and on nonlocal dependencies (Borsley & Crysmann 2021). Müller (2023a) deals with German clause structure within HPSG and discusses various alternative approaches that could not be discussed here (Generalized Phrase Structure Grammar, Dependency Grammar, Construction Grammar, linearization-based HPSG approaches).

7 Passive

This chapter deals with the passive. The passive is usually analyzed as the suppression of the subject. However, before I can develop an analysis, I have to ask what it is that constitutes a subject. This is a question that is the topic of edited volumes and dissertations and modest as I am, I will try and provide an answer at least for the Germanic languages. As we will see, the situation is rather clear in languages like Danish, English, and German, but there are exciting facts to be discovered about Icelandic.

7.1 The phenomenon

7.1.1 Subjects and other subjects

The situation in languages like Danish, English, and German is rather clear. For instance, many authors assume that non-predicative NPs in the nominative are subjects in German. So, *der Delphin* 'the dolphin' is the subject of the sentences in (1):

(1) a. Der   Delphin lacht.   (German)
         the.NOM dolphin laughs

     b. Der   Delphin hilft   dem   Kind.
         the.NOM dolphin helps the.DAT child

     c. Der   Delphin gibt   ihr   einen Ball.
         the.NOM dolphin gives her.DAT a.ACC ball

The restriction to non-predicative NPs is needed since otherwise, we would have to assume that both NPs in (2) are subjects, but *ein Lügner* 'a liar' is a predicative phrase and only *der Mann* 'the man' is the subject.

(2) Der   Mann ist ein   Lügner.   (German)
     the.NOM man   is a.NOM liar

     'The man is a liar.'

In addition, certain clausal arguments are treated as subjects.

Genitives and datives as in (3) are not counted among the subjects in German.

(3) a. Ihrer   wurde gedacht.   (German)
         they.GEN AUX   remembered
         'They were remembered.'

     b. Ihm   wurde geholfen.
         he.DAT AUX   helped
         'He/she was helped.'

Interestingly the question whether genitives and datives like those in (3) are subjects was answered quite differently for the SVO language Icelandic by researchers following the work of Zaenen, Maling & Thráinsson (1985). Although the sentences in (4) look like those in (2), the genitive and the dative element in (4a) and (4b) are claimed to be subjects.

(4) a. Hennar   var saknað.   (Icelandic)
         she.SG.GEN was missed

     b. Þeim   var hjálpað.
         they.PL.DAT was helped

Since Icelandic is a V2 language, the constituent order in such simple sentences does not help us to determine whether *hennar* 'her' and *Þeim* 'them' are subjects or not. These elements are fronted and since both subjects and objects can be fronted, the sentences in (4) do not help us in determining the grammatical function of these arguments. However, Zaenen, Maling & Thráinsson (1985) argued that these elements should be analyzed as subjects and provided a test battery. Among the tests are more elaborate positional tests and omitability in so-called control constructions. I will turn to these tests now.

7.1.1.1 The position of subjects in V2 and V1 sentences

The first test that was suggested uses the position of constituents in V2 sentences in which a non-subject is fronted (Zaenen, Maling & Thráinsson 1985: Section 2.3). For instance, consider the following examples:

(5) a. Með þessari byssu   skaut Ólafur   refinn.   (Icelandic)
         with this   shotgun shot Olaf.NOM the.fox.ACC

     b. * Með þessari byssu   skaut refinn   Ólafur.
         with this   shotgun shot the.fox.ACC Olaf.NOM

The nominative can appear directly after the finite verb *skaut* 'shot' as in (5a) but it cannot appear to the right of the accusative as in (5b).

The second test uses *w*-questions and checks the position of the subject with respect to the object and to non-finite verbs:

(6) a. Hvenær hafði Sigga   hjálpað Haraldi?   (Icelandic)
       when   has   Sigga.NOM helped Harald.DAT

     b. * Hvenær hafði Haraldi   Sigga   hjálpað?
       when   has   Harald.DAT Sigga.NOM helped

The object has to follow the participle *hjálpað* as in (6a) and the subject immediately follows the finite verb. Examples with the object before the subject as in (6b) are ungrammatical. The dative object can be fronted, but then it has to be realized in initial position to the left of the finite verb, not to its right:

(7)   Haraldi   hafði Sigga   aldrei hjálpað.   (Icelandic)
       Harald.DAT has   Sigga.NOM never helped

The same situation can be found in yes/no questions:

(8) a. Hafði Sigga   aldrei hjálpað Haraldi?   (Icelandic)
       has   Sigga.NOM never helped Harald.DAT

     b. * Hafði Haraldi   Sigga   aldrei hjálpað?
       has   Harald.DAT Sigga.NOM never helped

Zaenen, Maling & Thráinsson (1985: Section 2.3) observed that certain datives can appear in this postverbal position as well:

(9) a. Hefur henni   alltaf   þótt   Ólafur   leiðinlegur?   (Icelandic)
       has   she.DAT always thought Olaf.NOM boring.NOM
       'Has she always considered Olaf boring?'

     b. Ólafur   hefur henni   alltaf   þótt   leiðinlegur.
       Olaf.NOM has   she.DAT always thought boring.NOM
       'She always considered Olaf boring.'

     c. * Hefur Ólafur   henni   alltaf   þótt   leiðinlegur?
       has   Olaf.NOM her.DAT always thought boring.NOM

The German equivalent would be the sentence in (10):

(10)   ?? Mich dünkt der   Film   langweilig.   (German)
       I.ACC thinks the.NOM movie boring
       'I think the movie is boring.'

However, *dünkt* is archaic and is usually used with a *dass* 'that' clause – if it is used at all. But there is a non-archaic verb that has a similar form:

(11) Mir   scheint der   Mann langweilig.   (German)
      I.DAT seems the.NOM man   boring

      'The man seems boring to me.'

The experiencer of *scheinen* 'to seem' is expressed with the dative, while the subject of the embedded predicate *langweilig* 'boring' is in the nominative.

7.1.1.2 Subjects in control constructions

Zaenen, Maling & Thráinsson (1985: Section 2.7) discuss control structures in which the subject of the embedded verb is not expressed. (12a) shows an example of normal control in which the subject of the matrix verb *vonast* 'to hope' refers to the same discourse referent as the subject of the embedded verb *fara* 'to go'. (12b) is an example of so-called arbitrary control. In cases of arbitrary control there is no element depending on the head that governs the infinitive that refers to the same discourse referent as the subject of the infinitive. The unexpressed subject corresponds to a pronoun *one* that is used generically. In example (22b) *óvenjulegt* 'unusual' does not select for an argument that refers to the same referent as the subject of *fara* 'to go'. The subject of *að fara heim snemma* 'to go home early' is not expressed but is understood as the indefinite pronoun *one*.

(12) a. Ég vonast til að fara heim.   (Icelandic)
         I hope for to go   home

         'I hope to go home.'

      b. Að fara heim snemma er óvenjulegt.
         to go   home early   is unusual

         'It is unusual to go home early.'

Now, it can be observed that Icelandic allows verbs that do not take a nominative in such control constructions. An example is *vantar* ('lacks'), which takes two accusatives rather than a nominative and an accusative:

(13) Mig   vantar peninga.   (Icelandic)
      I.ACC lack   money.ACC

(14) shows that this verb can be embedded under *vonast* ('to hope'):

(14) Ég vonast til að vanta ekki peninga.   (Icelandic)
      I hope for to lack   not money.ACC

      'I hope that I do not lack money.'

This should be compared with German:

(15)   a. Mir fehlt kein   Geld.   (German)
          I.DAT lacks no.a.NOM money
          'I do not lack money.'

       b. * Ich hoffe, kein   Geld   zu fehlen.
          I   hope not.a.NOM money to lack
          Intended: 'I hope that I do not lack money.'

The question at the beginning of this section was whether the datives and genitives in sentences like (4), repeated here as (16), are subjects or not.

(16)   a. Hennar var saknað.   (Icelandic)
          she.GEN was missed
          'She was missed.'

       b. Þeim   var hjálpað.
          they.DAT was helped
          'They were helped.'

We are now able to use the tests to answer this question: the dative is right-adjacent to the finite verb in the question in (17) and, thus, in subject position.

(17)   a. Var hennar saknað?   (Icelandic)
          was she.GEN missed
          'Was she missed?'

       b. Var þeim   hjálpað?
          was they.DAT helped
          'Were they helped?'

Similarly, the dative follows the finite verb in the V2 sentence in (18):

(18) Í prófinu   var honum vist   hjálpað.   (Icelandic)
     in the.exam was he.DAT apparently helped
     'Apparently he was helped in the exam.'

In addition, these datives can be omitted in control constructions as the examples in (19) show:

(19)   a. Ég vonast til að verða hjálpað.   (Icelandic)
          I hope for to be   helped

       b. Að vera hjálpað i   prófinu   er óleyfilegt.
          to be   helped in the.exam is un.allowed
          'It is not allowed to be helped in the exam.'

This should be compared to German: while verbs like *unterstützen* 'to support' that govern a nominative and an accusative can appear in such control constructions, verbs like *helfen* 'to help' that take a nominative and a dative are ruled out in this construction:

(20) a. dass jemand   ihm   hilft   (German)
           that somebody him.DAT helps

      b. dass jemand   ihn   unterstützt
           that somebody him.ACC supports

      c. dass ihm   geholfen wird
           that him.DAT helped   AUX

      d. dass er   unterstützt wird
           that he.NOM supported AUX

(21) a.   Ich hoffe unterstützt zu werden.   (German)
           I   hope supported to AUX

      b. * Ich hoffe geholfen zu werden.
           I   hope helped   to AUX

The dative object cannot be omitted in such control constructions, as (21b) shows. The only way to realize a passive below *hoffen* 'to hope' in an infinitival clause is to use the dative passive with *erhalten/bekommen/kriegen*. The dative passive can turn a dative object into a nominative subject:[1]

(22)   Aicke   bekommt geholfen.   (German)
       Aicke.NOM AUX   helped

       'Aicke gets helped.'

Since the object of *helfen* is then nominative and, hence, undoubtedly a subject in German, it does not come as a surprise that it can be omitted in control constructions like (23):

(23)   Ich hoffe hier geholfen zu bekommen.[2]   (German)
       I   hope here helped   to AUX

       'I hope to get help here.'

---

[1]Not all speakers accept such sentences. We will return to them below when discussing the examples (57) and (58).

[2]http://www.photovoltaikforum.com/sds-allgemein-ueber-solar-log-f38/solarlog-1000-mit-wifi-anschliesen-t96371.html. 10.01.2014

7.1.2 Comparison between German, Danish, English, Icelandic

In the following subsections, I will compare several dimensions in which the Germanic languages vary:

- Danish and Icelandic have a morphological passive; English and German do not.

- German and Icelandic allow for subjectless constructions; Danish and English do not.

- Danish, German, and Icelandic allow for impersonal passives; English does not.

- Danish and Icelandic allow both objects to be promoted to subject; English and German do not.

- German has the remote passive, Danish the complex passive and Danish and English have the reportive passive.

7.1.2.1 Morphological and analytic forms

Danish has a morphological passive. It is formed by appending the suffix *-s* to the verb, and there are forms for the present tense (24b) and the past tense (24c):

(24) a. Peter læser avisen.   (Danish)
           Peter reads newspaper.DEF
           'Peter is reading the newspaper.'

      b. Avisen   læses   af Peter.
           newspaper.DEF read.PRES.PASS by Peter
           'The newspaper is read by Peter.'

      c. Avisen   læstes   af Peter.
           newspaper.DEF read.PAST.PASS by Peter
           'The newspaper was read by Peter.'

As the examples in (25) shows, the *af* phrase is not necessary:

(25) a. Avisen   læses hver dag.   (Danish)
           newspaper.DEF reads every day
           'The newspaper is read every day.'

b. Avisen   læstes hver dag.   (Danish)
   newspaper.DEF read   every day
   'The newspaper was read every day.'

Danish also has an analytic form with *blive* 'be' plus past participle:

(26) Avisen   bliver læst af Peter.   (Danish)
      newspaper.DEF is   read by Peter
      'The newspaper is read by Peter.'

The morphological passive may also apply to infinitives:

(27) Avisen   skal læses   hver dag.   (Danish)
      newspaper.def must read.INF.PASS every day
      'The newspaper must be read every day.'

English and German only have the analytic variant:

(28) a. The paper was read.
      b. Der   Aufsatz wurde gelesen.   (German)
          the.NOM paper   AUX   read

7.1.2.2 Personal and impersonal passive

All languages under consideration allow for the promotion of an accusative object to subject, an example of which is given in (29).

(29) a. Angehörige   haben den   Verdächtigen zuletzt am   (German)
          relatives.NOM have   the.ACC suspect   lastly at.the
          Montag gesehen.
          Monday seen
          'Relatives have seen the suspect for the last time on Monday.'
      b. Der   Verdächtige wurde zuletzt am   Montag gesehen.
          the.NOM suspect   AUX   lastly at.the Monday seen
          'The suspect was seen for the last time on Monday.'

As the following examples show, the subject can be an S or a VP:

(30) a. At regeringen   træder tilbage, bliver påstået.   (Danish)
          that government.DEF resigns PART   is   claimed
          'It is claimed that the government resigns.'

   b. At reparere bilen,   bliver forsøgt.
      to repair   car.DEF is   tried
      'It is tried to repair the car.'

In addition to such personal passives, Danish, German, and Icelandic have impersonal passives.[3] Since German does not require a subject, impersonal passives like (31) are expected:

(31) weil   noch getanzt wurde   (German)
      because still danced AUX

      'because there was still dancing there'

The following two examples from Icelandic show that Icelandic also has impersonal constructions (Thráinsson 2007: 264):

(32) a. Oft   var talað um   þennan mann.   (Icelandic)
         often was talked about this   Mann.ACC.SG.M

      b. Aldrei hefur verið sofið í þessu rúmi.
         never has   been slept in this   bed.DAT
         'This bed has never been slept in.'

Danish also allows for impersonal passives, but it differs from the languages discussed so far in that it requires an expletive subject:

(33) a. at   der   bliver danset   (Danish)
         that EXPL is   danced

         'that there is dancing'

---

[3]The labels "personal" and "impersonal passive" are misnomers, since both passives share the property of demoting the subject. So-called personal passives can have animate subjects or inanimate subjects:

  (i) Der   Diamant wurde zuletzt am   Montag gesehen.   (German)
      the.NOM diamond AUX   lastly at.the Monday seen
      'The diamond was seen for the last time on Monday.'

The big German grammar of the Institut für Deutsche Sprache tried to establish the new terms *Zweitakt-Passiv* 'two-phase passive' and *Eintakt-Passiv* 'one-phase passive' (Zifonun 1997: 1793). The first phase being the suppression of the subject and the second phase the promotion of the accusative object to subject for those verbs that govern an accusative. While these terms are more appropriate in principle, I will not use them here since the analysis suggested in what follows deals with both passives in a unified way: it just suppresses the subject. Personal and impersonal passives are analyzed the same way. The difference is due to differences in case assignment. Due to the lack of better terms, I continue to use the terms personal and impersonal passive.

b. at der danses
   that EXPL dance.PRES.PASS
   'that there is dancing'

c. *Bliver danset?
    is   danced

d. *Danses?
    dance.PASS

Thus, Danish is like English in always requiring a subject, but, while this constraint results in the impossibility of impersonal passives in English, Danish found a solution to the subject problem by inserting an expletive.

Expletives are excluded in German impersonal constructions:

(34) *weil   es noch gearbeitet wurde   (German)
       because it still worked   AUX

      Intended: 'because there was still working there'

7.1.2.3 Promotion of the primary and secondary object

English and German allow the promotion of one of the objects of a ditransitive verb only. (35) shows that the accusative object can be realized as subject, but the dative object cannot:

(35) a. weil   der   Mann dem   Jungen den   Ball   (German)
          because the.NOM man   the.DAT boy   the.ACC ball
          schenkt
          gives
          'because the man gives the boy a ball as a present'

      b. weil   dem   Jungen der   Ball geschenkt wurde
          because the.DAT boy   the.NOM ball given   AUX
          'because the ball was given to the boy'

      c. *weil   der   Junge den   Ball geschenkt wurde
          because the.NOM boy   the.ACC ball given   AUX

Similarly, English can realize the first object as subject, but the second object cannot be promoted to subject:

(36) a. because the man gave the child the ball

      b. because the child was given the ball

      c. *because the ball was given the child

The information structural effect can be reached with a different lexical variant of *give* though. *give* can be used with an NP object and a *to* PP instead of two NPs as in (37a). The first object of the ditransitive *give* is realized as PP in (37a) and the second object *the ball* is the first object in (37a). This alternation is also called dative-shift.

(37) a. because the man gave the ball to the child

  b. because the ball was given to the child

(37b) is the passive variant of (37a). As in (36b), the primary object is promoted to subject.

Danish and Icelandic differ from English and German. In the former languages, both objects can be promoted to subject without any previous alternation of valence frames like dative shift.

(38) a. fordi   manden giver barnet   bolden   (Danish)
    because man.DEF gives child.DEF ball.DEF

    'because the man gives the child the ball'

  b. fordi   barnet   bliver givet bolden
    because child.DEF is   given ball.DEF

    'because the child is given the ball'

  c. fordi   bolden bliver givet barnet
    because ball.DEF is   given child.DEF

    'because the ball is given to the child'

One could assume that it is always the first object (the primary object) that is promoted to subject and that Danish does not have an order of the objects, so that both objects are equally prominent and can be promoted to subject. Moro is a language that is said to have such properties (Ackerman et al. 2017). However, Danish differs from Moro in that the order of the objects in sentences is clearly fixed: while (38a) is possible, the reverse order of the objects is ungrammatical, as (39) shows.

(39) * fordi   manden giver bolden barnet
    because man.DEF gives ball.DEF child.DEF

As far as Icelandic is concerned, Zaenen, Maling & Thráinsson (1985: 460) note that, apart from the possibility to promote the accusative to nominative subject, the dative can become a quirky subject:

(40) Konunginum voru gefnar   ambáttir.   (Icelandic)
    the.king.DAT were given.F.PL maidservants.NOM.F.PL

    'The king was given female slaves.'

The structure of (40) is sketched in (41):

(41) [S$_i$ Aux $_{-i}$ V O]

Since the nominative is serialized after the participle, it cannot be the subject, which implies that the fronted dative element is the subject.

Alternatively, the accusative object is promoted to nominative subject:

(42) Ambáttin   var gefin   konunginum.   (Icelandic)
      the.maidservant.NOM.SG AUX given.F.SG the.king.DAT
      'The female slave was given to the king.'

This sentence, too, has the structure in (41).

In order to show that the dative is really promoted to subject in (40) and that the accusative is promoted to subject in (42), Zaenen, Maling & Thráinsson (1985: 460) apply a battery of tests. I only give the V2 examples with an adjunct in initial position, the questions, and the control structures here. The examples in (43) and (44) show that the sentences above really have the structure in (41). The first position in (43) is filled by an adjunct, which entails that the subject remains in subject position and hence shows that the dative *konunginum* 'the king' is the subject. Similarly, the nominative *ambáttin* 'the female slave' is the subject in (43b).

(43) a. Um veturinn   voru konunginum gefnar ambáttir.   (Icelandic)
         in   the.winter AUX the.king.DAT given slaves.NOM
         'In the winter, the king was given (female) slaves.'

      b. Um veturinn   var ambáttin   gefin konunginum.
         in   the.winter AUX the.slave.NOM given the.king.NOM
         'In the winter, the slave was given to the king.'

The questions in (44) are further evidence. The initial position is not filled, and the dative in (44a) and the nominative in (44b) are realized immediately following the finite verb.

(44) a. Voru konunginum gefnar ambáttir?   (Icelandic)
         AUX the.king.DAT given slaves.NOM
         'Was the king given slaves?'

      b. Var ambáttin   gefin konunginum?
         AUX the.slave.NOM given the.king.DAT
         'Was the slave given to the king?'

(45) shows the corresponding control examples:

(45)   a. Að vera gefnar ambáttir   var mikill heiður.   (Icelandic)
          to AUX given slaves.NOM was great honor
          'To be given slaves was a great honor.'

       b. Að vera gefin konunginum olli   miklum vonbrigðum.
          to AUX given the.king.DAT caused great   disappointment
          'To be given to the king caused great disappointment.'

In (45a) the dative is not expressed and in (45b) the nominative is omitted. This
shows that both the primary and the secondary object can be promoted to subject
in Icelandic, even though the primary object is in the dative and the case of the
NP does not change to nominative in passive examples.

7.2 The analysis

7.2.1 Structural and lexical case and the Case Principle

For the analysis of the passive, it is useful to distinguish between structural and
lexical case. Structural case is case that depends on the syntactic structure in
which arguments get realized, while lexical case is case that stays constant independent of the syntactic environment. In addition to lexical and structural case,
there is semantic case. This case is not assigned by a governing head like a verb,
adjective, or preposition but is due to a certain function of an adverbial. For instance, time expressions like *den ganzen Tag* 'the whole day' in (46) are in the
accusative in German.

(46)   Er   arbeitet den   ganzen Tag.   (German)
       he.NOM works   the.ACC whole day
       'He works the whole day.'

Since this chapter is about the passive and its variation in the Germanic languages, I will ignore semantic case here.

7.2.1.1 Nominatives and accusative objects

Up to now, the case that an argument gets assigned by its head has been represented in the valence list of the head. With such a representation, we would
need two different lexical items for the verb *lesen* 'to read': one in which the verb
takes a nominative and an accusative as in (47c), and one in which it takes two

accusatives as in (47d). (47c) would be used in the analysis of (47a), and (47d) in the analysis of (47b).

(47) a. Er   wird das   Buch lesen.   (German)
         he.NOM will   the.ACC book read
         'He will read the book.'

      b. Ich sah ihn das Buch lesen.
         I   saw him the book read
         'I saw him read the book.'

      c. ⟨ NP[*nom*], NP[*acc*] ⟩

      d. ⟨ NP[*acc*], NP[*acc*] ⟩

Rather than having two distinct, yet homophonous forms in the lexicon, one can propose just one lexical item and leave the actual case assignment to be resolved later when the syntactic context provides sufficient information. So, depending on whether the subject of *lesen* is realized as the subject of *wird* 'will' or as the object of *sah* 'saw', it gets nominative or accusative. Such cases are called structural cases. The distinction between structural and lexical case will play an important role in the analysis of the passive. It is this distinction that makes a unified analysis of the personal and impersonal passive possible.

(48) provides additional examples and involves different forms of the verb (finite vs. non-finite) and a nominalization:

(48) a. Der   Installateur kommt.
         the.NOM plumber   comes
         'The plumber comes.'

      b. Der Mann lässt den   Installateur kommen.
         the man   lets the.ACC plumber   come
         'The man lets the plumber come.'

      c. das Kommen des   Installateurs
         the coming   of.the.GEN plumber
         'the coming of the plumber'

The example in (48c) also shows that the subject of *kommen* 'to come' can be realized as genitive. Thus, nominative, genitive, and accusative are structural cases in German. (The question whether some or all datives should be treated as structural case is addressed below in Section 7.2.1.3).

The examples in (48) show that the case of subjects in German can change, those in (49) show that the case of accusative objects can change as well:

(49) a. Judit schlägt den   Weltmeister.
          Judit defeats the.ACC world.champion
          'Judit defeats the world champion.'

      b. Der   Weltmeister   wird geschlagen.
          the.NOM world.champion AUX beaten
          'The world champion is beaten.'

7.2.1.2 Genitive objects

The examples in (50) show instances of lexical case: genitive that depends on the verb is lexical since it does not change when the verb is passivized.

(50) a. Wir   gedenken der Opfer.
          we.NOM remember the victims.GEN
          'We remember the victims.'

      b. Der   Opfer wird gedacht.
          the.GEN victims AUX remembered
          'The victims are remembered.'

      c. * Die   Opfer wird   / werden gedacht.
          the.NOM victims AUX.3SG   AUX.3PL remembered

As the example in (50c) shows, the nominative is impossible. The genitive object remains in the genitive in passive constructions. As was explained in Section 7.1.2.2, passives without a subject as in (50b) are traditionally called "impersonal passives".

7.2.1.3 Dative objects

Let us now turn to the dative. If we consider examples like (51), we see that the dative does not change either in the passive:

(51) a. Der   Mann hat ihm   geholfen.
          theNOM man   has him.DAT helped
          'The man helped him.'

      b. Ihm   wird geholfen.
          him.DAT AUX helped
          'He is helped.'

So in analogy to the genitive examples above, the dative should be a lexical case.

But there are examples like those in (52) and, according to the view that structural cases are those cases that vary according to the syntactic environment, the dative should be a structural case.

(52) a. Der Mann hat den Ball dem Jungen geschenkt.
          the man   has the ball the boy   given
          'The man gave the boy the ball as a present.'

      b. Der Junge bekam den Ball geschenkt.
          the boy   got   the ball given
          'The boy got the ball as a present.'

The question whether the dative should be seen as a structural or a lexical case is a hotly debated one. In principle, there are three possibilities and all three of them have been suggested in the literature. One could assume that all datives are lexical (Haider 1985, 1986a: 9, Heinz & Matiasek 1994: 207, 217, 228, Müller 1999, 2001, 2003b: 289, Scherpenisse 1986: 97, Pollard 1994: 277, 291, Meurers 1999, Vogel & Steinbach 1998, Abraham 1995, McIntyre 2006: 187, Woolford 2006), that some are lexical and others are structural (Wegener 1985a, 1991, den Besten 1985b: 26, 1985a: page 55–56, Fanselow 1987: 161, 2000: 178, 205, 2003a: 181, 182, 206, Czepluch 1988: 286–287, Sternefeld 1995: 77, 80, von Stechow 1996: 102–103, Wunderlich 1997: 48, 51, Molnárfi 1998: 553), or that all datives are structural (Sternefeld 1995: 80, Ryu 1997: 203, 205–206, Gunkel 2003: 96–97).

I follow Haider (1986a) and treat all datives as lexical cases. Under this assumption, the contrast in Haider's examples (1986a: 20) in (53) is explained immediately:

(53) a. Er   streichelt den   Hund.
          he.NOM strokes   the.ACC dog

      b. Der   Hund wurde gestreichelt.
          the.NOM dog   AUX   stroked

      c. sein Streicheln des   Hundes
          his stroking   of.the.GEN dog

      d. Er hilft den   Kindern.
          he helps the.DAT children

      e. Den   Kindern wurde geholfen.
          the.DAT children AUX   helped

      f. das Helfen der   Kinder
          the helping of.the.GEN children

   g. * sein Helfen der Kinder
        his   helping the children

The accusative object of *streicheln* 'to stroke' can be realized as nominative in the passive, so it is clearly a structural case. Nominalizations allow this object to be realized in the genitive as (53c) shows. However, this does not work with datives. The dative object of *helfen* 'to help' cannot be realized in the genitive. (53f) is possible, but only with a reading in which the children are the agents, that is, the nominalization in (53f) corresponds to (54) rather than (53d):

(54)   Die   Kinder   helfen jemandem.
       the.NOM children help   somebody.DAT

If the agent is expressed by a prenominal possessive as in (53g) the genitive or dative *der Kinder* is ruled out.

   The only way to express the dative at all is prenominally:

(55)   das Den-Kindern-Helfen
       the the-children-helping
       'the children's helping'

Thus, authors who assume that all datives are structural have a problem explaining the differences in impersonal passives and nominalizations.[4] In addition, there is a problem with bivalent verbs. While some verbs take the dative, others take the accusative, though there is hardly any semantic difference or any other reason that could be made responsible.

(56)   a. Er hilft ihm.
          he helps him

---

[4] This problem can be solved by assuming more fine-grained distinctions among the structural cases (Gunkel 2003: 96) and/or additional features singling out accusative objects (Ryu 1997: 208). Gunkel's approach is equivalent to saying that primary objects must be nominative or dative and secondary objects must be nominative or accusative. For case assignment in verbal environments, he states that objects must be non-nominative (p. 112). However, he does not include the genitives in nominalizations. If this were included, the secondary object would be compatible to nominative, genitive, and accusative. Demanding non-nominative for objects would not be sufficient, since this would leave the option of realizing secondary objects as genitives in verbal environments, which is ungrammatical. Gunkel would have to state that objects have to be in the dative or accusative, which would result in a rather complex and unattractive account restating the facts at various places in the grammar. Ryu assumes features for singling out the subject and the secondary object and because of this he can distinguish between primary and secondary object in the principle responsible for case assignment (pp. 205–206). For detailed criticism of Ryu (1997) and Gunkel (2003) see Müller (2003b: Section 3.4) and Müller (2013b: Chapter 14.3.1), respectively.

    b. Er unterstützt ihn.
       he supports   him

The fact that *helfen* takes a dative object while *unterstützen* 'to support' takes an accusative is just an idiosyncrasy of German that speakers of German have to learn when they acquire the language. Thus, the information in the lexical entry for *helfen* 'to help' must be different from the one for *unterstützen*. Some authors acknowledge this difference and assume that the dative of bivalent verbs is lexical, while the dative of ditransitive verbs is structural (Wunderlich 1997: 48, 51). The assumption is that verbs assign the nominative to their first argument, the accusative to their last argument and if there is an additional argument that is neither the first nor the last, it gets dative. The prediction that such mixed accounts make is that the dative passive should be possible with ditransitive verbs but impossible with bivalent verbs, since the dative is structural for the former verbs and lexical for the latter. The empirical situation is not as clear-cut as one might wish. Some authors accept examples like (57); others reject them.

(57)   a. Er kriegte von vielen geholfen / gratuliert   / applaudiert.
          he got   by   many helped   congratulated applauded

    b. Man kriegt täglich gedankt.
       one gets daily   thanked

However, there are attested examples:[5]

(58)   a. „Da kriege ich geholfen."[6]
           there get I helped
        'Somebody helps me there.'

    b. Heute morgen bekam ich sogar schon gratuliert.[7]
       today morning AUX   I   even already congratulated
       'Somebody even wished me a happy birthday this morning already.'

    c. „Klärle" hätte es wirklich mehr als   verdient, auch mal zu einem
       Klärle had it really   more than deserved also once to a
       „unrunden" Geburtstag gratuliert   zu bekommen.[8]
       insignificant birthday   congratulated to AUX
       'Klärle would have more than deserved to be wished a happy
       birthday, even an insignificant birthday.'

---

[5]These examples were first discussed in Müller (2002: 134–135) and Müller (2007a: 293).

[6]Frankfurter Rundschau, 26.06.1998, p. 7.

[7]Brief von Irene G. an Ernst G. vom 10.04.1943, Feldpost-Archive mkb-fp-0270.

[8]Mannheimer Morgen, 28.07.1999, Lokales; „Klärle" feiert heute Geburtstag.

   d. Mit dem alten Titel von Elvis Presley „I can't help falling in love"
       with the old   song by Elvis Presley I can't help falling in love
       bekam Kassier Markus Reiß zum   Geburtstag gratuliert,   [...][9]
       got   cashier Markus Reiß to.the birthday   congratulated
       'The cashier Markus Reiß was wished a happy birthday with the old
       Elvis Presley song "I can't help falling in love with you".'

It appears that the verbs *kriegen, erhalten,* and *bekommen* are on the way to become auxiliaries. Their meaning is getting more and more bleached. Hence, there are almost no selectional restrictions left on the downstairs verb. The only requirement for the dative passive to apply is of course that the embedded verb governs a dative.

Now, if the dative passive is possible with bivalent verbs like *helfen* and if *helfen* has to govern a lexical dative (since otherwise the difference between *helfen* and *unterstützen* could not be explained)[10], it follows that the dative passive must be able to convert a lexical dative into a structural case (realized as nominative in the examples above). This means that one could assume that all datives are lexical, even the datives of ditransitive verbs. This explains why these datives are not realized as nominatives or accusatives in passives like (59):

(59)   a.   dass er   dem   Jungen den   Ball gegeben hat
           that he.NOM the.DAT boy   the.ACC ball given   has

       b.   dass dem   Jungen der   Ball gegeben wurde
           that the.DAT boy   the.NOM ball given   AUX

       c.   * dass der   Junge den   Ball gegeben wurde
           that the.NOM boy   the.ACC ball given   AUX

       d.   * dass den   Junge der   Ball gegeben wurde
           that the.ACC boy   the.NOM ball given   AUX

They simply remain in the dative. The only exception is the dative passive, and this has to be regarded as an exception.

After this discussion of lexical and structural case in German, let us now move on to the Case Principle, which is responsible for case assignment. As was explained in Section 4.9, it is assumed that all arguments of a head are represented in one list: the ARGUMENT STRUCTURE list (ARG-ST list). (60) shows the argument structure list of a ditransitive verb like *geben* 'to give':

---

[9]Mannheimer Morgen, 21.04.1999, Lokales; Motor des gesellschaftlichen Lebens.

[10]But see footnote 4. Additional features could be assumed or subtypes of structural case.

(60) $\langle$ NP[*str*], NP[*ldat*], NP[*str*] $\rangle$

As was argued above, dative is treated as a lexical case. *ldat* is an abbreviation for lexical dative and *str* stands for for structural case. The Case Principle has the following form (adapted from Przepiórkowski 1999; Meurers 1999):

Principle 1 (Case Principle)
- In a list that contains both the subject and the complements of a verbal head, the first element with structural case gets nominative unless it is raised by a higher head.

- All other elements in this list that have structural case and are not raised get accusative.

- In nominal environments elements with structural case get genitive.

This principle is inspired by Yip, Maling & Jackendoff (1987) and, as will be demonstrated below, it works for all of the languages analyzed here, in particular, for the complex case system of Icelandic. The case system assumed here differs in not assigning case to elements that are raised to a higher predicate. This point will be explained in more detail below.

The effect of this principle will be explained with respect to the verbs in (61):

(61) a. *schläft* 'sleep':   ARG-ST $\langle$ NP[*str*]$_i$ $\rangle$

     b. *unterstützt* 'support':   ARG-ST $\langle$ NP[*str*]$_i$, NP[*str*]$_j$ $\rangle$

     c. *hilft* 'help':   ARG-ST $\langle$ NP[*str*]$_i$, NP[*ldat*]$_j$ $\rangle$

     d. *schenkt* 'give as a present': ARG-ST $\langle$ NP[*str*]$_i$, NP[*ldat*]$_j$, NP[*str*]$_k$ $\rangle$

The first element in these lists that has structural case gets nominative and the second one accusative. This is exactly what one expects. The result is given in (62). *snom* stands for structural nominative, and *sacc* for structural accusative.

(62) a. *schläft* 'sleep':   ARG-ST $\langle$ NP[*snom*]$_i$ $\rangle$

     b. *unterstützt* 'support':   ARG-ST $\langle$ NP[*snom*]$_i$, NP[*sacc*]$_j$ $\rangle$

     c. *hilft* 'help':   ARG-ST $\langle$ NP[*snom*]$_i$, NP[*ldat*]$_j$ $\rangle$

     d. *schenkt* 'give as a present': ARG-ST $\langle$ NP[*snom*]$_i$, NP[*ldat*]$_j$, NP[*sacc*]$_k$ $\rangle$

7.2.2 Argument reduction and case assignment: The passive

Given the distinction between structural and lexical case, the analysis of the passive is really simple and directly corresponds to the intuition that the passive is the suppression of the subject (the most prominent, that is, the first argument in the ARG-ST list).[11] If the first argument is removed from the lists in (61), the following lists result:

(63) a. *geschlafen*: ARG-ST $\langle\,\rangle$

   b. *unterstützt*: ARG-ST $\langle$ NP[*str*]$_j$ $\rangle$

   c. *geholfen*: ARG-ST $\langle$ NP[*ldat*]$_j$ $\rangle$

   d. *geschenkt*: ARG-ST $\langle$ NP[*ldat*]$_j$, NP[*str*]$_k$ $\rangle$

The NPs that are in the first position in (63) where in the second position in (62). The first NP with structural case gets nominative and hence the following case assignments result:

(64) a. *geschlafen*: ARG-ST $\langle\,\rangle$

   b. *unterstützt*: ARG-ST $\langle$ NP[*snom*]$_j$ $\rangle$

   c. *geholfen*: ARG-ST $\langle$ NP[*ldat*]$_j$ $\rangle$

   d. *geschenkt*: ARG-ST $\langle$ NP[*ldat*]$_j$, NP[*snom*]$_k$ $\rangle$

As lexical case as in (64c–d) is not affected by the case principle, it stays the way it was specified, namely dative.

It should be noted here that this simple approach to the passive accounts both for the so-called personal and the impersonal passive. The passives of *schlafen* 'to sleep' and *helfen* 'to help' are called impersonal passives, as the respective clauses do not have a subject.

(65) a. dass geschlafen wurde
      that slept   AUX
      'that there was sleeping there'

   b. dass dem   Mann geholfen wurde
      that the.DAT man   helped   AUX
      'that the man was helped'

The passives of *unterstützen* 'to support' and *schenken* 'to give as a present' do have subjects, namely the arguments that are realized as accusative objects in the active:

---

[11]Some authors assume a demotion of the subject, that is, the subject is turned into a complement *by*-PP or a *von*-PP (Pollard & Sag 1987: 216). I follow Höhle (1978: 161), Sadziński (1987), von Stechow (1990: 174), Zifonun (1992: 255), Lieb (1992: 181), Wunderlich (1993: 740), Gunkel (2003: 65) and others, in assuming that the PPs for expressing the agent are adjuncts. See Müller (2003b: Section 5) for details.

(66) a. dass der   Mann unterstützt wurde
         that the.NOM man   supported   AUX
         'that the man was supported'
     b. dass dem   Jungen der   Ball geschenkt wurde
         that the.DAT boy   the.NOM ball given   AUX
         'that the ball was given to the boy as a present'

Those analyses that assign all cases lexically would have to assume that the case
of the objects (accusative) is changed into nominative in the passive. Hence, there
would be two variants of the passive: The impersonal passive just suppresses the
subject and the personal passive suppresses the subject and additionally changes
the case of the object into nominative. The analysis using the structural/lexical
case distinction just postpones the case assignment until the point where it is
clear what the right case will be. If we have a participle and use it with the
passive auxiliary it is clear what the case of the arguments has to be.

7.2.3 Argument extension and case assignment: AcI constructions

The case principle contains restrictions on case assignment that prohibit the assignment to elements that are raised. These restrictions have not been explained
yet. Consider the examples in (67):

(67) a. Der   Junge liest den   Aufsatz.
         the.NOM boy   reads the.ACC paper
         'The boy reads the paper.'
     b. Der   Mann lässt den   Jungen den   Aufsatz lesen.
         the.NOM man   lets the.ACC boy   the.ACC paper   read
         'The man lets the boy read the paper.'

The example (67a) shows that the subject of *lesen* is assigned nominative. However, the subject of *lesen* gets accusative in (67b). So, if one were to assign case
on the basis of the argument structure of *lesen* in (67b), one would assign nominative, but the AcI verb *lassen* 'to let' assigns accusative to its object. The point
is that the subject of *lesen* is raised to the object of *lassen*. The Case Principle is
set up in a way such that case is assigned only to those arguments that are not
raised to a higher head. Hence, *den Jungen* does not get case from *lesen*, but from
lässt.

   The analysis of (67b) is given in Figure 7.1. The arguments of *lesen* 'to read'
are taken over by *lässt*. Since *lässt* contributes its own argument, the causer

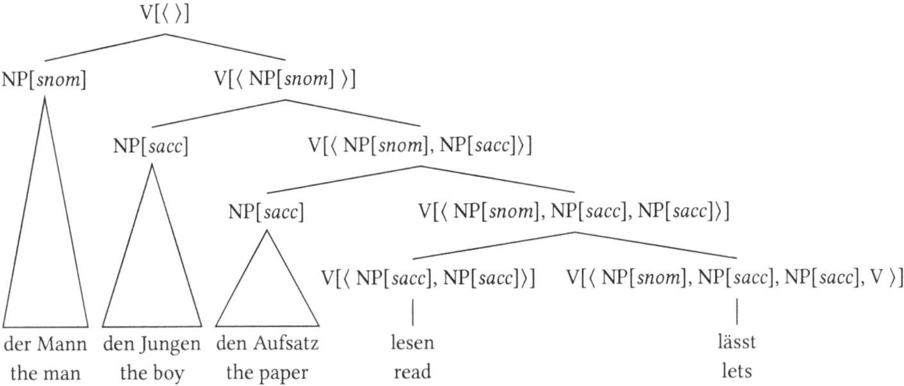

Figure 7.1: Analysis of AcI constructions as raising constructions and the verbal complex in German

or the one who gives the permission, *lässt* selects for three NPs with structural case and a verb in the specific sentence depicted in Figure 7.1. According to the Case Principle, the first NP with structural case gets nominative and the other NPs with structural case get accusative. This results in a list with one NP in the nominative and two NPs in the accusative.

(68) shows the ARG-ST list of *lässt* when it is combined with *schlafen*, *unterstützen*, *helfen*, or *schenken*, respectively.

(68) a. *lässt + schlafen:*   ARG-ST $\langle$ NP$[str]_l$, NP$[str]_i$, V$\rangle$

b. *lässt + unterstützen:* ARG-ST $\langle$ NP$[str]_l$, NP$[str]_i$, NP$[str]_j$, V $\rangle$

c. *lässt + helfen:*   ARG-ST $\langle$ NP$[str]_l$, NP$[str]_i$, NP$[ldat]_j$, V $\rangle$

d. *lässt + schenken:*   ARG-ST $\langle$ NP$[str]_l$, NP$[str]_i$, NP$[ldat]_j$, NP$[str]_k$, V $\rangle$

The NP that is added has the index *l*. As the first NP with structural case on these lists it gets nominative. All other elements of this list that have structural case get accusative. Hence the subject of the embedded verb is assigned accusative, the lexical cases stay the same and the accusative objects of the embedded verb get accusative as well, since their case is structural too.

Note that the question of whether a language has a verbal complex or not is orthogonal to issues of case assignment. Figure 7.2 shows the analysis of the English translation of (67b). *let* selects for the subject, the object and a VP. The subject of *read* is simultaneously the object of *let* and hence the Case Principle does

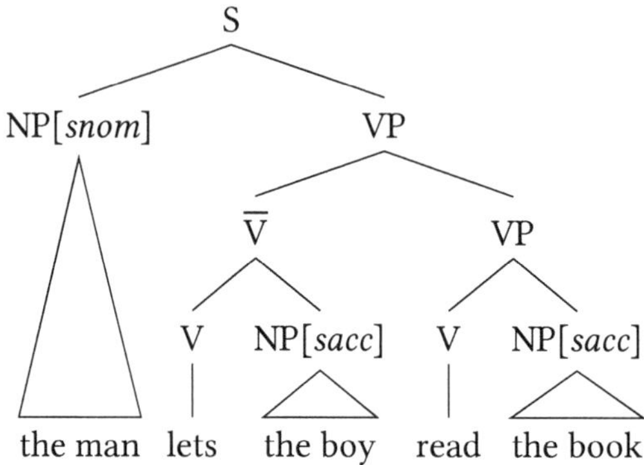

Figure 7.2: AcI constructions in English

not assign nominative to the subject of the embedded verb *read*, but accusative to the object of the matrix verb *let*.

7.2.4 Accounting for the crosslinguistic differences

As argument reduction and case assignment was already explained for German in Section 7.2.2, I would like now to speak more directly on and provide lexical items for the passive and perfect auxiliary for German. After this I discuss the other languages (e.g., Danish, English, and Icelandic) and explain how the differences can be accounted for analytically.

7.2.4.1 Designated argument reduction

Haider (1986a: 10) suggested marking the argument of a verb that has subject properties. He calls these special arguments *designated argument*. Heinz & Matiasek (1994) transferred this idea to HPSG and Müller (2003b) modified it slightly to get certain facts with modal infinitives right. One important use of the designated argument is to distinguish so-called unaccusative verbs from unergative verbs. Perlmutter (1978) pointed out that unaccusative verbs have remarkable properties and argued that their subjects are not really subjects but behave more like objects. One of their properties is that they do not allow for passives. Furthermore, their participles can be used attributively, which is not possible with unergative verbs:

(69) a. der angekommene Zug   (unaccusative)
          the arrived   train
          'the arrived train'

b. * der geschlafene Mann   (unergative)
    the slept   man

This is explained if one assumes that the subject of *ankommen* 'arrive' has object-like properties and hence patterns with the object of transitive verbs:

(70) der geliebte Mann
    the beloved man

Mann 'man' fills the object slot of *geliebte*. If the sole argument of *ankommen* is treated as an object, the similarity to the transitive *lieben* is explained immediately. Similarly, the fact that unaccusatives do not allow for passives is explained: If passive is the suppression of the subject and *ankommen* does not have a subject in that sense, passive cannot apply.

(71) a. Der Zug ist angekommen.
      the train is arrived

      'The train arrived.'

    b. * weil   angekommen wurde
      because arrived   AUX

In the HPSG analyses the authors assume that there is a list-valued feature DESIG-NATED ARGUMENT (DA). This list contains the subject of transitive and unergative verbs (intransitive verbs that are not unaccusative). The DA value of unaccusative verbs is the empty list, since these verbs do not have an argument with subject properties.

The passive is analyzed as a lexical rule that licenses a lexical item for the participle. The ARG-ST list of the participle is the ARG-ST list of the verb stem that is the input to the lexical rule minus the DA list. Since this is not the focus of this book, I will not discuss unaccusative verbs in the following. (72) provides some prototypical examples for unergative and transitive verbs:

(72)   ARG-ST   DA

    a. tanzen (dance): $\langle$ ①NP[*str*] $\rangle$ $\langle$ ① $\rangle$

    b. lesen (read): $\langle$ ①NP[*str*], NP[*str*] $\rangle$ $\langle$ ① $\rangle$

    c. schenken (give as a present): $\langle$ ①NP[*str*], NP[*ldat*], NP[*str*] $\rangle$ $\langle$ ① $\rangle$

    d. helfen (help): $\langle$ ①NP[*str*], NP[*ldat*] $\rangle$ $\langle$ ① $\rangle$

The lexical rule that forms the participle is sketched in (73):

(73) Lexical rule for the formation of the participle (preliminary):

$$\begin{bmatrix} stem \\ \text{HEAD} \begin{bmatrix} verb \\ \text{DA} \;\boxed{1} \end{bmatrix} \\ \text{ARG-ST} \;\boxed{1} \oplus \boxed{2} \end{bmatrix} \mapsto \begin{bmatrix} word \\ \text{ARG-ST} \;\boxed{2} \end{bmatrix}$$

This rule splits the ARG-ST list of the input into two lists $\boxed{1}$ and $\boxed{2}$. $\boxed{1}$ is identical to the DA value. Therefore the designated argument is taken off the ARG-ST list and is not present in the lexical item that is licensed by the rule.

The ARG-ST list of the participle that is licensed is either empty (74a) or starts with an object of the active form:

(74)   ARG-ST

  a. getanzt (danced, unerg): $\langle\rangle$

  b. gelesen (read, trans): $\langle\text{NP}[\mathit{str}]\rangle$

  c. geschenkt (given, ditrans): $\langle\text{NP}[\mathit{ldat}], \text{NP}[\mathit{str}]\rangle$

  d. geholfen (helped, unerg): $\langle\text{NP}[\mathit{ldat}]\rangle$

As was explained above, the first element in the ARG-ST list with structural case gets nominative and hence the accusative object of *lesen* in (75a) is realized as nominative in (75b):

(75) a. Er liest den Aufsatz.   (German)
    he.NOM reads the.ACC paper

  b. Der Aufsatz wurde gelesen.
     the.NOM paper AUX read

English differs from German in not having a dative case at all. I am talking about morphological markings here, not about semantics. Therefore, both objects of English ditransitive verbs are accusative objects. However, only one of the objects can be promoted to subject. This is modeled in the analysis at hand by assuming that the secondary object bears lexical accusative (see also Grewendorf (2002: 57) for the assumption of lexical accusative for the secondary object in English).[12]

---

[12] Admittedly this is just a restatement of the facts, since assigning lexical case means that the argument under consideration cannot have another case. But taken together with constraints on subjects in English the facts about promotion or non-promotion of arguments follow nicely.

(76) ARG-ST

   b. dance (unerg): $\langle NP[str]\rangle$

   c. read (trans): $\langle NP[str], NP[str]\rangle$

   d. give (ditrans): $\langle NP[str], NP[str], NP[lacc]\rangle$

   e. help (trans): $\langle NP[str], NP[str]\rangle$

German can promote the second object (accusative); English the first object. The commonality is that the object closer to the verb can be promoted. This is the accusative for German since nominative-dative-accusative is the unmarked order and German is a OV language, but the first accusative in English, as English is a VO language.

(77) a. dass dem   Kind der   Ball gegeben wurde   (German)
      that the.DAT child the.NOM ball given   AUX

      'that the ball was given to the child'

    b. because the child was given the ball

A further difference is the lexical item for *help*. Since there is no dative in English, the object is marked accusative as it is the case for *read*. As expected, English allows for the personal passive of *help*, while this is not possible in German:

(78) a.   because he was helped
    b.   weil   ihm   geholfen wurde   (German)
       because he.DAT helped   AUX

    c. * weil   er   geholfen wurde
       because he.NOM helped   AUX

7.2.4.2 Primary and secondary objects

In this section I want to look at languages that allow both objects to be promoted. Danish is like English in not having a dative. This is reflected in the following ARG-ST values:

(79) ARG-ST

   a. danse (dance, unerg): $\langle NP[str]_i\rangle$

   b. læse (read, trans): $\langle NP[str]_i, NP[str]_j\rangle$

   c. give (give, ditrans): $\langle NP[str]_i, NP[str]_j, NP[str]_k\rangle$

   d. hjælpe (help, trans): $\langle NP[str]_i, NP[str]_j\rangle$

Danish thus has two objects with structural case, while English and German have just one object with structural case and the other one with lexical accusative and lexical dative, respectively. Since English and German do not allow for subjects with lexical case, it is clear that the promotion to subject of the argument that bears lexical case is excluded. Danish also disallows subjects with lexical case, but since the two objects have structural case anyway, they can both be promoted.

Note however that the lexical rule in (73) does not account for the promotion of the secondary object. What it does is suppress the subject. Under the assumption that the first NP with structural case is the subject, the secondary object could never be realized as subject. Note that it would not help to say that any NP with structural case can be the subject, since this would admit wrong realizations. In addition to the correct (38a), the following two sentences would be admitted:

(80) a. * fordi   barnet   giver manden bolden
          because child.DEF gives man.DEF ball.DEF

      b. * fordi   bolden   giver manden barnet
          because ball.DEF gives man.DEF child.DEF

(80a) is ungrammatical with *barnet* 'child' as the recipient of the giving. Similarly, the transferred object *bolden* cannot be realized as subject in active sentences. This means that the promotion to subject has to be a part of the lexical rule that licenses the participle that is used in the passive. The lexical rule in (81) takes the ARG-ST list in the input of the lexical rule and splits it into two lists: ⒈ and ⒉. The first list ⒈ is identical to the value of DA. The second list ⒉ is the remainder of the ARG-ST list. ⒉ is related to ⒊, the ARG-ST value of the output of the lexical rule, by the relational constraint promote. ⒊ is either equal to ⒉ or it is a list in which another NP with structural case is positioned at the beginning of the list.

(81)   Lexical rule for the passive for Danish, English, German, and Icelandic:

$$\begin{bmatrix} \text{HEAD} & \begin{bmatrix} verb \\ \text{DA} & ⒈ \end{bmatrix} \\ \text{ARG-ST} & ⒈ \oplus ⒉ \end{bmatrix} \mapsto \begin{bmatrix} \text{ARG-ST} & ⒊ \end{bmatrix} \wedge \text{promote}(⒉, ⒊)$$

(82) shows the ARG-ST values of our prototypical verbs:

(82)   ARG-ST

     a. danset/-s (dance, unerg): $\langle\rangle$

     b. læst/-s (read, trans): $\langle\text{NP}[str]_j\rangle$

     c. givet/-s (give, ditrans): $\langle\text{NP}[str]_j, \text{NP}[str]_k\rangle$

                                $\langle\text{NP}[str]_k, \text{NP}[str]_j\rangle$

     d. hjulpet/-s (help, trans): $\langle\text{NP}[str]_j\rangle$

The NP$[str]_i$ that is the first element in (79) is suppressed. The effect of promote
is that there are two different ARG-ST values for the passive variants of *givet* 'to
give': one with an ARG-ST list in which NP$[str]_j$ precedes NP$[str]_k$ and another
one in which NP$[str]_j$ follows NP$[str]_k$. The first order corresponds to (38b) –
repeated here as (83a) – and the second corresponds to (38c) – repeated here as
(83b):

(83)   a.   fordi   barnet   bliver givet bolden
              because child.DEF is   given ball.DEF
              'because the child is given the ball'

       b.   fordi   bolden   bliver givet barnet
              because ball.DEF is   given child.DEF
              'because the ball is given to the child'

Before turning to impersonal passives in Danish in the next subsection, I discuss
the passive in double object constructions in Icelandic.

     The distribution of structural/lexical case in Icelandic is basically the same as
in German. The difference is that Icelandic allows for subjects with lexical case
and German does not. (84) shows our standard examples in Icelandic:

(84)   ARG-ST

     a. dansa (dance, unerg): $\langle\text{NP}[str]\rangle$

     b. lesa (read, trans): $\langle\text{NP}[str], \text{NP}[str]\rangle$

     c. gefa (give, ditrans): $\langle\text{NP}[str], \text{NP}[ldat], \text{NP}[str]\rangle$

     d. hjálpa (help, trans): $\langle\text{NP}[str], \text{NP}[ldat]\rangle$

The lexical rule in (81) licenses the following participles:

(85)

	ARG-ST	SPR	COMPS
a. dansað (danced, unerg):	$\langle\rangle$	$\langle\rangle$	$\langle\rangle$
b. lesið (read, trans):	$\langle NP[str]_j \rangle$	$\langle NP[str]_j \rangle$	$\langle\rangle$
c. gefið (given, ditrans):	$\langle NP[ldat]_j, NP[str]_k \rangle$	$\langle NP[ldat]_j \rangle$	$\langle NP[str]_k \rangle$
	$\langle NP[str]_k, NP[ldat]_j \rangle$	$\langle NP[str]_k \rangle$	$\langle NP[ldat]_j \rangle$
d. hjálpað (helped, trans):	$\langle NP[ldat]_j \rangle$	$\langle NP[ldat]_j \rangle$	$\langle\rangle$

In addition to the ARG-ST list, (85) shows the mapping to the SPR and COMPS features. Since Icelandic allows for quirky subjects the dative argument of 'to help' can be mapped to the SPR list (Wechsler 1995: 147–148). Similarly, the two orders of the ARG-ST of 'to give' result in participles with a dative subject and a nominative subject as it is required for the analysis of (44a) and (44b) repeated here as (86):

(86)   a. Voru konunginum gefnar ambáttir?
          were the.king.DAT given slaves.NOM
          'Was the king given slaves?'

       b. Var ambáttin   gefin konunginum?
          was the.slave.NOM given the.king.DAT
          'Was the slave given to the king?'

The impersonal passive with 'to dance' is parallel to the German impersonal passive, but the passivization of 'to help' differs since this is an instance of the personal passive in Icelandic.

7.2.4.3 Impersonal passive

As a final point in this subsection, let us have a look at the impersonal passive. German and Icelandic do not require subjects. So if there is no NP with structural case, the construction in German is subjectless. Similarly, Icelandic does not require a subject: If there is no NP argument, the result is an impersonal passive. An example of the latter case is the passivization of *dansa* 'to dance'. The ARG-ST list is the empty list and therefore the SPR list and the COMPS list are empty as well. Passive participles of verbs that govern an NP and a PP object will have an ARG-ST list that just contains the PP argument. This PP argument will be mapped to the COMPS list and hence a subjectless construction will result.

English does not allow for impersonal passives as it requires an NP or a sentential argument that can serve as a subject. Danish requires a subject as well, but allows for impersonal constructions. The trick that Danish employs is the insertion of an expletive. I assume that the expletive insertion happens during the mapping of the ARG-ST elements to SPR and COMPS. If there is an NP/VP/CP at the beginning of the ARG-ST list, it is mapped to SPR and all other elements are mapped to COMPS. If there is no element that can be mapped to SPR, an expletive is inserted.

(87) shows the mappings for Danish.

(87)

	ARG-ST	SPR	COMPS
a. danset/-s (unerg):	$\langle\rangle$	$\langle NP_{expl}\rangle$	$\langle\rangle$
b. læst/-s (trans):	$\langle NP[str]_j\rangle$	$\langle NP[str]_j\rangle$	$\langle\rangle$
c. givet/-s (ditrans):	$\langle NP[str]_j, NP[str]_k\rangle$	$\langle NP[str]_j\rangle$	$\langle NP[str]_k\rangle$
	$\langle NP[str]_k, NP[str]_j\rangle$	$\langle NP[str]_k\rangle$	$\langle NP[str]_j\rangle$
d. hjulpet/-s (trans):	$\langle NP[str]_j\rangle$	$\langle NP[str]_j\rangle$	$\langle\rangle$

7.2.4.4 The passive auxiliary

We now saw what the participle forms of the languages under considerations look like and how they are licensed from lexical entries for stems via lexical rules. What is missing is the lexical items for the auxiliary verbs. Chapter 5 dealt with the analysis of verbal complexes in SOV languages like German, Dutch, and Afrikaans, and it was pointed out that SVO languages like English and the Scandinavian languages do not form a verbal complex. With this background, it may come as a surprise that it is possible to formulate one general constraint covering all the passive auxiliaries in the Germanic languages. The following AVM shows a constraint holding on all ARG-ST lists for passive auxiliary in Germanic languages:[13]

(88)   Passive auxiliary for Germanic languages (*be, werden, believe,* etc.):

$$\left[\text{ARG-ST } \boxed{1} \oplus \boxed{2} \oplus \left\langle \begin{bmatrix} \text{VFORM} & ppp \\ \text{SPR} & \boxed{1} \\ \text{COMPS} & \boxed{2} \end{bmatrix} \right\rangle \right]$$

When the passive auxiliary in (88) is used in a German grammar, the arguments of the participle ($\boxed{1}$ and $\boxed{2}$) are attracted by the passive auxiliary (Hinrichs & Nakazawa 1989b, 1994). Auxiliaries in the SVO languages embed a VP. This

---

[13]The lexical item of the passive auxiliary used by Müller (2002: 147) and Müller & Ørsnes (2013a: 149) specifies the DA value of the embedded participle to be a referential NP. This excludes the passivization of unaccusative verbs, which have the empty list as the DA value.

means that the COMPS value of the embedded verb has to be the empty list. Therefore ② is the empty list and only the specifier (①) is taken over from the embedded verb.

With the lexical item for the auxiliary in place, we can have a look at some example analyses of passive sentences. Let's start with an English example. The analysis of (89) is shown in Figure 7.3.

(89) The child was given a novel.

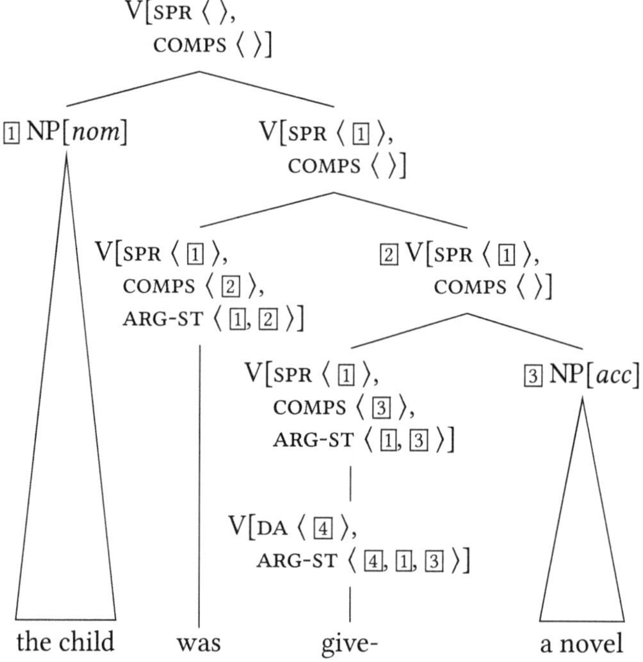

Figure 7.3: Analysis of *The child was given a novel.*

The lexical item for the stem *give-* is input to the passive lexical rule. The passive lexical rule licenses the participle *given*. The ARG-ST of *give-* is shortened by the element in the DA list of *give-* (④). The result is an ARG-ST list containing the two NPs that would be the objects in active sentences. The first one (①) is mapped to SPR and the second one (③) to COMPS. The combination of *given* and *a novel* forms a VP (something with an empty COMPS list and an element in the SPR list). The passive auxiliary *was* selects the VP *given a novel*. The specifier of the selected VP (①) is attracted. As the first argument of *was* with structural case, this NP gets nominative. Finally, the VP *was given a novel* is combined with *the child* and we have a complete sentence.

The analysis of the parallel German sentence in (90) is shown in Figure 7.4.

(90) dass dem   Kind ein   Roman gegeben wurde   (German)
      that the.DAT child a.NOM novel   given   AUX

      'that the child was given a novel'

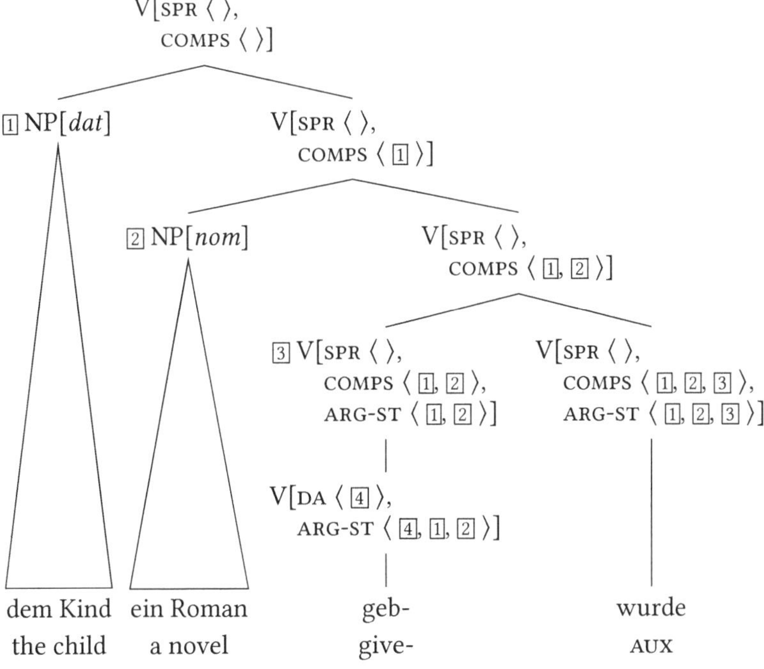

Figure 7.4: Analysis of *dass dem Kind ein Roman gegeben wurde* 'that the child was given a novel'

The analysis is similar to the one of the English example but it differs in that the auxiliary and the participle is forming a verbal complex. First, the passive lexical rule applies to a verb stem *geb-* and licenses the participle form *gegeben. gegeben* (③) is combined with *wurde* and *wurde* takes over the elements of the COMPS list of *gegeben* ⟨ ①, ② ⟩. The result of the combination of *gegeben* and *werden* has the COMPS list ⟨ ①, ② ⟩.

203

7.2.4.5 The morphological passive

A lexical rule similar to the one accounting for the participle forms can be used for the morphological passives in Danish. One difference is, of course, the affixal material that is added by the rule. Furthermore, it is assumed for the morphological passive that the DA of the input to the lexical rule has to contain a referential XP. As was discussed in the previous section, this excludes morphological passives of unaccusatives and weather verbs.

7.2.4.6 Perfect

Haider's (1986a) analysis of the passive is brilliant since it is sufficient to have one lexical item for the participle. The participle has a blocked designated argument, and the designated argument remains blocked in the passive, while the perfect auxiliary deblocks the designated argument.

(91) a. dass der   Aufsatz gelesen wurde
          that the.NOM paper   read   AUX
          'that the paper was read'

      b. dass Kirby den   Aufsatz gelesen hat
          that Kirby the.ACC paper   read   AUX
          'that Kirby has read the paper'

Deblocking of the designated argument is possible since the designated argument is encoded not just in the stem of a verb but also in the lexical item for the participle.

(92) Lexical item for perfect auxiliaries in SOV languages like Dutch and German:

$$\left[\text{ARG-ST } \boxed{1} \oplus \boxed{2} \oplus \boxed{3} \oplus \left\langle \begin{bmatrix} \text{VFORM} & ppp \\ \text{DA} & \boxed{1} \\ \text{SPR} & \boxed{2} \\ \text{COMPS} & \boxed{3} \end{bmatrix} \right\rangle \right]$$

Unfortunately Haider's approach does not work for SVO languages. If we wanted to use the argument blocking/deblocking approach, we would have to assume the structures in (93a–b):

(93) a. He [has given] the book to Mary.

      b. The book [was given] to Mary.

      c. He has [given the book to Mary].

      d. The book was [given to Mary].

If we assume that auxiliaries embed VPs as was argued on page 129, we run into problems since the subject of the participle is blocked and the only VP we can form with the participle is the one in (93d), but for the perfect we also need a VP containing the object as in (93c).

7.2.4.7 The remote passive

The so-called *remote passive* is a highlight of German syntax since several phenomena interact in a non-trivial way. It was first discussed by Höhle (1978: 175–176). Höhle observed that objects of German infinitives with *zu* appear in the nominative in certain contexts. (94) provides some constructed examples from the literature:

(94)   a. daß er   auch von mir zu überreden versucht wurde[14] (German)
           that he.NOM also from me to persuade tried   AUX

           'that an attempt to persuade him was also made by me'

    b. weil   der   Wagen oft   zu reparieren versucht wurde
        because the.NOM car   often to repair   tried   AUX
        'because many attempts were made to repair the car'

The examples in (95) are attested data collected from the COSMAS corpus by Müller (2002: 136–137):

(95)   a. Dabei darf jedoch nicht vergessen werden, daß in der Bundesrepublik, wo *ein Mittelweg zu gehen versucht wird*, die Situation der Neuen Musik allgemein und die Stellung der Komponistinnen im besonderen noch recht unbefriedigend ist.[15]

        'One should not forget that the situation of the New Music in general and the position of female composers in particular is rather unsatisfying in the Bundesrepublik, where one tries to follow a middle course.'

    b. Noch ist es nicht so lange her, da ertönten gerade aus dem Thurgau jeweils die lautesten Töne, wenn im Wallis oder am Genfersee im Umfeld einer Schuldenpolitik mit den unglaublichsten Tricks *der sportliche Abstieg zu verhindern versucht wurde.*[16]

        'It still is not too long ago that the loudest protests were heard in the Thurgau itself when the most unbelievable tricks in the sphere of

---

[14]Oppenrieder (1991: 212).

[15]Mannheimer Morgen, 26.09.1989, Feuilleton; Ist's gut, so unter sich zu bleiben?

[16]St. Galler Tagblatt, 09.02.1999, Ressort: TB-RSP; HCT und das Prinzip Hoffnung.

debt policies were applied to prevent relegation in the Valais or at Lake Geneva.'

c. Die Auf- und Absteigenden erzeugen ungewollt einen Ton, *der bewusst nicht als lästig zu eliminieren versucht wird*, sondern zum Eigenklang des Hauses gehören soll, so wünschen es sich die Architekten.[17]

'The people who go up and down produce a tune without intention which is not consciously sought to be eliminated but which, rather, belongs to the individual sound of the building, as the architects intended.'

Höhle's examples and other examples from the literature involved the verb *versuchen* 'to try', but Wurmbrand (2003b) showed that other verbs allow for the remote passive as well. (96) and (97) show some of her examples with *beginnen* 'to start', *vergessen* 'to forget', and *wagen* 'to dare':

(96) *der   zweite Entwurf* wurde zu bauen begonnen,[18]   (German)
      the.NOM second plan   AUX   to build started

'It was begun to build the second plan.'

While the case of *der zweite Entwurf* 'the second plan' is unambiguously nominative, this is not the case for the examples in (97), since the respective elements are in the plural and hence could be nominative or accusative. But due to agreement with the finite verb, it is clear that the relative pronoun are in the nominative.

(97) a. Anordnungen, die zu stornieren vergessen *wurden*[19]   (German)
         orders   that to cancel   forgotten were

      'orders that were forgotten to cancel'

      b. Aufträge [...], die zu drucken vergessen worden *sind*[20]
         orders that to print forgot were are

      'orders that somebody forgot to print'

      c. NUR Leere, oder doch noch Hoffnung, weil aus Nichts wieder Gefühle entstehen,

---

[17] Züricher Tagesanzeiger, 01.11.1997, p. 61.

[18] http://www.waclawek.com/projekte/john/johnlang.html, 28.07.2003.

[19] http://www.rlp-irma.de/Dateien/Jahresabschluss2002.pdf, 28.07.2003.

[20] http://www.iitslips.de/news.html, 28.07.2003.

> die so   vorher nicht mal zu träumen gewagt *wurden?*[21]
> that this.way before not   even to dream   dared   were
>
> 'that were not even dared to be dreamed of in this way before'

d. Dem Voodoozauber einer Verwünschung oder die gefaßte
Entscheidung zu einer Trennung,

> die   bis   dato noch nicht   auszusprechen gewagt *wurden*[22]
> which until now not   express dared   were
>
> 'which until now have not been dared to express'

The object of a verb that is embedded under a passive participle is promoted to subject of the sentence:

(98) a. weil   Aicke den   Wagen oft   zu reparieren   (German)
          because Aicke the.ACC car   often to repair
          versucht hat
          tried   has

   b. weil   der   Wagen oft   *zu reparieren versucht wurde*
       because the.NOM car   often to repair   tried   was
       'because many attempts were made to repair the car'

The remote passive is possible in verbal complexes only. If no verbal complex is formed as in (99a,c), the object of *reparieren* has to appear in the accusative:

(99) a. weil   oft   versucht wurde, den   Wagen zu reparieren.
          because often tried   AUX   the.ACC car   to repair
          'because many attempts were made to repair the car.'

   b. * weil   oft   versucht wurde, der   Wagen zu reparieren.
       because often tried   AUX   the.NOM car   to repair

   c. Den   Wagen zu reparieren wurde oft   versucht.
       the.ACC car   to repair   AUX   often tried

   d. * Der   Wagen zu reparieren wurde oft   versucht.
       the.NOM car   to repair   AUX   often tried

The difference between (98b) and (99a,c) are explained by an analysis that treats the remote passive as a passivization of a predicate complex, i.e., by an analysis that assigns the structure (100) to (98b).

---

[21]http://www.ultimaquest.de/weisheiten_kapitel1.htm, 28.07.2003.

[22]http://www.wedding-no9.de/adventskalender/advent23_shawn_colvin.html, 28.07.2003.

(100) weil   der   Wagen oft   [[zu reparieren versucht] wurde].
      because the.NOM car   often   to repair   tried   AUX
      'because many attempts were made to repair the car.'

In (99a,c) we do not have predicate complexes. The object of *zu reparieren* is part of the VP and therefore it gets accusative. The passives in (99a,c) are impersonal passives.

The verb *versuchen* 'to try' selects a subject, an infinitive with *zu* 'to' and the complements of the embedded verb.

(101) *versuch-* 'to try':
$$\left[\text{ARG-ST} \; \langle \text{NP}[str]_i \rangle \oplus \boxed{1} \oplus \langle V[\textit{inf}, \text{SUBJ} \; \langle \text{NP}[str]_i \rangle, \text{COMPS} \; \boxed{1}] \rangle \right]$$

In our example, the embedded verb is *reparieren* and has one complement. (102) shows the ARG-ST value of *versuch-*. The first NP is the subject of *versuchen* and the second NP is the attracted object of *zu reparieren*.

(102) ARG-ST value of *versuch-* with embedding of a strictly transitive verb:
$$\langle \; \text{NP}[str]_i, \text{NP}[str]_j, V[\textit{inf}] \; \rangle$$

When the passive lexical rule applies to this verb stem and licenses the respective participle, the resulting lexical item for *versucht* 'tried' will have the following ARG-ST value:

(103) ARG-ST of participle *versucht* with embedding of strictly transitive verb:
$$\langle \; \text{NP}[str]_j, V[\textit{inf}] \; \rangle$$

The first NP is mapped to SUBJ and V[*inf*] is mapped to COMPS. After combination with *zu reparieren*, we have a complex with NP[*str*]$_j$ in SUBJ and nothing in COMPS. *wurde* selects a verb or verbal complex with the verb form *ppp* and the arguments of the embedded verb. Hence, NP[*str*]$_j$ ends up as the first element of the ARG-ST list of *werden* where it gets nominative. Since *werden* is finite all ARG-ST elements are mapped to COMPS and have to be realized in the sentence. The analysis of the verbal complex in (100) is shown in Figure 7.5.

The remote passive is also possible with object control verbs, that is, verbs taking a subject and an object and a verbal projection the subject of which is coreferential with the object. An example is *erlauben* 'to permit'. (104a) shows the verb in the active and without verbal complex formation. The object of *erlauben* 'to permit' *uns* 'us' is coreferential with the subject of *den Erfolg auszukosten* 'to enjoy the success'. (104b,c) show that the object of *auszukosten* can be realized in the nominative, if the verbs are forming a verbal complex:

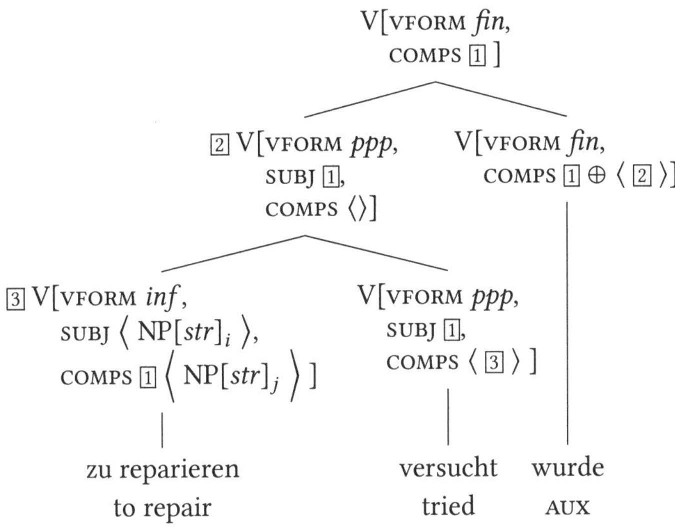

Figure 7.5: The analysis of the remote passive as passivization of a complex forming verb

(104) a. Sie erlauben uns nicht, den Erfolg auszukosten.
　　　 they permitted us.DAT not the.ACC success to.enjoy
　　　 'They did not permit us to enjoy the success.'

　　 b. Keine Zeitung wird ihr zu lesen erlaubt.[23]
　　　 no newspaper.NOM AUX her.DAT to read allowed
　　　 'She is not allowed to read any newspapers.'

　　 c. Der Erfolg wurde uns nicht auszukosten erlaubt.[24]
　　　 the success.NOM AUX us.DAT not to.enjoy permitted
　　　 'We were not permitted to enjoy our success.'

The passive of the construction without verbal complex is an impersonal passive:

(105) Uns wurde erlaubt, den Erfolg auszukosten.
　　　 us.DAT AUX allowed the.ACC success to.enjoy

(106) shows the ARG-ST value of *erlaub-*: *erlauben* takes a subject and a dative object. The dative object is coindexed with the subject of the embedded verb, that is, the two NPs have the same index, namely j.

---

[23]Stefan Zweig. *Marie Antoinette.* Leipzig: Insel-Verlag. 1932, p. 515, quoted from Bech (1955: 309). That this is an instance of the remote passive was noted by Askedal (1988: 13).

[24]Haider (1986b: 110)

(106) *erlaub-* 'to permit':
  $\left[\text{ARG-ST}\ \langle\text{NP}[\textit{str}]_i, \text{NP}[\textit{ldat}]_j\rangle\oplus\boxed{1}\oplus\langle\text{V}[\textit{inf},\ \text{SUBJ}\ \langle\text{NP}[\textit{str}]_j\rangle, \text{COMPS}\ \boxed{1}]\rangle\right]$

The complements of the embedded verb ($\boxed{1}$) are taken over by the embedding verb. (107) shows the ARG-ST value of the respective highest verb:

(107)   a. *zu lesen erlauben:* $\langle\ \text{NP}[\textit{str}]_i, \text{NP}[\textit{ldat}]_j, \text{NP}[\textit{str}]_k, \text{V}[\text{COMPS}\ \langle\ \text{NP}[\textit{str}]_k\ \rangle]\ \rangle$

       b. *zu lesen erlaubt wird:* $\langle\ \text{NP}[\textit{ldat}]_j, \text{NP}[\textit{str}]_k, \text{V}[\text{COMPS}\ \langle\ \text{NP}[\textit{str}]_k\ \rangle]\ \rangle$

(107a) shows how the object of *lesen* is attracted so that the combined ARG-ST contains three NPs. (107b) shows the passive variant in which the subject of *erlauben* is suppressed. The result is a ARG-ST list starting with a dative NP, an NP with lexical case. Since the first NP with structural case gets nominative and agrees with the finite verb, the theory makes the right predictions even in situations as complex as the remote passive with object control verbs. The first NP with structural case is the subject in German.

7.3 Alternatives

As with the sections about alternatives in previous chapters, this section is for advanced readers only. It is not necessary to read it in order to understand the rest of the book.

7.3.1 Government & Binding analyses

The analysis adopted here was developed out of proposals by Hubert Haider (1986a). Haider developed analyses within the framework of Government & Binding (Chomsky 1981) and his analyses of various phenomena – not just passive – are to a large extent compatible with HPSG views and are adopted by many researchers working in German within the framework of HPSG. The most common analysis of the passive in GB is different though. Grewendorf 1988: 155–157, 1995: 1311 adapted Chomsky's analysis of the passive in English (Chomsky 1981: 124) to German (see also Lohnstein 2014: 180 for a more recent suggestion along these lines in a textbook). This analysis is based on the CP/TP/VP system (see Section 4.10.1 for a discussion of scrambling in this system). The discussion of this analysis of the passive is based on Müller (2023b: Section 3.4).

GB's passive analysis is similar to the analysis suggested here in that it is a lexical analysis: the lexical item for the participle is special in not assigning case to the accusative object. There is a Case Filter requiring that every NP in a sentence must have case. Since the verb does not assign case, the NP that would have accusative in the active has to get case elsewhere. There are two ways to get case: the subject receives case from (finite) T and the case of the remaining arguments comes from V (Chomsky 1981: 50; Haider 1984: 26; Fanselow & Felix 1987: 71–73). This is stated as the Case Principle:

Principle 2 (Case Principle)

- V assigns objective case (accusative) to its complement if it bears structural case.

- When finite, Tense assigns case to the subject.

Figure 7.6 shows the Case Principle in action with the example in (108a).[25]

(108) a. [dass] der Delphin dem   Kind den   Ball gibt
           that   the dolphin the.DAT child the.ACC ball gives
        'that the dolphin gives the child the ball'

     b. [dass] der Ball   dem   Kind gegeben wird
           that   the ball.NOM the.DAT child given   AUX
        'that the ball is given to the child'

The passive morphology of *gegeben* 'given' blocks the subject and absorbs the structural accusative. In GB, it is assumed that semantic roles are assigned to certain tree positions. These positions are determined in the so-called base-configuration, which is the configuration before any movement and reorganization of trees takes place. The object that would get accusative in the active receives only a semantic role in its base position in the passive, but it does not get the absorbed case. Therefore, it has to move to a position where case can be assigned to it (Chomsky 1981: 124). Figure 7.7 shows how this works for example (108b).

This movement-based analysis works well for English since the underlying object always has to move:

(109) a. The dolphin gave [the child] [a ball].

     b. [The child] was given [a ball] (by the dolphin).

     c. * It was given [the child] [a ball].

---

[25]The figure does not correspond to $\overline{\text{X}}$ theory in its classic form, since *der Frau* 'the woman' is a complement which is combined with V′. In classical $\overline{\text{X}}$ theory, all complements have to be combined with V^0. This leads to a problem in ditransitive structures since the structures have to be binary (see Larson (1988) for a treatment of double object constructions). Furthermore, in the following figures the verb has been left in V^0 for reasons of clarity. In order to create a well-formed S-structure, the verb would have to move to its affix in I^0. Note also that the assignment of the subject theta-role by the verb crosses a phrase boundary. This problem can be solved by assuming that the subject is generated within the VP, gets a theta role there and then moves to SpecIP. An alternative suggestion was to assume that the VP assigns a semantic role to SpecIP (Chomsky 1981: 104–105, Aoun & Sportiche 1983: 229).

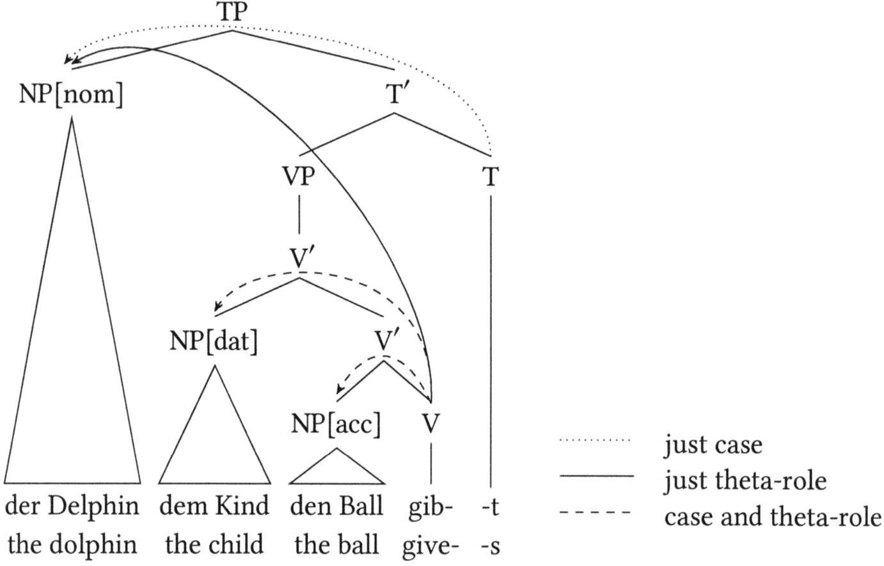

Figure 7.6: Case and theta-role assignment in active clauses

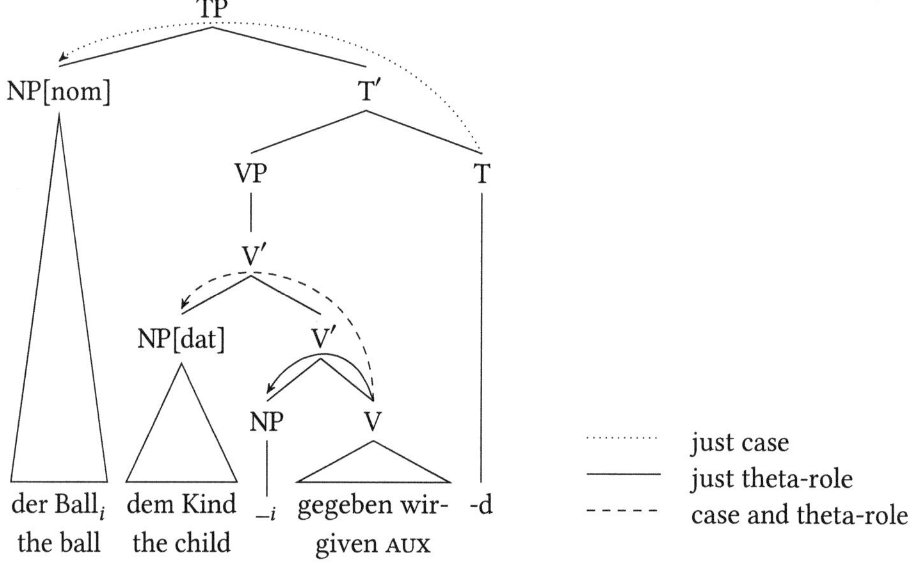

Figure 7.7: Case and theta-role assignment in passive clauses

(109c) shows that filling the subject position with an expletive is not possible, and hence, since English requires a subject, the object really has to move. However, Lenerz (1977: Section 4.4.3) showed that such a movement is not obligatory in German. (110) illustrates:

(110) a. weil der Delphin dem Kind den Ball gab
because the.NOM dolphin the.DAT child the.ACC ball gave
'because the dolphin gave the ball to the child'

b. weil dem Kind der Ball gegeben wurde
because the.DAT child the.NOM ball given AUX
'because the ball was given to the child'

c. weil der Ball dem Kind gegeben wurde
because the.NOM ball the.DAT child given AUX

In comparison to (110c), (110b) is the unmarked order. *der Ball* 'the ball' in (110b) occurs in the same position as *den Ball* in (110a), that is, no movement is necessary. Only the case differs. (110c) is, however, somewhat marked in comparison to (110b). So, if one assumed (110c) to be the normal order for passives and (110b) is derived from this by movement of *dem Kind* 'the child', (110b) should be more marked than (110c), contrary to the facts. To solve this problem, an analysis involving abstract movement has been proposed for cases such as (110b): the elements stay in their positions, but are connected to the subject position and receive their case information from there. Grewendorf (1988: 155–157, 1995: 1311) assumes that there is an empty expletive pronoun in the subject position of sentences such as (110b) and in the subject position of sentences with an impersonal passive such as (111):[26]

(111) weil heute nicht gearbeitet wird
because today not worked AUX
'because there will be no work done today'

A silent expletive pronoun is something that one cannot see or hear and that does not carry any meaning. Such empty elements are rejected by many researchers, since it is unclear how their existence is to be acquired by language learners. It seems to be necessary to assume rich innate linguistic knowledge for this, something that not even Chomsky assumes nowadays (Hauser, Chomsky

---

[26]See Koster (1986: 11–12) for a parallel analysis for Dutch as well as Lohnstein (2014: 180) for a movement-based account of the passive that also involves an empty expletive for the analysis of the impersonal passive.

& Fitch 2002). For discussion of this kind of empty element, see Müller (2023b: Section 13.1.3 and Chapter 19) and Müller (2022: Section 7).

Koster (1986: 12) has pointed out that the passive in English cannot be derived by Case Theory, that is, lack of case and movement to the specifier position of TP due to the Case Filter, since if one allowed empty expletive subjects for English as well as German and Dutch, then it would be possible to have analyses such as the following in (112) where np is an empty expletive:

(112)   np was read the book.

The object would not have to move to subject position and could just stay there, contrary to the facts. Koster rather assumes that subjects in English are either bound by other elements (that is, non-expletive) or lexically filled, that is, filled by visible material. Therefore, the structure in (112) would be ruled out and it would be ensured that *the book* would have to be placed in front of the finite verb so that the subject position is filled.

Concluding, one can say that passive should not be explained by movement. Chomsky's analysis works, but this is only due to the fact that English requires a subject. Two phenomena are mixed that should be treated separately. In the analysis suggested here, passive is the suppression of the subject in the argument structure list. This works for all examined languages. It depends on the language under consideration whether there has to be a subject and whether it has to be realized in a certain position. In English, we have to have something in the specifier position, in German, all arguments are listed on the COMPS list. No movement is involved. Note that the equivalent to the base-order for semantic role assignment is the ARG-ST list. The ARG-ST list has a certain fixed order. This fact can be used for linking, since it is clear on which position of the list which argument is represented. Passive sentences involve a passivized verb. The passivized verb is related to a verb stem with an ARG-ST list corresponding to the active form. So this ARG-ST list is somehow accessible for semantic role assignment but the analysis of the passive clause does not involve the analysis of an active clause and some movement. For all what is known about human language processing up to now, this is the right approach from a psycholinguistic point of view (Wasow 2021: Section 3.2).

7.4 Summary

In conclusion, it can be said that this chapter provides a unified account of the passive in Danish, English, German, and Icelandic. The lexical rule accounts both for the morphological and the analytical passives. The first element on the ARG-ST list is suppressed and a relational constraint `promote` promotes any NP with structural case. The languages differ in what cases they use and which cases are structural/lexical. Danish inserts expletives to allow for impersonal passives and fulfilling the need of a subject. This expletive insertion is done in the ARG-ST mapping when arguments are mapped from ARG-ST to the valence lists.

The SVO languages seem to require different items for the perfect/passive participles, but Haider's (1986a) passive analysis for German using just one participle form for both perfect and passive can be maintained.

Comprehension questions

1. What tests do you know for subjecthood?

2. Do these tests work for all Germanic languages?

3. In which way is German different from Icelandic in terms of subjects?

4. What is structural case? What is lexical case?

5. What is an impersonal passive?

6. Does Icelandic have impersonal passives?

Exercises

1. Which NPs in (113) have structural and which lexical case?

(113) a. Der   Junge lacht.
            the.NOM boy   laughs

        b. Mich friert.
            I.ACC freeze
            'I am cold.'

   c. Er   zerstört die   Umwelt.
      he.NOM destroys the.ACC environment
      'He destroys the environment.'

   d. Das   dauert ein   ganzes Jahr.
      this.NOM takes a.ACC whole year
      'This takes a whole year.'

   e. Er   hat nur einen   Tag dafür   gebraucht.
      he.NOM has just one.ACC day there.for needed
      'He needed a day for this.'

   f. Er   denkt an den   morgigen Tag.
      he.NOM thinks at the.ACC tomorrow day
      'He thinks about tomorrow.'

2. Give ARG-ST lists for the following verbs:

(114)   a. show, eat, meet   (English)

          b. zeigen 'show', essen 'eat', begegnen 'meet', treffen 'meet'
                                           (German)

If you are uncertain as far as case is concerned, you may use the Wiktionary: https://de.wiktionary.org/.

3. Draw the analysis tree for the following clause:

(115)   that the box was opened

Please provide valence features (SPR and COMPS) and part of speech information. You may abbreviate the NP using a triangle.

8 Clause types and expletives

Chapter 6 discussed the analysis of verb-initial and verb-second clauses. This chapter deals with embedded clauses with complementizers (e.g., *that* in English) and embedded interrogative clauses.

8.1 The phenomena

This first section introduces the phenomenon and consists of three parts: Section 8.1.1 deals with embedded clauses introduced by a complementizer, Section 8.1.2 describes the structure of interrogative clauses and Section 8.1.3 deals with expletives in V2 and interrogative clauses.

8.1.1 Embedded clauses introduced by a complementizer

As was already mentioned, Afrikaans, Dutch, German are SOV languages and this is also shown in embedded clauses that are introduced by a complementizer. (1) is an example:

(1)   Ich weiß, dass Aicke das Buch heute gelesen hat.   (German)
     I   know that Aicke the book today read   has
     'I know that Aicke read the book today.'

English, being an SVO non-V2 language, allows for SVO order only.

(2)   I know that Kim has read the book yesterday.   (English)

However, elements can be fronted in *that* clauses:

(3)   a.   I know that yesterday Peter came.
     b. ? I know that bagels, he likes.

Interestingly, Danish, also an SVO language, allows both SVO order (4) and V2 order (5) in clauses preceded by a complementizer:

(4)   Jeg ved, at   Gert ikke har læst bogen   i dag.   (Danish)
           I   know that Gert not has read book.DEF today
           'I know that Gert did not read the book today.'

(5)   a.   Jeg ved, at   i dag har Gert ikke læst bogen.   (Danish)
            I   know that today has Gert not read book.DEF

      b.   Jeg ved, at   bogen   har Gert ikke læst i dag.
            I   know that book.DEF has Gert not read today

The example in (4) includes the negation in order to show that we do indeed deal with the SVO order here. Without the negation it is not clear whether non-V2 clauses are allowed in clauses that are introduced by a complementizer since (6a) has the finite verb in second position. With the negation present, it is clear that we have a V2 clause if the negation follows the finite verb as in (6b) and that we do not have a V2 clause if the finite verb follows the negation as in (4) and hence is in third position.

(6)   a. at   Gert har læst bogen   (V2 or SVO)
         that Gert has read book.DEF

         'that Gert has read the book'

      b. at   Gert har ikke læst bogen   (V2)
         that Gert has not read book.DEF

For complementizerless clauses, the V2 order is the only order that is possible:

(7)   a.   Gert har ikke læst bogen   (V2)
         Gert has not read book.DEF

      b. * Gert ikke har læst bogen   (SVO)
        Gert not has read book.DEF

Yiddish and Icelandic are SVO languages as well. The clauses that are combined with a complementizer are V2:

(8)   a. Ikh meyn az   haynt hot Max geleyent dos bukh.[1]   (Yiddish)
         I   think that today has Max read   the book
         'I think that Max read the book today.'

      b. Ikh meyn az   dos bukh hot Max geleyent.
         I   think that the book has Max read

---

[1]Diesing (1990: 58)

(9) Engum   datt í hug,   að vert væri að reyna til   að   (Icelandic)
     no.one.DAT fell to mind that worth was to try   PREP to
     kynnast honum.[2]
     know   him
     'It didn't occur to anyone that it was worth trying to get to know him.'

8.1.2 Interrogative clauses

The OV languages form subordinated interrogative clauses by preposing a phrase containing an interrogative pronoun[3] from an otherwise SOV clause. (10) shows a German example:

(10) a. Ich weiß, wer heute das Buch gelesen hat.   (German)
          I   know who today the book read   has
          'I know who read the book today.'

      b. Ich weiß, was   Aicke heute gelesen hat.
          I   know what Aicke today read   has
          'I know what Aicke has read today.'

Since languages like German allow for scrambling, sentences like those in (10) could just be due to the permutation of arguments of a head. However, the generalization about these *w*-clauses is that an arbitrary *w*-element can be fronted. (11) gives a German example involving a nonlocal dependency:

(11) Ich weiß nicht, [über welches Thema]$_i$ sie versprochen   (German)
      I   know not   about which   topic   she promised
      hat, [[einen Vortrag $_{-i}$] zu   halten].
      has   a   talk   to hold
      'I do not know about which topic she promised to give a talk.'

Here, the phrase *über welches Thema* 'about which topic' is an argument of *Vortrag*, which is embedded in the VP containing *zu halten* 'to hold', which is in turn embedded under *versprochen hat* 'promised has'. The generalization about interrogative clauses is that an interrogative clause consists of an interrogative phrase (*über welches Thema* 'about which topic') and a clause in which this interrogative phrase is missing somewhere (*sie versprochen hat, einen Vortrag zu halten* 'she promised to give a talk').

---

[2]Maling (1990: 75)

[3]Most interrogative pronouns start with *w* in German and *wh* in English. Phrases containing an interrogative pronoun are called *w*-phrases or *wh*-phrases, respectively. Interrogative clauses are sometimes called *w*-clauses or *wh*-clauses.

In German the order of the other constituents is free as in assertive main clauses and embedded clauses with a complementizer that were discussed earlier.

(12)   a. Ich weiß, was   keiner   diesem Eichhörnchen geben würde. (German)
       I   know what nobody this   squirrel   give would

       'I know what nobody would give this squirrel.'

   b. Ich weiß, was   diesem Eichhörnchen keiner   geben würde.
       I   know what this   squirrel   nobody give   would

This follows from what was said so far, since interrogatives are just SOV clauses from which one constituent has been extracted. The possibility of scrambling constituents is not affected by extracting a phrase.

In Danish and English, the interrogative clauses consist of an interrogative phrase and an SVO clause in which the interrogative phrase is missing:

(13)   a. Gert har givet ham bogen.   (Danish)
       Gert has given him book.DEF

       'Gert gave him the book.'

   b. Jeg ved,   hvad$_i$ [Gert har givet ham $_i$].
       I   know what   Gert has given him

       'I know what Gert gave him.'

   c. Jeg ved,   hvem$_i$ [Gert har givet $_i$ bogen].
       I   know who   Gert has given   book.DEF

       'I know who Gert has given the book.'

(13a) shows the clause with SVO order and (13b) is an example with the secondary object as interrogative pronoun and (13c) is an example with the primary object as interrogative pronoun. The position that the respective objects have in non-interrogative clauses like (13a) is marked with $_i$.

Yiddish is special in that it has V2 order in interrogative clauses as well (Diesing 1990: Sections 4.1, 4.2): interrogatives consist of an interrogative phrase that is extracted from a V2 clause:

(14)   Ir   veyst efsher [avu   do   voynt Roznblat der goldshmid]?[4]
       you know maybe where there lives Roznblat the goldsmith

       'Do you perhaps know where Roznblat the goldsmith lives?'

So the variation is *w*-phrase + SOV, *w*-phrase + SVO, and *w*-phrase + V2.

---

[4]Diesing (1990: 65). Quoted from Olsvanger, *Royte Pomerantsn*, 1949.

In addition to the question regarding the order within the embedded clause (SOV, SVO, V2), there is variation in finiteness of the embedded clause:

(15) a. I wonder what to read.

    b. I wonder what I should read.

    c. * Ich frage mich, was   zu lesen.   (German)
       I   ask   myself what to read

    d. Ich frage mich, was   ich lesen soll / kann.   (German)
       I   ask   myself what I   read shall can

      'I wonder what I shall/can read.' or 'I wonder what to read.'

English allows for infinitives with *to*. In comparison to finite interrogative clauses, the infinitival form adds a modal meaning. German does not allow for non-finite interrogatives, as (15c) illustrates.

8.1.3 The use of expletives to mark the clause type

The Germanic languages use constituent order to code the clause type: V2 main clauses can be assertions or questions, depending on the content of the preverbal material and intonation. Similarly, embedded interrogative clauses consist of a *w*-phrase and an SVO, SOV, or V2 clause. The fronting of a constituent in a V2 clause comes with certain information-structural effects: something is the topic or the focus of an utterance. For embedded clauses, it is important in some languages that the structure is transparent, that is, that we have *w* + SVO or *w* + V2 order. There are situations in which it is inappropriate to front an element, and in such situations the Germanic languages use expletives, that is, pronouns that do not make a semantic contribution, to maintain a certain order.

German uses the expletive *es* to fill the position in front of the finite verb, if no other constituent is to be fronted.

(16) a. Drei Reiter ritten zum   Tor hinaus.   (German)
      three riders rode   to.the gate out

      'Three riders rode out of the gate.'

    b. Es   ritten drei Reiter zum   Tor hinaus.
      EXPL rode   three riders to.the gate out

Danish uses the expletive *der* to make it clear that an extraction of a constituent took place (Müller & Ørsnes 2011: 169):[5]

---

[5]Examples marked with DK are extracted from KorpusDK, a corpus of 56 Million words documenting contemporary Danish (http://ordnet.dk/korpusdk).

(17) a. Politiet   ved   ikke, hvem der   havde placeret   (Danish)
        police.DEF knows not   who EXPL has   placed
        bomben.[6]
        bomb.DEF
        'The police does not know who placed the bomb.'

   b. * Politiet   ved   ikke, hvem havde placeret bomben.
        police.DEF knows not   who has   placed bomb.DEF

Without the expletive, one would have a pattern like the one in (17b). In (17b) we
have the normal SVO order and it is not obvious to the hearer that the pattern
consists of an extracted element (the subject) and an SVO clause from which it
is missing. This is more transparent if an expletive is inserted into the subject
position as in (17a). (18) shows this using the analysis that will be suggested
in Section 8.2.3: (18a) shows the hypothetical structure that would result if one
assumed that the subject *hvem* 'who' is extracted. So-called *string-vacuous movement* would result: the subject is moved to a place right next to it. In (18b), on the
other hand, the subject position is taken by the expletive and hence it is clear that
the embedded clause has a special structure. The expletive *der* is an overt marker
for the hearer or reader of the clause marking it as an embedded interrogative
clause.

(18) a. * [hvem$_i$ [$_{-i}$ havde placeret bomben]]   (Danish)
          who   has   placed bomb.DEF

   b.   [hvem$_i$ [der   havde $_{-i}$ placeret bomben]]
          who   EXPL has   placed bomb.DEF

Similarly, Yiddish uses an expletive in embedded interrogatives (w + V2) if
there is no other element that is information-structurally appropriate for the
preverbal position. (19) shows examples from Prince (1989: 403–404):

(19) a. ikh hob zi gefregt ver es   iz beser far ir.   (Yiddish)
         I   have her asked   who EXPL is better for her
         'I have asked her who is better for her.'

   b.   ikh hob im gefregt vemen es   kenen ale dayne khaverim.
        I   have him asked   whom EXPL know all your   friends
        'I asked him whom all your friends know.'

(19a) is an example involving an interrogative pronoun that is the subject, and
(19b) is an example in which the preverbal position is not filled by an argument

---

[6]DK

of *kenen* 'know' but by an expletive. The subject *ale dayne khaverim* 'all your friends' stays behind and the object *vemen* 'whom' is extracted as it is the interrogative pronoun.

8.2 The analysis

This section will first deal with clauses introduced by a complementizer (Subsection 8.2.1) and then discuss embedded interrogative clauses in Subscetion 8.2.2. Subsection 8.2.3 discusses a lexical rule for the introduction of expletives that play a role in various languages in marking the clause type.

8.2.1 Embedded clauses introduced by a complementizer

The analysis of Afrikaans, Dutch, German and English complementizer phrases is straightforward: the complementizer is combined with an uninverted verbal projection. For the first three languages, this is a verb-final clause (SOV), and for English it is an SVO clause. The respective analyses are given in Figure 8.1 and 8.2.

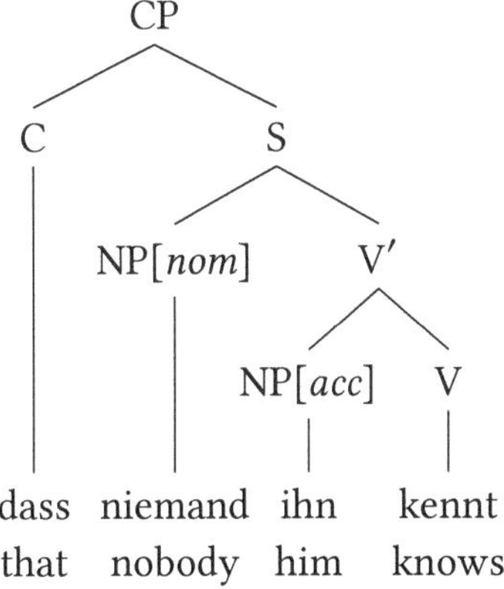

Figure 8.1: Analysis of German complementizer phrase as C + SOV

Yiddish complementizers select a V2 clause. The analysis of the example in (20) is shown in Figure 8.3.

(20) Ikh meyn az   haynt hot Max geleyent dos bukh.[7]   (Yiddish)
      I   think that today has Max read   the book

      'I think that Max read the book today.'

---

[7]Diesing (1990: 58)

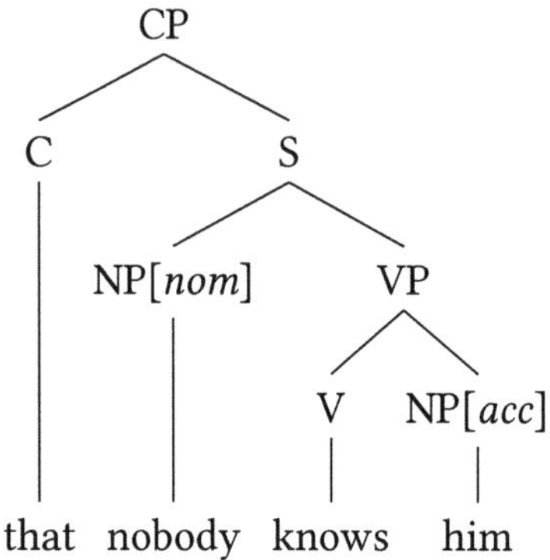

Figure 8.2: Analysis of English complementizer phrase as C + SVO

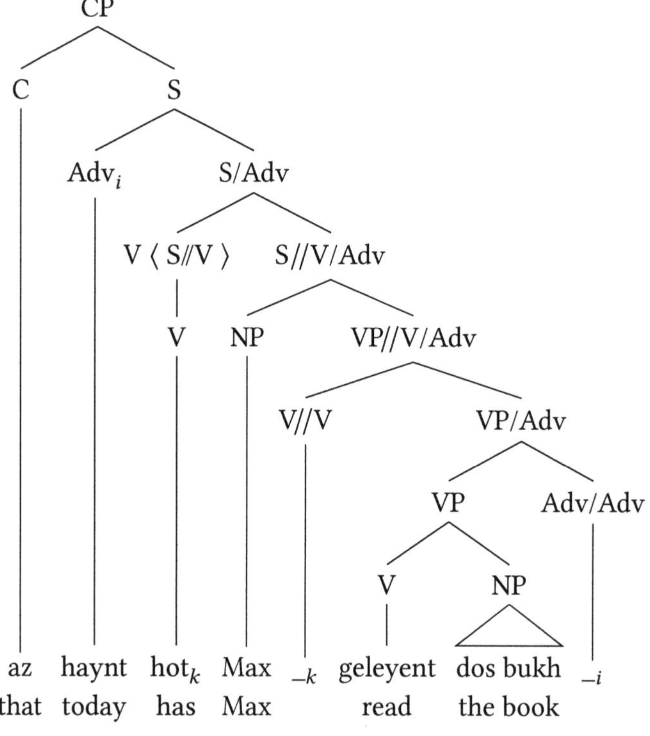

Figure 8.3: Analysis of the Yiddish complementizer phrase as C + V2

The analysis looks complicated, but it is really just the combination of a complementizer with a V2 clause. The V2 clause has *haynt* 'today' extracted and the finite auxiliary *hot* 'has' is moved to V1 position.

The differences between languages can be accounted for by letting the complementizer select Ses with different feature–value combinations. While complementizers in SOV languages select verb-final projections (INITIAL−), Yiddish selects V2+ clauses (the result of applying the Filler-Head Schema) and Danish does not specify any of such features on the selected clause. Since nothing is specified in Danish, the embedded clause can have the form that the rest of the Danish grammar permits: it can be SVO or V2.

8.2.2 Interrogative clauses

As the data discussion showed, the phrase containing the interrogative pronoun is extracted from the remaining clause. The fronting of the *w*-phrase is like fronting in V2 clauses. In the topological fields model, the fronted phrase in German relative clauses and interrogative clauses is assigned to the *Vorfeld* (Müller 2023b: 48–49). The difference between interrogative clauses and V2 clauses is the position of the verb: V2 clauses have the verb in initial position while it is in final position in interrogatives and relatives. Figure 8.4 shows the analysis of the interrogative clause in (21). The pronominal adverb *worüber* 'about what' is extracted from the rest of the clause.

(21) Ich weiß, [worüber]$_i$ [$\_i$ sie spricht].
      I   know where.about   she speaks
      'I know what she speaks about.'

Figure 8.4 uses the slash notation that I have been using so far. In order to account for more complex *w*-phrases I will use the same trick as for other nonlocal dependencies and pass information about *w*-pronouns on to mother nodes. For modeling this I will use list-valued features like SPR and COMPS. Figure 8.5 shows the same clause as Figure 8.4 but with two features that are traditionally used in the analysis of nonlocal dependencies (Pollard & Sag 1994: Chapter 4 and 5): QUE and SLASH. By convention, the boxed numbers are put in front of XPs if the XP is an argument and they follow the XP if the XP is involved in a nonlocal dependency. The reason for this is that different parts of information are shared. A full explanation of the difference requires some deeper understanding of the mechanisms and cannot be given here. The interested reader is referred to Müller (2013b: Chapter 10) or to Borsley & Crysmann (2021). PP₁[SLASH ⟨ 1 ⟩] means

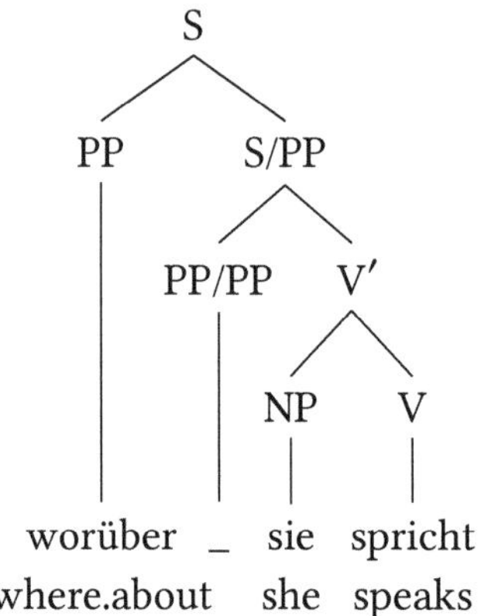

Figure 8.4: Analysis of simple interrogative clause

that the relevant information about the PP is put into SLASH, that is, into the list that is percolated upwards until a matching filler is found (a PP whose relevant properties can be identified with the element in the SLASH list). Once a filler has been found no SLASH element is passed upwards. The SLASH list of the top-most node is the empty list.

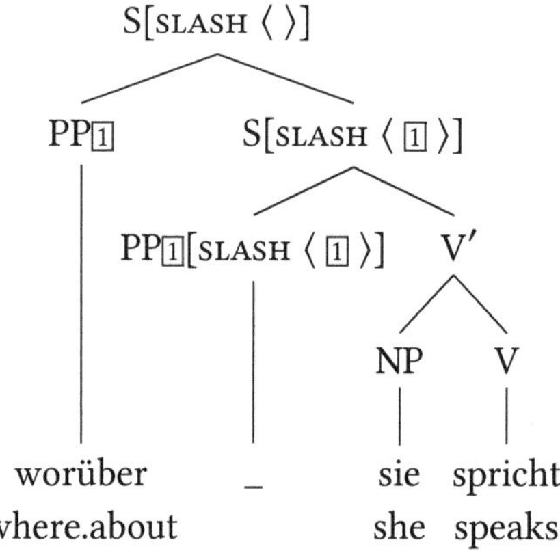

Figure 8.5: Analysis of simple interrogative clause using the SLASH feature

Now, this machinery can be extended to cover nonlocal dependencies for interrogative pronouns. Figure 8.6 shows how the information about the interrogative within the complex *w*-phrase can be passed upwards in a tree by using the QUE feature.

(22) Ich weiß, [über welches Thema]$_i$ [_$_i$ sie spricht].
      I   know about which   topic   she speaks

      'I know which topic she speaks about.'

Figure 8.6 is completely parallel to Figure 8.4 except that information about the
w-word is added. The content of QUE is not provided here but the QUE list of *w*-
words contains information that is needed for semantics: the *w*-word indicates
what is asked for and this information is passed up to the level of the complete
clause (see Ginzburg & Sag 2000 on interrogatives in general and on their semantics in particular).

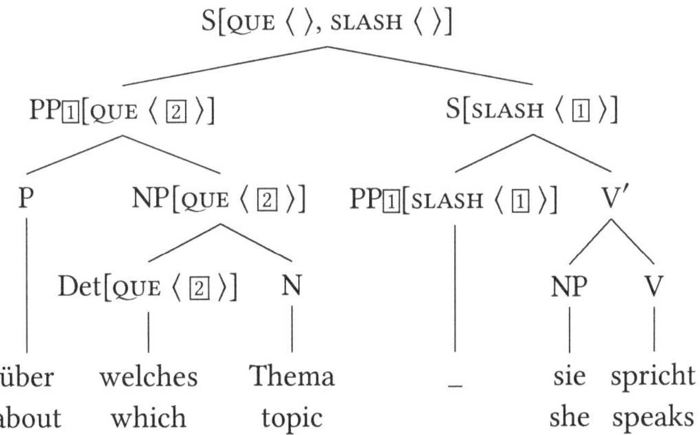

Figure 8.6: Analysis of simple interrogative clause using SLASH and QUE

Interrogative clauses are licensed by a special variant of the Filler-Head Schema,
namely a schema that requires the initial daughter (the filler) to have something
in its QUE list (Figure 8.7). This entails that the filler has to contain a *w*-word.

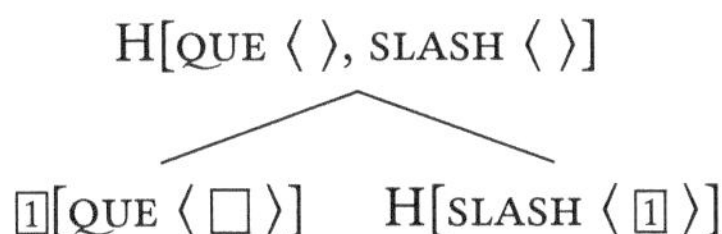

Figure 8.7: Interrogative Clause Schema

The languages differ as far as the order of the verb and its arguments are concerned, so further specifications have to be added to what is given in Figure 8.7.
For example, German interrogative clauses are verb final, while Yiddish interrogatives involve an extraction out of a V2 clause. In addition, constraints regarding

the verb form have to be specified. German allows for finite verbs only, while English allows for finite verbs and infinitives with *to* (see (15) on p. 221).

Up to now, we have looked at German examples with prepositional objects fronted. Figure 8.8 shows the analysis of (23) with a subject as a *w*-phrase:

(23)   wer das Buch liest   (German)
       who the books reads

       'who reads the book'

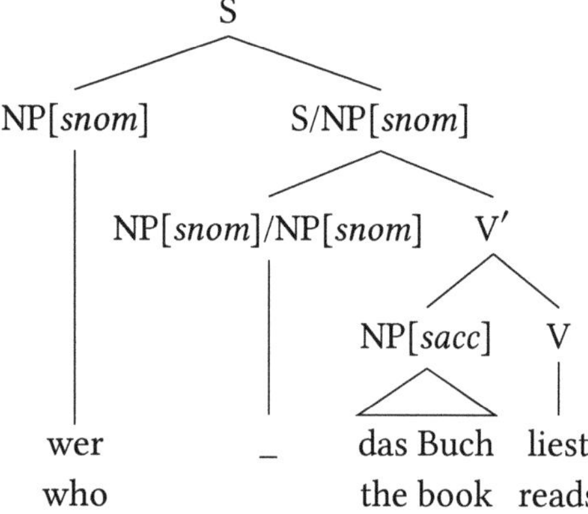

Figure 8.8: Analysis of German interrogative clause with the subject as *w*-word

So, with what we have so far, we can analyze interrogatives in German and other SOV languages but there are still open questions in languages like Danish where expletive insertion in subject position is required when a subject is questioned (see (17)). Similarly, Yiddish may insert expletives in the preverbal position in interrogatives (see (19)). So, to account for this data, we have to deal with expletives. Expletives are the topic of the next section.

8.2.3 A lexical rule for the introduction of expletives

The various types of expletives introduced in Section 8.1.3 can – maybe somewhat surprisingly – be accounted for by a simple lexical rule that adds an expletive to the ARG-ST list of lexical items (Müller & Ørsnes 2011: 180):

(24)   Expletive Insertion Lexical Rule:

$$\begin{bmatrix} \text{HEAD} & \begin{bmatrix} verb \\ \text{VFORM } fin \end{bmatrix} \\ \text{ARG-ST } \boxed{1} \end{bmatrix} \mapsto \begin{bmatrix} \text{ARG-ST } \left\langle \text{NP}[lnom]_{expl} \right\rangle \oplus \boxed{1} \end{bmatrix}$$

The application of the lexical rule is restricted to finite verbs since positional expletives occur in V2 clauses and these are always finite. Expletives in interrogative clauses are used to fill the subject position to mark extraction and of course this is something that is necessary in finite clauses only.

The case of the expletive pronoun is specified as lexical nominative, which means that it is invisible to case assignment principles. Nominative is assigned to the first NP with structural case (see p. 190) and since the expletive has lexical case, nothing changes. The same is true for structural accusatives: the first NP with structural case gets nominative and all others accusative. The expletive does not interfere with this.

Similarly, the theory of agreement entertained so far is not affected: the verb agrees with the first NP with structural case. This makes the right predictions for agreement in Icelandic, where the verb agrees with objects in the nominative (Zaenen et al. 1985: 460).

(25) a. Hefur henni   alltaf þótt   Ólafur   leibinlegur?[8]   (Icelandic)
          has   she.DAT always thought Olaf.NOM boring.NOM

      'Has she always considered Olaf boring?'

      b. Konunginum voru gefnar   ambáttir.[9]
         the.king.DAT were given.F.PL maidservants.NOM.F.PL

      'The king was given female slaves.'

And the approach to agreement also works for cases of remote passive in German, where the subject is not the first element in an ARG-ST list. One of the examples in (104) on p. 208 is repeated below:

(26) a. Sie erlauben uns   nicht, den   Erfolg auszukosten.
         they permitted us.DAT not   the.ACC success to.enjoy

      'They did not permit us to enjoy the success.'

      b. Der Erfolg   wurde uns   nicht auszukosten erlaubt.[10]
         the success.NOM was   us.DAT not   to.enjoy   permitted

      'We were not permitted to enjoy our success.'

See p. 210 for the respective ARG-ST lists.

As far as the position in the clause is concerned, the expletive is a subject in Danish. This is exactly what we want and what follows from the general mapping

---

[8] Zaenen, Maling & Thráinsson (1985: 451)

[9] Zaenen, Maling & Thráinsson (1985: 460)

[10] Haider (1986b: 110)

from ARG-ST to SPR and COMPS in SVO languages. The analysis of (27) is shown in Figure 8.9.

(27) hvem der   læser bogen   (Danish)
      who   EXPL reads book.DEF

      'who reads the book'

The lexical item for *læser* 'to read' is given in (28):

(28) Lexical item for *læser* 'to read' with expletive subject:

$$
\begin{bmatrix}
\text{SPR} & \langle\, \text{NP}[\mathit{lnom}]_{\mathit{expl}} \,\rangle \\
\text{COMPS} & \langle\, \text{NP}[\mathit{str}], \text{NP}[\mathit{str}] \,\rangle \\
\text{ARG-ST} & \langle\, \text{NP}[\mathit{lnom}]_{\mathit{expl}}, \text{NP}[\mathit{str}], \text{NP}[\mathit{str}] \,\rangle
\end{bmatrix}
$$

The case assignment principles assign nominative to the first NP with structural case and accusative to the second. As Figure 8.9 shows, the expletive subject is realized as specifier in the subject position and the nominative and accusative on the COMPS list are realized as objects. The "nominative object" is extracted and realized as the interrogative pronoun.

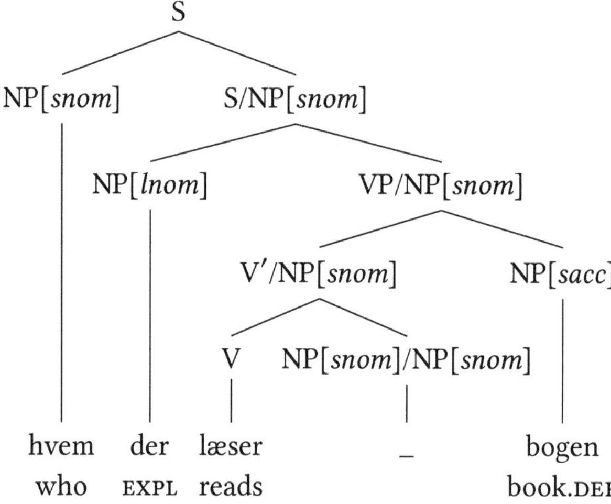

Figure 8.9: Analysis of interrogative clauses in Danish with subject extraction

Similarly, the analysis of interrogatives in Yiddish may involve an initial expletive in the V2 clause if the speaker finds the subject or any other element inappropriate for this position for information structural reasons. Figure 8.10 shows the analysis of (29):

(29) ver es   leyent dos bukh   (Yiddish)
      who EXPL reads the book

'who reads the book'

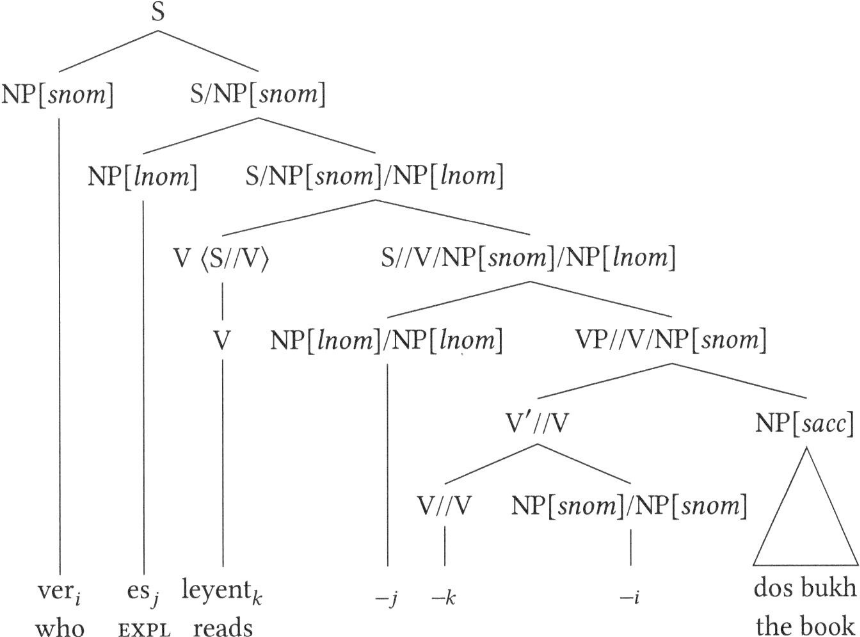

Figure 8.10: Analysis of a Yiddish interrogative clause involving a fronted expletive pronoun

The analysis is more complex than the Danish one, but this is due to the fact that Yiddish has V2 clauses in interrogatives involving verb movement in addition to extraction. Interrogatives have two extracted elements: one for V2, the expletive in the example, and another one which is the interrogative phrase (*ver* 'who' in the example). The figure shows two elements after a /. In the notation using the SLASH feature, there would be a list with two elements.

This completes the analysis of finite interrogative clauses with and without expletives, but there is more to be said about expletives in general. I stipulated a lexical rule adding an expletive element above and this accounts for expletives in Yiddish interrogatives. It not just works for interrogatives but for V2 in general.

Yiddish declarative V2 clauses can have initial expletives as well, as can German V2 clauses. (30a) is a German example. As (30b) shows, the expletive is not allowed to appear in the *Mittelfeld*.

(30) a. Es   lachen drei Kinder.
          EXPL laugh three children
          'Three children laugh.'

      b. * dass es   drei Kinder   lachen
            that EXPL three children laugh

In German descriptive grammars, this expletive is called "positional *es*" and it is emphasized that it is not the subject and not an argument of the verb (Eisenberg 2004: 129, 177, 371, Eisenberg et al. 2005: §1263). The fact that the *es* cannot appear in the *Mittelfeld* is seen as support for the non-argumenthood of it. However, we have seen that the expletive is realized in the subject position in Danish, so there is some appeal to the idea to treat it uniformly as the initial element of the ARG-ST list across the Germanic languages. Nevertheless it is undeniable that the *Vorfeld* is the only place in which this expletive can appear in German and Yiddish. The problem can be solved by adding the following constraint to the Expletive Insertion Lexical Rule in the grammars of German and Yiddish:

(31) Constraint on the output of the Expletive Insertion Lexical Rule for German and Yiddish:
$$\left[\text{ARG-ST} \ \left\langle \ \text{NP}_{\boxed{1}}[\text{SLASH} \ \langle \boxed{1} \rangle] \ \right\rangle \oplus \Box \right]$$

This constraint says that the first element in the ARG-ST list (the expletive) has to have a SLASH element with the relevant properties of the expletive. Since the expletive pronoun does not have anything in SLASH, it cannot be combined directly with the respective lexical items. The trace has something in SLASH, this is its very nature. So a trace can combine with the lexical item for *lachen* 'to laugh' and then the expletive can function as the filler.

One problem remains: extraction of expletives must be clause-bound:

(32) * Es$_i$ glaube ich, dass _$_i$ drei Kinder   lachen.   (German)
        EXPL believe I   that   three children laugh

      Intended: 'I believe that three children laugh.'

While extraction may cross clause boundaries in principle (see (11) on p. 219), this is excluded in (32). However, this is not a particular problem of the analysis of the positional *es* at hand but it is a general property of expletive elements. (33)

shows an example with the weather *es*, which clearly is an argument of the verb *regnen* 'to rain':

(33) * Es$_i$ glaube ich, dass $_i$ regnet.
      EXPL believe I   that   rains
      Intended: 'I believe that it rains.'

So, whatever rules out examples like (33) also accounts for (32).

Finally, there is one problem left: I provided a lexical rule that licenses lexical item for interrogatives with an expletive in subject position, but what is still missing is a constraint that rules out clauses without the expletive. There is nothing in the grammar so far that does this. It is possible to formulate something like this but the formal tools have not been introduced in this book. The reader is referred to Müller & Ørsnes (2011: 185) for details.

8.3 Summary

This chapter provided an analysis of dependent clauses introduced by a complementizer and of interrogative clauses. Together with the V1 and V2 clauses dealt with in Chapter 6, this covers the main clause types in the Germanic languages. The variation in these subordinated clauses is connected to what we saw before: the SOV languages have SOV order in embedded languages and some SVO languages have SVO order, some allow for both SVO and V2 and some allow for V2 only. Interrogative clauses involve a clause with a gap and the filler is the interrogative phrase containing a *wh*-word in English and a corresponding word in the other Germanic languages. The *wh* phrase may consist of a single interrogative pronoun or may be internally complex. The information about the interrogative pronoun has to be present at the top-most node of the interrogative phrase for semantic and syntactic reasons. The syntactic reason is of course that one has to make sure that the fronted phrase contains an interrogative pronoun at all. The information is passed up from the interrogative pronoun by the same mechanism that is also used for extraction: like SLASH, QUE is used to pass the information up. Danish and Yiddish use expletive pronouns in interrogatives. To account for this, Müller & Ørsnes (2011) suggested a lexical rule that introduced the expletive into the ARG-ST list. This expletive can function as subject in Danish and as positional expletive in German and Yiddish.

Comprehension questions

1. Where are expletives used in Germanic languages for clause type marking?

2. Is the clause following the complementizer in (34) a SVO or V2 clause?

    (34)   at   Gert har ikke læst bogen   (Danish)
             that Gert has not read book.DEF

Exercises

1. Analyze the interrogative clauses in (35):

    (35)   a. Ich weiß, wen   Kim kennt.   (German)
                I   know who.ACC Kim knows
                'I know who Kim knows.'
          b. Jeg ved, hvem der kende Kim.   (Danish)
                I   know who EXPL knows Kim
                'I know who knows Kim.'

2. Analyze the clause in (36). Use triangles for the NP and the PP.

    (36)   Es   schwammen zwei Delphine neben dem Boot.
             EXPL swam   two dolphins next.to the boat
             'Two dolphins were swimming next to the boat.'

9 Outlook

This book has sketched fragments of grammars of several Germanic languages. The theory lurking in the background is Head-Driven Phrase Structure Grammar (HPSG) (Pollard & Sag 1987, 1994, Müller 2013b, Müller et al. 2021). We had a look at valence and how it is represented in valence lists like SPR and COMPS. We also looked at adjuncts, which are not represented in lists: adjuncts select the heads they modify. HPSG assumes that there are schemata for the combination of linguistic material. We dealt with the Specifier-Head Schema, the Head-Complements Schema, the Head-Adjunct Schema and also the Predicate Complex Schema. Verbal complexes in the Germanic OV languages have been analyzed as predicate complex formation.

The Germanic languages vary as far as their basic order is concerned (VO or OV). Apart from English, all Germanic languages are V2 languages. V2 sentences are analyzed via head-movement: there is an empty verb in final position which is related to the fronted verb.

All analyses are implemented in computer-processable grammar fragments. They are fully formalized – otherwise they would not be processable – but they have been given here in simplified and sketchy form. I briefly talked about the connection between syntax and semantics in Section 4.9, but of course all implementations come with semantic representations.

Due to space limitations, it is not possible to carefully introduce all concepts of HPSG, but the interested reader is invited to have a look at the HPSG monographs (Pollard & Sag 1987, 1994, Ginzburg & Sag 2000, Müller 2013b), overview articles (Levine & Meurers 2006, Przepiórkowski & Kupść 2006, Bildhauer 2014, Müller 2015a, Müller & Machicao y Priemer 2019), Chapter 9 in the Grammatical Theory textbook (Müller 2023b) or the handbook on HPSG (Müller et al. 2021). Especially the latter volume is an up-to-date book with more than 1600 pages dealing in 32 chapters with almost every aspect one could be interested in.

Appendix A: Solutions

A.1 Phrase structure grammars and $\overline{\text{X}}$ theory

1. Draw trees for the following phrases. You may use the symbol NP for proper names and $\overline{\text{N}}$ for nouns not requiring complements (as in Figure 3.13).

(1) a. eine Stunde vor   der Ankunft des   Zuges
        one hour   before the arrival   of.the train
        'one hour before the arrival of the train'

     b. kurz   nach der Ankunft in Paris
        shortly after the arrival   in Paris
        'shortly after the arrival in Paris'

     c. das ein Lied singende Kind aus   dem Allgäu
        this a   song singing   child from the   Allgäu
        'the child from the Allgäu singing a song'

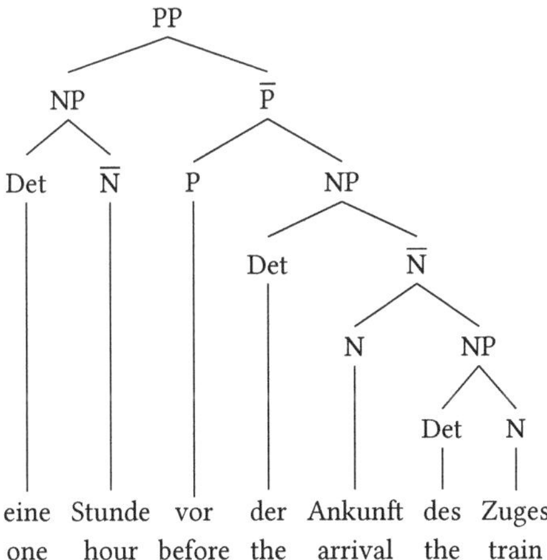

Figure A.1: Analysis of *eine Stunde vor der Ankunft des Zuges* 'one hour before the arrival of the train'

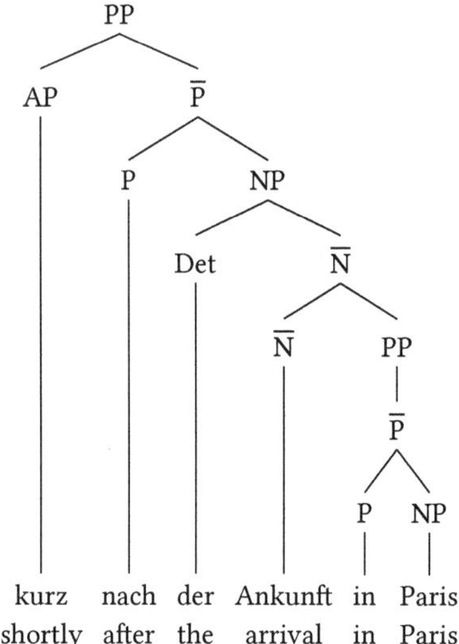

Figure A.2: Analysis of *kurz nach der Ankunft in Paris* 'shortly after the arrival in Paris'

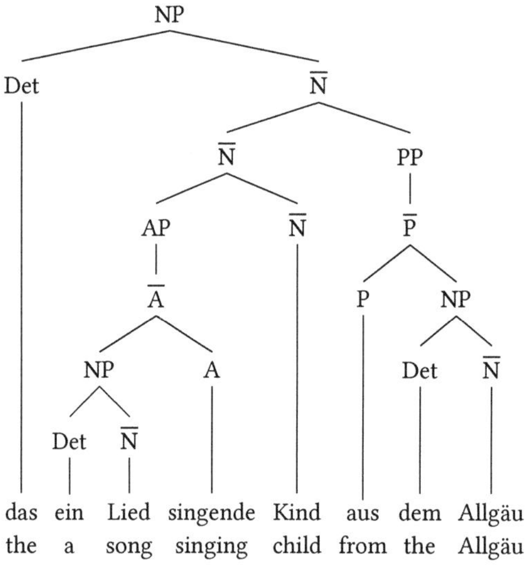

Figure A.3: Analysis of *das ein Lied singende Kind aus dem Allgäu* 'the child from the Allgäu singing a song'

A.2 Valency, argument order and adjunct placement

1. Provide the valence lists for the following words:

    (2) a. laugh   SPR ⟨ NP[*nom*] ⟩
         b. eat   SPR ⟨ NP[*nom*] ⟩, COMPS ⟨ NP[*acc*] ⟩
         c. to douse   SPR ⟨ NP[*nom*] ⟩, COMPS ⟨ NP[*acc*] ⟩
         d. bezichtigen SPR ⟨⟩, COMPS ⟨ NP[*nom*], NP[*gen*] ⟩   (German)
            accuse
         e. he   SPR ⟨⟩, COMPS ⟨⟩
         f. the   SPR ⟨⟩, COMPS ⟨⟩
         g. Ankunft   SPR ⟨ DET ⟩, COMPS ⟨ NP ⟩   (German)
            arrival   SPR ⟨ DET ⟩, COMPS ⟨⟩

    If you are uncertain as far as case assignment is concerned, you may use
    the Wiktionary: https://de.wiktionary.org/.

2. Draw trees for the NPs that were also used in Exercise 1 on page 62 in
   Chapter 3.

    (3) a. eine Stunde vor   der Ankunft des   Zuges
             one hour   before the arrival of.the train
             'one hour before the arrival of the train'

         b. kurz   nach der Ankunft in Paris
             shortly after the arrival in Paris
             'shortly after the arrival in Paris'

         c. das ein Lied singende Kind aus   dem Allgäu
             this a   song singing child from the Allgäu
             'the child from the Allgäu singing a song'

3. Draw trees for the following examples. NPs can be abbreviated.

    (4) a. weil   Aicke dem   Kind ein   Buch schenkt   (German)
             because Aicke the.DAT child a.ACC book gives.as.a.present
             'because Aicke gives the child a book as a present'

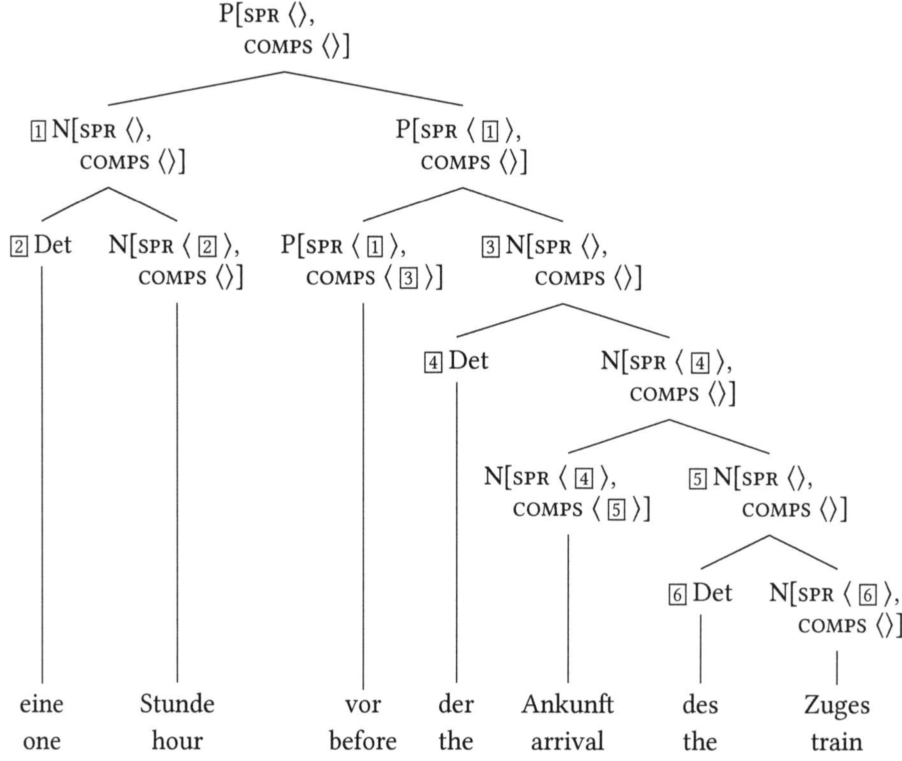

Figure A.4: Analysis of *eine Stunde vor der Ankunft des Zuges* 'one hour before the arrival of the train'

    b. weil   dem   Kind solch ein   Buch niemand
       because the.DAT child such a.ACC book nobody.NOM
       schenkt
       gives.as.a.present
       'because nobody gives the child such a book as a present'

    c. because Kim gave a book to him

    d. Sandy saw this yesterday.

    e. at   Bjarne læste bogen   (Danish)
       that Bjarne read book.DEF
       'that Bjarne read the book'

The trees with the solutions are given in the following. Figure A.8 differs

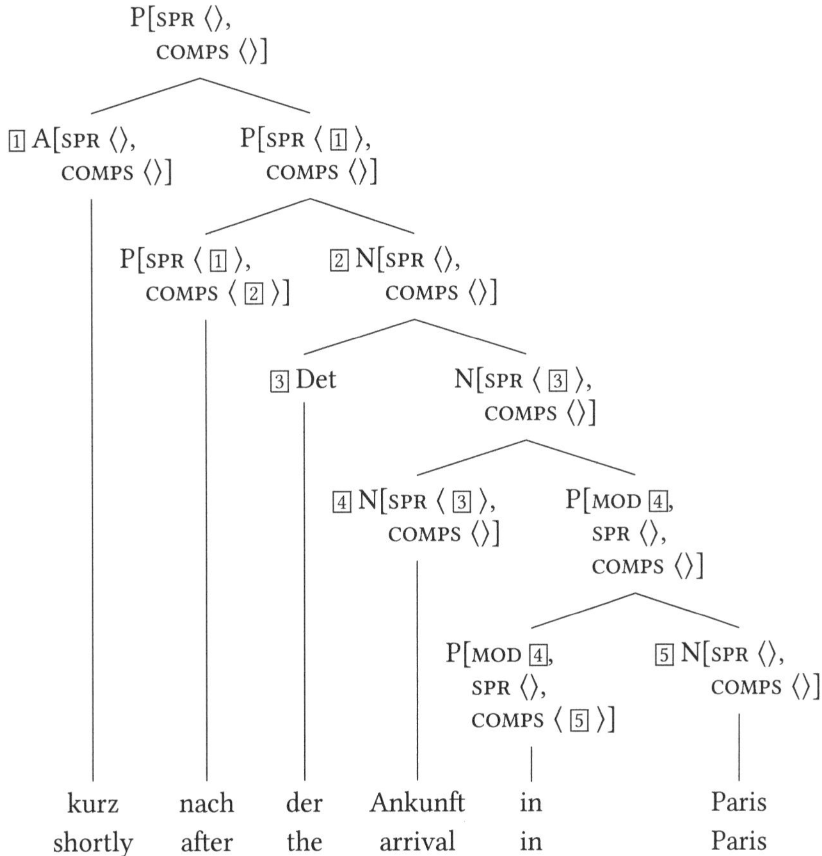

Figure A.5: Analysis of *kurz nach der Ankunft in Paris* 'shortly after the arrival in Paris'

from Figure A.7 in the way the elements in the COMPS list are numbered, but in each case the order of the elements in the COMPS list of *schenkt* 'gives as a present' is ⟨ NP[*nom*], NP[*dat*], NP[*acc*]⟩. The different numbering is due to the order in which the elements are combined. If the numbering is done consistently from top to bottom, Figure A.8 is the result. If one is more liberal in the way the numbers are assigned, the same situation can be depicted as in Figure A.9. Figure A.9 has the same numbering in the valence list as Figure A.7 and maybe easier to grasp because of this.

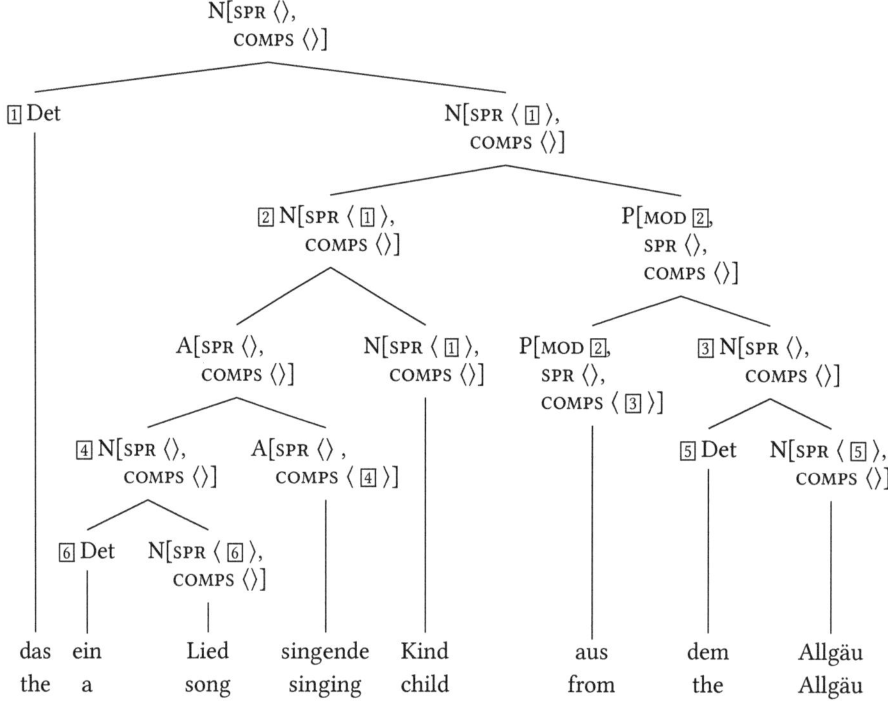

Figure A.6: Analysis of *das ein Lied singende Kind aus dem Allgäu* 'the child from the Allgäu singing a song'

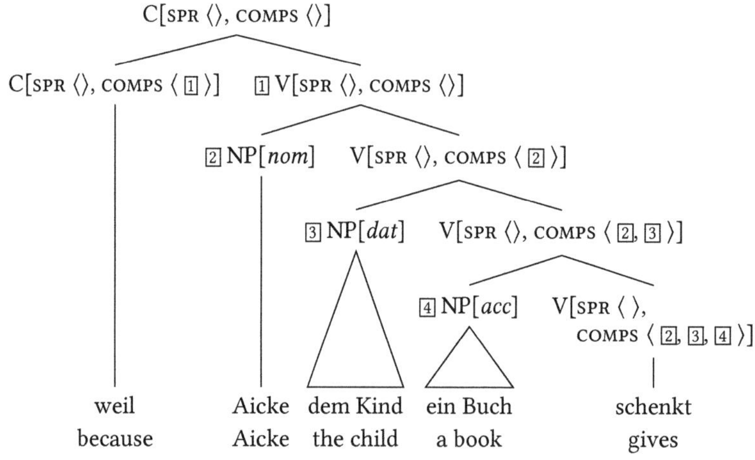

Figure A.7: The analysis of *weil Aicke dem Kind ein Buch schenkt* 'because Aicke gives the child a book as a present'

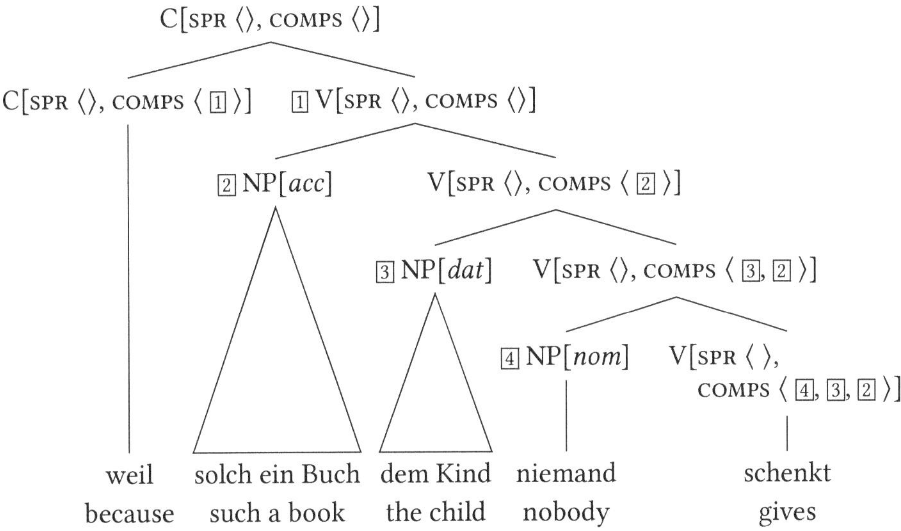

Figure A.8: The analysis of *weil dem Kind solch ein Buch niemand schenkt* 'because nobody gives the child such a book as a present'

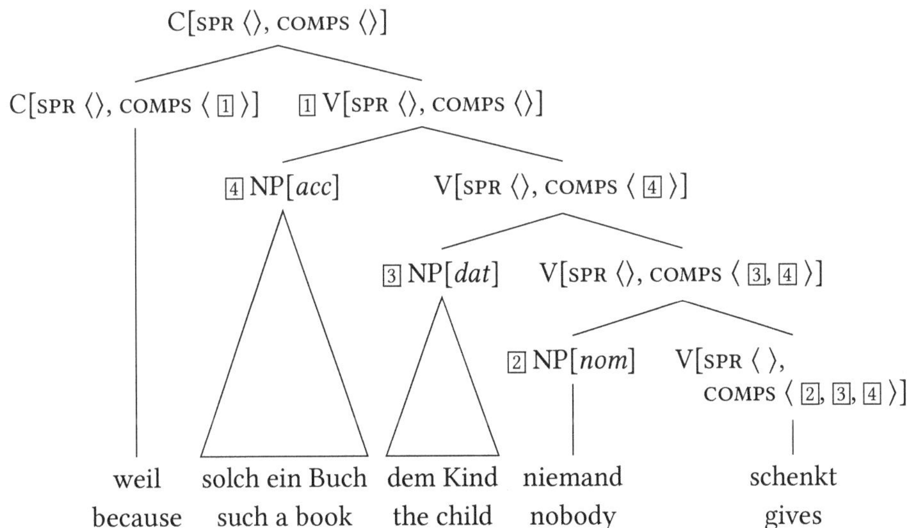

Figure A.9: The analysis of *weil dem Kind solch ein Buch niemand schenkt* 'because nobody gives the child such a book as a present'

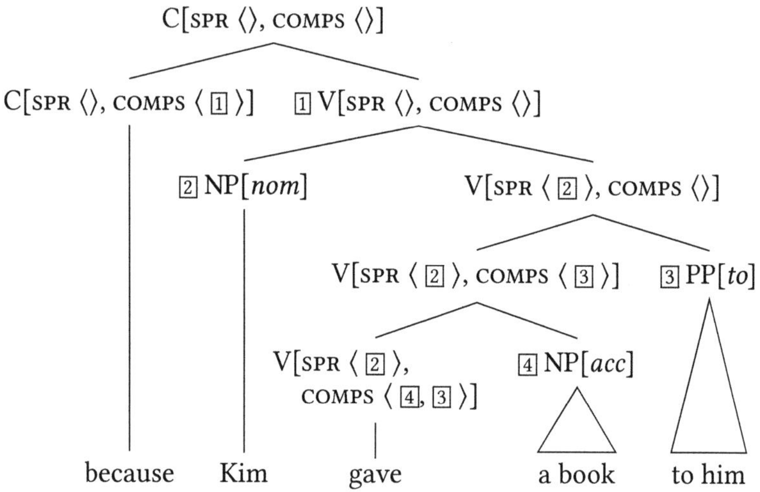

Figure A.10: The analysis of *because Kim gave a book to him*

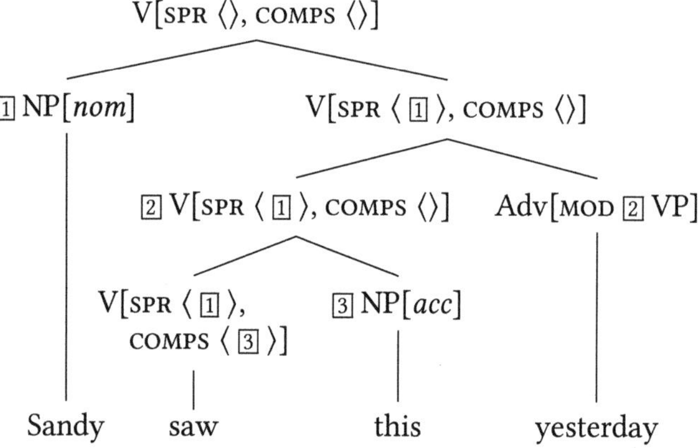

Figure A.11: Analysis of *Sandy saw this yesterday.*

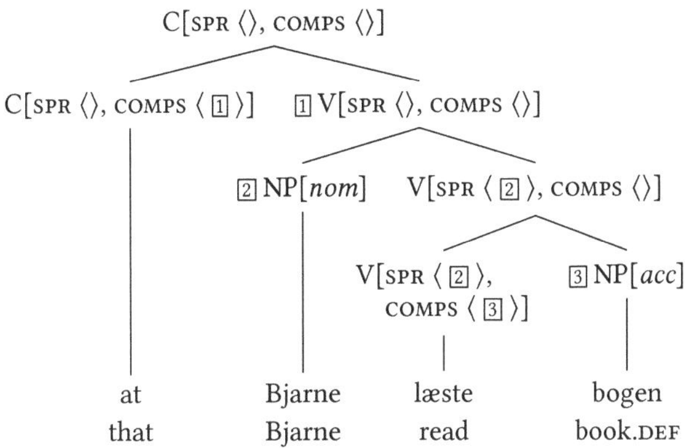

Figure A.12: Analysis of *at Bjarne læste bogen* 'that Bjarne read the book'

A.3 The verbal complex

1. Sketch the analysis of the verbal complexes in the following examples:

(5) a. dass sie darüber   lachen muss   (German)
         that she there.about laugh   must

         'that she has to laugh about it'

     b. dass sie darüber   hat lachen müssen
         that she there.about has laugh   must

         'that she had to laugh about it'

     c. dass sie darüber   wird haben lachen müssen
         that she there.about will   have   laugh must

         'that it will be the case that she had to laugh about it'

You may omit the SPR values, since they are the empty list for all German
verbs anyway.

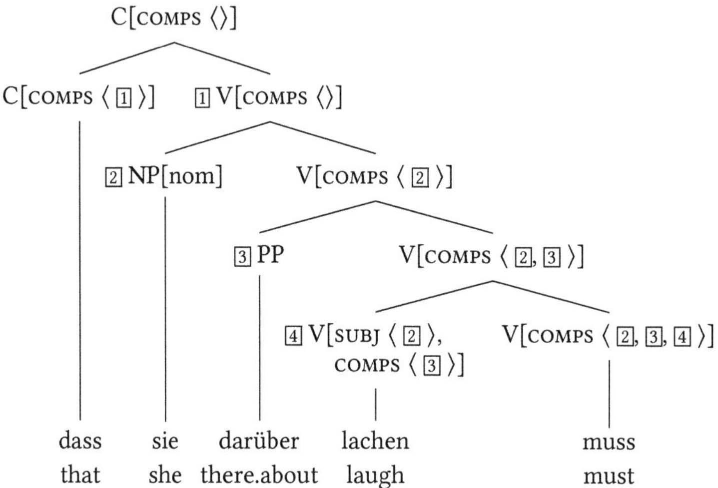

Figure A.13: Analysis of *dass sie darüber lachen muss* 'that she has to laugh about this'

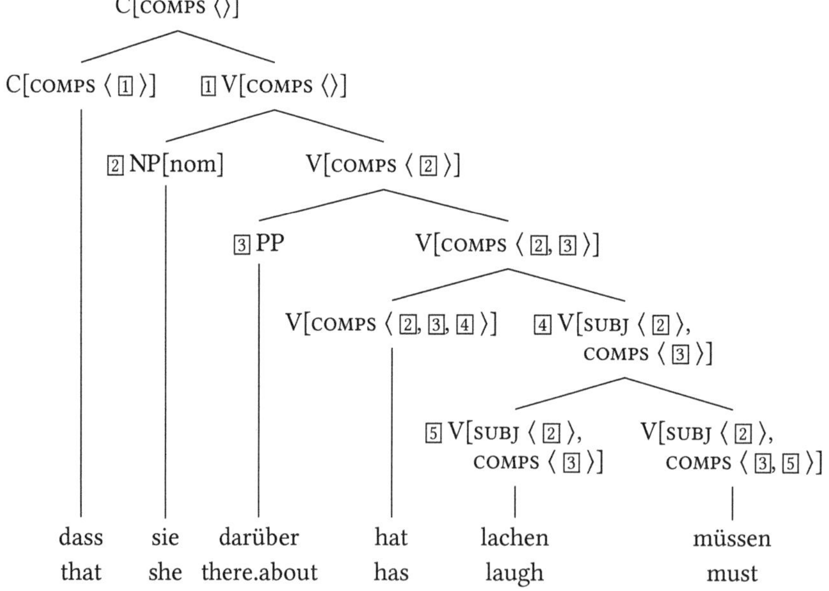

Figure A.14: Analysis of *dass sie darüber hat lachen müssen* 'that she had to laugh about this'

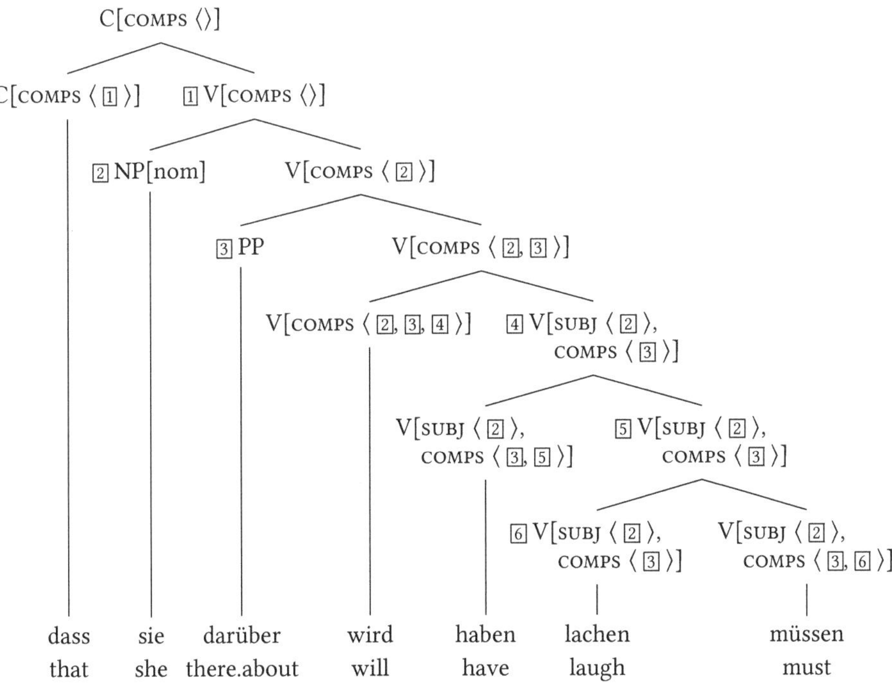

Figure A.15: Analysis of *dass sie darüber wird haben lachen müssen* 'that it will be the case that she had to laugh about this'

A.4 Verb position: Verb-first and verb-second

1. Classify the Germanic languages according to their basic constituent order (SVO, SOV, VSO, …) and V2 assuming that you know that one of the following patterns exists in the language:

(6) a. NP[acc] V-Aux NP[nom] V NP[dat]   V2 SVO

    b. NP[acc] V-Aux NP[nom] NP[dat] V   V2 SOV

    c. NP[acc] NP[nom] V NP[acc]   −V2 SVO

    d. NP[acc] NP[nom] V-Aux V NP[acc]   −V2 SVO

    e. NP[acc] V-Aux NP[nom] V PP   not classifiable

The pattern in (6a) cannot be English, since English does not have a dative. Hence it is a V2 language. The dative object follows the verb, so it must be an SVO language. An example would be Icelandic:

(7) Bókina   hafa ég   gefið honum.   (Icelandic)
     book.the.ACC have I.NOM given he.DAT
     'I gave him the book.'

(6b) has an auxiliary and two NPs followed by a verb. Since the dative object would follow the verb in an SVO language, it must be a SOV language. Since all Germanic SOV languages are also V2 languages, (6b) must be a V2 language. German and Dutch would be examples.

(8) Den   Roman hat jemand   dem   Kind gegeben.
     the.ACC novel   has somebody.NOM the.DAT child given
     'Somebody has given the child the novel.'

Ignoring multiple frontings in German (Müller 2003a), (6c) must be a non-V2 pattern. The language can only be English:

(9) This book, Kim gave Sandy.

For the same reason, (6d) is non-V2 and SVO. The language must be English:

(10) This book, Kim had given Sandy.

The pattern in (6e) cannot be unambiguously classified with respect to V2 and SOV/SVO. Since PPs can be extraposed easily, it could be an SOV langauge with extraposition (e.g., German) or it could be English with question formation (residual V2):

(11) a. Wen hat Aicke gesehen bei   der Demonstration?
        who has Aicke seen   during the rally
        'Who has Aicke seen during the rally.'

     b. Who did Kim see during the rally?

2. Sketch the analysis for the following examples. Use the abbreviations used in this chapter; that is, do not go into the details regarding SPR and COMPS values but use S, VP, and V′.

(12) a. Arbejder Bjarne ihærdigt på bogen?   (Danish)
        works   Bjarne seriously at book.DEF

        'Does Bjarne work seriously on the book?'

     b. Arbeitet Bjarne ernsthaft an dem Buch?   (German)
        works   Bjarne seriously at the book

        'Does Bjarne work seriously on the book?'

     c. Wird sie darüber   nachdenken?   (German)
        will   she there.upon PART.think

        'Will she think about this?'

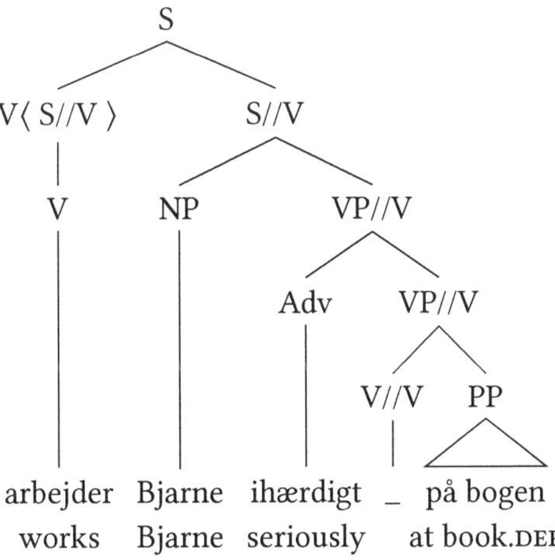

Figure A.16: Analysis of *Arbejder Bjarne ihærdigt på bogen?* 'Does Bjarne work seriously on the book?'

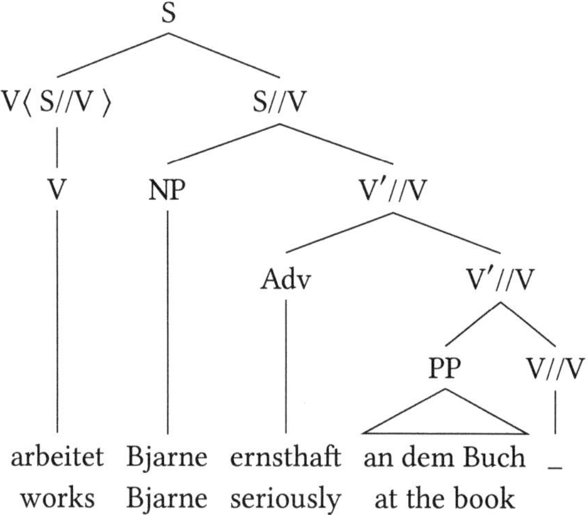

Figure A.17: Analysis of *Arbejder Bjarne ihærdigt på bogen?* 'Does Bjarne work seriously on the book?'

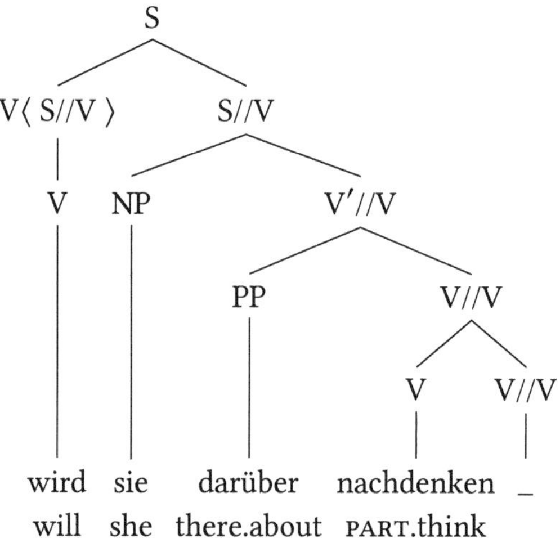

Figure A.18: Analysis of *Wird sie darüber nachdenken?* 'Will she think about this?'

3. Sketch the analysis for the following examples. Use the valence features SPR and COMPS rather than the abbreviations S, VP, and V′. Since the value of SPR in German is always the empty list, you may omit it in the German examples. NPs and PPs can be abbreviated as NP and PP, respectively.

(13) a. dass sie darüber   nachdenkt   (German)
         that she there.upon PART.thinks

         'that she thinks about this'

     b. dass sie darüber   nachdenken wird
        that she there.upon PART.think   will

        'that she will think about this'

     c. Wird sie darüber   nachdenken?
        will she there.upon PART.think

        'Will she think about this?'

(14) a. Arbejder Bjarne ihærdigt på bogen?   (Danish)
         works   Bjarne seriously at book.DEF

         'Does Bjarne work seriously on the book?'

     b. Arbeitet Bjarne ernsthaft an dem Buch?   (German)
        works   Bjarne seriously at the book

        'Does Bjarne work seriously on the book?'

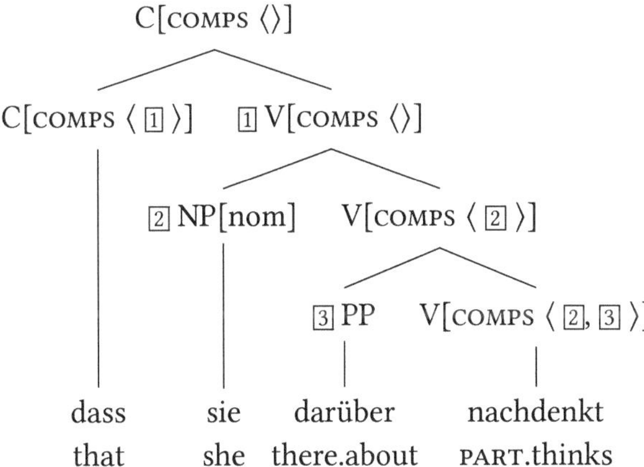

Figure A.19: Analysis of *dass sie darüber nachdenkt* 'that she thinks about this'

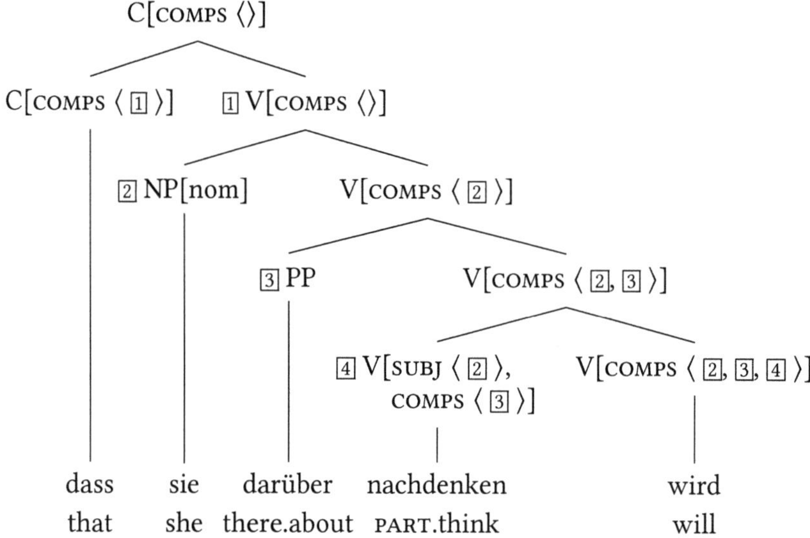

Figure A.20: Analysis of *dass sie darüber nachdenken wird* 'that she will think about this'

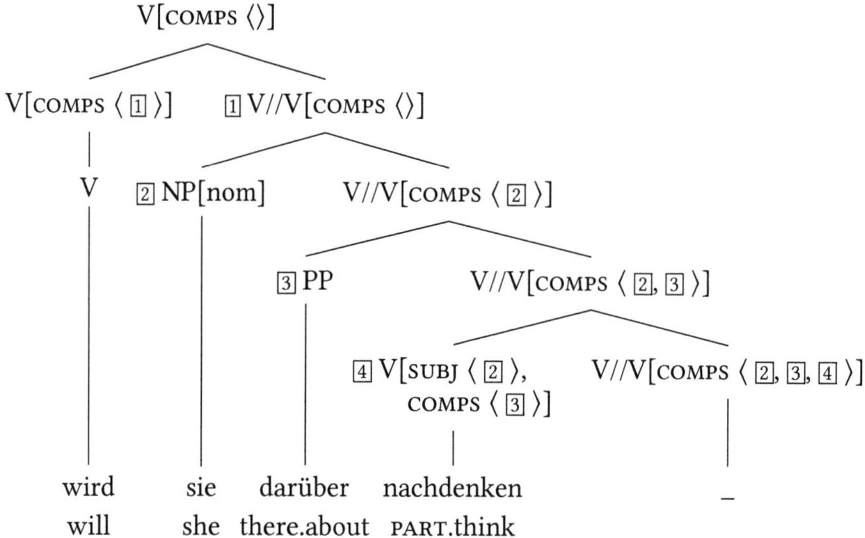

Figure A.21: Analysis of *Wird sie darüber nachdenken?* 'Will she think about this?'

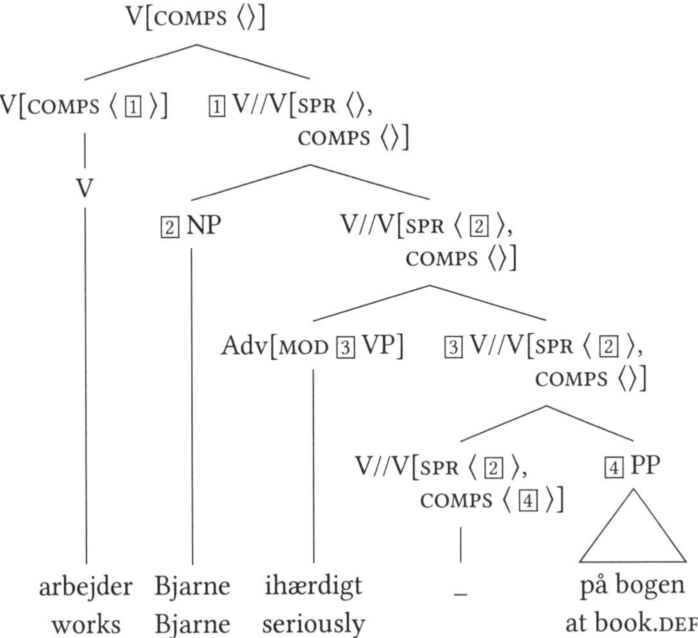

Figure A.22: Analysis of *Arbejder Bjarne ihærdigt på bogen?* 'Does Bjarne work seriously on the book?'

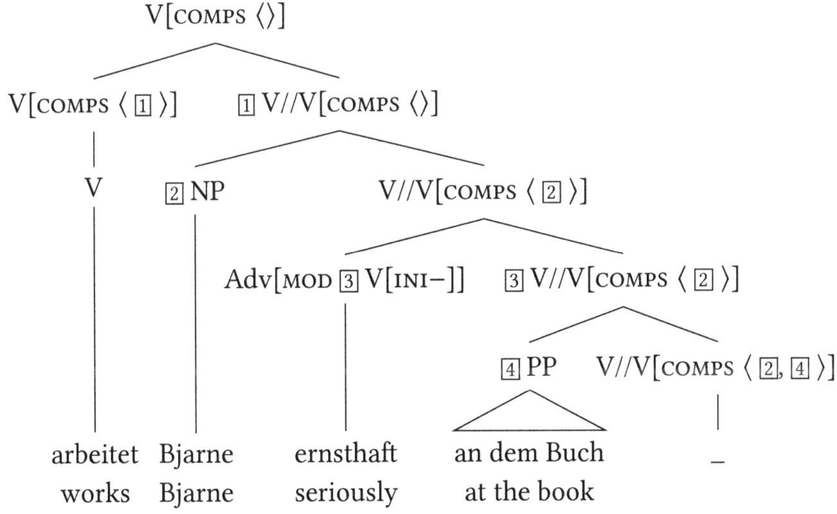

Figure A.23: Analysis of *Arbeitet Bjarne ernsthaft an dem Buch?* 'Does Bjarne work seriously on the book?'

4. Sketch the analysis of the following examples. NPs may be abbreviated. Valence features should not be given, but node labels like V, V′, VP and S should be used instead. If non-local dependencies are involved indicate them using the '/' symbol.

(15) a. Such books, I like.

  b. Solche Bücher mag ich.   (German)
     such books like I

     'I like such books.'

  c. Boger som det elsker jeg.   (Danish)
     books like this like   I

     'I like such books.'

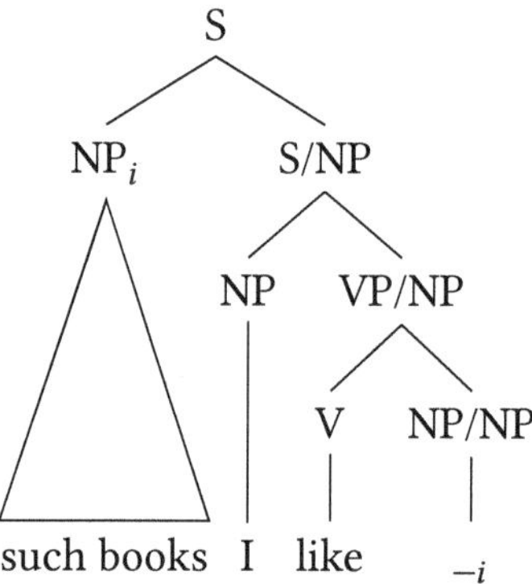

Figure A.24: Analysis of *Such books, I like.*

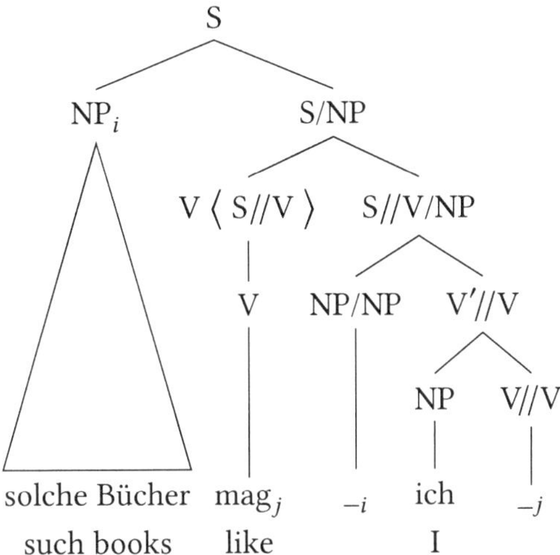

Figure A.25: Analysis of the German example *Solche Bücher mag ich.* 'I like such books.'

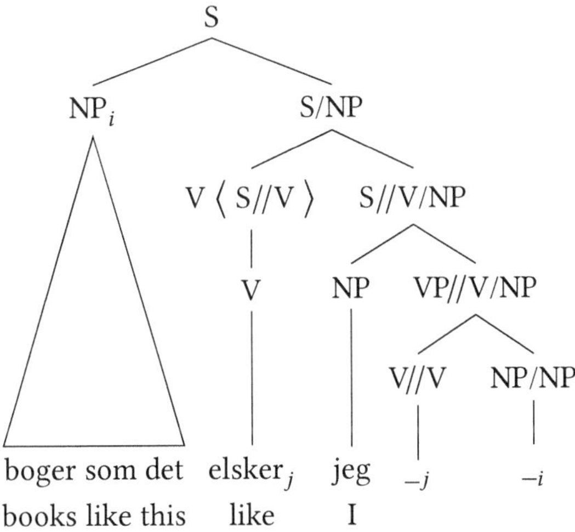

Figure A.26: Analysis of the Danish example *Boger som det elsker jeg.* 'I like such books.'

A.5 Passive

1. Which NPs in (16) do have structural and which lexical case?

   (16) a. Der   Junge lacht.
          the.NOM boy   laughs
          'The boy laughs.'

      b. Mich friert.
          I.ACC freeze
          'I am cold.'

      c. Er   zerstört die   Umwelt.
          he.NOM destroys the.ACC environment
          'He destroys the environment.'

      d. Das   dauert ein   ganzes Jahr.
          this.NOM takes   a.ACC whole year
          'This takes a whole year.'

      e. Er   hat nur einen   Tag dafür   gebraucht.
          he.NOM has just one.ACC day there.for needed
          'He needed a day for this.'

      f. Er   denkt an den   morgigen Tag.
          he.NOM thinks at the.ACC tomorrow day
          'He thinks about tomorrow.'

   All nominatives in (16) are structural cases. The accusatives in (16b, d, f) are lexical, the ones in (16c, e) are structural.

2. Give ARG-ST lists for the following verbs. Provide the ARG-ST list with the maximum amount of arguments.

   (17) a. show, eat, meet   (English)

      b. zeigen 'show', essen 'eat', begegnen 'meet', treffen 'meet'
                                                                      (German)

   (18) a. *show:* ⟨ NP[*str*], NP[*str*], NP[*lacc*] ⟩

      b. *eat:* ⟨ NP[*str*], NP[*str*] ⟩

      c. *meet:* ⟨ NP[*str*], NP[*str*] ⟩

   (19) a. *zeigen:* ⟨ NP[*str*], NP[*ldat*], NP[*str*] ⟩

b. *essen:* ⟨ NP[*str*], NP[*str*] ⟩

c. *begegnen:* ⟨ NP[*str*], NP[*ldat*] ⟩

d. *treffen:* ⟨ NP[*str*], NP[*str*] ⟩

If you are uncertain as far as case is concerned, you may use the Wiktionary: https://de.wiktionary.org/.

3. Draw the analysis tree for the following clause:

(20) that the box was opened

Please provide valence features (SPR and COMPS) and part of speech information. You may abbreviate the NP using a triangle.

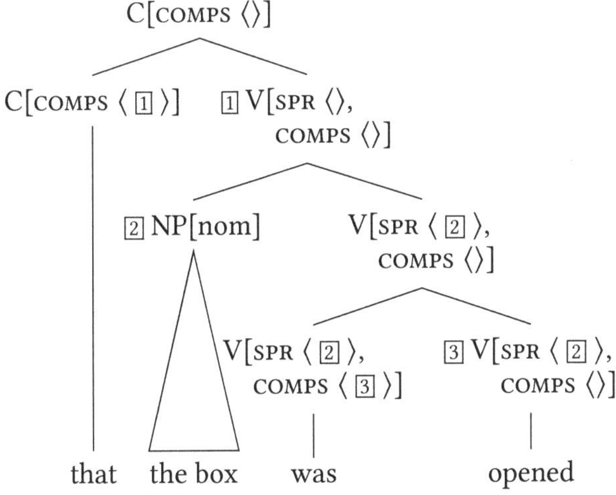

Figure A.27: Analysis of the passive clause *that the box was opened*

The transitive verb *open* takes a subject and an object. The ARG-ST list contains two NPs with structural case. The passive lexical rule removes one argument. For the passive participle this leaves us with one element on the ARG-ST list. This element gets mapped to the SPR list of *opened.* The passive auxiliary takes a VP in passive form and takes over its element from SPR. After combination of auxiliary and passive VP, we have the VP *was opened* still selecting for a specifier. The NP *the box* functions as the specifier and the combination of *the box* and *was opened* is a complete sentence.

A.6 Clause types and expletives

1. Analyze the interrogative clauses in (21):

(21) a. Ich weiß, wen Kim kennt. (German)
   I   know who Kim knows

   'I know who Kim knows.'

   b. Jeg ved, hvem det kende Kim (Danish)
   I   know who   EXPL knows Kim

   'I know who knows Kim.'

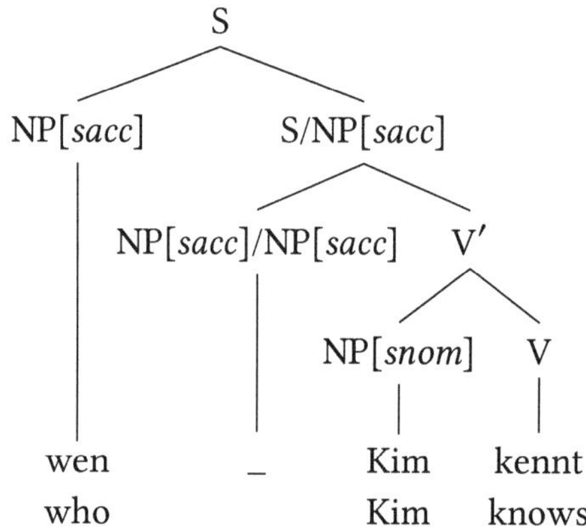

Figure A.28: Analysis of *wen Kim kennt* 'who Kim knows'

2. Analyze the clause in (22). Use triangles for the NP and the PP.

(22) Es   schwammen zwei Delphine neben dem Boot.
   EXPL swam   two dolphins next.to the boat

   'Two dolphins were swimming next to the boat.'

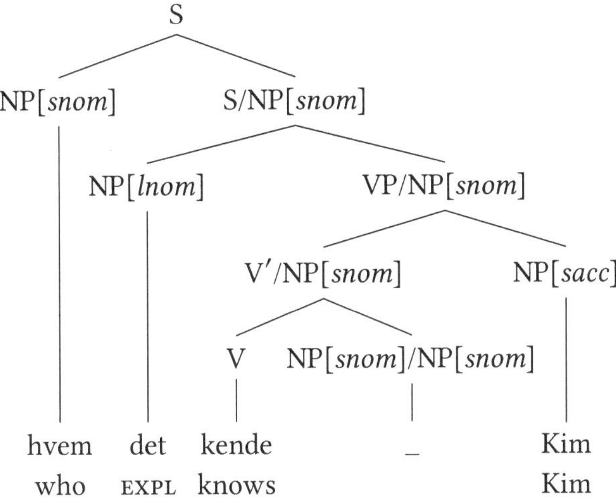

Figure A.29: Analsis of *hvem det knows Kim* 'who knows Kim'

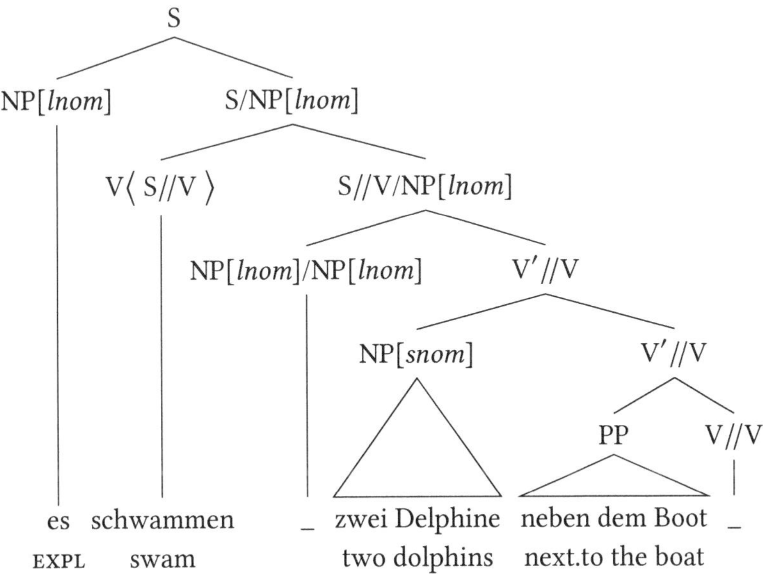

Figure A.30: Analysis of *Es schwammen zwei Delphine neben dem Boot.* 'Two dolphins were swimming next to the boat.'

References

Abeillé, Anne & Robert D. Borsley. 2021. Basic properties and elements. In Stefan Müller, Anne Abeillé, Robert D. Borsley & Jean-Pierre Koenig (eds.), *Head-Driven Phrase Structure Grammar: The handbook* (Empirically Oriented Theoretical Morphology and Syntax 9), 3–45. Berlin: Language Science Press. DOI: 10.5281/zenodo.5599818.

Abeillé, Anne & Rui P. Chaves. 2021. Coordination. In Stefan Müller, Anne Abeillé, Robert D. Borsley & Jean-Pierre Koenig (eds.), *Head-Driven Phrase Structure Grammar: The handbook* (Empirically Oriented Theoretical Morphology and Syntax 9), 725–776. Berlin: Language Science Press. DOI: 10.5281/zenodo.5599848.

Abraham, Werner. 1995. *Deutsche Syntax im Sprachenvergleich: Grundlegung einer typologischen Syntax des Deutschen.* 1st edn. (Studien zur deutschen Grammatik 41). Tübingen: Stauffenburg Verlag.

Abraham, Werner. 2005. *Deutsche Syntax im Sprachenvergleich: Grundlegung einer typologischen Syntax des Deutschen.* 2nd edn. (Studien zur deutschen Grammatik 41). Tübingen: Stauffenburg Verlag.

Ackerman, Farrell, Robert Malouf & John Moore. 2017. Symmetrical objects in Moro: Challenges and solutions. *Journal of Linguistics* 53(1). 3–50. DOI: 10.1017/S0022226715000353.

Adams, Marianne. 1987. From Old French to the theory of pro-drop. *Natural Language & Linguistic Theory* 5(1). 1–32. DOI: 10.1007/BF00161866.

Adger, David. 2003. *Core syntax: A Minimalist approach* (Oxford Core Linguistics 1). Oxford: Oxford University Press.

Allwood, Jens, Lars-Gunnar Anderson & Östen Dahl. 1973. *Logik für Linguisten* (Romanistische Arbeitshefte 8). Tübingen: Max Niemeyer Verlag.

Alsina, Alex. 1996. Resultatives: A joint operation of semantic and syntactic structures. In Miriam Butt & Tracy Holloway King (eds.), *Proceedings of the LFG '96 conference, Rank Xerox, Grenoble*, 1–15. Stanford, CA: CSLI Publications. http://csli-publications.stanford.edu/LFG/1/ (10 February, 2021).

Anderson, Stephen R. 2006. Verb second, subject clitics, and impersonals in Surmiran (Rumantsch). In Zhenya Antić, Charles B. Chang, Emily Cibelli, Jisup

Hong, Michael J. Houser, Clare S. Sandy, Maziar Toosarvandani & Yao Yao (eds.), *Proceedings of the 32nd Annual Meeting of the Berkeley Linguistics Society: Theoretical approaches to argument structure*, vol. 32, 3–21. Berkeley, CA: Berkeley Linguistics Society. DOI: 10.3765/bls.v32i1.3435.

Aoun, Joseph & Dominique Sportiche. 1983. On the formal theory of government. *The Linguistic Review* 2(3). 211–236.

Askedal, John Ole. 1988. Über den Infinitiv als Subjekt im Deutschen. *Zeitschrift für Germanistische Linguistik* 16(1). 1–25. DOI: 10.1515/zfgl.1988.16.1.1.

Asudeh, Ash, Mary Dalrymple & Ida Toivonen. 2008. Constructions with lexical integrity: Templates as the lexicon-syntax interface. In Miriam Butt & Tracy Holloway King (eds.), *Proceedings of the LFG '08 conference, University of Sydney*, 68–88. Stanford, CA: CSLI Publications. http://csli-publications.stanford.edu/LFG/13/papers/lfg08asudehetal.pdf (10 February, 2021).

Asudeh, Ash, Mary Dalrymple & Ida Toivonen. 2013. Constructions with lexical integrity. *Journal of Language Modelling* 1(1). 1–54. DOI: 10.15398/jlm.v1i1.56.

Bartsch, Renate & Theo Vennemann. 1972. *Semantic structures: A study in the relation between semantics and syntax* (Athenäum-Skripten Linguistik 9). Frankfurt/Main: Athenäum.

Bayer, Josef & Jaklin Kornfilt. 1990. Restructuring effects in German. In Elisabet Engdahl, Mike Reape, Martin Mellor & Richard Cooper (eds.), *Parametric variation in Germanic and Romance* (Edinburgh Working Papers in Cognitive Science 6), 21–42. Edinburgh: Center for Cognitive Science & Department of Artificial Intelligence.

Bech, Gunnar. 1955. *Studien über das deutsche Verbum infinitum* (Historisk-filologiske Meddelelser udgivet af Det Kongelige Danske Videnskabernes Selskab. Bind 35, no. 2, 1955; Bind 36, no. 6, 1957). København: Det Kongelige Danske Videnskabernes Selskab. Reprint as: *Studien über das deutsche Verbum infinitum*. 2nd edn. (Linguistische Arbeiten 139). Tübingen: Max Niemeyer Verlag, 1983.

Beck, Sigrid & Remus Gergel. 2014. *Contrasting English and German grammar: An introduction to syntax and semantics* (Mouton Textbook). Berlin: de Gruyter Mouton. DOI: 10.1515/9783110346190.

Behaghel, Otto. 1932. *Die deutsche Syntax: Eine geschichtliche Darstellung: Wortstellung. Periodenbau*, vol. 4 (Germanische Bibliothek 1: Sammlung germanischer Elementar- und Handbücher. R. 1: Grammatiken 10). Heidelberg: Carl Winters Universitätsbuchhandlung.

Berman, Judith. 2003. *Clausal syntax of German* (Studies in Constraint-Based Lexicalism 12). Stanford, CA: CSLI Publications.

Bhatt, Rakesh Mohan. 1999. *Verb movement and the syntax of Kashmiri* (Studies in Natural Language and Linguistic Theory 46). Dordrecht: Kluwer Academic Publishers. DOI: 10.1007/978-94-015-9279-6.

Bierwisch, Manfred. 1963. *Grammatik des deutschen Verbs* (studia grammatica 2). Berlin: Akademie-Verlag.

Bildhauer, Felix. 2014. Head-Driven Phrase Structure Grammar. In Andrew Carnie, Yosuke Sato & Dan Siddiqi (eds.), *The Routledge handbook of syntax* (Routledge Handbooks 1), 526–555. London: Routledge. DOI: 10.4324/9781315796604.

Bildhauer, Felix & Philippa Cook. 2010. German multiple fronting and expected topic-hood. In Stefan Müller (ed.), *Proceedings of the 17th International Conference on Head-Driven Phrase Structure Grammar, Université Paris Diderot*, 68–79. Stanford, CA: CSLI Publications. DOI: 10.21248/hpsg.2010.4.

Birnbaum, Salomo A. 1915. *Praktische Grammatik der Jiddischen Sprache für den Selbstunterricht: mit Lesestücken und einem Wörterbuch* (Die Kunst der Polyglottie 128). Wien: A. Hartleben's Verlag.

Bishop, Dorothy V. M. 2002. Putting language genes in perspective. *TRENDS in Genetics* 18(2). 57–59. DOI: 10.1016/S0168-9525(02)02596-9.

Bjerre, Anne & Tavs Bjerre. 2007. Perfect and periphrastic passive constructions in Danish. *Nordic Journal of Linguistics* 30(1). 5–53. DOI: 10.1017/S0332586507001643.

Blackburn, Patrick & Johan Bos. 2005. *Representation and inference for natural language: A first course in computational semantics* (Studies in Computational Linguistics). Stanford, CA: CSLI Publications.

Bloomfield, Leonard. 1926. A set of postulates for the science of language. *Language* 2(3). 153–164. DOI: 10.2307/408741. Reprint as: A set of postulates for the science of language. In Charles F. Hockett (ed.), *A Leonard Bloomfield anthology* (Indiana University Studies in the History and Theory of Linguistics), 128–138. Bloomington, IN: Indiana University Press, 1970.

Bloomfield, Leonard. 1933. *Language*. New York, NY: Holt, Rinehart, & Winston.

Bonami, Olivier, Danièle Godard & Brigitte Kampers-Manhe. 2004. Adverb classification. In Francis Corblin & Henriëtte de Swart (eds.), *Handbook of French semantics* (CSLI Lecture Notes 170), 143–184. Stanford, CA: CSLI Publications.

Borsley, Robert D. 1987. *Subjects and complements in HPSG*. Report No. CSLI-87-107. Stanford, CA: Center for the Study of Language & Information.

Borsley, Robert D. 1989. Phrase-Structure Grammar and the Barriers conception of clause structure. *Linguistics* 27(5). 843–863. DOI: 10.1515/ling.1989.27.5.843.

Borsley, Robert D. 1991. *Syntactic theory: A unified approach.* London: Edward Arnold.

Borsley, Robert D. 2005. Against ConjP. *Lingua* 115(4). 461–482. DOI: 10.1016/j. lingua.2003.09.011.

Borsley, Robert D. & Berthold Crysmann. 2021. Unbounded dependencies. In Stefan Müller, Anne Abeillé, Robert D. Borsley & Jean-Pierre Koenig (eds.), *Head-Driven Phrase Structure Grammar: The handbook* (Empirically Oriented Theoretical Morphology and Syntax 9), 537–594. Berlin: Language Science Press. DOI: 10.5281/zenodo.5599842.

Borsley, Robert D. & Andreas Kathol. 2000. Breton as a V2 language. *Linguistics* 38(4). 665–710. DOI: 10.1515/ling.2000.002.

Borsley, Robert D. & Stefan Müller. 2021. HPSG and Minimalism. In Stefan Müller, Anne Abeillé, Robert D. Borsley & Jean-Pierre Koenig (eds.), *Head-Driven Phrase Structure Grammar: The handbook* (Empirically Oriented Theoretical Morphology and Syntax 9), 1253–1329. Berlin: Language Science Press. DOI: 10.5281/zenodo.5599874.

Borsley, Robert D., Maggie Tallerman & David Willis. 2007. *The syntax of Welsh* (Cambridge Syntax Guides 7). Cambridge: Cambridge University Press. DOI: 10.1017/CBO9780511486227.

Bošković, Željko. 2009. Unifying first and last conjunct agreement. *Natural Language & Linguistic Theory* 27(3). 455–496. DOI: 10.1007/s11049-009-9072-6.

Bouma, Gosse. 2003. Verb clusters and the scope of adjuncts in Dutch. In Pieter A. M. Seuren & Gerard Kempen (eds.), *Verb constructions in German and Dutch* (Current Issues in Linguistic Theory 242), 5–42. Amsterdam: John Benjamins Publishing Co. DOI: 10.1075/cilt.242.02bou.

Bouma, Gosse, Robert Malouf & Ivan A. Sag. 2001. Satisfying constraints on extraction and adjunction. *Natural Language & Linguistic Theory* 19(1). 1–65. DOI: 10.1023/A:1006473306778.

Bresnan, Joan (ed.). 1982. *The mental representation of grammatical relations* (MIT Press Series on Cognitive Theory and Mental Representation). Cambridge, MA: MIT Press.

Bresnan, Joan. 2001. *Lexical-Functional Syntax.* 1st edn. (Blackwell Textbooks in Linguistics 16). Oxford: Blackwell Publishers Ltd.

Bresnan, Joan, Ash Asudeh, Ida Toivonen & Stephen Wechsler. 2016. *Lexical-functional syntax.* 2nd edn. (Blackwell Textbooks in Linguistics 16). Oxford: Wiley-Blackwell. DOI: 10.1002/9781119105664.

Chomsky, Noam. 1957. *Syntactic structures* (Janua Linguarum / Series Minor 4). Berlin: Mouton de Gruyter. DOI: 10.1515/9783112316009.

Chomsky, Noam. 1970. Remarks on nominalization. In Roderick A. Jacobs & Peter S. Rosenbaum (eds.), *Readings in English Transformational Grammar*, 184–221. Waltham, MA: Ginn & Company.

Chomsky, Noam. 1973. Conditions on transformations. In Stephen R. Anderson & Paul Kiparsky (eds.), *A Festschrift for Morris Halle*, 232–286. New York, NY: Holt, Rinehart & Winston.

Chomsky, Noam. 1980. *Rules and representations* (Woodbridge lectures delivered at Columbia University 11). New York, NY: Columbia University Press.

Chomsky, Noam. 1981. *Lectures on government and binding* (Studies in Generative Grammar 9). Dordrecht: Foris Publications. DOI: 10.1515/9783110884166.

Chomsky, Noam. 1986. *Barriers* (Linguistic Inquiry Monographs 13). Cambridge, MA: MIT Press.

Chomsky, Noam. 1995. *The Minimalist Program* (Current Studies in Linguistics 28). Cambridge, MA: MIT Press. DOI: 10.7551/mitpress/9780262527347.001.0001.

Christie, Elizabeth. 2010. Using templates to account for English resultatives. In Miriam Butt & Tracy Holloway King (eds.), *Proceedings of the LFG '10 conference, Carleton University, Ottawa*, 155–164. Stanford, CA: CSLI Publications. http://csli-publications.stanford.edu/LFG/15/ (10 February, 2021).

Cinque, Guglielmo. 1994. On the evidence for partial N movement in the Romance DP. In Guglielmo Cinque, Jan Koster, Jean-Yves Pollock, Luigi Rizzi & Raffaella Zanuttini (eds.), *Paths towards Universal Grammar: Studies in honor of Richard S. Kayne* (Georgetown studies in Romance literature), 85–110. Washington, D.C.: Georgetown University Press.

Cinque, Guglielmo. 1999. *Adverbs and functional heads: A cross-linguistic perspective* (Oxford Studies in Comparative Syntax 15). New York, NY: Oxford University Press.

Cinque, Guglielmo & Luigi Rizzi. 2010. The cartography of syntactic structures. In Bernd Heine & Heiko Narrog (eds.), *The Oxford handbook of linguistic analysis* (Oxford Handbooks in Linguistics), 51–65. Oxford: Oxford University Press. DOI: 10.1093/oxfordhb/9780199544004.013.0003.

Citko, Barbara. 2011. *Symmetry in syntax: Merge, move and labels* (Cambridge Studies in Linguistics 129). Cambridge, UK: Cambridge University Press. DOI: 10.1017/CBO9780511794278.

Cook, Philippa. 2006. The datives that aren't born equal: Beneficiaries and the dative passive. In Daniel Hole, André Meinunger & Werner Abraham (eds.), *Datives and similar cases: Between argument structure and event structure* (Studies in Language Companion Series 75), 141–184. Amsterdam: John Benjamins Publishing Co. DOI: 10.1075/slcs.75.08coo.

Copestake, Ann, Dan Flickinger, Carl Pollard & Ivan A. Sag. 2005. Minimal Recursion Semantics: An introduction. *Research on Language and Computation* 3(2–3). 281–332. DOI: 10.1007/s11168-006-6327-9.

Crysmann, Berthold. 2004. Underspecification of intersective modifier attachment: Some arguments from German. In Stefan Müller (ed.), *Proceedings of the 11th International Conference on Head-Driven Phrase Structure Grammar, Center for Computational Linguistics, Katholieke Universiteit Leuven*, 378–392. Stanford, CA: CSLI Publications. DOI: 10.21248/hpsg.2004.21.

Culicover, Peter W. & Ray Jackendoff. 2005. *Simpler Syntax* (Oxford Linguistics). Oxford: Oxford University Press. DOI: 10.1093/acprof:oso/9780199271092.001.0001.

Czepluch, Hartmut. 1988. Kasusmorphologie und Kasusrelationen: Überlegungen zur Kasustheorie des Deutschen. *Linguistische Berichte* 116. 275–310.

Dąbrowska, Ewa. 2004. *Language, mind and brain: Some psychological and neurological constraints on theories of grammar*. Washington, D.C.: Georgetown University Press.

Dalrymple, Mary. 2001. *Lexical Functional Grammar* (Syntax and Semantics 34). Bingley, UK: Emerald Group Publishing. DOI: 10.1163/9781849500104.

Daniels, Michael W. 2002. On a type-based analysis of feature neutrality and the coordination of unlikes. In Frank Van Eynde, Lars Hellan & Dorothee Beermann (eds.), *Proceedings of the 8th International Conference on Head-Driven Phrase Structure Grammar, Norwegian University of Science and Technology*, 137–147. Stanford, CA: CSLI Publications. DOI: 10.21248/hpsg.2001.9.

Davis, Anthony R. 2001. *Linking by types in the hierarchical lexicon* (Studies in Constraint-Based Lexicalism 10). Stanford, CA: CSLI Publications.

Davis, Anthony R., Jean-Pierre Koenig & Stephen Wechsler. 2021. Argument structure and linking. In Stefan Müller, Anne Abeillé, Robert D. Borsley & Jean-Pierre Koenig (eds.), *Head-Driven Phrase Structure Grammar: The handbook* (Empirically Oriented Theoretical Morphology and Syntax 9), 315–367. Berlin: Language Science Press. DOI: 10.5281/zenodo.5599834.

De Kuthy, Kordula. 2021. Information structure. In Stefan Müller, Anne Abeillé, Robert D. Borsley & Jean-Pierre Koenig (eds.), *Head-Driven Phrase Structure Grammar: The handbook* (Empirically Oriented Theoretical Morphology and Syntax 9), 1043–1078. Berlin: Language Science Press. DOI: 10.5281/zenodo.5599864.

De Kuthy, Kordula, Vanessa Metcalf & Detmar Meurers. 2004. *Documentation of the implementation of the Milca English Resource Grammar in the Trale system.* Ohio State University, ms.

den Besten, Hans. 1985a. Some remarks on the Ergative Hypothesis. In Werner Abraham (ed.), *Erklärende Syntax des Deutschen* (Studien zur deutschen Grammatik 25), 53–74. Tübingen: Gunter Narr Verlag.

den Besten, Hans. 1985b. The Ergative Hypothesis and free word order in Dutch and German. In Jindřich Toman (ed.), *Studies in German grammar* (Studies in Generative Grammar 21), 23–64. Dordrecht: Foris Publications. DOI: 10.1515/9783110882711-004.

den Besten, Hans. 2012. From Khoekhoe foreigner talk via Hottentot Dutch to Afrikaans: The creation of a novel grammar. In Ton van der Wouden (ed.), *Roots of Afrikaans: Selected writings of Hans Den Besten* (Creole Language Library 44), 257–287. Amsterdam: John Benjamins Publishing Co. DOI: 10.1075/cll.44. Reprint from: From Khoekhoe foreigner talk via Hottentot Dutch to Afrikaans: The creation of a novel grammar. In *Wheels within wheels. Papers of the Duisburg Symposium on Pidgin and Creole Languages,* 207–209. Frankfurt a. M.: Peter Lang, 1989. Reprint as: From Khoekhoe foreigner talk via Hottentot Dutch to Afrikaans: The creation of a novel grammar. In Ton van der Wouden (ed.), *Roots of Afrikaans: Selected writings of Hans Den Besten* (Creole Language Library 44), 257–287. Amsterdam: John Benjamins Publishing Co., 2012. DOI: 10.1075/cll.44.

den Besten, Hans & Jerold A. Edmondson. 1983. The verbal complex in Continental West Germanic. In Werner Abraham (ed.), *On the formal syntax of the Westgermania: Papers from the 3rd Groningen Grammar Talks, Groningen, January 1981* (Linguistik Aktuell/Linguistics Today 3), 155–216. Amsterdam: John Benjamins Publishing Co. DOI: 10.1075/la.3.

den Besten, Hans & Corretje Moed-van Walraven. 1986. The syntax of verbs in Yiddish. In Hubert Haider & Martin Prinzhorn (eds.), *Verb second phenomena in Germanic languages* (Publications in Language Sciences 21), 111–135. Dordrecht: Foris Publications. DOI: 10.1515/9783110846072.111.

Diesing, Molly. 1990. Verb movement and the subject position in Yiddish. *Natural Language & Linguistic Theory* 8(1). 41–79. DOI: 10.1007/BF00205531.

Diesing, Molly. 1997. Yiddish VP order and the typology of object movement in Germanic. *Natural Language & Linguistic Theory* 15(2). 369–427. DOI: 10.1023/A:1005778326537.

Dowty, David. 1991. Thematic proto-roles and argument selection. *Language* 67(3). 547–619. DOI: 10.2307/415037.

Dryer, Matthew S. 2013a. Determining dominant word order. In Matthew S. Dryer & Martin Haspelmath (eds.), *The world atlas of language structures online*. Leipzig: Max Planck Institute for Evolutionary Anthropology. https://wals.info/chapter/s6 (19 December, 2022).

Dryer, Matthew S. 2013b. Order of subject, object and verb. In Matthew S. Dryer & Martin Haspelmath (eds.), *The world atlas of language structures online*. Leipzig: Max Planck Institute for Evolutionary Anthropology. http://wals.info/chapter/81 (10 February, 2021).

Eisenberg, Peter. 1994. German. In Ekkehard König & Johan van der Auwera (eds.), *The Germanic languages* (Routledge Language Family Descriptions 3), 349–387. London: Routledge. DOI: 10.4324/9781315812786.

Eisenberg, Peter. 2004. *Grundriß der deutschen Grammatik: Der Satz*. 2nd edn., vol. 2. Stuttgart, Weimar: Verlag J. B. Metzler.

Eisenberg, Peter, Jörg Peters, Peter Gallmann, Cathrine Fabricius-Hansen, Damaris Nübling, Irmhild Barz, Thomas A. Fritz & Reinhard Fiehler. 2005. *Duden: Die Grammatik*. 7th edn., vol. 4. Mannheim: Dudenverlag.

Elman, Jeffrey L., Elizabeth A. Bates, Mark H. Johnson, Annette Karmiloff-Smith, Domenico Parisi & Kim Plunkett. 1996. *Rethinking innateness: A connectionist perspective on development* (Neural Network Modeling and Connectionism 10). Cambridge, MA: Bradford Books/MIT Press. DOI: 10.7551/mitpress/5929.001.0001.

Engdahl, Elisabet & Enric Vallduví. 1994. Information packaging and grammar architecture: A constraint-based approach. In Elisabet Engdahl (ed.), *Integrating information structure into constraint-based and categorial approaches* (DYANA-2 Report R.1.3.B), 41–79. Amsterdam: ILLC.

Engdahl, Elisabet & Enric Vallduví. 1996. Information packaging in HPSG. In Claire Grover & Enric Vallduví (eds.), *Studies in HPSG* (Edinburgh Working Papers in Cognitive Science 12), 1–32. Edinburgh: Centre for Cognitive Science, University of Edinburgh. ftp://ftp.cogsci.ed.ac.uk/pub/CCS-WPs/wp-12.ps.gz (10 February, 2021).

Ernst, Thomas. 1992. The phrase structure of English negation. *The Linguistic Review* 9(2). 109–144. DOI: 10.1515/tlir.1992.9.2.109.

Fanselow, Gisbert. 1987. *Konfigurationalität* (Studien zur deutschen Grammatik 29). Tübingen: Gunter Narr Verlag.

Fanselow, Gisbert. 2000. Optimal exceptions. In Barbara Stiebels & Dieter Wunderlich (eds.), *The lexicon in focus* (studia grammatica 45), 173–209. Berlin: Akademie Verlag. DOI: 10.1515/9783050073712-009.

Fanselow, Gisbert. 2001. Features, θ-roles, and free constituent order. *Linguistic Inquiry* 32(3). 405–437. DOI: 10.1162/002438901750372513.

Fanselow, Gisbert. 2003a. Free constituent order: A Minimalist interface account. *Folia Linguistica* 37(1–2). 191–231. DOI: 10.1515/flin.2003.37.1-2.191.

Fanselow, Gisbert. 2003b. Münchhausen-style head movement and the analysis of verb second. In Anoop Mahajan (ed.), *Syntax at sunset 3: Head movement and syntactic theory* (UCLA Working Papers in Linguistics 10), 40–76. Los Angeles: UCLA, Linguistics Department. Published as Münchhausen-style head movement and the analysis of verb second. In Ralf Vogel (ed.), *Three papers on German verb movement* (Linguistics in Potsdam 22), 9–49. Potsdam: Universität Potsdam, 2004.

Fanselow, Gisbert. 2006. On pure syntax (uncontaminated by information structure). In Patrick Brandt & Eric Fuß (eds.), *Form, structure, and grammar: A festschrift presented to Günther Grewendorf on occasion of his 60th birthday* (studia grammatica 63), 137–157. Berlin: Akademie Verlag. DOI: 10.1524/9783050085555.

Fanselow, Gisbert & Sascha W. Felix. 1987. *Sprachtheorie 2. Die Rektions- und Bindungstheorie* (UTB für Wissenschaft: Uni-Taschenbücher 1442). Tübingen: A. Francke Verlag.

Fillmore, Charles J., Russell R. Lee-Goldmann & Russell Rhomieux. 2012. The FrameNet constructicon. In Hans C. Boas & Ivan A. Sag (eds.), *Sign-Based Construction Grammar* (CSLI Lecture Notes 193), 309–372. Stanford, CA: CSLI Publications.

Fisher, Simon E. & Gary F. Marcus. 2005. The eloquent ape: Genes, brains and the evolution of language. *Nature Reviews Genetics* 7(1). 9–20. DOI: 10.1038/nrg1747.

Fitch, W. Tecumseh. 2007. Linguistics: An invisible hand. *Nature* 449(11). 665–667. DOI: 10.1038/449665a.

Flickinger, Dan, Emily M. Bender & Stephan Oepen. 2003. *MRS in the LinGO Grammar Matrix: A practical user's guide.* Ms. University of Washington. http://faculty.washington.edu/ebender/papers/userguide.pdf (20 December, 2022).

Fontana, Josep M. 1997. On the integration of second position phenomena. In Ans van Kemenade & Nigel Vincent (eds.), *Parameters of morphosyntactic change,* 207–249. Cambridge, UK: Cambridge University Press.

Fortmann, Christian. 2007. Bewegungsresistente Verben. *Zeitschrift für Sprachwissenschaft* 26(1). 1–40. DOI: 10.1515/ZFS.2007.009.

Frey, Werner. 1993. *Syntaktische Bedingungen für die semantische Interpretation: Über Bindung, implizite Argumente und Skopus* (studia grammatica 35). Berlin: Akademie Verlag.

Frey, Werner. 2004a. A medial topic position for German. *Linguistische Berichte* 198. 153–190.

Frey, Werner. 2004b. *The grammar-pragmatics interface and the German prefield.* Forschungsprogramm Sprache und Pragmatik 52. Germanistisches Institut der Universität Lund. 1–39.

Fries, Norbert. 1988. *Über das Null-Topik im Deutschen.* Forschungsprogramm Sprache und Pragmatik 3. Germanistisches Institut der Universität Lund. 19–49.

Gazdar, Gerald. 1981. Unbounded dependencies and coordinate structure. *Linguistic Inquiry* 12(2). 155–184.

Gazdar, Gerald, Ewan Klein, Geoffrey K. Pullum & Ivan A. Sag. 1985. *Generalized Phrase Structure Grammar.* Cambridge, MA: Harvard University Press.

Gazdar, Gerald, Geoffrey K. Pullum & Ivan A. Sag. 1982. Auxiliaries and related phenomena in a restrictive theory of grammar. *Language* 58(3). 591–638. DOI: 10.2307/413850.

Geach, Peter Thomas. 1970. A program for syntax. *Synthese* 22(1–2). 3–17. DOI: 10.1007/BF00413597.

Geerts, Guido, Walter Haeseryn, Jaap de Rooij & Maarten C. van den Toorn. 1984. *Algemene nederlandse spraakkunst.* Groningen: Wolters-Noordhoff.

Geilfuß, Jochen. 1990. Jiddisch als SOV-Sprache. *Zeitschrift für Sprachwissenschaft* 9(1–2). 170–183. DOI: 10.1515/zfsw.1990.9.1-2.170.

Ginzburg, Jonathan & Ivan A. Sag. 2000. *Interrogative investigations: The form, meaning, and use of English interrogatives* (CSLI Lecture Notes 123). Stanford, CA: CSLI Publications.

Godard, Danièle & Pollet Samvelian. 2021. Complex predicates. In Stefan Müller, Anne Abeillé, Robert D. Borsley & Jean-Pierre Koenig (eds.), *Head-Driven Phrase Structure Grammar: The handbook* (Empirically Oriented Theoretical Morphology and Syntax 9), 419–488. Berlin: Language Science Press. DOI: 10.5281/zenodo.5599838.

Goldberg, Adele E. 1995. *Constructions: A Construction Grammar approach to argument structure* (Cognitive Theory of Language and Culture). Chicago, IL: The University of Chicago Press.

Goldberg, Adele E. & Ray Jackendoff. 2004. The English resultative as a family of constructions. *Language* 80(3). 532–568.

Greenberg, Joseph H. 1963. Some universals of grammar with particular reference to the order of meaningful elements. In Joseph H. Greenberg (ed.), *Universals in language*, 58–90. Cambridge, MA: MIT Press.

Grewendorf, Günther. 1988. *Aspekte der deutschen Syntax: Eine Rektions-Bindungs-Analyse* (Studien zur deutschen Grammatik 33). Tübingen: Gunter Narr Verlag.

Grewendorf, Günther. 1989. *Ergativity in German* (Studies in Generative Grammar 35). Dordrecht: Foris Publications. DOI: 10.1515/9783110859256.

Grewendorf, Günther. 1995. German: A grammatical sketch. In Joachim Jacobs, Arnim von Stechow, Wolfgang Sternefeld & Theo Vennemann (eds.), *Syntax – Ein internationales Handbuch zeitgenössischer Forschung*, vol. 2 (Handbücher zur Sprach- und Kommunikationswissenschaft 9), 1288–1319. Berlin: Walter de Gruyter. DOI: 10.1515/9783110142631.2.

Grewendorf, Günther. 2002. *Minimalistische Syntax* (UTB für Wissenschaft: Uni-Taschenbücher 2313). Tübingen: A. Francke Verlag.

Grewendorf, Günther. 2005. The discourse configurationality of scrambling. In Joachim Sabel & Mamoru Saito (eds.), *The free word order phenomenon: Its syntactic sources and diversity* (Studies in Generative Grammar 69). Mouton de Gruyter. DOI: 10.1515/9783110197266.

Grewendorf, Günther. 2009. The left clausal periphery: Clitic left dislocation in Italian and left dislocation in German. In Benjamin Shear, Philippa Cook, Werner Frey & Claudia Maienborn (eds.), *Dislocated elements in discourse: Syntactic, semantic, and pragmatic perspectives* (Routledge Studies in Germanic Linguistics 12), 49–94. New York: Routledge. DOI: 10.4324/9780203929247.

Grimshaw, Jane. 2000. Locality and extended projection. In Peter Coopmans, Martin Everaert & Jane Grimshaw (eds.), *Lexical specification and insertion* (Current Issues in Linguistic Theory 197), 115–134. Amsterdam: John Benjamins Publishing Co. DOI: 10.1075/cilt.197.07gri.

Gunji, Takao. 1986. Subcategorization and word order. In William J. Poser (ed.), *Papers from the Second International Workshop on Japanese Syntax*, 1–21. Stanford, CA: CSLI Publications.

Gunkel, Lutz. 2003. *Infinitheit, Passiv und Kausativkonstruktionen im Deutschen* (Studien zur deutschen Grammatik 67). Tübingen: Stauffenburg Verlag.

Haegeman, Liliane. 1994. *Introduction to Government and Binding Theory*. 2nd edn. (Blackwell Textbooks in Linguistics 1). Oxford: Blackwell Publishers Ltd.

Haftka, Brigitta. 1995. Syntactic positions for topic and contrastive focus in the German middlefield. In Inga Kohlhof, Susanne Winkler & Hans-Bernhard Drubig (eds.), *Proceedings of the Göttingen Focus Workshop, 17 DGfS, March 1–3* (Arbeitspapiere des SFB 340 No. 69), 137–157. Tübingen: Universität Tübingen.

Haftka, Brigitta. 1996. Deutsch ist eine V/2-Sprache mit Verbendstellung und freier Wortfolge. In Ewald Lang & Gisela Zifonun (eds.), *Deutsch – typologisch* (Institut für Deutsche Sprache, Jahrbuch 1995), 121–141. Berlin: Walter de Gruyter. DOI: 10.1515/9783110622522-007.

Haider, Hubert. 1984. Was zu haben ist und was zu sein hat – Bemerkungen zum Infinitiv. *Papiere zur Linguistik* 30(1). 23–36.

Haider, Hubert. 1985. The case of German. In Jindřich Toman (ed.), *Studies in German grammar* (Studies in Generative Grammar 21), 65–101. Dordrecht: Foris Publications. DOI: 10.1515/9783110882711-005.

Haider, Hubert. 1986a. Fehlende Argumente: Vom Passiv zu kohärenten Infinitiven. *Linguistische Berichte* 101. 3–33.

Haider, Hubert. 1986b. Nicht-sententiale Infinitive. *Groninger Arbeiten zur Germanistischen Linguistik* 28. 73–114.

Haider, Hubert. 1991. Pro-bleme? In Gisbert Fanselow & Sascha W. Felix (eds.), *Strukturen und Merkmale syntaktischer Kategorien* (Studien zur deutschen Grammatik 39), 121–143. Tübingen: Gunter Narr Verlag.

Haider, Hubert. 1993. *Deutsche Syntax – generativ: Vorstudien zur Theorie einer projektiven Grammatik* (Tübinger Beiträge zur Linguistik 325). Tübingen: Gunter Narr Verlag.

Haider, Hubert. 1997a. Projective economy: On the minimal functional structure of the German clause. In Werner Abraham & Elly van Gelderen (eds.), *German: Syntactic problems—Problematic syntax* (Linguistische Arbeiten 374), 83–103. Tübingen: Max Niemeyer Verlag. DOI: 10.1515/9783110914726-006.

Haider, Hubert. 1997b. Typological implications of a directionality constraint on projections. In Artemis Alexiadou & T. Alan Hall (eds.), *Studies on Universal Grammar and typological variation* (Linguistik Aktuell/Linguistics Today 13), 17–33. Amsterdam: John Benjamins Publishing Co. DOI: 10.1075/la.13.

Haider, Hubert. 2000. OV is more basic than VO. In Peter Svenonius (ed.), *The derivation of VO and OV* (Linguistik Aktuell/Linguistics Today 31), 45–67. Amsterdam: John Benjamins Publishing Co. DOI: 10.1075/la.31.03hai.

Haider, Hubert. 2010. *The syntax of German* (Cambridge Syntax Guides). Cambridge: Cambridge University Press. DOI: 10.1017/CBO9780511845314.

Haider, Hubert. 2020. VO/OV-base ordering. In Michael T. Putnam & B. Richard Page (eds.), *Cambridge handbook of Germanic linguistics* (Cambridge Handbooks in Language and Linguistics 33), 339–364. Cambridge, UK: Cambridge University Press. DOI: 10.1017/9781108378291.016.

Haider, Hubert. 2021. A null theory of scrambling. *Zeitschrift für Sprachwissenschaft* 39(3). 375–405. DOI: 10.1515/zfs-2020-2019.

Haider, Hubert. 2022. The Left-Left Constraint: A structural constraint on adjuncts. In Ulrike Freywald, Horst J. Simon & Stefan Müller (eds.), *Headedness and/or grammatical anarchy?* (Empirically Oriented Theoretical Morphology and Syntax 11), 199–232. Berlin: Language Science Press. DOI: 10.5281/zenodo.7142712.

Haider, Hubert & Martin Prinzhorn (eds.). 1986. *Verb second phenomena in Germanic languages* (Publications in Language Sciences 21). Dordrecht: Foris Publications. DOI: 10.1515/9783110846072.

Hall, Beatrice. 1979. Accounting for Yiddish word order or what's a nice NP like you doing in a place like this? In Jürgen M. Meisel & Martin D. Pam (eds.), *Linear order and Generative theory* (Current Issues in Linguistic Theory 7), 253–287. Amsterdam: John Benjamins Publishing Co. DOI: 10.1075/cilt.7.08hal.

Harbert, Wayne. 2006. *The germanic languages* (Cambridge Language Surveys). Cambridge University Press. DOI: 10.1017/CBO9780511755071.

Harman, Gilbert H. 1963. Generative grammars without transformation rules: A defense of phrase structure. *Language* 39(4). 597–616. DOI: 10.2307/411954.

Harris, Zellig S. 1946. From morpheme to utterance. *Language* 22(3). 161–183. DOI: 10.2307/410205.

Haspelmath, Martin. 2010a. Comparative concepts and descriptive categories in crosslinguistic studies. *Language* 86(3). 663–687.

Haspelmath, Martin. 2010b. The interplay between comparative concepts and descriptive categories (reply to Newmeyer). *Language* 86(3). 696–699. DOI: 10.1353/lan.2010.0004.

Haugereid, Petter. 2007. Decomposed phrasal constructions. In Stefan Müller (ed.), *Proceedings of the 14th International Conference on Head-Driven Phrase Structure Grammar, Stanford Department of Linguistics and CSLI's LinGO Lab*, 120–129. Stanford, CA: CSLI Publications. DOI: 10.21248/hpsg.2007.7.

Haugereid, Petter. 2009. *Phrasal subconstructions: A constructionalist grammar design, exemplified with Norwegian and English* (Doctoral Theses at NTNU 122). Trondheim: Norwegian University of Science & Technology. http://hdl.handle.net/11250/243990 (20 December, 2022).

Hauser, Marc D., Noam Chomsky & W. Tecumseh Fitch. 2002. The faculty of language: What is it, who has it, and how did it evolve? *Science* 298(5598). 1569–1579. DOI: 10.1126/science.298.5598.1569.

Heather, Peter. 1999. *The Goths* (The Peoples of Europe). Blackwell Publishers Ltd.

Heinz, Wolfgang & Johannes Matiasek. 1994. Argument structure and case assignment in German. In John Nerbonne, Klaus Netter & Carl Pollard (eds.), *German in Head-Driven Phrase Structure Grammar* (CSLI Lecture Notes 46), 199–236. Stanford, CA: CSLI Publications.

Hendriksen, Hans. 1990. Sentence position of the verb in Himachali. *Acta Linguistica Hafniensia* 22(1). 159–171. DOI: 10.1080/03740463.1990.10411526.

Henriksen, Carol & Johan van der Auwera. 1994. The Germanic languages. In Ekkehard König & Johan van der Auwera (eds.), *The Germanic languages* (Routledge Language Family Descriptions 3), 1–18. London: Routledge. DOI: 10.4324/9781315812786.

Hinrichs, Erhard W. & Sandra Kübler. 2005. Treebank profiling of spoken and written German. In Montserrat Civit, Sandra Kübler & Maria Antònia Martí (eds.), *Proceedings of the Fourth Workshop on Treebanks and Linguistic Theories (TLT)*. Barcelona, Spain.

Hinrichs, Erhard W. & Tsuneko Nakazawa. 1989a. Flipped out: AUX in German. In Erhard W. Hinrichs & Tsuneko Nakazawa (eds.), *Aspects of German VP structure* (SfS-Report-01-93), 13–23. Tübingen: Universität Tübingen.

Hinrichs, Erhard W. & Tsuneko Nakazawa. 1989b. Subcategorization and VP structure in German. In Erhard W. Hinrichs & Tsuneko Nakazawa (eds.), *Aspects of German VP structure* (SfS-Report-01-93), 1–12. Tübingen: Universität Tübingen.

Hinrichs, Erhard W. & Tsuneko Nakazawa. 1994. Linearizing AUXs in German verbal complexes. In John Nerbonne, Klaus Netter & Carl Pollard (eds.), *German in Head-Driven Phrase Structure Grammar* (CSLI Lecture Notes 46), 11–38. Stanford, CA: CSLI Publications.

Hoberg, Ursula. 1981. *Die Wortstellung in der geschriebenen deutschen Gegenwartssprache* (Heutiges Deutsch. Linguistische Grundlagen. Forschungen des Instituts für Deutsche Sprache 10). München: Max Hueber Verlag.

Höhle, Tilman N. 1978. *Lexikalische Syntax: Die Aktiv-Passiv-Relation und andere Infinitkonstruktionen im Deutschen* (Linguistische Arbeiten 67). Tübingen: Max Niemeyer Verlag. DOI: 10.1515/9783111345444.

Höhle, Tilman N. 1982. Explikationen für „normale Betonung" und „normale Wortstellung". In Werner Abraham (ed.), *Satzglieder im Deutschen – Vorschläge zur syntaktischen, semantischen und pragmatischen Fundierung* (Studien zur deutschen Grammatik 15), 75–153. Tübingen: Gunter Narr Verlag. Republished as Explikationen für „normale Betonung" und „normale Wortstellung". In Stefan Müller, Marga Reis & Frank Richter (eds.), *Beiträge zur deutschen Gramma-*

tik: Gesammelte Schriften von Tilman N. Höhle, 2nd edn. (Classics in Linguistics 5), 107–191. Berlin: Language Science Press, 2019. DOI: 10.5281/zenodo.2588383.

Höhle, Tilman N. 1988. *Verum-Fokus*. Netzwerk Sprache und Pragmatik 5. Lund: Universität Lund, Germananistisches Institut. 2–7. Reprint as: Über Verum-Fokus im Deutschen. In Stefan Müller, Marga Reis & Frank Richter (eds.), *Beiträge zur deutschen Grammatik: Gesammelte Schriften von Tilman N. Höhle*, 2nd edn. (Classics in Linguistics 5), 381–416. Berlin: Language Science Press, 2019. DOI: 10.5281/zenodo.2588365.

Höhle, Tilman N. 1991a. On reconstruction and coordination. In Hubert Haider & Klaus Netter (eds.), *Representation and derivation in the theory of grammar* (Studies in Natural Language and Linguistic Theory 22), 139–197. Dordrecht: Kluwer Academic Publishers. DOI: 10.1007/978-94-011-3446-0_5. Republished as On reconstruction and coordination. In Stefan Müller, Marga Reis & Frank Richter (eds.), *Beiträge zur deutschen Grammatik: Gesammelte Schriften von Tilman N. Höhle*, 2nd edn. (Classics in Linguistics 5), 311–368. Berlin: Language Science Press, 2019. DOI: 10.5281/zenodo.2588383.

Höhle, Tilman N. 1991b. Projektionsstufen bei V-Projektionen: Bemerkungen zu F/T. Ms. Universität Tübingen. Published as Projektionsstufen bei V-Projektionen: Bemerkungen zu F/T. In Stefan Müller, Marga Reis & Frank Richter (eds.), *Beiträge zur deutschen Grammatik: Gesammelte Schriften von Tilman N. Höhle*, 2nd edn. (Classics in Linguistics 5), 369–379. Berlin: Language Science Press, 2019. DOI: 10.5281/zenodo.2588383.

Höhle, Tilman N. 1997. Vorangestellte Verben und Komplementierer sind eine natürliche Klasse. In Christa Dürscheid, Karl Heinz Ramers & Monika Schwarz (eds.), *Sprache im Fokus: Festschrift für Heinz Vater zum 65. Geburtstag*, 107–120. Tübingen: Max Niemeyer Verlag. Reprint as: Vorangestellte Verben und Komplementierer sind eine natürliche Klasse. In Stefan Müller, Marga Reis & Frank Richter (eds.), *Beiträge zur deutschen Grammatik: Gesammelte Schriften von Tilman N. Höhle*, 2nd edn. (Classics in Linguistics 5), 417–433. Berlin: Language Science Press, 2019. DOI: 10.5281/zenodo.2588383.

Höhle, Tilman N. 2019. Topologische Felder. In Stefan Müller, Marga Reis & Frank Richter (eds.), *Beiträge zur deutschen Grammatik: Gesammelte Schriften von Tilman N. Höhle*, 2nd edn. (Classics in Linguistics 5), 7–89. First circulated as draft in 1983. Berlin: Language Science Press. DOI: 10.5281/zenodo.2588383.

Holmberg, Anders. 2015. Verb second. In Tibor Kiss & Artemis Alexiadou (eds.), *Syntax – theory and analysis: An international handbook*, vol. 1 (Handbooks of Linguistics and Communication Science 42), 342–383. Berlin: Mouton de Gruyter. DOI: 10.1515/9783110377408.342.

Huddleston, Rodney & Geoffrey K. Pullum (eds.). 2002. *The Cambridge grammar of the English language*. Cambridge, UK: Cambridge University Press. DOI: 10. 1017/9781316423530.

Hudson, Richard. 1992. So-called "double objects" and grammatical relations. *Language* 68(2). 251–276. DOI: 10.2307/416941.

Jackendoff, Ray. 1977. $\overline{X}$ *syntax: A study of phrase structure* (Linguistic Inquiry Monographs 2). Cambridge, MA: MIT Press.

Jacobs, Joachim. 2003. Die Problematik der Valenzebenen. In Vilmos Ágel, Ludwig M. Eichinger, Hans-Werner Eroms, Peter Hellwig, Hans Jürgen Heringer & Henning Lobin (eds.), *Dependency and valency: An international handbook of contemporary research*, vol. 1 (Handbooks of Linguistics and Communication Science 25), 378–399. Berlin: Walter de Gruyter. DOI: 10.1515/9783110141900.1. 4.378.

Jacobson, Pauline. 1987a. Phrase structure, grammatical relations, and discontinuous constituents. In Geoffrey J. Huck & Almerindo E. Ojeda (eds.), *Discontinuous constituency* (Syntax and Semantics 20), 27–69. New York, NY: Academic Press.

Jacobson, Pauline. 1987b. Review of Gerald Gazdar, Ewan Klein, Geoffrey K. Pullum, and Ivan A. Sag, 1985: Generalized Phrase Structure Grammar. *Linguistics and Philosophy* 10(3). 389–426. DOI: 10.1007/BF00584132.

Johannessen, Janne Bondi. 1996. Partial agreement and coordination. *Linguistic Inquiry* 27(4). 661–676.

Johannessen, Janne Bondi. 1998. *Coordination* (Oxford Studies in Comparative Syntax). Oxford: Oxford University Press.

Johnson, Mark. 1986. A GPSG account of VP structure in German. *Linguistics* 24(5). 871–882. DOI: 10.1515/ling.1986.24.5.871.

Jurafsky, Daniel. 1996. A probabilistic model of lexical and syntactic access and disambiguation. *Cognitive Science* 20(2). 137–194. DOI: 10 . 1207 / s15516709cog2002_1.

Kasper, Robert T. 1994. Adjuncts in the Mittelfeld. In John Nerbonne, Klaus Netter & Carl Pollard (eds.), *German in Head-Driven Phrase Structure Grammar* (CSLI Lecture Notes 46), 39–70. Stanford, CA: CSLI Publications.

Kayne, Richard S. 1994. *The antisymmetry of syntax* (Linguistic Inquiry Monographs 25). Cambridge, MA: MIT Press.

Kim, Jong-Bok. 2021. Negation. In Stefan Müller, Anne Abeillé, Robert D. Borsley & Jean-Pierre Koenig (eds.), *Head-Driven Phrase Structure Grammar: The handbook* (Empirically Oriented Theoretical Morphology and Syntax 9), 811–845. Berlin: Language Science Press. DOI: 10.5281/zenodo.5599852.

Kim, Jong-Bok & Ivan A. Sag. 2002. Negation without head-movement. *Natural Language & Linguistic Theory* 20(2). 339–412. DOI: 10.1023/A:1015045225019.

Kim, Jong-Bok & Peter Sells. 2008. *English syntax: An introduction* (CSLI Lecture Notes 185). Stanford, CA: CSLI Publications.

Kiss, Tibor. 1995a. *Infinite Komplementation: Neue Studien zum deutschen Verbum infinitum* (Linguistische Arbeiten 333). Tübingen: Max Niemeyer Verlag. DOI: 10.1515/9783110934670.

Kiss, Tibor. 1995b. *Merkmale und Repräsentationen: Eine Einführung in die deklarative Grammatikanalyse.* Opladen/Wiesbaden: Westdeutscher Verlag.

Kiss, Tibor. 2001. Configurational and relational scope determination in German. In W. Detmar Meurers & Tibor Kiss (eds.), *Constraint-based approaches to Germanic syntax* (Studies in Constraint-Based Lexicalism 7), 141–175. Stanford, CA: CSLI Publications.

Kiss, Tibor & Birgit Wesche. 1991. Verb order and head movement. In Otthein Herzog & Claus-Rainer Rollinger (eds.), *Text understanding in LILOG* (Lecture Notes in Artificial Intelligence 546), 216–240. Berlin: Springer-Verlag. DOI: 10.1007/3-540-54594-8_63.

Koenig, Jean-Pierre & Frank Richter. 2021. Semantics. In Stefan Müller, Anne Abeillé, Robert D. Borsley & Jean-Pierre Koenig (eds.), *Head-Driven Phrase Structure Grammar: The handbook* (Empirically Oriented Theoretical Morphology and Syntax 9), 1001–1042. Berlin: Language Science Press. DOI: 10.5281/zenodo.5599862.

König, Ekkehard & Johan van der Auwera (eds.). 1994. *The Germanic languages* (Routledge Language Family Descriptions 3). London: Routledge. DOI: 10.4324/9781315812786.

Koster, Jan. 1975. Dutch as an SOV language. *Linguistic Analysis* 1(2). 111–136.

Koster, Jan. 1986. The relation between pro-drop, scrambling, and verb movements. *Groningen Papers in Theoretical and Applied Linguistics* 1. 1–43.

Koster, Jan. 1999. The word orders of English and Dutch. Collective vs. individual checking. *Groninger Arbeiten zur Germanistischen Linguistik* 43. 1–42.

Laenzlinger, Christoph. 2004. A feature-based theory of adverb syntax. In Jennifer R. Austin, Stefan Engelberg & Gisa Rauh (eds.), *Adverbials: The interplay between meaning, context, and syntactic structure* (Linguistik Aktuell/Linguistics Today 70), 205–252. Amsterdam: John Benjamins Publishing Co. DOI: 10.1075/la.70.08lae.

Larson, Richard K. 1988. On the double object construction. *Linguistic Inquiry* 19(3). 335–391.

Larson, Richard K. 1990. Double objects revisited: Reply to Jackendoff. *Linguistic Inquiry* 21(4). 589–632.

Lenerz, Jürgen. 1977. *Zur Abfolge nominaler Satzglieder im Deutschen* (Studien zur deutschen Grammatik 5). Tübingen: Gunter Narr Verlag.

Levine, Robert D. & Walt Detmar Meurers. 2006. Head-Driven Phrase Structure Grammar: Linguistic approach, formal foundations, and computational realization. In Keith Brown (ed.), *The encyclopedia of language and linguistics*, 2nd edn., 237–252. Oxford: Elsevier Science Publisher B.V. (North-Holland). DOI: 10.1016/B0-08-044854-2/02040-X.

Lieb, Hans-Heinrich. 1992. Zur Polyfunktionalität des deutschen Vorgangspassivs. *Zeitschrift für Phonetik, Sprachwissenschaft und Kommunikationsforschung* 45(2). 178–188. DOI: 10.1524/stuf.1992.45.14.178.

Lohnstein, Horst. 2014. Artenvielfalt in freier Wildbahn: Generative Grammatik. In Jörg Hagemann & Sven Staffeldt (eds.), *Syntaxtheorien: Analysen im Vergleich* (Stauffenburg Einführungen 28), 165–185. Tübingen: Stauffenburg Verlag.

Machicao y Priemer, Antonio. 2022. Konstituententest. In Stefan J. Schierholz & Pál Uzonyi (eds.), *Grammatik: Syntax*, vol. 2 (Wörterbücher zur Sprach- und Kommunikationswissenschaft 1), 482–487. Berlin: De Gruyter. DOI: 10.1515/9783110698527.

Machicao y Priemer, Antonio & Stefan Müller. 2021. NPs in German: Locality, theta roles, and prenominal genitives. *Glossa: a journal of general linguistics* 6(1). 1–38. DOI: 10.5334/gjgl.1128.

Maling, Joan. 1990. Inversion in embedded clauses in Modern Icelandic. In Joan Maling & Annie Zaenen (eds.), *Modern Icelandic syntax* (Syntax and Semantics 24), 71–91. Bingley, UK: Brill. DOI: 10.1163/9789004373235_004.

Marslen-Wilson, William D. 1975. Sentence perception as an interactive parallel process. *Science* 189(4198). 226–228. DOI: 10.1126/science.189.4198.226.

McIntyre, Andrew. 2006. The interpretation of German datives and English *have*. In Daniel Hole, André Meinunger & Werner Abraham (eds.), *Datives and other cases: Between argument structure and event structure* (Studies in Language Companion Series 75), 185–212. Amsterdam: John Benjamins Publishing Co. DOI: 10.1075/slcs.75.09mci.

Meinunger, André. 2001. Restrictions on verb raising. *Linguistic Inquiry* 32(4). 732–740.

Meurers, Walt Detmar. 1999. Raising spirits (and assigning them case). *Groninger Arbeiten zur Germanistischen Linguistik (GAGL)* 43. 173–226. http://www.sfs.uni-tuebingen.de/~dm/papers/gagl99.html (10 February, 2021).

Meurers, Walt Detmar. 2000. *Lexical generalizations in the syntax of German non-finite constructions.* Arbeitspapiere des SFB 340 No. 145. Tübingen: Universität Tübingen. http://www.sfs.uni-tuebingen.de/~dm/papers/diss.html (2 February, 2021).

Molnárfi, László. 1998. Kasusstrukturalität und struktureller Kasus – zur Lage des Dativs im heutigen Deutsch. *Linguistische Berichte* 176. 535–580.

Müller, Gereon & Wolfgang Sternefeld. 1993. Improper movement and unambiguous binding. *Linguistic Inquiry* 24(3). 461–507.

Müller, Stefan. 1999. *Deutsche Syntax deklarativ: Head-Driven Phrase Structure Grammar für das Deutsche* (Linguistische Arbeiten 394). Tübingen: Max Niemeyer Verlag. DOI: 10.1515/9783110915990.

Müller, Stefan. 2001. Case in German: Towards an HPSG analysis. In W. Detmar Meurers & Tibor Kiss (eds.), *Constraint-based approaches to Germanic syntax* (Studies in Constraint-Based Lexicalism 7), 217–255. Stanford, CA: CSLI Publications.

Müller, Stefan. 2002. *Complex predicates: Verbal complexes, resultative constructions, and particle verbs in German* (Studies in Constraint-Based Lexicalism 13). Stanford, CA: CSLI Publications.

Müller, Stefan. 2003a. Mehrfache Vorfeldbesetzung. *Deutsche Sprache* 31(1). 29–62.

Müller, Stefan. 2003b. Object-to-subject-raising and lexical rule: An analysis of the German passive. In Stefan Müller (ed.), *Proceedings of the 10th International Conference on Head-Driven Phrase Structure Grammar, Michigan State University*, 278–297. Stanford, CA: CSLI Publications. DOI: 10.21248/hpsg.2003.16.

Müller, Stefan. 2005. Zur Analyse der scheinbar mehrfachen Vorfeldbesetzung. *Linguistische Berichte* 203. 297–330.

Müller, Stefan. 2006. Phrasal or lexical constructions? *Language* 82(4). 850–883. DOI: 10.1353/lan.2006.0213.

Müller, Stefan. 2007a. *Head-Driven Phrase Structure Grammar: Eine Einführung.* 1st edn. (Stauffenburg Einführungen 17). Tübingen: Stauffenburg Verlag.

Müller, Stefan. 2007b. The Grammix CD Rom: A software collection for developing typed feature structure grammars. In Tracy Holloway King & Emily M. Bender (eds.), *Proceedings of the Grammar Engineering Across Frameworks (GEAF07) workshop* (Studies in Computational Linguistics ONLINE 2), 259–266. Stanford, CA: CSLI Publications. http://csli-publications.stanford.edu/GEAF/2007/ (2 February, 2021).

Müller, Stefan. 2010. Persian complex predicates and the limits of inheritance-based analyses. *Journal of Linguistics* 46(3). 601–655. DOI: 10.1017/S0022226709990284.

Müller, Stefan. 2012. A personal note on open access in linguistics. *Journal of Language Modelling* (1). 9–39. DOI: 10.15398/jlm.v0i1.52.

Müller, Stefan. 2013a. *Grammatiktheorie*. 2nd edn. (Stauffenburg Einführungen 20). Tübingen: Stauffenburg Verlag.

Müller, Stefan. 2013b. *Head-Driven Phrase Structure Grammar: Eine Einführung.* 3rd edn. (Stauffenburg Einführungen 17). Tübingen: Stauffenburg Verlag.

Müller, Stefan. 2013c. Unifying everything: Some remarks on Simpler Syntax, Construction Grammar, Minimalism and HPSG. *Language* 89(4). 920–950. DOI: 10.1353/lan.2013.0061.

Müller, Stefan. 2014. Kernigkeit: Anmerkungen zur Kern-Peripherie-Unterscheidung. In Antonio Machicao y Priemer, Andreas Nolda & Athina Sioupi (eds.), *Zwischen Kern und Peripherie* (studia grammatica 76), 25–39. Berlin: de Gruyter. DOI: 10.1524/9783050065335.

Müller, Stefan. 2015a. HPSG – A synopsis. In Tibor Kiss & Artemis Alexiadou (eds.), *Syntax – theory and analysis: An international handbook*, vol. 2 (Handbooks of Linguistics and Communication Science 42), 937–973. Berlin: Mouton de Gruyter. DOI: 10.1515/9783110363708-004.

Müller, Stefan. 2015b. Satztypen: Lexikalisch oder/und phrasal. In Rita Finkbeiner & Jörg Meibauer (eds.), *Satztypen und Konstruktionen im Deutschen* (Linguistik – Impulse & Tendenzen 65), 72–105. Berlin: de Gruyter. DOI: 10.1515/9783110423112-004.

Müller, Stefan. 2015c. The CoreGram project: Theoretical linguistics, theory development and verification. *Journal of Language Modelling* 3(1). 21–86. DOI: 10.15398/jlm.v3i1.91.

Müller, Stefan. 2016. *Grammatical theory: From Transformational Grammar to constraint-based approaches.* 1st edn. (Textbooks in Language Sciences 1). Berlin: Language Science Press. DOI: 10.17169/langsci.b25.167.

Müller, Stefan. 2017. Head-Driven Phrase Structure Grammar, Sign-Based Construction Grammar, and Fluid Construction Grammar: Commonalities and differences. *Constructions and Frames* 9(1). 139–173. DOI: 10.1075/cf.9.1.05mul.

Müller, Stefan. 2018. *A lexicalist account of argument structure: Template-based phrasal LFG approaches and a lexical HPSG alternative* (Conceptual Foundations of Language Science 2). Berlin: Language Science Press. DOI: 10.5281/zenodo.1441351.

Müller, Stefan. 2019. Complex predicates: Structure, potential structure and underspecification. *Linguistic Issues in Language Technology* 17(3). 1–8. DOI: 10.33011/lilt.v17i.1423.

Müller, Stefan. 2021a. Constituent order. In Stefan Müller, Anne Abeillé, Robert D. Borsley & Jean-Pierre Koenig (eds.), *Head-Driven Phrase Structure Grammar: The handbook* (Empirically Oriented Theoretical Morphology and Syntax 9), 369–417. Berlin: Language Science Press. DOI: 10.5281/zenodo.5599836.

Müller, Stefan. 2021b. HPSG and Construction Grammar. In Stefan Müller, Anne Abeillé, Robert D. Borsley & Jean-Pierre Koenig (eds.), *Head-Driven Phrase Structure Grammar: The handbook* (Empirically Oriented Theoretical Morphology and Syntax 9), 1497–1553. Berlin: Language Science Press. DOI: 10.5281/zenodo.5599882.

Müller, Stefan. 2022. Headless in Berlin: Headless (nominal) structures in Head-Driven Phrase Structure Grammar. In Ulrike Freywald, Horst J. Simon & Stefan Müller (eds.), *Headedness and/or grammatical anarchy?* (Empirically Oriented Theoretical Morphology and Syntax 11), 73–121. Berlin: Language Science Press. DOI: 10.5281/zenodo.7142691.

Müller, Stefan. 2023a. *German clause structure: An analysis with special consideration of so-called multiple fronting* (Empirically Oriented Theoretical Morphology and Syntax). Berlin: Revise and resubmit Language Science Press.

Müller, Stefan. 2023b. *Grammatical theory: From Transformational Grammar to constraint-based approaches.* 5th edn. (Textbooks in Language Sciences 1). Berlin: Language Science Press. DOI: 10.5281/zenodo.7376662.

Müller, Stefan, Anne Abeillé, Robert D. Borsley & Jean-Pierre Koenig (eds.). 2021. *Head-Driven Phrase Structure Grammar: The handbook* (Empirically Oriented Theoretical Morphology and Syntax 9). Berlin: Language Science Press. DOI: 10.5281/zenodo.5543318.

Müller, Stefan, Jong-Bok Kim & Alain Kihm. 2019. *Predicate topicalization in Korean and Yiddish: A construction-based HPSG approach.* Talk given at HPSG 2019 in Bucharest.

Müller, Stefan & Antonio Machicao y Priemer. 2019. Head-Driven Phrase Structure Grammar. In András Kertész, Edith Moravcsik & Csilla Rákosi (eds.), *Current approaches to syntax: A comparative handbook* (Comparative Handbooks of Linguistics 3), 317–359. Berlin: Mouton de Gruyter. DOI: 10.1515/9783110540253-012.

Müller, Stefan & Bjarne Ørsnes. 2011. Positional expletives in Danish, German, and Yiddish. In Stefan Müller (ed.), *Proceedings of the 18th International Con-*

ference on Head-Driven Phrase Structure Grammar, University of Washington, 167–187. Stanford, CA: CSLI Publications. DOI: 10.21248/hpsg.2011.10.

Müller, Stefan & Bjarne Ørsnes. 2013a. Passive in Danish, English, and German. In Stefan Müller (ed.), *Proceedings of the 20th International Conference on Head-Driven Phrase Structure Grammar, Freie Universität Berlin*, 140–160. Stanford, CA: CSLI Publications. DOI: 10.21248/hpsg.2013.8.

Müller, Stefan & Bjarne Ørsnes. 2013b. Towards an HPSG analysis of object shift in Danish. In Glyn Morrill & Mark-Jan Nederhof (eds.), *Formal Grammar: 17th and 18th International Conferences, FG 2012, Opole, Poland, August 2012, revised selected papers, FG 2013, Düsseldorf, Germany, August 2013: Proceedings* (Lecture Notes in Computer Science 8036), 69–89. Berlin: Springer-Verlag. DOI: 10.1007/978-3-642-39998-5_5.

Müller, Stefan & Bjarne Ørsnes. 2015. *Danish in Head-Driven Phrase Structure Grammar*. Ms. Freie Universität Berlin. To be submitted to Language Science Press. Berlin.

Müller, Stefan & Stephen Wechsler. 2014a. Lexical approaches to argument structure. *Theoretical Linguistics* 40(1–2). 1–76. DOI: 10.1515/tl-2014-0001.

Müller, Stefan & Stephen Wechsler. 2014b. Two sides of the same slim Boojum: Further arguments for a lexical approach to argument structure. *Theoretical Linguistics* 40(1–2). 187–224. DOI: 10.1515/tl-2014-0009.

Muysken, Pieter. 1982. Parametrizing the notion of "head". *Journal of Linguistic Research* 2. 57–75.

Neeleman, Ad. 1994. Scrambling as a D-structure phenomenon. In Norbert Corver & Henk van Riesdijk (eds.), *Studies on scrambling: Movement and non-movement approaches to free word-order phenomena* (Studies in Generative Grammar 41), 387–429. Berlin: Mouton de Gruyter. DOI: 10.1515/9783110857214.387.

Neeleman, Ad & Hans van de Koot. 2008. Dutch scrambling and the nature of discourse templates. *The Journal of Comparative Germanic Linguistics* 11(2). 137–189. DOI: 10.1007/s10828-008-9018-0.

Nerbonne, John. 1986. 'Phantoms' and German fronting: Poltergeist constituents? *Linguistics* 24(5). 857–870. DOI: 10.1515/ling.1986.24.5.857.

Netter, Klaus. 1992. On non-head non-movement: An HPSG treatment of finite verb position in German. In Günther Görz (ed.), *Konvens 92. 1. Konferenz „Verarbeitung natürlicher Sprache". Nürnberg 7.–9. Oktober 1992* (Informatik aktuell), 218–227. Berlin: Springer-Verlag. DOI: 10.1007/978-3-642-77809-4_23.

Netter, Klaus. 1994. Towards a theory of functional heads: German nominal phrases. In John Nerbonne, Klaus Netter & Carl Pollard (eds.), *German in Head-*

Driven Phrase Structure Grammar (CSLI Lecture Notes 46), 297–340. Stanford, CA: CSLI Publications.

Netter, Klaus. 1998. *Functional categories in an HPSG for German* (Saarbrücken Dissertations in Computational Linguistics and Language Technology 3). Saarbrücken: Deutsches Forschungszentrum für Künstliche Intelligenz and Universität des Saarlandes.

Newmeyer, Frederick J. 2010. On comparative concepts and descriptive categories: A reply to Haspelmath. *Language* 86(3). 688–695. DOI: 10.1353/lan.2010.0000.

Oppenrieder, Wilhelm. 1991. *Von Subjekten, Sätzen und Subjektsätzen* (Linguisitische Arbeiten 241). Tübingen: Max Niemeyer Verlag. DOI: 10.1515/9783111356426.

Ørsnes, Bjarne. 2009. Das Verbalfeldmodell: Ein Stellungsfeldermodell für den kontrastiven DaF-Unterricht. *Deutsch als Fremdsprache* 46(3). 143–149. DOI: 10.37307/j.2198-2430.2009.03.03.

Paul, Hermann. 1919. *Deutsche Grammatik. Teil IV: Syntax*, vol. 3. 2nd unchanged edition 1968, Tübingen: Max Niemeyer Verlag. Halle an der Saale: Max Niemeyer Verlag. DOI: 10.1515/9783110929805.

Penn, Gerald. 2004. Balancing clarity and efficiency in typed feature logic through delaying. In Donia Scott (ed.), *Proceedings of the 42nd Meeting of the Association for Computational Linguistics (ACL'04)*, 239–246. Barcelona, Spain: Association for Computational Linguistics. DOI: 10.3115/1218955.1218986.

Perlmutter, David M. 1978. Impersonal passives and the Unaccusative Hypothesis. In Jeri J. Jaeger, Anthony C. Woodbury, Farrell Ackerman, Christine Chiarello, Orin D. Gensler, John Kingston, Eve E. Sweetser, Henry Thomson & Kenneth W. Whistler (eds.), *Proceedings of the 4th Annual Meeting of the Berkeley Linguistics Society*, 157–189. Berkeley: Berkeley Linguistic Society. https://escholarship.org/uc/item/73h0s91v (5 December, 2021).

Plank, Frans (ed.). 2003. *Das grammatische Raritätenkabinett*. Konstanz: Universität Konstanz. https://typo.uni-konstanz.de/rara/ (21 December, 2022).

Poletto, Cecilia. 2002. The left-periphery of V2-Rhaetoromance dialects: A new view on V2 and V3. In Sjef Barbiers, Leonie Cornips & Susanne van der Kleij (eds.), *Syntactic microvariation* (Meertens Institute Electronic Publications in Linguistics 2), 214–242. Amsterdam: Meertens Instituut. https://www.meertens.knaw.nl/books/synmic/pdf/poletto.pdf (27 April, 2020).

Pollard, Carl. 1994. Toward a unified account of passive in German. In John Nerbonne, Klaus Netter & Carl Pollard (eds.), *German in Head-Driven Phrase Struc-*

ture Grammar (CSLI Lecture Notes 46), 273–296. Stanford, CA: CSLI Publications.

Pollard, Carl & Ivan A. Sag. 1987. *Information-based syntax and semantics* (CSLI Lecture Notes 13). Stanford, CA: CSLI Publications.

Pollard, Carl & Ivan A. Sag. 1994. *Head-Driven Phrase Structure Grammar* (Studies in Contemporary Linguistics 4). Chicago, IL: The University of Chicago Press.

Pollard, Carl J. 1996. On head non-movement. In Harry Bunt & Arthur van Horck (eds.), *Discontinuous constituency* (Natural Language Processing 6), 279–305. Veröffentlichte Version eines Ms. von 1990. Berlin: Mouton de Gruyter. DOI: 10.1515/9783110873467.279.

Pollock, Jean-Yves. 1989. Verb movement, Universal Grammar and the structure of IP. *Linguistic Inquiry* 20(3). 365–424.

Prince, Ellen F. 1989. Yiddish *Wh*-clauses, subject-postposing, and topicalization. In Joyce Powers & Kenneth de Jong (eds.), *Proceedings of ESCOL 5 1988*, 403–415. Columbus, OH: Ohio State University.

Przepiórkowski, Adam. 1999. On case assignment and "adjuncts as complements". In Gert Webelhuth, Jean-Pierre Koenig & Andreas Kathol (eds.), *Lexical and constructional aspects of linguistic explanation* (Studies in Constraint-Based Lexicalism 1), 231–245. Stanford, CA: CSLI Publications.

Przepiórkowski, Adam & Anna Kupść. 2006. HPSG for slavicists. *Glossos* 8. 1–68.

Quirk, Randolph, Sidney Greenbaum, Geoffrey Leech & Jan Svartvik. 1985. *A comprehensive grammar of the English language.* London: Longman.

Radford, Andrew. 1993. Head-hunting: On the trail of the nominal Janus. In Greville G. Corbett, Norman M. Fraser & Scott McGlashan (eds.), *Heads in grammatical theory*, 73–113. Cambridge: Cambridge University Press. DOI: 10.1017/CBO9780511659454.005.

Ratkus, Artūras. 2018. Greek ἀρχιερεύς in Gothic translation: Linguistics and theology at a crossroads. *NOWELE. North-Western European Language Evolution* 71(1). 3–34. DOI: 10.1075/nowele.00002.rat.

Reis, Marga. 1980. On justifying topological frames: 'Positional field' and the order of nonverbal constituents in German. *Documentation et Recherche en Linguistique Allemande Contemporaine. Revue de Linguistique* 22/23. 59–85. DOI: 10.3406/drlav.1980.957.

Reis, Marga. 1982. Zum Subjektbegriff im Deutschen. In Werner Abraham (ed.), *Satzglieder im Deutschen – Vorschläge zur syntaktischen, semantischen und pragmatischen Fundierung* (Studien zur deutschen Grammatik 15), 171–211. Tübingen: Gunter Narr Verlag.

Richter, Frank. 2021. Formal background. In Stefan Müller, Anne Abeillé, Robert D. Borsley & Jean-Pierre Koenig (eds.), *Head-Driven Phrase Structure Grammar: The handbook* (Empirically Oriented Theoretical Morphology and Syntax 9), 89–124. Berlin: Language Science Press. DOI: 10.5281/zenodo.5599822.

Riemsdijk, Henk van. 1998. Categorial feature magnetism: The endocentricity and distribution of projections. *The Journal of Comparative Germanic Linguistics* 2(1). 1–48. DOI: 10.1023/A:1009763305416.

Rizzi, Luigi. 1990. Speculations on verb-second. In Joan Mascaró & Marina Nespor (eds.), *Grammar in progress: GLOW essays for Henk van Riemsdijk* (Studies in Generative Grammar 36), 375–386. Dordrecht: Foris Publications. DOI: 10.1515/9783110867848.375.

Rizzi, Luigi. 1997. The fine structure of the left periphery. In Liliane Haegeman (ed.), *Elements of grammar: Handbook of Generative Syntax* (Kluwer International Handbooks of Linguistics 1), 281–337. Dordrecht: Kluwer Academic Publishers. DOI: 10.1007/978-94-011-5420-8_7.

Roberts, Ian. 1993. *Verbs and diachronic syntax: A comparative history of English and French* (Studies in Natural Language and Linguistic Theory 28). Dordrecht: Kluwer Academic Publishers. DOI: 10.1007/978-94-011-2910-7.

Robinson, Orrin W. 1992. *Old English and its closest relatives: A survey of the earliest Germanic languages.* Stanford, CA: Stanford University Press.

Ross, Malcolm D. 2004. The morphosyntactic typology of Oceanic languages. *Language and Linguistics* 5(2). 491–541.

Ryu, Byong-Rae. 1997. *Argumentstruktur und Linking im constraint-basierten Lexikon: Ein Zwei-Stufen-Modell für eine HPSG-Analyse von Ergativität und Passivierung im Deutschen.* Arbeitspapiere des SFB 340 No. 124. Tübingen: Universität Tübingen.

Sadock, Jerrold M. 1998. A vestige of verb final syntax in Yiddish. *Monatshefte* 90(2). 220–226.

Sadziński, Roman. 1987. Zur valenztheoretischen Wertung des Agensanschlusses im deutschen Passiv. In Centre de Recherche en Linguistique Germanique (Nice) (ed.), *Das Passiv im Deutschen: Akten des Kolloquiums über das Passiv im Deutschen, Nizza 1986* (Linguistische Arbeiten 183), 147–159. Tübingen: Max Niemeyer Verlag. DOI: 10.1515/9783111357683.147.

Sag, Ivan A. 1997. English relative clause constructions. *Journal of Linguistics* 33(2). 431–483. DOI: 10.1017/S002222679700652X.

Sag, Ivan A. 2007. Remarks on locality. In Stefan Müller (ed.), *Proceedings of the 14th International Conference on Head-Driven Phrase Structure Grammar, Stan-*

ford Department of Linguistics and CSLI's LinGO Lab*, 394–414. Stanford, CA: CSLI Publications. DOI: 10.21248/hpsg.2007.23.

Sag, Ivan A. 2010. English filler-gap constructions. *Language* 86(3). 486–545.

Sag, Ivan A. 2012. Sign-Based Construction Grammar: An informal synopsis. In Hans C. Boas & Ivan A. Sag (eds.), *Sign-Based Construction Grammar* (CSLI Lecture Notes 193), 69–202. Stanford, CA: CSLI Publications.

Sag, Ivan A., Hans C. Boas & Paul Kay. 2012. Introducing Sign-Based Construction Grammar. In Hans C. Boas & Ivan A. Sag (eds.), *Sign-Based Construction Grammar* (CSLI Lecture Notes 193), 1–29. Stanford, CA: CSLI Publications.

Sag, Ivan A., Rui Chaves, Anne Abeillé, Bruno Estigarribia, Frank Van Eynde, Dan Flickinger, Paul Kay, Laura A. Michaelis-Cummings, Stefan Müller, Geoffrey K. Pullum & Thomas Wasow. 2020. Lessons from the English auxiliary system. *Journal of Linguistics* 56(1). 87–155. DOI: 10.1017/S002222671800052X.

Sag, Ivan A. & Thomas Wasow. 2011. Performance-compatible competence grammar. In Robert D. Borsley & Kersti Börjars (eds.), *Non-transformational syntax: Formal and explicit models of grammar: A guide to current models*, 359–377. Oxford: Wiley-Blackwell. DOI: 9781444395037.ch10.

Sag, Ivan A., Thomas Wasow & Emily M. Bender. 2003. *Syntactic theory: A formal introduction.* 2nd edn. (CSLI Lecture Notes 152). Stanford, CA: CSLI Publications.

Santorini, Beatrice. 1993. Jiddish als gemischte OV/VO-Sprache. In Werner Abraham (ed.), *Dialektsyntax* (Linguistische Berichte Sonderheft 5), 230–245. Opladen: Westdeutscher Verlag.

Schäfer, Lea. 2023. Yiddish. In *The oxford encyclopedia of germanic linguistics*. To appear. Oxford: Oxford University Press.

Schallert, Oliver. 2007. *Wortstellungstypologie des Jiddischen im Spannungsfeld zwischen den germanischen und den slawischen Sprachen.* Ms. Philipps–Universität Marburg.

Scherpenisse, Wim. 1986. *The connection between base structure and linearization restrictions in German and Dutch* (Europäische Hochschulschriften, Reihe XXI, Linguistik 47). Frankfurt/M.: Peter Lang.

Scott, Gary-John. 2002. Stacked adjectival modification and the structure of nominal phrases. In Guglielmo Cinque (ed.), *Functional structure in DP and IP: The cartography of syntactic structures* (Oxford Studies in Comparative Syntax), 91–120. Oxford: Oxford University Press.

Sternefeld, Wolfgang. 1995. Voice phrases and their specifiers. *FAS Papers in Linguistics* 3. 48–85.

Sternefeld, Wolfgang. 2006. *Syntax: Eine morphologisch motivierte generative Beschreibung des Deutschen* (Stauffenburg Linguistik 31). Tübingen: Stauffenburg Verlag.

Stiles, Patrick V. 2013. The Pan-West Germanic isoglosses and the subrelationships of West Germanic to other branches. *NOWELE. North-Western European Language Evolution* 66(1). 5–38. DOI: 10.1075/nowele.66.1.02sti.

Storto, Luciana R. 2003. Interactions between verb movement and agreement in Karitiana (Tupi stock). *Revista Letras* 60. 411–433. DOI: 10.5380/rel.v60i0.2876.

Struckmeier, Volker. 2017. Against information structure heads: a relational analysis of german scrambling. *Glossa: a journal of general linguistics* 2(1). 1–29. DOI: 10.5334/gjgl.56.

Tanenhaus, Michael K., Michael J. Spivey-Knowlton, Kathleen M. Eberhard & Julie C. Sedivy. 1996. Using eye movements to study spoken language comprehension: Evidence for visually mediated incremental interpretation. In Toshio Inui & James L. McClelland (eds.), *Information integration in perception and communication* (Attention and Performance XVI), 457–478. Cambridge, MA: MIT Press.

Tesnière, Lucien. 2015. *Elements of structural syntax.* Translated by Timothy Osborne and Sylvain Kahane. Amsterdam: John Benjamins Publishing Co. DOI: 10.1075/z.185.

Thráinsson, Höskuldur. 2007. *The syntax of Icelandic* (Cambridge Syntax Guides). Cambridge, UK: Cambridge University Press. DOI: 10.1017/CBO9780511619441.

Thuilier, Juliette, Margaret Grant, Benoît Crabbé & Anne Abeillé. 2021. Word order in French: The role of animacy. *Glossa: a journal of general linguistics* 6(1). 1–21. DOI: 10.5334/gjgl.1155.

Uszkoreit, Hans. 1987. *Word order and constituent structure in German* (CSLI Lecture Notes 8). Stanford, CA: CSLI Publications.

Van Eynde, Frank. 2021. Nominal structures. In Stefan Müller, Anne Abeillé, Robert D. Borsley & Jean-Pierre Koenig (eds.), *Head-Driven Phrase Structure Grammar: The handbook* (Empirically Oriented Theoretical Morphology and Syntax 9), 275–313. Berlin: Language Science Press. DOI: 10.5281/zenodo.5599832.

Van Koppen, Marjo. 2005. *One probe–two goals: Aspects of agreement in Dutch dialects* (LOT Dissertation Series 105). Utrecht Institute of Linguistics: Netherlands Graduate School of Linguistics.

Vance, Barbara S. 1997. *Syntactic change in Medieval French: Verb-second and null subjects* (Studies in Natural Language and Linguistic Theory 41). Dordrecht: Kluwer Academic Publishers. DOI: 10.1007/978-94-015-8843-0.

Vikner, Sten. 2001. *Verb movement variation in Germanic and Optimality Theory.* University of Tübingen. (Habilitationsschrift).

Vogel, Ralf & Markus Steinbach. 1998. The dative – An oblique case. *Linguistische Berichte* 173. 65–90.

von Stechow, Arnim. 1990. Status government and coherence in German. In Günther Grewendorf & Wolfgang Sternefeld (eds.), *Scrambling and barriers* (Linguistik Aktuell/Linguistics Today 5), 143–198. Amsterdam: John Benjamins Publishing Co. DOI: 10.1075/la.5.

von Stechow, Arnim. 1996. The different readings of *wieder* 'again': A structural account. *Journal of Semantics* 13(2). 87–138. DOI: 10.1093/jos/13.2.87.

Wasow, Thomas. 2021. Processing. In Stefan Müller, Anne Abeillé, Robert D. Borsley & Jean-Pierre Koenig (eds.), *Head-Driven Phrase Structure Grammar: The handbook* (Empirically Oriented Theoretical Morphology and Syntax 9), 1081–1104. Berlin: Language Science Press. DOI: 10.5281/zenodo.5599866.

Wechsler, Stephen. 1995. *The semantic basis of argument structure* (Dissertations in Linguistics). Stanford, CA: CSLI Publications.

Wegener, Heide. 1985a. „Er bekommt widersprochen" – Argumente für die Existenz eines Dativpassivs im Deutschen. *Linguistische Berichte* 96. 127–139.

Wegener, Heide. 1985b. *Der Dativ im heutigen Deutsch* (Studien zur deutschen Grammatik 28). Tübingen: Gunter Narr Verlag.

Wegener, Heide. 1991. Der Dativ – ein struktureller Kasus? In Gisbert Fanselow & Sascha W. Felix (eds.), *Strukturen und Merkmale syntaktischer Kategorien* (Studien zur deutschen Grammatik 39), 70–103. Tübingen: Gunter Narr Verlag.

Weinreich, Max. 1945. Der YIVO un di problemen fun undzer tsayt [the yivo faces the post-war world]. *YIVO Bleter* 25(1). 3–18.

Weiß, Helmut. 2005. Inflected complementizers in Continental West Germanic dialects. *Zeitschrift für Dialektologie und Linguistik* 72(2). 148–166.

Weiß, Helmut. 2018. The Wackernagel complex and pronoun raising. In Agnes Jäger, Gisella Ferraresi & Helmut Weiß (eds.), *Clause structure and word order in the history of German* (Oxford Studies in Diachronic and Historical Linguistics 31), 132–154. Oxford: Oxford University Press.

Wells, Rulon S. 1947. Immediate constituents. *Language* 23(2). 81–117. DOI: 10.2307/410382.

Willis, David W. E. 1998. *Syntactic change in Welsh: A study of the loss of verb-second.* Oxford: Clarendon Press.

Wolfe, Sam. 2015. The nature of old spanish verb second reconsidered. *Lingua* 164(1). 132–155. DOI: 10.1016/j.lingua.2015.06.007.

Wolfe, Sam. 2016. On the left periphery of V2 languages: Evidence from Romance Fin and Force V2 systems. *Rivista di Grammatica Generativa* 38. 287–310.

Woolford, Ellen. 2006. Lexical case, inherent case, and argument structure. *Linguistic Inquiry* 37(1). 111–130.

Wunderlich, Dieter. 1993. Diathesen. In Joachim Jacobs, Arnim von Stechow, Wolfgang Sternefeld & Theo Vennemann (eds.), *Syntax: An international handbook of contemporary research*, vol. 1 (Handbooks of Linguistics and Communication Science 9), 730–747. Berlin: Walter de Gruyter. DOI: 10.1515/9783110095869.1.12.730.

Wunderlich, Dieter. 1997. Cause and the structure of verbs. *Linguistic Inquiry* 28(1). 27–68.

Wurmbrand, Susanne. 2003a. *Infinitives: Restructuring and clause structure* (Studies in Generative Grammar 55). Berlin: Mouton de Gruyter. DOI: 10.1515/9783110908329.

Wurmbrand, Susanne. 2003b. *Long passive (corpus search results)*. Ms. University of Connecticut.

Yip, Moira, Joan Maling & Ray Jackendoff. 1987. Case in tiers. *Language* 63(2). 217–250. DOI: 10.2307/415655.

Zaenen, Annie, Joan Maling & Höskuldur Thráinsson. 1985. Case and grammatical functions: The Icelandic passive. *Natural Language & Linguistic Theory* 3(4). 441–483. DOI: 10.1007/BF00133285.

Zifonun, Gisela. 1992. Das Passiv im Deutschen: Agenten, Blockaden und (De-)gradierungen. In Ludger Hoffmann (ed.), *Deutsche Syntax: Ansichten und Aussichten* (Jahrbuch des Instituts für Deutsche Sprache; 1991), 250–275. Berlin: de Gruyter. DOI: 10.1515/9783110622447.

Zifonun, Gisela. 1997. Das Passiv (und die Familie der grammatischen Konversen). In Gisela Zifonun, Ludger Hoffmann & Bruno Strecker (eds.), *Grammatik der deutschen Sprache*, vol. 3 (Schriften des Instituts für deutsche Sprache 7), 1788–1858. Berlin: Walter de Gruyter. DOI: 10.1515/9783110872163.

Name index

Language index

Subject index